MW00677829

KIERKEGAARD AND THE RENAISSANCE AND MODERN TRADITIONS

TOME III: LITERATURE, DRAMA AND MUSIC

Kierkegaard Research: Sources, Reception and Resources
Volume 5, Tome III

Kierkegaard Research: Sources, Reception and Resources
is a publication of the Søren Kierkegaard Research Centre

This volume was published with the generous financial support
of the Danish Agency for Science, Technology and Innovation

Kierkegaard and the Renaissance and Modern Traditions

Tome III: Literature, Drama and Music

Edited by
JON STEWART

ASHGATE

Published by
Ashgate Publishing Limited
Wey Court East
Union Road
Farnham
Surrey, GU9 7PT
England

Ashgate Publishing Company
Suite 420
101 Cherry Street
Burlington
VT 05401-4405
USA

www.ashgate.com

British Library Cataloguing in Publication Data
Kierkegaard and the Renaissance and modern traditions
  Vol. 5 Tome 3: Literature, drama and music. –
  (Kierkegaard research : sources, reception and resources)
  1. Kierkegaard, Soren, 1813–1855 2. Philosophy, Renaissance
  3. Philosophy, Modern
  I. Stewart, Jon (Jon Bartley)
  198.9

Library of Congress Cataloging-in-Publication Data
Kierkegaard and the Renaissance and modern traditions / [edited by] Jon Stewart.
     p. cm. — (Kierkegaard research: sources, reception and resources ; v. 5)
  Includes bibliographical references and indexes.
  ISBN 978-0-7546-6820-6 (hardcover : v. 3 : alk. paper)
  1. Kierkegaard, Soren, 1813–1855—Sources.
  I. Stewart, Jon (Jon Bartley)

  B4377.K45527 2008
  198'.9—dc22

2008050992

ISBN 978-0-7546-6820-6

Cover design by Katalin Nun

Mixed Sources
Product group from well-managed forests and other controlled sources
www.fsc.org Cert no. SGS-COC-2482
© 1996 Forest Stewardship Council

Printed and bound in Great Britain by
TJ International Ltd, Padstow, Cornwall

Contents

List of Contributors   *vii*

List of Abbreviations   *ix*

Lord George Gordon Byron:
Seduction, Defiance, and Despair in the Works of Kierkegaard
Bartholomew Ryan   1

Miguel de Cervantes:
The Valuable Contribution of a Minor Influence
Óscar Parcero Oubiña   13

François-René de Chateaubriand:
The Eloquent Society of Συμπαρανεκρωμενοι
Ingrid Basso   31

Johannes Ewald:
Poetic Fire
Kim Ravn   63

Ludvig Holberg:
Kierkegaard's Unacknowledged Mentor
Julie K. Allen   77

Alphonse de Lamartine:
The Movement "*en masse*" versus the Individual Choice
Ingrid Basso   93

Prosper Mérimée:
A New Don Juan
Nataliya Vorobyova   109

Molière:
An Existential Vision of Authenticity in Man Across Time
Jeanette Bresson Ladegaard Knox   125

Wolfgang Amadeus Mozart:
The Love for Music and the Music of Love
Elisabete M. de Sousa   137

Eugène Scribe:
The Unfortunate Authorship of a Successful Author
Elisabete M. de Sousa   169

William Shakespeare:
Kierkegaard's Post-Romantic Reception of "the Poet's Poet"
Joel D.S. Rasmussen   185

Percy Bysshe Shelley:
Anxious Journeys, the Demonic, and "Breaking the Silence"
Bartholomew Ryan   215

Richard Brinsley Sheridan:
A Story of One Review—Kierkegaard on *The School for Scandal*
Nataliya Vorobyova   225

Johan Herman Wessel:
Kierkegaard's Use of Wessel, or The Crazier the Better
Tonny Aagaard Olesen   245

Edward Young:
Kierkegaard's Encounter with a Proto-Romantic Religious Poet
Joseph Ballan   273

Index of Persons   *283*
Index of Subjects   *291*

List of Contributors

Julie K. Allen, College of Letters and Science, Department of Scandinavian Studies, 1302 Van Hise Hall, 1220 Linden Dr., Madison, WI 53706, USA.

Joseph Ballan, University of Chicago Divinity School, Swift Hall, 1025 East 58th St., Chicago, IL 60637, USA.

Ingrid Basso, Università Cattolica del Sacro Cuore, Dipartimento di Filosofia, Largo A. Gemeli, 1-20123 Milano, Italy.

Jeanette Bresson Ladegaard Knox, DIS, Danish Institute for Study Abroad, Vestergade 5–7, 1456 Copenhagen K, Denmark.

Tonny Aagaard Olesen, Søren Kierkegaard Research Centre, Farvergade 27 D, 1463 Copenhagen K, Denmark.

Óscar Parcero Oubiña, Facultade de Filosofía, Universidade de Santiago de Compostela, Praza de Mazarelos, 15782 Santiago de Compostela, Spain.

Joel D.S. Rasmussen, Mansfield College, Oxford University, Mansfield Road, Oxford, OX1 3TF, UK.

Kim Ravn, Søren Kierkegaard Research Centre, Farvergade 27 D, 1463 Copenhagen K, Denmark.

Bartholomew Ryan, European College of Liberal Arts, Platanenstraße 24, 13156 Berlin, Germany.

Elisabete M. de Sousa, Centro de Filosofia da Universidade de Lisboa, Faculdade de Letras, Alameda da Universidade, 1600-214 Lisboa, Portugal.

Nataliya Vorobyova, Instytut Anglistyki Uniwersytetu Warzawskeigo, Nowy Swiat 4, Warsaw 00-497, Poland.

List of Abbreviations

Danish Abbreviations

B&A   *Breve og Aktstykker vedrørende Søren Kierkegaard*, ed. by Niels
            Thulstrup, vols. I–II, Copenhagen: Munksgaard 1953–54.

Bl.art.   *S. Kierkegaard's Bladartikler, med Bilag samlede efter Forfatterens Død,
            udgivne som Supplement til hans øvrige Skrifter*, ed. by Rasmus Nielsen,
            Copenhagen: C.A. Reitzel 1857.

EP   *Af Søren Kierkegaards Efterladte Papirer*, vols. 1–9, ed. by H.P. Barfod
            and Hermann Gottsched, Copenhagen: CA. Reitzel 1869–81.

Pap.   *Søren Kierkegaards Papirer*, vols. I to XI–3, ed. by Peter Andreas
            Heiberg, Victor Kuhr and Einer Torsting, Copenhagen: Gyldendalske
            Boghandel, Nordisk Forlag 1909–48; second, expanded ed., vols. I to
            XI–3, by Niels Thulstrup, vols. XII to XIII supplementary volumes, ed.
            by Niels Thulstrup, vols. XIV to XVI index by Niels Jørgen Cappelørn,
            Copenhagen: Gyldendal 1968–78.

SKS   *Søren Kierkegaards Skrifter*, vols. 1-28, K1-K28, ed. by Niels Jørgen
            Cappelørn, Joakim Garff, Jette Knudsen, Johnny Kondrup, Alastair
            McKinnon and Finn Hauberg Mortensen, Copenhagen: Gads Forlag
            1997ff.

SV1   *Samlede Værker*, vols. I–XIV, ed. by A.B. Drachmann, Johan Ludvig
            Heiberg and H.O. Lange, Copenhagen: Gyldendal 1901–06.

English Abbreviations

AN   *Armed Neutrality*, trans. by Howard V. Hong and Edna H. Hong, Princeton:
            Princeton University Press 1998.

AR   *On Authority and Revelation*, *The Book on Adler*, trans. by Walter Lowrie,
            Princeton: Princeton University Press 1955.

ASKB   *The Auctioneer's Sales Record of the Library of Søren Kierkegaard*, ed.
            by H.P. Rohde, Copenhagen: The Royal Library 1967.

BA   *The Book on Adler*, trans. by Howard V. Hong and Edna H. Hong, Princeton: Princeton University Press 1998.

C   *The Crisis and a Crisis in the Life of an Actress*, trans. by Howard V. Hong and Edna H. Hong, Princeton: Princeton University Press 1997.

CA   *The Concept of Anxiety*, trans. by Reidar Thomte in collaboration with Albert B. Anderson, Princeton: Princeton University Press 1980.

CD   *Christian Discourses*, trans. by Howard V. Hong and Edna H. Hong, Princeton: Princeton University Press 1997.

CI   *The Concept of Irony*, trans. by Howard V. Hong and Edna H. Hong, Princeton: Princeton University Press 1989.

CIC   *The Concept of Irony*, trans. with an Introduction and Notes by Lee M. Capel, London: Collins 1966.

COR   *The Corsair Affair; Articles Related to the Writings*, trans. by Howard V. Hong and Edna H. Hong, Princeton: Princeton University Press 1982.

CUP1   *Concluding Unscientific Postscript*, vol. 1, trans. by Howard V. Hong and Edna H. Hong, Princeton: Princeton University Press 1992.

CUP2   *Concluding Unscientific Postscript*, vol. 2, trans. by Howard V. Hong and Edna H. Hong, Princeton: Princeton University Press 1992.

EO1   *Either/Or*, Part I, trans. by Howard V. Hong and Edna H. Hong, Princeton: Princeton University Press 1987.

EO2   *Either/Or*, Part II, trans. by Howard V. Hong and Edna H. Hong, Princeton: Princeton University Press 1987.

EOP   *Either/Or*, trans. by Alastair Hannay, Harmondsworth: Penguin Books 1992.

EPW   *Early Polemical Writings*, among others: *From the Papers of One Still Living; Articles from Student Days; The Battle Between the Old and the New Soap-Cellars*, trans. by Julia Watkin, Princeton: Princeton University Press 1990.

EUD   *Eighteen Upbuilding Discourses*, trans. by Howard V. Hong and Edna H. Hong, Princeton: Princeton University Press 1990.

FSE   *For Self-Examination*, trans. by Howard V. Hong and Edna H. Hong, Princeton: Princeton University Press 1990.

FT	*Fear and Trembling*, trans. by Howard V. Hong and Edna H. Hong, Princeton: Princeton University Press 1983.
FTP	*Fear and Trembling*, trans. by Alastair Hannay, Harmondsworth: Penguin Books 1985.
JC	*Johannes Climacus, or De omnibus dubitandum est*, trans. by Howard V. Hong and Edna H. Hong, Princeton: Princeton University Press 1985.
JFY	*Judge for Yourself!*, trans. by Howard V. Hong and Edna H. Hong, Princeton: Princeton University Press 1990.
JP	*Søren Kierkegaard's Journals and Papers*, vols. 1–6, ed. and trans. by Howard V. Hong and Edna H. Hong, assisted by Gregor Malantschuk (vol. 7, Index and Composite Collation), Bloomington and London: Indiana University Press 1967–78.
KAC	*Kierkegaard's Attack upon "Christendom," 1854–1855*, trans. by Walter Lowrie, Princeton: Princeton University Press 1944.
KJN	*Kierkegaard's Journals and Notebooks*, vols. 1–11, ed. by Niels Jørgen Cappelørn, Alastair Hannay, David Kangas, Bruce H. Kirmmse, George Pattison, Vanessa Rumble, and K. Brian Söderquist, Princeton and Oxford: Princeton University Press 2007ff.
LD	*Letters and Documents*, trans. by Henrik Rosenmeier, Princeton: Princeton University Press 1978 (A translation of *B&A*).
LR	*A Literary Review*, trans. by Alastair Hannay, Harmondsworth: Penguin Books 2001.
M	*The Moment and Late Writings*, trans. by Howard V. Hong and Edna H. Hong, Princeton: Princeton University Press 1998.
P	*Prefaces*, trans. by Todd W. Nichol, Princeton: Princeton University Press 1997.
PC	*Practice in Christianity*, trans. by Howard V. Hong and Edna H. Hong, Princeton: Princeton University Press 1991.
PF	*Philosophical Fragments*, trans. by Howard V. Hong and Edna H. Hong, Princeton: Princeton University Press 1985.
PJ	*Papers and Journals: A Selection*, trans. by Alastair Hannay, Harmondsworth: Penguin Books 1996.

PLR   *Prefaces: Light Reading for Certain Classes as the Occasion May Require*,
            trans. by William McDonald, Tallahassee: Florida State University Press
            1989.

PLS   *Concluding Unscientific Postscript*, trans. by David F. Swenson and
            Walter Lowrie, Princeton: Princeton University Press 1941.

PV   *The Point of View* including *On My Work as an Author, The Point of View
            for My Work as an Author*, and *Armed Neutrality*, trans. by Howard V.
            Hong and Edna H. Hong, Princeton: Princeton University Press 1998.

PVL   *The Point of View for My Work as an Author* including *On My Work
            as an Author*, trans. by Walter Lowrie, New York and London: Oxford
            University Press 1939.

R   *Repetition*, trans. by Howard V. Hong and Edna H. Hong, Princeton:
            Princeton University Press 1983.

SBL   *Notes of Schelling's Berlin Lectures*, trans. by Howard V. Hong and Edna
            H. Hong, Princeton: Princeton University Press 1989.

SLW   *Stages on Life's Way*, trans. by Howard V. Hong and Edna H. Hong,
            Princeton: Princeton University Press 1988.

SUD   *The Sickness unto Death*, trans. by Howard V. Hong and Edna H. Hong,
            Princeton: Princeton University Press 1980.

SUDP   *The Sickness unto Death*, trans. by Alastair Hannay, London and New
            York: Penguin Books 1989.

TA   *Two Ages: The Age of Revolution and the Present Age. A Literary Review*,
            trans. by Howard V. Hong and Edna H. Hong, Princeton: Princeton
            University Press 1978.

TD   *Three Discourses on Imagined Occasions*, trans. by Howard V. Hong and
            Edna H. Hong, Princeton: Princeton University Press 1993.

UD   *Upbuilding Discourses in Various Spirits*, trans. by Howard V. Hong and
            Edna H. Hong, Princeton: Princeton University Press 1993.

WA   *Without Authority* including *The Lily in the Field and the Bird of the Air,
            Two Ethical-Religious Essays, Three Discourses at the Communion on
            Fridays, An Upbuilding Discourse, Two Discourses at the Communion
            on Fridays*, trans. by Howard V. Hong and Edna H. Hong, Princeton:
            Princeton University Press 1997.

WL   *Works of Love*, trans. by Howard V. Hong and Edna H. Hong, Princeton: Princeton University Press 1995.

WS   *Writing Sampler*, trans. by Todd W. Nichol, Princeton: Princeton University Press 1997.

Lord George Gordon Byron:

Seduction, Defiance, and Despair in the Works of Kierkegaard

Bartholomew Ryan

> Soon, soon you will be mine. When the sun shuts its vigilant eye, when history is over and the myths begin, I will not only throw my cloak around me but I will throw the night around me like a cloak and hurry to you and listen in order to find you—listen not for your footsteps but for the beating of your heart.[1]

Søren Kierkegaard never read English, but he did keep a German edition of the complete works of Byron, the English Romantic poet, in his personal library.[2] Lord George Gordon Byron was born in 1788 and died in 1824. He is the image of the Romantic poet *par excellence*: reckless, brilliant, handsome, prolific, polemical, and forever young. Byron was born in London to a Scotswoman, Catherine Gordon, and the penniless but titled widower, Captain John Byron. Byron's charming and reckless father soon abandoned both wife and child. He died in 1791, perhaps of tuberculosis or poison, but not before appointing his son as heir to his non-existent estate.

The young Byron, educated at Harrow School and the University of Cambridge, soon became well-known for his volatile temperament and wild antics of promiscuity with both sexes. Byron's first collection of poems, *Hours of Idleness*, was published in 1807. The Cantos I and II of *Childe Harold Pilgrimage* in 1812 brought him instant celebrity. Suddenly Byron became a handsome hero, lauded by the aristocracy and pursued by countless women. Thus the Byron legend was born.

The significance of this cannot be underestimated. Already in 1818, six years before Byron's death, the German philosopher Arthur Schopenhauer (1788–1860) was quoting directly from Byron's *Childe Harold's Pilgrimage* and referring to him as one of "the great men of genius."[3] Lady Caroline Lamb (1785–1828) memorably

---

[1]   *SKS* 2, 428 / *EO1*, 441.

[2]   *Lord Byron's sämmtliche Werke. Nach den Anforderungen unserer Zeit neu übersetzt von Mehreren*, vols. 1–10, Stuttgart: Hoffman 1839 (*ASKB* 1868–1870).

[3]   Arthur Schopenhauer, *The World as Will and Representation*, vols. 1–2, London: Dover 1969, vol. 1, p. 181; p. 191; p. 251. (Kierkegaard owned the second edition of Schopenhauer's work in German, see *Die Welt als Wille und Vorstellung*, vols. 1–2, 2nd revised and enlarged ed., Leipzig: F.A. Brockhaus 1844 [1819] (*ASKB* 773–773a).) Byron is also quoted and referred to on numerous occasions (such as the poems *Don Juan*, *Lara*, *The Prophecy of Dante*, *Childe*

remarked that Byron was "mad, bad and dangerous to know."[4] Byron's *The Corsair* (1814) was also hugely popular with its dashing, enigmatic hero and pirate adventure.[5] The poems *The Prisoner of Chillon* (which was imitated by Alexander Pushkin (1799–1837), the darling of Russian letters, in *The Prisoner of the Caucasus* (1822), in its title and inset portrait of the poet[6]) and the Faustian *Manfred* were published in 1816. *Cain: A Mystery* was published in 1821, while the unfinished *Don Juan*, considered Byron's masterpiece, was published in its episodic Cantos (16 in all) in the years 1819–23. In his final year, Byron joined the revolt of the Greeks against the Ottoman Empire. He died of a fever in Missolonghi, Greece, in 1824.

II.

Among Kierkegaard's published works, Byron is mentioned in *Either/Or* (1843) and *The Concept of Anxiety* (1844). It is no surprise that Kierkegaard would refer to Byron in *Either/Or*, since the English poet might well have been a model for the aesthete depicted in Part One of that book. We will now examine the passages in which Byron is explicitly named. In his reflections on Mozart's *Don Giovanni*, the aesthetician A comments:

> That Byron was in many ways particularly endowed to present Don Juan is certain enough, and therefore one can be sure that when that undertaking failed, the reason was not in Byron but in something far deeper: Byron has ventured to bring Don Juan into existence for us, to tell us of his childhood and youth, to construct him out of context for his finite life-relationships. But Don Juan thereby became a reflective personality who loses the ideality he has in the traditional picture.[7]

Two pages later, A draws the following conclusion about Byron's *magnum opus*: "Therefore, Byron's *Don Juan* must be regarded as a failure because it stretches out epically."[8] In Part Two of *Either/Or*, on "The Aesthetic Validity of Marriage," the pseudonym Judge William also comments on Byron: "What I am saying here does not apply only to some seducer prowling about in the world like a beast of prey. No, it fits a goodly chorus of often highly gifted people, and it is not only Byron who

---

Harolde's Pilgrimage again, *Cain* and *Euthanasia*) in the second volume of Schopenhauer's major work, but this volume was added and expanded later in 1844 and 1859.

[4]   Fiona MacCarthy, *Byron: Life and Legend*, London: Faber and Faber 2003, p. 164.

[5]   There seems to be no connection between Byron's poem and Goldschmidt's satirical weekly paper of the same name. Goldschmidt's *Corsair* (*Corsaren*) heralds from Paris. For more on this, see Joakim Garff, *Søren Aabye Kierkegaard. A Biography*, trans. by Bruce H. Kirmmse, Princeton, New Jersey: Princeton University Press 2005, p. 326. The image of the pirate though fits both Byron's image and Goldschmidt's paper; a travelling, seafaring outlaw was an image that Kierkegaard was equally fascinated and repelled by.

[6]   T.J. Binyon, *Pushkin: A Biography*, London: HarperCollins 2002, p. 151. We might view Pushkin, in his own masterpiece *Eugene Onegin*, as attempting to overcome his debt to Byron, by directly mocking him.

[7]   *SKS* 2, 110 / *EO1*, 106.

[8]   *SKS* 2, 111 / *EO1*, 108.

declares that love is heaven and marriage hell."[9] Twenty pages afterward, Judge William mentions Byron for the second and final time: "For the person who reflects temporally, the first kiss, for example, will be a past (just as Byron has put it in a short poem); for the person who reflects eternally, there will be an eternal possibility."[10] From these references, it can be ascertained that Kierkegaard at least read some of *Don Juan* and Byron's first collection of poems, *Hours of Idleness*.

All of Kierkegaard's remaining substantive references to Byron are to be found in his journals and notebooks. In what may be called Kierkegaard's Faustian period (1836–37), Byron is mentioned three times in the journals. In this period, Kierkegaard explores the aesthetics of Mozart's *Don Giovanni*, the concept of irony, the idea of mythology, and Goethe's *Faust*. Byron makes his first appearance in connection with Kierkegaard's reading of Karl Ernst Schubarth's (1796–1860) comparative analysis of Goethe's *Faust* and Byron's *Manfred*:[11] "He [sc. Schubarth] shows that some have simply understood the poem to be a complaint that he was denied the highest pleasures of life, and that Lord Byron has reproduced the matter and content in F.[aust] from this standpoint."[12] Further on, Kierkegaard refers to Byron as among the "great poets," claiming that Byron's dramatic piece, *Cain*, "has understood the Devil from another side."[13] Still reading Schubarth's work on *Faust* and *Manfred*, Kierkegaard jots down in another journal entry a few days later, "Probably Lord Byron's Manfred is Faust without a Goethean *educating* Mephisto?"[14] The last mention of Byron in Kierkegaard's journals is 14 years later; "Yes, one who wishes to enjoy life on a grand scale (a Lord Byron, for example) could certainly wish to be healed—but not on the condition that he has to die to the world once and for all."[15]

The final section of teasing out the works and general myth of Byron in Kierkegaard's writings concludes with interpretations of their place in Kierkegaard's body of work. I will briefly mention five aspects in Kierkegaard's writings that invite an interpretation of his use of Byron: his use of Byron's *Manfred* alongside Goethe's *Faust*, the role and image of the poet, the creation and critique of the seducer, the critique of *Don Juan*, and finally, the essay "The Rotation of Crops."

III.

A.

As mentioned, Kierkegaard's interest in Byron began during his Faustian phase. In journal entries from this period, Kierkegaard refers to both *Manfred* and *Cain*. His interest in *Cain* lies in the presentation of Lucifer, and *Manfred* is likened to a *Faust*

---

9   *SKS* 3, 31 / *EO2*, 22.
10   *SKS* 3, 48 / *EO2*, 41.
11   K.E. Schubarth, *Ueber Goethe's Faust. Vorlesungen*, Berlin: Enslin 1830, especially pp. 45–6; pp. 81–2 (*ASKB* U 96).
12   *SKS* 17, 89, BB:7 / *KJN* 1, 82.
13   *SKS* 17, 89, BB:7 / *KJN* 1, 83.
14   *Pap.* I C 102, p. 277 / *JP* 5, 5160.
15   *SKS* 23, 424, NB20:57 / *JP* 2, 1872.

without Mephistopheles. Kierkegaard's interest and avid note-taking on different versions and interpretations of the Faust story fades once his former tutor Hans Lassen Martensen (1808–84) published an extended essay on Lenau's *Faust*.[16] But there are aspects of Byron's *Manfred* that are akin to Kierkegaard and his project on *Faust*. The poem's epigraph is from Hamlet—surely one of Kierkegaard's most cherished fictional characters.[17] Both *Manfred* and *Cain* can be related to *Faust*, with respect to their content; this can be seen from Kierkegaard's reading of Schubarth and Faust's own efforts to overcome the classic notion of good and evil.

B.

The second aspect of the presence of Byron in Kierkegaard's writings might be seen in the whole image and mythology of this very charismatic poet, and in Kierkegaard's own ongoing complex depiction of the use and abuse of a being a poet. This image is reflective of the reception of Byron outside England, in continental Europe. One influential image is Napoleonic in kind: not simply in evoking a battlefield and territorial conquest, but as a tribute to one's own art and to the triumph over one's god. Nietzsche, for example, salutes Byron's *Manfred* as follows: "There thus arises the danger that man may bleed to death from knowledge of truth. This was expressed by Byron in immortal verse: 'Sorrow is knowledge: they who know the most / Must mourn the deepest o'er the fatal truth, / The Tree of Knowledge is not that of Life.' "[18] Others' images of Byron are of the revolutionary fighter, the great seducer, and the colossal poet of despair and restless wanderer.

Byron served as a leader of Italy's revolutionary organization "the Carbonari" which fought against Austria, and, as already mentioned, he fought against the Turks in the Greek War of Independence. There are many odes to various women throughout his works, from Marion to Lesbia, Emma to Caroline, Eliza to Anne, not to mention the erotic eulogies to all those in *Don Juan*. Byron's poem *Childe Harold's Pilgrimage* is enough to create the image of the restless wandering poet, and the anguish and despair of the poet can also be felt throughout his writings from "My Soul is Dark" to "Darkness," from "Parisina" to *Manfred*. One can begin to see the disparity between Byron (and the image of Byron) and Kierkegaard; this gives us a clue to Kierkegaard's own constant conflict with what a poet ought to be.

---

[16]   Hans Lassen Martensen, "Betragtninger over Ideen af Faust med Hensyn til Lenaus Faust," *Perseus, Journal for den speculative Idee*, no. 1, 1837, pp. 91–164. Nicolaus Lenau was the pseudonym for the Austro-Hungarian poet Nicolaus Niembsch von Strehlenau (1802–50). See Kierkegaard's journal entry in *Pap.* II A 597 / *JP* 5, 5225: "How unhappy I am—Martensen has written an essay on Lenau's *Faust*."

[17]   *SKS* 7, 151 / *CUP1*, 163 "...to pray is just as difficult as to play the role of Hamlet, of which the greatest actor is supposed to have said that only once had he been close to playing it well; nevertheless he would devote all his ability and his entire life to continued study of this role." See also *SKS* 6, 417–19 / *SLW*, 442–54.

[18]   Friedrich Nietzsche, *Human, All Too Human*, trans. by R.J. Hollingdale, Cambridge: Cambridge University Press 1996, vol. 1, p. 109; pp. 60–1; Byron, *Manfred: A Dramatic Poem*, Act I, Scene i; quoted from *Byron: Poetical Works*, ed. by Frederick Page, Oxford: Oxford University Press 1970 (the piece was first published in 1817), p. 390.

When one arrives at *Either/Or* with its opening question, "What is a poet?," one finds an answer that applies best to the typical portrait of a Romantic poet: "An unhappy person who conceals profound anguish in his heart but whose lips are so formed that as sighs and cries pass over them they sound like beautiful music."[19] Byron embodies Kierkegaard's tortured aesthetic man, that seducer and larger-than-life figure of *Either/ Or*, Part I; this figure is a reflection of the cult of Byron that was then cultivated by French, German, and Russian men of letters. On a Kierkegaardian reading, Byron remains a slave to aestheticism and defiant despair. The poet suffers, as does the poetic character of *Either/Or*, in order to alleviate his sufferings; he loses himself in Mozart's sensual masterpiece, and in the seduction and conquest of women. Close to the end of *Stages on Life's Way*, Frater Taciturnus clarifies the distinction that Kierkegaard is himself trying to make: "The aesthetic hero is great by conquering, the religious hero is great by suffering."[20] This first part of this sentence succinctly affirms the Byronic way of life. Byron's poet, in the tradition of the Romantic idea of its day, is the living embodiment of poetry as life lived to the fullest and amid a great outpouring of work. In *The Sickness unto Death*, the suffering poet as religious poet is presented most directly by Kierkegaard's Anti-Climacus.[21] In this same text, the Byronic character with whom Kierkegaard empathizes is confronted in the section "Despair as Defiance," which is the final and most potent stage of despair. Here are a few examples of Manfred's defiant despair from a Kierkegaardian perspective:

> I plunged deep,
> But, like an ebbing wave, it dashed me back
> Into the gulf of my unfathom'd thought
> ...I dwell in my despair—
> And live—and live for ever.[22]

> I have sunk before my vain despair, and knelt
> To my own desolation.[23]

> There is no power in holy men,
> Nor charm in prayer, nor purifying form
> Of penitence, nor outward look, nor fast,
> Nor agony—nor, greater than all these,
> The innate tortures of that deep despair,
> Which is remorse without the fear of hell.[24]

Anti-Climacus' descriptions of the person of defiant despair reflect the manner in which the characters Manfred, Cain, Don Juan, and the poet Byron himself, sense,

---

[19]   *SKS* 2, 27 / *EO1*, 19.
[20]   *SKS* 6, 420 / *SLW*, 454.
[21]   *SKS* 11, 191–2 / *SUD*, 77–8. These first two pages of the second section of *The Sickness unto Death* offer a fascinating glimpse into the dilemmas of the poet in the face of the poet's muse.
[22]   *Manfred*, Act II, Scene ii.
[23]   Ibid., Act II, Scene iv.
[24]   Ibid., Act III, Scene i.

feel and act: "The self is its own master, absolutely its own master, so-called; and precisely this is the despair, but also what it regards as its pleasure and delight."[25] Anti-Climacus could well be speaking for Byron's Cain when Cain abandons all that he loves to agree with Lucifer, in his defiance of God, whom he sees as having shamed his family. Here Anti-Climacus' defiant despairer begins to understand that he treads a very dangerous path, yet he proceeds with ever more fury:

> By now, even if God in heaven and all the angels offered to help him out of it—no, he does not want that, now it is too late. Once he would gladly have given everything to be rid of his agony, but he was kept waiting; now it is too late, now he would rather rage against everything and be the wronged victim of the whole world and of all life, and it is of particular significance to him to make sure that no one takes it away from him—for then he would not be able to demonstrate and to prove to himself that he is right.[26]

Byron's friend and contemporary, Percy Bysshe Shelley (1792–1822), displays his own perception of this demonic defiance and rage embodied in the Byronic figure in a three-line fragment for Byron published posthumously: "O Mighty mind, in whose deep stream this age / Shakes like a reed in the unheeding storm, / Why dost thou curb not thine own sacred rage?"[27] A comparison of Shelley's fragment to Kierkegaard's analysis of defiant despair in *The Sickness unto Death* allows us to attain a more nuanced understanding of Byron in terms of this image of the poet full of creativity, defiance, and rage. Nevertheless, in *The Concept of Anxiety*, Byron is described alongside Shelley and Shakespeare as one of the few poets who are able to "break the silence."[28] This silence is usually approached with awe and terror by Kierkegaard, especially in *Fear and Trembling* and *The Concept of Anxiety*. Yet both the poet and the seducer have the potential to "break" this silence.[29] Silence, however, will always have the last word, whether that be in Agnete's silent faith in the face of the charismatic Merman in *Fear and Trembling*, or as one of the three guides in the discourse on the lily and the birds of 1849.

C.

Kierkegaard's third use of Byron can be discovered through his creation and critique of the pseudonym A and the seducer in *Either/Or*. In the second part of *Either/Or*, Judge William connects the writer (who is referred to as A) of Part One to Byron in his attitude towards commitment to marriage and women in general, and in his being a slave to romantic love and nothing more. Judge William alludes to Byron's poem,

---

[25]   *SKS* 11, 183 / *SUD*, 69.
[26]   Ibid.
[27]   Percy Bysshe Shelley, "Fragment: To Byron" in *The Complete Poems of Percy Bysshe Shelley*, New York: The Modern Library Edition 1994 (written in 1818), p. 608.
[28]   *SKS* 4, 432 / *CA*, 131.
[29]   *SKS* 2, 317 / *EO1*, 327: "Let her hate me, scorn me, be indifferent to me, love someone else—I do not fear; but stir up the water, break the silence."

"To Eliza," which reads, "Though women are angels, yet wedlock's the devil."[30] Again, A is compared to Byron in the priority of the first kiss, and the slow fading away of the first stirrings of love. Byron writes: "Give me the mild beam of the soul-breathing glance, / Or the rapture which dwells on the first kiss of love."[31] Does Judge William interpret Byron correctly? For Byron, the first kiss of love seems to be greater than the actual muse: "The earnest remembrance will still be the last, / Our sweetest memorial the first kiss of love."[32]

Judge William had written: "for the person who reflects eternally, there will be an eternal possibility."[33] Byron's lines seem to indicate that the first kiss is eternal, in that it will always be remembered and thereby resonant. As long as one reflects on the first kiss, there is the eternal possibility. This is something that Judge William overlooks. The poem reveals the religiosity that pervades the true poet, and the first kiss itself is equated with the divine sphere: "Some portion of paradise still is on earth, / What are visions like these to the first / Kiss of love?"[34] Like Byron, the seducer in *Either/Or*, Part One, also speaks of a divine kiss: "a kiss, unlike a human kiss, which subtracts something, but rather a divine kiss, which gives everything."[35] Finally, the seducer invokes the literary image of a vampire, which again brings to mind Byron or the Byronic figure. The protagonist comes across as a kind of vampire, residing in the shadows of the city streets, deftly moving in and out of the city crowds, and always alert with the sleepless eye. The references to this image are numerous: "living in a kingdom of mist," "eyes in a cape," and "continually seek[ing] my prey."[36] Through the use of the cape (*Kappe*) or cloak (*Kaabe*) throughout the essay,[37] the seducer's shadow world is vividly evoked.

D.

Next, mention should be made of the critique of Byron's *Don Juan* in the essay on Mozart's *Don Giovanni* in *Either/Or*, Part One. For Kierkegaard's pseudonymous

---

[30]   Judge William is referring to Byron's poem "To Eliza," in *Lord Byron's sämmtliche Werke*, vol. 1, p. 83; quoted from *Byron: Poetical Works*, ed. by Frederick Page, p. 29.

[31]   Byron, "The First Kiss of Love," in *Byron: Poetical Works*, ed. by Frederick Page, p. 8.

[32]   Ibid.

[33]   *SKS* 3, 48 / *EO2*, 41.

[34]   Byron, "The First Kiss of Love," in *Byron: Poetical Works*, ed. by Frederick Page, p. 8.

[35]   *SKS* 2, 362 / *EO1*, 374.

[36]   *SKS* 2, 299 / *EO1*, 310. *SKS* 2, 305 / *EO1*, 314. *SKS* 2, 314 / *EO1*, 324.

[37]   See, for example, *SKS* 2, 321 / *EO1*, 314. *SKS* 2, 310 / *EO1*, 321. *SKS* 2, 14 / *EO1*, 323. *SKS* 2, 341 / *EO1*, 352. *SKS* 2, 352 / *EO1*, 363. *SKS* 2, 428 / *EO1*, 441. The seducer is the hunter with his cape (*Kappe*) chasing Cordelia as the prey with her green cloak (*Kaabe*) *SKS* 2, 315 / *EO1*, 325. *SKS* 2, 317, *EO1*, 327. *SKS* 2, 319–21 / *EO1*, 329–31. In a passage deleted from the final draft, Kierkegaard actually does write: "this vampiric tendency of his. Just as the shadows of the underworld sucked the blood out of the real human beings and lived so long, so did he." *Pap.* III B 45 / *EO1*, Supplement, p. 553. This vampire image is also apparent in *Repetition* where, in Berlin, Constantin relishes watching the city by a window at moonlight, and desiring to throw on a cape after midnight, looks out his window and "sees the shadows of passersby hurrying along the walls." *SKS* 4, 28 / *R*, 151–2.

aesthetician, Byron's *Don Juan* is a failure because it does not treat Don Juan himself as an ideality; instead, it presents him as a human being who was born, had a childhood, and developed relationships. The argument in *Either/Or* is that when Don Juan is interpreted musically, the true splendor of the character is revealed, as the "total infinitude of passion," "the infinite power that nothing can resist," "the wild craving of desire," and the "absolute victoriousness of this desire."[38] Music represents Don Juan as a power, not as an individual. Here, Kierkegaard's aesthetician's interpretation can be affiliated with the power of an abyss-like religiosity, abyss-like in that its demonism (Don Juan is described as "demonically powerful"[39]) is such that Don Juan cannot come into conflict with the world but is to be forever lost to the infinite. A makes this point: "If Don Juan is interpreted as an individual, then he is *eo ipso* in conflict with the world about him."[40]

E.

Finally, one might attribute the framework of the essay "The Rotation of Crops" in *Either/Or* to one of the verses of Canto XIII in *Don Juan*. I quote the verse in full:

> Our ridicules are kept in the back ground—
>   Ridiculous enough, but also dull;
> Professions, too, are no more to be found
>   Professional; and there is nought to cull
> Of folly's fruit; for though your fools abound,
>   They're barren and not worth the pains to pull.
> Society is now one polish'd horde,
> Form'd of two mighty tribes, the *Bores* and *Bored*.[41]

The last lines closing with "the *Bores* and *Bored*" strikingly bring to mind Kierkegaard's "The Rotation of Crops." Kierkegaard's aesthete practically repeats this idea:

> The word "boring" can designate just as well a person who bores others as someone who bores himself....How remarkable it is that those who do not bore themselves generally bore others; those, however, who bore themselves entertain others. Generally, those who do not bore themselves are busy in the world in one way or another, but for that reason they are, of all people, the most boring of all, the most unbearable....The other class of human beings, the superior ones, are those who bore themselves.[42]

Indeed: so much of *Don Juan* conjures up a world where most men and women sleepwalk through life, busying themselves with vacuous conversation to cover up the abyss of "civilized" existence. This is the world-view of the superior aesthete both

---

[38]   *SKS* 2, 110 / *EO1*, 107.
[39]   Ibid.
[40]   Ibid.
[41]   *Don Juan*, Canto XIII, verse 95; quoted from *Byron: Poetical Works*, ed. by Frederick Page, p. 819.
[42]   *SKS* 2, 278 / *EO1*, 288.

in *Don Juan* and *Either/Or*. The poet who moves through *Either/Or* is at times the sufferer of his sonorous art, the triumphant seducer of women, the graveyard wanderer and the bored aristocrat. In Kierkegaard's own vivid imagination, all of these aspects of the poet of *Either/Or* embody perfectly the Romantic poet Lord Byron.

In this same section from *Don Juan* we can see also the influence of—or at least parallels with—Goethe's *Faust*, to which both Byron and Kierkegaard are indebted. When Byron writes, "Society is now one polish'd horde,"[43] I am reminded of Mephistopheles' remarks in the "Witch's Kitchen" Scene in *Faust*: "Besides, civilisation, which now licks / Us all smooth, has taught even the Devil tricks."[44]

The name Byron is mentioned only a handful of times in Kierkegaard's published works, and yet he made his mark as one of the "real poets" in the works of Kierkegaard, most notably in Byron's "demonic" works, *Cain* and *Manfred*, and in his story of a seducer, *Don Juan*. Though Byron never attained a place as substantial as Shakespeare in the works of Kierkegaard, it is nonetheless the despair of "real poets" such as Byron that Kierkegaard recognized as needing to be confronted in the journey toward the religious realm. It is not simply a cliché to place Byron in the role of the seducer that we think we understand; instead, one is tempted to be seduced by the troubled seducer whose power enters into the religious realm of Kierkegaard's probing thought. In the philosopher's own words: "He who *could* not seduce men *cannot* save them either. This is the qualification of reflection."[45]

---

[43]   *Don Juan*, Canto XIII, verse 95; quoted from *Byron: Poetical Works*, ed. by Frederick Page, p. 819.
[44]   Goethe, *Faust I* (1808), lines 2495–6; quoted from Johann Wolfgang von Goethe, *Faust: Part One*, trans. by David Luke, Oxford: Oxford University Press 1987, p. 78.
[45]   *SKS* 21, 148, NB8:8 / *JP* 3, 3706.

Bibliography

I. Byron's Works in The Auction Catalogue *of Kierkegaard's Library*

Lord Byron's sämmtliche Werke. Nach den Anforderungen unserer Zeit neu übersetzt von Mehreren, vols. 1–10, Stuttgart: Hoffman 1839 (*ASKB* 1868–1870).

II. Works in The Auction Catalogue *of Kierkegaard's Library that Discuss Byron*

Adler, Adolph Peter, *Populaire Foredrag over Hegels objective Logik*, Copenhagen: C.A. Reitzel 1842, p. 61, note (*ASKB* 383).

[Becker, Karl Friedrich], *Karl Friedrich Beckers Verdenshistorie, omarbeidet af Johan Gottfried Woltmann*, vols. 1–12, trans. by J. Riise, Copenhagen: Fr. Brummer 1822–29, vol. 10, p. 238 (*ASKB* 1972–1983).

Heiberg, Johan Ludvig, "Lyrisk Poesie," in *Intelligensblade*, vol. 3, nos. 25–6, 1843, pp. 25–72, see p. 38 (*ASKB* U 56).

—— *Om Philosophiens Betydning for den nuværende Tid. Et Indbydelses-Skrift til en Række af philosophiske Forelæsninger*, Copenhagen: C.A. Reitzel 1833, p. 43 (*ASKB* 568).

Møller, Poul Martin, "Drømmen. (Efter Lord Byron)," in *Efterladte Skrifter af Poul M. Møller*, vols. 1–3, ed. by Christian Winther, F.C. Olsen and Christen Thaarup, Copenhagen: C.A. Reitzel 1839–43, vol. 1, pp. 25–33 (*ASKB* 1574–1576).

Rosenkranz, Karl, *Psychologie oder die Wissenschaft vom subjectiven Geist*, Königsberg: Bornträger 1837, p. 15 (*ASKB* 744).

Schopenhauer, Arthur, *Die Welt als Wille und Vorstellung*, vols. 1–2, 2nd revised and enlarged ed., Leipzig: F.A. Brockhaus 1844 [1819], vol. 2, p. 216; vol. 2, pp. 81–2; p. 146; p. 221; p. 433; p. 574; p. 585 (*ASKB* 773–773a).

Steffens, Henrich, *Was ich erlebte. Aus der Erinnerung niedergeschrieben*, vols. 1–10, Breslau: Josef Max 1840–44, vol. 9, p. 9; p. 351; vol. 10, p. 9 (*ASKB* 1834–1843).

Schubarth, Karl Ernst, *Ueber Goethe's Faust. Vorlesungen*, Berlin: Enslin 1830 (*ASKB* U 96)

Thiele, Just M., *Om den danske Billedhugger Bertel Thorvaldsen. Tilligemed en Fortegnelse paa de Arbeider, hvilke han indtil nærværende Tid har udført*, Copenhagen: Trykt i det Berlingske Bogtrykkeri 1837 (*ASKB* A II 198).

Thiersch, Friedrich, *Allgemeine Aesthetik in akademischen Lehrvorträgen*, Berlin: G. Reimer 1846, p. 507 (*ASKB* 1378).

Thomsen, Grimur, *Om den nyfranske Poesi, et Forsøg til Besvarelse af Universitetets æsthetiske Priisspørgsmaal for 1841: "Har Smag og Sands for Poesi gjort*

Frem- eller Tilbageskridt i Frankrig i de sidste Tider og hvilken er Aarsagen?,"
Copenhagen: Wahlske Boghandlings Forlag 1843, pp. 21–4; p. 38; p. 63;
pp. 67–73 passim; pp. 89–92; p. 95; p. 105; p. 108; p. 112; pp. 113ff.; p. 119;
p.127; p. 145; p. 150; p. 159; p. 162 (*ASKB* 1390).

Weiße, Christian Hermann, *System der Aesthetik als Wissenschaft von der Idee der
Schönheit. In drei Büchern*, vols. 1–2, Leipzig: C.H.F. Hartmann 1830, vol. 1,
pp. 182–3 (*ASKB* 1379–1380).

III. Secondary Literature on Kierkegaard's Relation to Byron

Fenger, Henning, "Kierkegaard: A Literary Approach," in *Kierkegaard and His
Contemporaries. The Culture of Golden Age Denmark*, ed. by Jon Stewart,
Berlin and New York: Walter de Gruyter 2003 (*Kierkegaard Studies. Monograph
Series*, vol. 10), pp. 301–18, see pp. 312–13.

Hertel, Hans, "P.L. Møller and Romanticism in Danish Literature," in *Kierkegaard
and His Contemporaries. The Culture of Golden Age Denmark*, ed. by Jon
Stewart, Berlin and New York: Walter de Gruyter 2003 (*Kierkegaard Studies.
Monograph Series*, vol. 10), pp. 356–72, see pp. 361–6 passim.

Pattison, George, "The Joy of Birdsong or Lyrical Dialectics," in *Without Authority*,
ed. by Robert L. Perkins, Macon, Georgia: Mercer University Press 2007
(*International Kierkegaard Commentary*, vol. 18), pp. 111–25.

Shilstone, Frederick, "Byron, Kierkegaard and the Irony of 'Rotation,' " *Colby
Library Quarterly*, no. 25, 1989, pp. 237–44.

Thorlby, Anthony, "Imagination and Irony in English Romantic Poetry," in *Romantic
Irony*, ed. by Frederick Garber, Budapest: Akadémiai Kiadó 1988, pp. 131–55,
see pp. 143–9.

Miguel de Cervantes:

The Valuable Contribution of a Minor Influence

Óscar Parcero Oubiña

To talk about the presence of Cervantes in the work of Kierkegaard is virtually equivalent to tracing the diverse references to *Don Quixote* which are strewn throughout both Kierkegaard's published works and the *Nachlass*. Most of these citations seem to indicate that the influence of the Spanish author in Kierkegaard was no more than the occasional rhetorical use of a very well-known literary figure. There are, however, a few other mentions of *Don Quixote*, plus a significant allusion to one of Cervantes' *Exemplary Novels,* that seem to suggest that Kierkegaard might have had a closer relation to the Spanish author. This article attempts to investigate the real extent of Cervantes' influence on Kierkegaard by means of an analysis of all the references found in the latter's writings.

I. An Overview of Cervantes' Life and Kierkegaard's Context of the Quixote

Cervantes' life was, one could say, the antithesis of Kierkegaard's. Whereas the latter enjoyed the privileges of a comfortable, carefree bourgeois life, living almost exclusively in the small world of nineteenth-century Copenhagen, the Spanish author suffered all kinds of tribulations in all the different cities and countries in which he lived his troubled 69 years.

Miguel de Cervantes Saavedra was born in 1547 in Alcalá de Henares, a town near Madrid. He lived his adolescence between Madrid and Seville, but left soon for Italy. Even though he started early to write, literature was not yet his main concern. In Italy, Cervantes joined the Spanish army and participated in the decisive battle of Lepanto. This famous battle would prove to be decisive not only for the decline of Turkish power on the Mediterranean, but also for Cervantes himself. He would always be very proud of having been part of such "glorious episode." Moreover, during the battle he was wounded on his left arm, which left his hand disabled for the rest of his days and gave him the nickname of "*El manco de Lepanto,*" that is "The Cripple of Lepanto."

When he was returning to Spain in 1575, Berberisque pirates attacked the ship in which Cervantes was travelling, and he was made prisoner. Cervantes spent five years as a captive in Algiers, trying day in and day out to escape and preparing escape plans for other prisoners as well. In 1580 he was finally released from his imprisonment by some Spanish friars and could at last return to Spain. Luck, however, would continue to be against him. Back home, Cervantes found his family bankrupt and no one willing to offer him much help, despite the letters of recommendation that he carried with him from Italy. Thus economic troubles started pressing Cervantes, who then decided to devote himself to letters. He started writing plays, mostly; more than twenty comedies of Cervantes were performed in Madrid between 1583 and 1587. But luck turned again against him: the powerful literary figure of Lope de Vega (1562–1635)—who would become Cervantes' greatest enemy—arose, outshining everyone around him.

Cervantes moved then to Seville, where he would stay until 1600. He traveled all around Andalusia, working, among other things, as a tax collector. During these years, he spent most of his time living in the Sevillian underworld, among burglars, gamblers, and swindlers. This gave him the opportunity to get to know first-hand the world that Spanish Golden Age literature would describe so brilliantly in what has been known as "Picaresca." As a matter of fact, the work *Rinconete and Cortadillo* can be considered an excellent example of both "Picaresca" in general, and Cervantes' own experiences in particular. But Cervantes' contact with the underworld went further. During his employment as a tax collector, some irregularities were found in his account book, and he was imprisoned. Apart from strengthening bonds with the aforementioned Sevillian underworld, Cervantes started in jail to write his masterpiece, the *Quixote*.

What would become probably the most important novel ever, began as just one of Cervantes' brief *Exemplary Novels*. Little did he know when he started that the simple mockery of books of chivalry would develop into a long and complex novel, followed later by a second part. Out of jail, Cervantes moved to Valladolid, where he continued and finished the novel. In 1605—Cervantes was then 58—the first edition of *The Ingenious Gentleman Don Quixote de La Mancha* appeared in Madrid. The book enjoyed an immediate success, which soon put its author to work on a second part. This would eventually appear in 1615, spurred on especially by the publication, one year before, of an unauthorized second part of the *Quixote*, signed by the pseudonymous Alonso Fernández de Avellaneda. Meanwhile, Cervantes had published his *Exemplary Novels* (1613) and *Voyage to Parnassus* (1614), works that, together with the early *The Galatea* (1585) and the posthumous *The Trials of Persiles and Sigismunda* (1617), constitute the core of his production.

On April 23, 1616, the very same day Shakespeare died, Cervantes was buried in Madrid. His life had never been a quiet one. Apart from the two imprisonments mentioned above, he still had to suffer a third one, together with his family, as suspects of murder. The early success of his *Quixote* would help Cervantes' troubled life very little. All the erratic experiences he lived, however, became significant influences for his works, which have plenty of autobiographical references, in a way similar to Kierkegaard's.

Before starting to analyze the references to Cervantes in Kierkegaard's writings, we need to take into consideration the context in which Kierkegaard received the work of the Spanish author. Kierkegaard had two different versions of the *Quixote* in his personal library. The first one was a Danish translation by Charlotte Dorothea

Biehl (1731–88),[1] and the second one Heine's German version.[2] If we consider that the latter was issued in 1837, then we will easily conclude that Kierkegaard's initial approach to the *Quixote* was made based on the Danish version, since his first references to the novel date back to 1835. Apart from the *Quixote*, we do not find any other work of Cervantes listed in the catalogue of Kierkegaard's personal library. And yet, it is possible that he might have had some kind of access to a translation of the *Exemplary Novels*, perhaps also Biehl's, since he refers to one of these brief novels in one of his journalistic articles (we will analyze this question below).

Together with the direct reading of Cervantes' work, it is very likely that the general atmosphere created around the *Quixote* by the Romantics had somehow also influenced Kierkegaard. When Kierkegaard came into contact for the first time with Cervantes' *Don Quixote*, a number of Romantic authors in different countries had already developed a new reading of the novel that not only consolidated it as a masterpiece of *serious* literature but also revolutionized the way the *Quixote* was read. To authors like Tieck, Schelling or the brothers Schlegel—to mention the most representative ones—the book of Cervantes was more than a capital work. They considered it to be an outstanding piece of Romantic literature *avant la lettre,* as well as the greatest work in which seriousness and parody were combined in a masterly fashion.

In his *Philosophy of Art*, Schelling developed what can be regarded as the culmination of this new conception of the book.[3] There, the German author denounced the hitherto standard reading of the story as a satire and defended the idea—essential for the Romantics—that Cervantes' *Quixote* was a unique portrait of the fight between the actual and the ideal.[4] Furthermore, *Don Quixote* was, together

---

[1]   Charlotte Dorothea Biehl (1731–88) translated several works into Danish, mainly French comedies, and she was a writer herself. As far as her translation of Cervantes is concerned, she not only translated the *Quixote* (*Don Quixote af Manchas Levnet og Bedrifter*, vols. 1–4, Copenhagen: M. Hallager 1776–77 (*ASKB* 1937–1940)) but also the *Exemplary Novels* (*Lærerige Fortællinger af Cervantes*, vols. 1–2, Copenhagen: Nicolaus Møller, Kongel. Hofbogtrykker 1780–1). Her translations of the Spanish writer do not seem to have reached a great significance, and Biehl has been mainly recollected for her own writings (see *Dansk biografisk Lexikon*, vols. 1–19, ed. by C. F. Bricka, Copenhagen: Gyldendal 1887–1905, vol. 2, pp. 188–9).

[2]   Heine's edition of *Don Quixote* (*Don Quixote von La Mancha*, vols. 1–2, Stuttgart: Verlag der Classiker 1837–38 (*ASKB* 1935–1936)) was of great importance for the novel's spread in German Romanticism. It must be said, however, that, contrary to what is often stated, Heinrich Heine was not translator of *Don Quixote* into German but solely responsible for the introduction to an anonymous translation (see J.-J.A. Bertrand, *Cervantes et le romantisme allemand*, Paris: Librairie Félix Alcan 1914, p. 578).

[3]   This is how Anthony Close characterizes Schelling's comments on the *Quixote* in his illustrative article "Las interpretaciones del Quijote" (Anthony Close, "Las interpretaciones del Quijote," in *Don Quijote de la Mancha*, ed. by Instituto Cervantes and Francisco Rico, Madrid: Crítica 1998, pp. CXLII–CLXV; pp. CLIII–CLIV).

[4]   [Schelling], *Friedrich Wilhelm Joseph von Schellings sämmtliche Werke*, vols. 1–14, ed. by Carl Friedrich August Schelling, Stuttgart: J.G. Cotta 1856–61, vol. 5, p. 667; p. 681.

with Goethe's *Wilhelm Meister*, the only novel that existed, according to Schelling.[5] If we think that for Schelling, in particular, and the Romantics, in general, the novel was a genre that they considered as essentially theirs and fully expressive of the Romantic sensibility, then we will easily understand the high significance of such statement. No wonder, then, that Schelling praised Cervantes as the greatest author for modernity, the way Homer was it for antiquity.[6]

We could also refer to other authors, such as Richter or Friedrich Schlegel, who, in line with Schelling's interpretation, called Cervantes "the real Romantic artist."[7] In short, all these interpreters brought a new way of reading and understanding to the novel that gave rise to what has been called the "Romantic approach" to the *Quixote*.[8]

In this way, Cervantes' novel and its main characters had become in the times of Kierkegaard an unavoidable reference as models of Romantic sensibility. We can be certain that such a new way of reading the novel cannot have been totally unknown to Kierkegaard, since he possessed the German edition that included an introduction to the *Quixote* written by one of those revolutionary readers, namely Heinrich Heine.

The mentions that Kierkegaard makes of Don Quixote and Sancho Panza have, therefore, to be understood taking this framework into account. Nonetheless, the whole context of Kierkegaard's reading of the *Quixote* is actually broader than Romanticism. In the nineteenth century, Cervantes' characters were also paradigms of comic *personae*. Together with Romanticism's *revolution* in the interpretations of the *Quixote*, we also have to bear in mind that the knight-errant and his squire were already regarded as the epitome of a purely comic couple. Even though Romanticism did bring about a revolution in reading the *Quixote*—stressing the seriousness in the novel—it did not completely eliminate a certain *popular*, strictly comic reading of its characters that had existed from the very beginning, when Cervantes first wrote his masterpiece. This means that Kierkegaard's references to these characters cannot be understood exclusively within the particular context of Romanticism but must also be considered from a broader perspective, which sees Don Quixote and Sancho Panza as a standard comic couple of burlesque.

To be able to follow Kierkegaard's relation to the *Quixote* we must not ignore either of these two perspectives of reading the novel. If there is something that characterizes Kierkegaard's reception of Cervantes' work, it is precisely the harmonious coexistence of those two levels of interpretation, which otherwise seem to be mutually exclusive. But let us take a look at the references.

---

[5]   Ibid., p. 679. The brothers Schlegel shared also this idea (see J.-J.A. Bertrand, "Renacimiento del cervantismo romántico alemán," *Anales Cervantinos*, vol. 9, 1961–62, pp. 143–67; p. 154).

[6]   [Schelling], *Friedrich Wilhelm Joseph von Schellings sämmtliche Werke*, vol. 5, p. 681.

[7]   Bertrand, *Cervantes et le romantisme allemand*, p. 120.

[8]   Anthony Close, *The Romantic Approach to* Don Quixote. *A Critical History of the Romantic Tradition in* Quixote *Criticism*, Cambridge: Cambridge University Press 1978. Germany and Great Britain were the places where the *Quixote* had the greatest impact in the nineteenth century, but also in other countries the admiration was highly significant. Curiously enough, Spain was rather an exception.

II. Kierkegaard's References to Cervantes

As already stated, the first time Kierkegaard refers to Cervantes' world is in 1835. There are two texts from this year in which Don Quixote is alluded to by Kierkegaard. The first one belongs to the *Journal AA*, from an entry in which Kierkegaard criticizes the so-called Christians for refusing to submit their faith to true trials. Instead—Kierkegaard denounces—they put those trials aside and concentrate on a fixed idea, on which they base all their supposedly Christian existences. Thus such existences become a "happy madness." Don Quixote is used to illustrate precisely this "happy madness":

> For what strikes me as among Don Quixote's most excellent traits is the ease with which when, say, he sees that he has mistaken windmills for giants, he discovers that it must have been the evil demon that is always on his tail. I wonder whether he ever doubted his knightly destiny, whether he lacked peace and contentment?[9]

There are two things to highlight in this first reference. The first one is that Kierkegaard makes here a rather *traditional* approach to the character. Not only does he quote the most popular episode of the novel (Don Quixote's attack on the windmills-giants), but also gives a no less *popular*, standard reading of that episode. The second important aspect is that he relates Don Quixote's madness to the notion of a finite, fixed idea, which Christendom embraces instead of Christianity's truth. Climacus will return back to this relation in the *Postscript*, as we will see.

The other fragment from this year is from "Our Journalistic Literature," a talk given to the Student Association.[10] It is curious to see that the passage of the *Quixote* alluded to by Kierkegaard on this occasion is exactly the same one as before: the famous charge at windmills, which Don Quixote mistakes for giants. What Kierkegaard adds here is a very first mention to Sancho Panza, who is also presented in his stereotype as the sane counterpart to Don Quixote's madness.

The journals from 1836 register, in all, four references to the *Quixote*. The first one, in line with the one we have just seen, alludes to Don Quixote and Sancho Panza as a couple of opposed characters that work complementarily, the one providing a deeper meaning to the other. The two are here listed together with other equivalent couples.[11] Only one month after this entry, Kierkegaard turns again to the two characters with exactly the same kind of comment. Sancho Panza is again mentioned along with Leporello and Wagner, and all of them are put in relation to fools of the Middle Ages.[12] For us, it is interesting to point here to, first, Kierkegaard's stress on the relevance of the couple in the novel and, second, the connection he establishes between the novel and the Middle Ages, an idea that he will take up again later on.

Next to this fragment, also from March 1836, we find one of the most significant passages about Don Quixote:

---

9   *SKS* 17, 33, AA:14 / *KJN* 1, 28.
10   *Pap.* I B 2, p. 173 / *JP* 5, 5116.
11   *Pap.* I A 122 / *JP* 4, 4387.
12   *Pap.* I A 145 / *JP* 2, 1670.

> I believe it could be a very interesting idea to work out a comic *novel*, "A Literary *Don Quixote*." A complete misunderstanding of the significance of books has developed in the learned world. Instead of their being regarded as a necessary supplement to life, primary stress is placed on reading as many as possible. The comic would then lie in the hopeless struggle to "go along with this" and, paralleling this, in the absolute failure, nevertheless, of accomplishing anything in the world, because the learned people are forever producing learned works and losing themselves in footnotes.[13]

For the first time, Kierkegaard alludes not to Don Quixote as a character, but to the novel as epitome of a particular work, namely, a satire. It is important for us that Kierkegaard suggests the possibility of other *Quixotes*, since this will prove to be a central idea in his use of the novel.

Still another entry from 1836 completes the series of references to the *Quixote* in these early years.[14] It is curious to notice that after these six remarks in a period of hardly two years, Cervantes will not appear again in Kierkegaard's writings until *Either/Or*, that is to say, seven years later. There is no explicit mention anywhere that could give us some information about when Kierkegaard read the *Quixote*. However, given this peculiar concentration of references followed by a considerable lapse of time, one could think that he might have read the novel for the first time in these years and then came back to it with a second reading later on. If we think that one of the editions he had of the novel—Heine's German version—was from 1837, we could conclude that that second reading must have actually taken place, at some time between 1837 and 1843, the year Kierkegaard resumes his use of Don Quixote.

It is reasonable to think, therefore, that Kierkegaard returned to the *Quixote* after an early first reading, and that he did so with the German edition. What there is no doubt about is the fact that his return to Cervantes' novel came together with a renewed reading of the text and its main character.

It is difficult to interpret this apparent point of inflection. As far as the quantity and frequency of references are concerned, we must not forget that it is precisely in 1843 when Kierkegaard really starts his huge series of publications. In this sense, the apparent "new stage" of Cervantes' presence could simply correspond, after all, to the "new stage" of Kierkegaard's production, and not to a real turning point in his reading of the *Quixote*. On the other hand, however, it is no less true that from 1843 on Kierkegaard's comments on the *Quixote* patently reveal a new and more mature way of reading the novel. Therefore, it does make sense to speak of a point of inflection.

We must not forget the aforementioned fact that some time after 1837 Kierkegaard purchased Heine's edition of *Don Quixote*. It is at least tempting to think, accordingly, that this event and such a new way of reading the book are closely connected. What we cannot venture to say is whether such renewal was the consequence of a direct influence of Heine's "Romantic" introduction to the German translation or rather the

---

[13]   *Pap.* I A 146 / *JP* 1, 770.
[14]   *SKS* 17, 38, AA:21 / *KJN* 1, 32.

result of a second and perhaps more thorough reading of the novel itself, Heine's text being a secondary or even minimal influence.[15]

But let us first come to the references. *Either/Or* contains two passages in which Don Quixote is mentioned. The first one recalls previous reflections, since it presents Don Quixote and Sancho Panza as a couple of opposed characters who operate complementarily in the novel. In addition to this, Kierkegaard depicts the two characters as incarnations of ideas, which are regarded by him as typical of the Middle Ages.[16] This is precisely the most significant element of Kierkegaard's comments here: the fact that he reads the *Quixote* as a work of the Middle Ages. It is a very well-known fact that nowadays the *Quixote* is considered to be the first modern novel, one that precisely distances itself from letters of the Middle Ages and lays the foundations for modern literature. As we saw before, this was a turn made by the Romantics, who had isolated the *Quixote* from its actual context and claimed it to be Romantic literature, the first example of a genre, the novel, that was fundamental for them. But Kierkegaard ignores here such reading and portrays Don Quixote and Sancho Panza as typical literary products of the Middle Ages. In this way, he shows a significant distance from the Romantics, which proves him to be, at least, not fully identified with the Romantic reading of the *Quixote*.

The second entry from *Either/Or* is also in connection with a previous remark. If in one of his early references Kierkegaard suggested the benefit of "a literary Don Quixote," now he wonders about the absence of a feminine equivalent to the novel in European literature.[17] It must be said, however, that Kierkegaard is wrong, since there did already exist a feminine version of the *Quixote*, namely *The Female Quixote or the Adventures of Arabella*, by Charlotte Lennox (1730–1804).[18]

Stages in Life's Way is the next work in which Don Quixote appears. This time it is not an allusion in passing, but rather a more detailed analysis of Cervantes' portrayal of the knight-errant's madness:

> It is well known that Don Quixote believed that he himself was a knight-errant. His madness by no means reaches its climax in this idea—Cervantes is much more profound than that. When Don Quixote had been healed of his sickness and the licenciate is already beginning to hope he has recovered his mind, he wants to test him a little. He

---

[15]   We do not find in Kierkegaard's writings much help to answer this question. Nevertheless, the possibility that Heine's text had at least some level of responsibility seems to be too obvious to deny. But, unfortunately, we cannot go beyond this weak statement. Among other reasons, the group of references to the *Quixote* made before Kierkegaard had access to Heine's text is too small and too weak to be regarded as an *interpretation* of the novel that existed previously and was later substituted by a new one under the influence of Heine. Moreover, Kierkegaard's use of Don Quixote after 1843 still shows the presence of a *popular* reading, which would contradict the hypothesis of a strong influence of Heine's interpretation.

[16]   *SKS* 2, 93 / *EO1*, 88.

[17]   *SKS* 2, 249 / *EO1*, 256.

[18]   This novel tried to "repeat" Cervantes' satire upon French heroic romances, instead of books of chivalry. The book enjoyed popular success, with an early second edition and translations into German, Spanish, and French (Charlotte Lennox, *The Female Quixote or the Adventures of Arabella*, London: R. Snagg 1752).

speaks to him about different things and then suddenly intersperses the news that the Moors have invaded Spain. Then there is only one way to save Spain, answers Don Quixote. "What is that?" asks the licenciate. Don Quixote refuses to tell; only to His Faithful Majesty, the King of Spain, will he disclose his secret. Finally he yields to the licenciate's pleas and, sworn to secrecy and with the solemnity of a father confessor, he receives that famous knight's confession: "The only way is for His Faithful Majesty to send out a call to arms to all the knights-errant." To be a knight-errant oneself is, if you please, the work of a half-mad man, but to populate all Spain with knights-errant is truly a *delirium furibundum*.[19]

What we find here is already a reflection on the novel and the character as such. It is not a mere allusion to the paradigmatic figure of Don Quixote, which we found in previous references, but rather a more elaborate analysis that proves clearly a closer reading of the novel. In this way, now Don Quixote is not only that paradigmatic comic figure, but also a comic figure upon which Kierkegaard reflects. The combination of regarding Don Quixote as a model of comicalness and reflecting upon it begins to give Cervantes' character a more significant role in Kierkegaard's writings.

On December 27, 1845 Kierkegaard published an article in *The Fatherland* entitled "The Activity of a Traveling Esthetician and How He still Happened to Pay for the Dinner." This article, in which Kierkegaard criticizes Peder Ludvig Møller (1814–65) and which would give rise to the polemic with *The Corsair*, contains probably the most curious reference to Cervantes. What makes the reference peculiar is the fact that it does not belong to the *Quixote* but to one of Cervantes' *Exemplary Novels*.[20] Thus this reference raises the question: Did Kierkegaard know any of Cervantes' other works apart from the *Quixote*? Initially, the answer should be simple: Kierkegaard would have read other Cervantes' works, since he mentions one. But a little bit of research will warn us to be cautious with such conclusion.

A Danish translation of Cervantes' *Exemplary Novels* existed in Kierkegaard's time.[21] There is no evidence, however, that Kierkegaard had read such a translation. It is clear that the catalogue of his personal library that was made on account of the auction of his books—in which no such translation of Cervantes appears—cannot be considered a totally accurate rendition of the books that Kierkegaard actually possessed, not to mention those he read. And yet, it *is* questionable that Kierkegaard read the *Exemplary Novels*, even though he refers to one of them. And the reason for this is not the absence of that book in the catalogue, but rather what surrounds Kierkegaard's passing—and sole—reference to that novel.

The article in which *The Glass Graduate* (Cervantes' *Exemplary Novel*) is slightly mentioned, was written by Kierkegaard in response to P.L. Møller's "A Visit in Sørø." In this writing, the man behind *The Corsair* referred to precisely *The Glass Graduate*. In Møller's article, it is clear that the man had read the novel and

---

[19]   *SKS* 6, 373 / *SLW*, 402.
[20]   *SV1* XIII, 426 / *COR*, 42 (See also *Pap.* VII–1 B 1, p. 166). Kierkegaard does not mention where the reference is taken from, although it obviously belongs to *The Glass Graduate* [*El Licenciado Vidriera*].
[21]   Cervantes, *Don Quixote af Manchas Levnet og Bedrifter*, vols. 1–4, trans. by Charlotte Dorothe Biehl.

was familiar with it, since his comment refers expressly to what Cervantes' story is about. On the contrary, Kierkegaard's passing allusion does not convincingly prove that he really knew this novel. Could it not have been the case that Kierkegaard just followed Møller's reference without really knowing what it was about? In such case, Kierkegaard's indirect allusion would simply be part of his response to Møller, rather than a reference to Cervantes, properly speaking.

It is not possible to offer a convincing and definitive answer to this issue, and it is a shame, since it involves one of the major questions regarding Kierkegaard's reception of Cervantes, namely, whether he only read the *Quixote* or knew also some other works. Nonetheless, the fact that we do not find any other trace of the *Exemplary Novels* in Kierkegaard's writings makes us suspect that the *Quixote* might have been, after all, his only connection to Cervantes.

The following series of entries related to Cervantes are surely the most significant ones in the whole authorship. They are those in Johannes Climacus' *Concluding Unscientific Postscript.* Climacus not only refers to Don Quixote three times throughout his work, but also elaborates the *Postscript* in a close connection to Cervantes' capital novel. In one of the references, the idea stressed is the same one that Kierkegaard had pointed out in his very first mention to *Don Quixote.* The knight-errant's mad conviction of being "persecuted by a nisse, who spoiled everything for him" is turned by Kierkegaard upside down by being used to contrast that other madness which is, for Climacus, to believe *world-historically* in one's own ethical merit.[22] The second reference to Don Quixote is central to Climacus' theses, since it serves to illustrate the greatest risk of his well-known claim "Truth is Subjectivity." Don Quixote is mentioned here as example of "subjective madness," which is, for Climacus, what a mere subjectivism would imply.[23]

But the most important reference of the three in the *Postscript* is the one that appears first in the book. In the section devoted to the church in Climacus' reflection on the historical point of view on the truth of Christianity, we read:

> Letter-zealotry, which did have passion, has vanished. Its merit was that it had passion. In another sense, it was comic. And just as the age of chivalry actually concluded with Don Quixote (the comic conception is always the concluding one), a poet, by comically eternalizing such an unfortunate servant of the letter in his tragic-comic romanticism, could still make it plain that literalist theology is something of the past.[24]

This idea recalls the early entry from 1836 in which Kierkegaard noted the interest of writing "a literary *Don Quixote.*" Now, instead of a literary one, Climacus suggests rather a "philosophical-theological" version of the satire, but the idea of *repeating* the *Quixote* is again presented. The question is now, could we not say that Climacus' enterprise is precisely one of those claimed new versions of the *Quixote*? There are various similarities between the two books, and Climacus is, after all, writing

---

[22]   *SKS* 7, 130 / *CUP1*, 140.

[23]   *SKS* 7, 179 / *CUP1*, 195.

[24]   *SKS* 7, 42 / *CUP1*, 35. Kierkegaard had already written a similar connection between Don Quixote and Letter-zealotry in a passage for Climacus' *Philosophical Fragments* which eventually did not appear in the final version of the work (See *Pap.* V B 1, 6 / *JP* 3, 3047).

comically a work that is meant to be *concluding*—"the comic conception is always the concluding one."[25] Satire is clearly a central element in the *Postscript*, as it is in the *Quixote*. And when we read Cervantes' prologue to his novel, the echoes of the *Postscript* become quite difficult to ignore: "to undermine the ill-founded edifice"[26] constituted by books of chivalry is clearly analogous to what Climacus aims to do towards books of speculative theology. And, in order to do so, both Climacus and Cervantes resort to the "proper use of imitation."[27] The two authors make use of satire, but note, a kind of *double-faced* satire in which *serious* readings are not necessarily excluded. For all this, the presence of the *Quixote* in Climacus' work can be regarded as far deeper than what the three particular references mentioned directly imply.[28]

One year after Climacus' *Postscript*, Kierkegaard writes in one of his journals another interesting comment on *Don Quixote*:

> It is a sad mistake for Cervantes to end *Don Quixote* by making him sensible and then letting him die. Cervantes, who himself had the superb idea of having him become a shepherd! It ought to have ended there. That is, Don Quixote should not come to an end; he ought to be presented as going full speed, so that he opens vistas upon an infinite series of new fixed ideas. Don Quixote is endlessly perfectible in madness, but the one thing he cannot become (for otherwise he could become everything and anything) is sensible. Cervantes seems not to have been dialectical enough to bring it to this romantic conclusion (that there is no conclusion).[29]

Like other previous references, this note shows us that Kierkegaard does not simply use Don Quixote as a comic stereotype, but he is also interested in the novel as such and develops his own interpretations of it. Thus, we can say that Kierkegaard is a *reader* of Cervantes, properly speaking. But what kind of reader is he? The following fragment invites us to regard Kierkegaard as a full-fledged Romantic interpreter:

> Alas, when I look at my own life! How rare the man who is so endowed for the life of the spirit and above all so rigorously schooled with the help of spiritual suffering—in the eyes of all my contemporaries I am fighting like a Don Quixote—it never occurs to them that it is Christianity; indeed, they are convinced of just the opposite.[30]

By identifying himself with the character, Kierkegaard stresses the *serious* side of *Don Quixote*, as Romanticism in general did. All the comic situations featured in the novel are now regarded simply as an intensification of Don Quixote's suffering: not only does he have to suffer because of the nature of his solitary task, but he is also

---

[25]   *SKS* 7, 42 / *CUP1*, 35.
[26]   *The Ingenious Gentleman Don Quixote de la Mancha*, trans. by Samuel Putnam, vols. 1–2, New York: The Viking Press 1949, vol. 1, pp. 15–16.
[27]   Ibid.
[28]   For a more detailed analysis of this relation between the two works, see Óscar Parcero Oubiña, "The Autonomy of the Comic: on Kierkegaard and *Don Quixote*," *Kierkegaardiana*, vol. 24, 2007, pp. 163–82.
[29]   *SKS* 20, 107, NB:170 / *JP* 1, 771.
[30]   *SKS* 22, 199, NB12:103 / *JP* 2, 1781.

mocked for it, and the mockery redoubles the suffering. Seriousness becomes the central aspect, and the comic, sentenced to be regarded as depending on it.

This identification with the character is very tempting to propose as an interpretation of the whole work of Kierkegaard. As a Romantic emblem of existence, *Don Quixote* might arise as a key for reading the life and work of the Dane: the knight of faith, who suffers in his solitary strength the impossibility of being understood, and uses his humoristic outwardness as an *incognito* to preserve the authenticity of his religious inwardness. But the next reference found in the writings forces us to reject such a suggestive interpretation:

> Christianity does not really exist. Christendom is waiting for a comic poet *a la* Cervantes, who will create a counterpart to Don Quixote out of the essentially Christian.
>
> The only difference will be that no poetic exaggerations will be required at all, as in Don Quixote—no, all he needs to do is to take any essentially true Christian life, not to mention simply taking Christ or an apostle. The comic element arises because the age has changed so enormously that it regards this as comic.
>
> That a person actually is earnest about renouncing this life, literally, that he *voluntarily* gives up the happiness of erotic love offered to him, that he endures all kinds of earthly privation, although the opposite is offered to him, that he thus exposes himself to all the anguish of spiritual trial [*Anfægtelse*], for spiritual trial comes only to the voluntary—and then that he, suffering all this, submits to being mistreated for it, hated, persecuted, scorned (the unavoidable consequence of essential Christianity in this world)—to our entire age such a life appears to be comic. It is a Don Quixote life.[31]

It is clear that Kierkegaard does not fully develop a Romantic reading of the *Quixote*. For him, the character of Cervantes still stands as a model of ludicrousness, even though it can *also* exemplify the ideal of a true Christian existence. This is precisely the most remarkable feature of Kierkegaard's reading of *Don Quixote*: whereas Romanticism stresses solely the conflict between the knight-errant's idealism and reality, in Kierkegaard, Cervantes' character embodies reality as well. The Romantic interpretation of the novel coexists in Kierkegaard's evaluation with a *popular* reading in which Don Quixote is merely a ludicrous figure. This duplicity, far from discrediting Kierkegaard's view of the novel, makes it more interesting, since it gives an excellent example of the duplicity of the comic in his work.[32]

The next references to Cervantes' novel confirm Kierkegaard's non-Romantic reading. In 1850, he uses for the first time the episode of Sancho Panza's self-administered blows to his own bottom to illustrate the lack of earnestness.[33] In this same year, Don Quixote is referred to once more as paradigm of mere ludicrousness, when Kierkegaard compares him to the Professor: "Eureka, I have it! The 'professor' is really the analogue

---

[31]   *SKS* 22, 242–3, NB12:164 / *JP* 2, 1762.

[32]   Don Quixote is, after all, the paradigm of a comic figure. I have studied this parallelism between Don Quixote and the comic in Kierkegaard elsewhere (Óscar Parcero Oubiña, "The Autonomy of the Comic: On Kierkegaard and *Don Quixote*," and "O *Quijote* e o Cómico na obra de Kierkegaard," *Ágora. Papeles de Filosofía*, vol. 24, no. 1, 2005, pp. 155–76).

[33]   *SKS* 23, 45–6, NB15:66 / *JP* 1, 188. Kierkegaard will use this example again in his journals (See *SKS* 24, 425f., NB24:159 / *JP* 4, 3902).

to Don Quixote. Perhaps he will become an even more profound comic figure."[34] It is certainly very difficult to find here any trace of a Romantic reading.

But there *are* traces of a Romantic reading elsewhere. After still another reference originally from the pen of Johannes Climacus,[35] Kierkegaard writes as follows:

> What our age would really be most inclined to regard as a counterpart of Don Quixote would be an ascetic in the old sense, an ascetic who fasts and prays and accuses himself of even the slightest sinful thought and imposes punishment upon himself for it—and then we are all Christians![36]

Here, Don Quixote appears as the incarnation of an ideal in a struggle with reality, which is precisely the Romantic view *par excellence*. But we can also give a different reading of this same fragment. We might just as well consider that Don Quixote would be the counterpart of "the ascetic in the old sense," that is to say *the ideal*, only in so far as "our age" sees it that way. In other words, "our age" makes Don Quixote be an ideal, although he essentially embodies actuality. It is the age that, being ludicrous, turns everything upside down, and the ludicrous Don Quixote appears as a serious ideal. In this way—as mentioned above—Don Quixote emerges as the perfect incarnation of the ambivalence of the comic in Kierkegaard. It depends on the point of view one takes to decide whether the knight-errant represents the pure ludicrousness of, say, a speculative professor or rather the high comicalness of a true religious individual who has in the comic the *incognito* to the world's ludicrousness.

The last reference to Cervantes we find in Kierkegaard's writings repeats the idea previously suggested that the Spanish author made a mistake ending the novel by letting Don Quixote die as a rational man.[37] According to Kierkegaard, the *Quixote* demands rather a "Romantic end," the kind of end that Cervantes himself suggested with the idea of making Don Quixote a shepherd. This would mean to turn the novel into what it essentially is, namely, a Romantic comedy, instead of the "kind of moral tale" which constitutes the actual end of the novel.[38]

---

[34]   *SKS* 23, 201, NB17:59 / *JP* 4, 3568.

[35]   See *Pap.* X–6 B 72.

[36]   *SKS* 24, 278, NB23:146 / *JP* 1, 175.

[37]   See *SKS* 26, 121, NB32:3 / *JP* 2, 1562.

[38]   It is not clear why Cervantes let Don Quixote die sane. Some circumstances that surround the novel suggest that Cervantes' declared interest in avoiding a new unauthorized "second part" like Avellaneda's might have had much to do with his decision. Whatever the case, I want to call into question the so-called "moral tale" that constitutes the novel's actual end. It is not true that Cervantes puts an end to Don Quixote's madness by letting him die after becoming sane. Important details such as the significant epitaph of Sansón Carrasco suggest to us that the death of the sane could be precisely the non-death of the mad knight-errant. After all, it is Alonso Quijano el Bueno who *dies*, not Don Quixote. A good analysis of this question can be found in James Iffland, *De fiestas y aguafiestas: risa, locura e ideología en Cervantes y Avellaneda*, Madrid: Universidad de Navarra 1999, pp. 547–68.

III. General Interpretation of Kierkegaard's Reception of Cervantes

Cervantes is certainly not a major influence in Kierkegaard, but he is not without importance either. The fact that Kierkegaard had two different editions of the *Quixote* in his personal library should be an indication that he paid particular attention to Cervantes' novel. As we have seen, as a reader of the book, he is influenced by the Romantics' interpretation, and yet he is not a Romantic reader himself. It is true that his comments reflect the new conception of the *Quixote* that arose in his time, but they also echo another way of reading the novel in which the ludicrous situations and characters are not linked to a serious or profound background.

Thus the first thing that stands out in Kierkegaard's use of Cervantes is its heterogeneity. The several references to the *Quixote* spread throughout Kierkegaard's writings differ from each other considerably. Sometimes, they are mere allusions to the well-known and paradigmatic comic figures of Don Quixote and Sancho Panza—commonplaces in which one cannot find any trace of serious reflection on the novel or the characters. At other times, however, we do find such reflections, and Kierkegaard appears as a careful reader of Cervantes, in line with his Romantic contemporaries.

The *superficial* comments on the *Quixote*, however, do not simply show Kierkegaard's treatment of a literary cliché. They also manifest his familiarity with a popular but no less literary tradition that comes from afar. Already in the early seventeenth century, Cervantes' novel had enjoyed a great popular success, which would immediately establish Don Quixote and Sancho Panza as paradigmatic burlesque figures. The eighteenth century would but sanction such status. Regardless of the Romantic emphasis upon the serious dimension of the novel, the popular and burlesque reading of it would still be of great importance in Kierkegaard's time, as it is still nowadays. Kierkegaard's treatment of the *Quixote* reflects significant echoes of this burlesque tradition of reading the novel. When Kierkegaard compares Don Quixote to the speculative professor or alludes to the well-known episode of the windmills, he is patently reading the novel on a purely burlesque level, and not necessarily just falling into stereotypes.

On the other hand, the various references to Don Quixote's idealism, to his fight with the *plainness* of actuality or, especially, the parallelism between the knight-errant and the authentic Christian, make evident that Kierkegaard also develops a *serious* interpretation of the novel, which is clearly distant from the burlesque one. In these references, Kierkegaard stands very close to his Romantic contemporaries, in so far as he stresses the *spiritual* dimension of Don Quixote and the seriousness that lies below the burlesque surface of the novel.

There is still a third group of references, namely, those in which Kierkegaard reflects upon the novel as a piece of literature. Rather than the content of the book, it is now its form which attracts the attention of Kierkegaard. In other words, instead of referring to Don Quixote in any of his multiple dimensions, Kierkegaard focuses on Cervantes as an author and his novel as a text. These references, as we saw, are of great significance, since they offer the possibility of comparing Cervantes' work with Kierkegaard's. From such a comparison, the use that Kierkegaard makes of the Spanish author comes into a new light, and, far from being a mere occasional allusion, it emerges as a possible object for a more fertile interpretation. Moreover, since Kierkegaard also *criticizes* Cervantes for not being fully coherent with the *spirit* of his novel, we can enrich such an interpretation by considering how *a Quixote* should operate, according to Kierkegaard. As we have seen, an interpretation like this would be to propose a parallelism between Cervantes' novel and Climacus' *Postscript*.

But the most attractive point in Kierkegaard's use of Cervantes does not lie in any single reference or even group of them. It is *the whole* of the heterogeneous allusions spread throughout the writings that makes Kierkegaard's use of the Spanish author most interesting. For Kierkegaard, Don Quixote is the embodiment of a comic figure. Regardless of what particular reference we choose, there is one thing that all of them have in common, and that is precisely the fact that the knight-errant is a paradigm of the comic. Therefore, to trace the heterogeneity of Don Quixote in Kierkegaard's writings becomes analogous to tracing the heterogeneity of the comic. The entire range of variants of the comic in Kierkegaard is represented by his use of Don Quixote. From the low burlesque to the connections with a true religiosity, Don Quixote incarnates every single form that the comic presents in the work of Kierkegaard. Thus, Cervantes' character becomes a highly appropriate guide to approach Kierkegaard's conception and use of the comic.

It is not surprising that Cervantes can be of great value to understand Kierkegaard's use of the comic. Both authors agree on a conception of the comic that combines burlesque with more *profound* interpretations. And that heterogeneous coexistence of the different levels makes their use of the comic highly rich and thought-provoking. As Anthony Close puts it, "Cervantes made little use of the easy comic formulae which lay to hand in the types of the macaronic knight and the *miles gloriosus*, and chose a more mature kind of comedy based on the hero's being plausibly able to visualise himself, from his own mad viewpoint, as a hero."[39] That "more mature kind of comedy" that presents Don Quixote as *both* a ludicrous character and the incarnation of noble ideals is precisely what we find in Kierkegaard's use of the comic: it can be *both* in the ludicrous fantasies of speculative professors and in the true religious experience of a Christian.

It goes without saying that all that has been stated here does not change the status of Cervantes as an influence for Kierkegaard, but it certainly affects the understanding of the significance of this otherwise minor presence in the writings of the Danish author.

---

[39]   Close, *The Romantic Approach to* Don Quixote, p. 248.

Bibliography

I. Cervantes' Works in The Auction Catalogue *of Kierkegaard's Library*

Der sinnreiche Junker Don Quixote von La Mancha, ed. by Heinrich Heine, vols.
1–2, Stuttgart: Verlag der Classiker 1837–38 (*ASKB* 1935–1936).
Den sindrige Herremands Don Quixote af Mancha Levnet og Bedrifter, vols. 1–4,
trans. by Charlotte Dorothea Biehl, Copenhagen: M. Hallager 1776–77 (*ASKB*
1937–1940).

II. Works in The Auction Catalogue *of Kierkegaard's Library
that Discuss Cervantes*

[Becker, Karl Friedrich], *Karl Friedrich Beckers Verdenshistorie, omarbeidet
af Johan Gottfried Woltmann*, vols. 1–12, trans. by J. Riise, Copenhagen: Fr.
Brummer 1822–29, vol. 6, p. 141 (*ASKB* 1972–1983).
Döring, Heinrich, *Joh. Gottfr. von Herder's Leben*, 2nd enlarged and revised ed.,
Weimar: Wilhelm Hoffmann 1829, p. 126 (*ASKB* A I 134).
Flögel, Karl Friedrich, *Geschichte der komischen Litteratur*, vols. 1–4, Liegnitz
and Leipzig: David Siegert 1784–87, vol. 1, p. 307; vol. 2, pp. 280–96; vol. 4,
pp. 167–9 (*ASKB* 1396–1399).
[Hamann, Johann Georg], *Hamann's Schriften*, vols. 1–8, ed. by Friedrich Roth,
Berlin: G. Reimer 1821–43, vol. 5, p. 17; vol. 2, p. 223; vol. 4, p. 20; pp. 468–71;
vol. 7, p. 92; p. 212 (*ASKB* 536–544).
[Hegel, Georg Wilhelm Friedrich], *Georg Wilhelm Friedrich Hegel's Vorlesungen
über die Aesthetik*, vols. 1–3, ed. by von Heinrich Gustav Hotho, Berlin: Verlag
von Duncker und Humblot 1835–38 (vols. 10.1–10.3 in *Georg Wilhelm Friedrich
Hegel's Werke. Vollständige Ausgabe*, vols. 1–18, ed. by Philipp Marheineke et
al., Berlin: Verlag von Duncker und Humblot 1832–45), vol. 1, p. 252; vol. 2,
pp. 214–15; p. 232 (*ASKB* 1384–1386).
Heiberg, Johan Ludvig, *Prosaiske Skrifter*, vol. 3, Copenhagen: J.H. Schubothe 1843
(vol. 3, in Johan Ludvig Heiberg, *Prosaiske Skrifter*, vols. 1–3, Copenhagen:
J.H. Schubothe 1841–43 which is Part of *Johan Ludvig Heiberg's Samlede
Skrifter* consisting of *Skuespil*, vols. 1–7, Copenhagen: J.H. Schubothe 1833–41
and *Digte og Fortællinger*, vols. 1–2, Copenhagen: J.H. Schubothe 1834–35),
pp. 79–107 (*ASKB* 1560).
[Lichtenberg, Georg Christoph], *Georg Christoph Lichtenberg's auserlesene
Schriften*, Baireuth: bei Iohann Andreas Lübecks Erben 1800, p. 18; p. 35;
p. 319; p. 359 (*ASKB* 1775).

Nielsen, Rasmus, *Forelæsningsparagrapher til Kirkehistoriens Philosophie. Et Schema for Tilhørere*, Copenhagen: P.G. Philipsen 1843, p. 50 (*ASKB* 698).

[Richter, Johann Paul Friedrich], Jean Paul, *Vorschule der Aesthetik nebst einigen Vorlesungen in Leipzig über die Parteien der Zeit*, vols. 1–3, 2nd revised ed., Stuttgart and Tübingen: J.G. Cotta'sche Buchhandlung 1813, vol. 1, p. 7; p. 140; p. 172; p. 205; p. 240; p. 295; p. 315; vol. 2, p. 572 (*ASKB* 1381–1383).

Rosenkranz, Karl, *Psychologie oder die Wissenschaft vom subjectiven Geist*, Königsberg: Bornträger 1837, p. 47; p. 262 (*ASKB* 744).

Schlegel, August Wilhelm, *Ueber dramatische Kunst und Litteratur. Vorlesungen*, vols. 1–2 [vol. 2 in 2 Parts], Heidelberg: Mohr und Zimmer 1809–11, vol. 2.2, pp. 343–5 (*ASKB* 1392–1394).

Schlegel, Friedrich, *Sämmtliche Werke*, vols. 1–10, Vienna: Jakob Mayer and Company 1822–25, vol. 2, 1822, pp. 72–107 (*ASKB* 1816–1825).

Schopenhauer, Arthur, *Die Welt als Wille und Vorstellung*, vols. 1–2, 2nd revised and enlarged ed., Leipzig: F.A. Brockhaus 1844 [1819]; vol. 2, p. 72; p. 96 (*ASKB* 773–773a).

——*Parerga und Paralipomena: kleine philosophische Schriften*, vols. 1–2, Berlin: A.W. Hayn 1851, vol. 1, p. 303; vol. 2, p. 385 (*ASKB* 774–775).

[Solger, Karl Wilhelm Ferdinand], *K.W.F. Solger's Vorlesungen über Aesthetik*, ed. by K.W.L. Heyse, Leipzig: F.A. Brockhaus 1829, p. 233; p. 296 (*ASKB* 1387).

Sulzer, Johann Georg, *Allgemeine Theorie der Schönen Künste, in einzeln, nach alphabetischer Ordnung der Kunstwörter auf einander folgenden, Artikeln abgehandelt*, vols. 1–4 and a register volume, 2nd revised ed., Leipzig: Weidmann 1792–99, vol. 1, p. 502; p. 534–41 passim; p. 638; vol. 2, p. 140; p. 611; vol. 3, p. 264; vol. 4, p. 165 (*ASKB* 1365–1369).

Thiersch, Friedrich, *Allgemeine Aesthetik in akademischen Lehrvorträgen*, Berlin: G. Reimer 1846, p. 507 (*ASKB* 1378).

Thomsen, Grimur, *Om den nyfranske Poesi, et Forsøg til Besvarelse af Universitetets æsthetiske Priisspørgsmaal for 1841: "Har Smag og Sands for Poesi gjort Frem- eller Tilbageskridt i Frankrig i de sidste Tider og hvilken er Aarsagen?,"* Copenhagen: Wahlske Boghandlings Forlag 1843, p. 112 (*ASKB* 1390).

Weiße, Christian Hermann, *System der Aesthetik als Wissenschaft von der Idee der Schönheit. In drei Büchern*, vols. 1–2, Leipzig: C.H.F. Hartmann 1830, vol. 1, p. 232 (*ASKB* 1379–1380).

III. Secondary Literature on Kierkegaard's Relation to Cervantes

Brandt, Frithiof, "Søren Kierkegaard som Don Quijote," *Ekstrabladet*, February 14, 1950.

Grimsley, Ronald, "Cervantes," *Kierkegaard Literary Miscellany*, ed. by Niels Thulstrup and Marie Mikulová Thulstrup, Copenhagen: C.A. Reitzel 1981 (*Bibliotheca Kierkegaardiana*, vol. 9), pp. 158–9.

Parcero Oubiña, Óscar, "O *Quijote* e o Cómico na obra de Kierkegaard," *Ágora. Papeles de Filosofía*, vol. 24, no. 1, 2005, pp. 155–76.

—— "The Autonomy of the Comic: On Kierkegaard and *Don Quixote*," *Kierkegaardiana*, vol. 24, 2007, pp. 163–82.

Thust, Martin, "Das Vorbild der Schwärmerei, der Ehrgeiz der Lächerlichkeit: der Wegweiser Don Quijote," in his *Sören Kierkegaard. Der Dichter des Religiösen. Grundlagen eines Systems der Subjektivität*, Munich: C.H. Beck'sche Verlagsbuchhandlung 1931, pp. 126–49.

Ziolkowski, Eric J., *The Sanctification of Don Quixote. From Hidalgo to Priest*, Pennsylvania: Pennsylvania State University Press 1991, p. xi; p. 275.

—— "Don Quixote and Kierkegaard's Understanding of the Single Individual in Society," in *Foundations of Kierkegaard's Vision of Community*, ed. by George B. Connell and C. Stephen Evans, New Jersey and London: Humanities Press 1992, pp. 130–43.

François-René de Chateaubriand:

The Eloquent Society of Συμπαρανεκρωμενοι

Ingrid Basso

> The mind is captivated by perceiving the links which connect so many men who remain unknown to one another.[1]

Anyone who would like to draw a comparison between the Danish thinker and the French poet will soon realize that two lines of inquiry are equally open in this direction: that of the explicit traces of Kierkegaard's reading of Chateaubriand, and that of the unconscious consonances. The former is the most complicated, even if it could appear to be the easier one, since even if it is based on something "visible"—that is, Kierkegaard's explicit references to Chateaubriand's words in his writings—there is no real certain criterion to establish whether Kierkegaard actually read the works he quotes, or simply had a second-hand knowledge of them, as sometimes seems to be the case. Further, we cannot know whether some references to the poet merely have the value of a simple literary allusion, or whether, on the contrary, they hide much more than what they immediately reveal, like the tip of an iceberg. This latter hypothesis, for example, has previously received detailed attention by H.P. Rohde, in his work *Gaadefulde stadier paa Kierkegaards vej*,[2] which we will consider in more detail below.

Moreover, it is also true that Kierkegaard did not quote Chateaubriand very frequently. He merely quotes, as is well known, a passage from the poet's most famous work *Atala*, as a "motto" at the beginning of the second part of *Either/Or*, and this in fact constitutes the only instance in which the philosopher mentions a work by the French poet in his own published works. He subsequently does so again some years later in two passages from his papers, once very briefly when he talks about Chateaubriand's *Mémoires* (in 1848),[3] and then again when he mentions *Génie du christianisme, ou les Beautés de la religion chrétienne, apologie de la religion*

---

[1] François-René de Chateaubriand, *Mémoires d'outre-tombe*, vols. 1–2, ed. by Maurice Levaillant and Georges Moulinier, vol. 2, Book XXVI, Chapter, p. 50 (the present English translation has been done by A.S. Kline).

[2] Hermann Peter Rohde, "Ørkenens sønner," in *Gaadefulde stadier paa Kierkegaards vej*, Copenhagen: Rosenkilde og Bagger 1974, pp. 64–80.

[3] *SKS* 21, 100, NB7:52.

(in 1850).[4] Finally, we find the name of the poet mentioned in a letter to Kierkegaard written by one of his friends, the professor of jurisprudence at the Copenhagen University, Janus Lauritz Andreas Kolderup-Rosenvinge (1792–1850),[5] with whom the philosopher at times used to promenade around the city, discussing politics. The last explicit trace of Chateaubriand in Kierkegaard's documents appears in the list of the books of his library, where we find a German translation of the work *Les Martyrs ou le Triomphe de la religion Chrétienne*.[6]

We will examine all these passages below, but for now let us also take into account the second line of inquiry in the comparison between these two writers. This is a very interesting possibility, because even if in some cases one could state with great certainty that Kierkegaard could not have read certain specific works by Chateaubriand, the consonances between the two authors are nevertheless at times truly amazing, even in terms of precise verbal expressions, and not only in the sense of a vague shared romantic, melancholic mood, since Chateaubriand—as Théophile Gautier wrote—"*inventa la mélancolie et la passion moderne*."[7] Accordingly, we would like to begin by analyzing this second perspective, only subsequently turning to the critical examination of the explicit traces of the French writer in Kierkegaard's works.

I. The Hidden Links: Unconscious Similarities between Kierkegaard and Chateaubriand

Certainly François-René de Chateaubriand could not imagine that—even if at the time[8] he was already the celebrated writer and popular defender of the Christian religion (read, Catholic[9]), who both the intellectuals and the common people knew[10]—*he himself* would so soon become the *object* of that "mind-capturing"

---

[4]   *SKS* 24, 122, NB22:34 / *JP* 1, 681.

[5]   See letter of August 1, 1849, in *B&A*, vol. 1, p. 240 / *LD*, Letter 216, p. 306.

[6]   Chateaubriand, *Die Martyren oder der Triumph der Christlichen Religion*, vols. 1–2, trans. by T. von Haupt, Darmstadt: Leske 1810 (*ASKB* 465), a book which seems to have been purchased by the philosopher in 1852.

[7]   Théophile Gautier, *Histoire du Romantisme*, Charpentier et Cie, Paris: Charpentier 1874, p. 4.

[8]   Chateaubriand wrote the passage we quoted, during his stay in Berlin in 1821 (from January to April) as Foreign Minister at Frederick William III's court, while the legitimate monarch Louis XVIII reigned in France and, thanks to Chateaubriand's maneuvering, the "ultras" Villèle and Corbière had been admitted to the cabinet.

[9]   The French writer E.P. de Senancour, for example, was the most bitter critic to emphasize Chateaubriand's identification of Christianity and Catholicism: see *Observations critiques sur l'ouvrage intitulé "Génie du Christianisme," suivies de réflexions sur les écrits de Monsieur de Bonald*, Paris: Delaunay 1816.

[10]   In particular concerning *Atala*'s extraordinary success, the writer tells that: "Atala became so popular that, in company with the Marquise de Brinvilliers, she went to swell Curtius' waxworks collection. The carters' taverns were decked with engravings in red, green and blue representing Chactas, Father Aubry, and the daughter of Simaghan. In the wooden booths, on the *quais*, they displayed my characters modeled in wax, as images of the Virgin

passion which perceives the hidden links connecting so many contemporary men unknown to one another. He could not know during the writing of his *Mémoires*, with which he intended simply "to talk from the bottom of the grave"[11] because "life suits me ill; perhaps death will become me better,"[12] that in the same years[13] a young unknown Danish thinker had addressed his words to an eloquent society of Συμπαρανεκρωμενοι,[14] or "Fellowship of the Dead"—as the Hongs' translation has it[15]—an odd society that the author approaches in these terms: "dear Συμπαρανεκρωμενοι, we, like the Roman soldiers, do not fear death; we know a worse calamity, and first and last, above all—it is to live."[16] These words appear in the very brief essay in the first part of *Either/Or* entitled "The Unhappiest One," an expression—*"le plus malheureux des hommes"*[17]—that Chateaubriand also used in his *Mémoires*, in a chapter originally written in 1836, and revised ten years later. Further, also in the *Mémoires*, we find the story of the author who describes how, during his exile in England, he used to meditate upon his unhappiness, walking inside Westminster Cathedral and, looking at that "labyrinth of tombs," thought of his own grave, *"ready to open."*[18] One day it happened that he did not realize that the

---

and the saints are displayed at fairs. I saw my savage lady in a street theater plumed with a cockerel's feathers, speaking of the *soul of solitude* to a savage of her tribe, in a manner such as to make me sweat with embarrassment. At the Varieties they performed a piece in which a young boy and girl, leaving their lodgings, traveled by stagecoach to marry in their little village; on arrival they spoke of nothing but alligators, egrets and forests, their parents believing they had gone mad. Parodies, caricatures, lampoons showered on me" (*Mémoires*, Book XIII, Chapter VII). It is also interesting to observe that *Atala* obtained the same success in Denmark: Georg Brandes informs us that at that time Chateaubriand was well known. See his *Hovedstrømninger i det 19. Aarhundredes Literatur—Emigrantliteraturen* (1872), in *Samlede Skrifter*, vols. 1–18, Copenhagen: Gyldendal 1900, vol. 4, pp. 22–3.

[11]   Chateaubriand, "Avant-Propos," in *Mémoires*, vol. 1, p. 2.

[12]   Chateaubriand, "Préface testamentaire," in *Mémoires*, vol. 1: "I have had no peace except for the nine months when my being lay in my mother's belly: it is probable that I shall never recover that ante-natal peace, except in the womb of our communal mother, after death."

[13]   I am now only referring to the above-mentioned *Preface* to *Mémoires* written in 1846; the entire work was subsequently published from October 21, 1848 to July 5, 1850 as a *feuilleton* in the review *La Presse*; then in 12 volumes by the publisher Penaud from January 1849 to October 1850. But, as is well known, the author had already started writing his *Mémoires* in October 1811, and in 1817 began reading his manuscript in public, first to the circle of his friends, then during the meetings of the French exiles in England, and, finally, in 1834, in the literary salon of Abbaye-aux-Bois, Madame J. Récamier, he inaugurated a long and successful series of public readings of the work, which the best-known intellectuals of the time frequently attended.

[14]   Cf. *SKS* 2, 137 / *EO1*, 137 (see also *SKS* K2–3, 142–3). *SKS* 2, 213–23 / *EO1*, 217–30.

[15]   *EO1*, 137 and *EO1*, 165, but also the Hongs' commentary, p. 623.

[16]   *SKS* 2, 214 / *EO1*, 220.

[17]   See Chateaubriand, *Mémoires*, vol. 1, Book XIII, Chapter 10, p. 462.

[18]   See ibid., Book X, Chapter 5, p. 354 (written in 1822). The imagine of the solitary grave returns again in Chateaubriand in the short novel *Les aventures du dernier Abencérage*, in *Œuvres Complètes de M. le Vicomte de Chateaubriand*, Paris: Pourrat frères 1836–39,

"usher"—as he wrote, using the English term—had already closed the gate, so that he had to spend a long part of the night inside the cathedral.

The image of an open grave could easily remind us of Kierkegaard's description of the English grave, which he presents at the beginning of "The Unhappiest One":

> As is well known, there is said to be a grave somewhere in England that is distinguished not by a magnificent monument or a mournful setting but a short inscription—"The Unhappiest One." It is said that the grave was opened, but no trace of a corpse was found. Which is the more amazing—that no corpse was found or that the grave was opened? It is indeed strange that someone took the time to see whether anyone was in it. When one reads a name in an epitaph, one is easily tempted to wonder how he passed his life on earth; one might wish to climb down into the grave for a conversation with him. But this inscription—it is so freighted with meaning![19]

Later Kierkegaard will tell us that this grave is empty simply because "the unhappiest one" is actually still alive, since real unhappiness consists in living, so that the existence of a hypothetical "unhappy" *dead* person would be a contradiction. This seems to be a kind of answer to Chateaubriand's story: the poet is looking at his own open grave inside the cathedral; he cannot descend, and this is, paradoxically, exactly the reason why the unhappiest one's grave belongs to him. The similarity between the two texts is striking in this regard.

The question of whether Kierkegaard really did not read anything from these *Mémoires* is difficult: the very first edition of the definitive version of this text began to appear between 1848 and 1850 (first as *feuilleton* in the review *La Presse*, then as a book in 12 volumes), and so Kierkegaard obviously could not have read the passages we quoted prior to 1843, that is, the year in which *Either/Or* appeared. However, it is nevertheless true that Chateaubriand started to write his work in 1811 and already from 1817 began giving frequent public readings of it, first in England during his exile, then in France, where the most important social gatherings of the best-known intellectuals of that time for the purpose of listening to Chateaubriand's

---

p. 205 (written during the eleven-month journey begun in 1806 with which the author had planned to visit the Holy Land, leaving from Venice, then going through the ruins of Athens, Sparta, Carthage, and finally coming back through Spain. The aim of this journey was supposed to be the gathering of images and information for the novel *Les martyrs* (1809). However, he ended up writing two other works, *L'Itinéraire de Paris à Jérusalem* (1811) and *Les aventures du dernier Abencérage*, which were published in 1826 in the complete works edited by Ladvocat): "Leaving from Tunis through the door which leads to the ruins of Carthage, one meets a cemetery: under a palm, in a corner of this cemetery, one grave was shown to me, it was called "the last of Abencerages' grave." It has nothing particularly interesting; the tombstone is smooth; according to Moorish custom, just a little hollow has been chiseled in the middle of the stone. The rainwater stagnated within this funereal bowl, and it serves—in that torrid climate—to quench the birds' thirst."

[19]   *SKS* 2, 213, *EO1*, 219. The Danish commentaries to this passage (*SKS* K2–3, 169) refer to Worcester Cathedral, where a grave exists with an epitaph in Latin which says only "*miserrimus*." Kierkegaard also quoted the same reference in *SKS* 19, 186, Not5:24.

Mémoires dates from 1834.[20] At the same time, numerous extracts of these readings were distributed to the reviews or journals like *Revue des Deux Mondes*, *Revue de Paris*, *Écho de la Jeune France*, for the sake of publicity,[21] and the most significant of them, along with the extracts of the readings, were already published collectively in 1834, in a volume entitled *Lectures des "Mémoires" de M. de Chateaubriand, ou recueil d'articles publié sur ces "Mémoires," avec des fragments originaux.*[22]

It is more than plausible to assume that anyone who was in some way interested or involved in literary criticism and discussion at that time, and not only in France, could not help but be aware of the importance of Chateaubriand. This is made clear merely from considering the example of Charles Augustin Sainte-Beuve (1804–69), who already in 1834 had defined him as the founder of imaginative poetry, or "*l'Homère du jeune siècle*"[23] and emphasized that all modern literary schools descended more or less directly from him. At the time, the *Revue des Deux Mondes*, a literary and widely cultural review founded in Paris in 1829 by François Buloz (1803–77), held a particularly important position both in France and the rest of Europe, and it is not unlikely that Kierkegaard read it during these years, even if it cannot be demonstrated.

We should merely consider, for example—as the Danish commentator of Kierkegaard's *Journal NB7* quotes[24]—that when Kierkegaard in 1848 wrote down in this journal, "Chateaubriand's *Memoirs* has a superb motto taken from Job: *sicut nubes...quasi naves—velut umbra*,"[25] he did it after having read Louis de Loménie's article "Chateaubriands Memoirer," in *Fædrelandet* in 1848,[26] which was a Danish translation of the French article "Chateaubriand et ses *Mémoires*," published between July 1 and September 1 in, precisely, the *Revue des Deux Mondes*.[27] This does not mean that Kierkegaard could not also have read this same review in the original language even before 1848—that is, from the first time that Chateaubriand began to read his *Mémoires* in public (and about this we can point out, in fact, that the

---

[20]   One could quote the name of some very important critics and journalist of the time, such as Charles-Augustin Sainte-Beuve, Edgar Quinet, Léonce de Lavergne, Désiré Nisard, and Alfred Nettement.

[21]   Some laudatory articles concerning the public readings of 1834 include those of Jules Janin in the *Revue de Paris* (March 1); Sainte-Beuve in the *Revue des Deux Mondes* (April 15); Quinet in the *Revue de Paris* (April 26); Nettement in the *Écho de la Jeune France*.

[22]   Chateaubriand, *Lectures des "Mémoires" de M. de Chateaubriand, ou recueil d'articles publié sur ces "Mémoires," avec des fragments originaux*, Paris: Lefèvre 1834, with a laudatory introduction by D. Nisard.

[23]   See his above-mentioned article of April 15, 1834, then republished in the volume *Portraits contemporains*, Paris: Didier 1855 [1834], vol. 1, p. 9. Some years prior, however, Saint-Beuve had already indicated Chateaubriand as the father of Romanticism (see *Revue de Paris*, September 25, 1831), even if he relegated him to the very beginning of the movement.

[24]   *SKS* 21, 100, NB7:52 / *JP* 4, 4150; see also *SKS* K21, 91.

[25]   *SKS* 21, 100, NB7:52 / *JP* 4, 4150.

[26]   *Fædrelandet*, nos. 272–6, October 25–30, 1848, columns 2157–94.

[27]   Louis de Loménie, "Chateaubriand et ses *Mémoires*," *Revue des Deux Mondes*, vol. 23, pp. 133–67 (first part), 674–707 (second part).

first time that the *incipit* of the *Mémoires*, that is, the already mentioned *Préface Testamentaire*[28]—where Job's words appear—was published, it was precisely also in the *Revue des Deux Mondes*, in March 1834). It is well known, among other things, that Kierkegaard often drew upon the University of Copenhagen Library, and especially the Students Association's book collection, whose catalogue is still preserved at the Royal Library of Copenhagen, and which, of course, included the above-mentioned review.[29]

However, we could also add that even if Kierkegaard himself did not read the review, he could have known something about the passages from Chateaubriand's *Mémoires* through conversations with his friends, such as, for example, the writer and literary critic Peder Ludvig Møller (1814–65), who, among other things, in 1840 won the literary prize offered by the University of Copenhagen on the theme of the modernity of the French taste for poetry, with a text in which Chateaubriand is naturally also quoted.[30]

These are, nevertheless, merely interesting hypotheses, but, as was said before, nothing in fact tells us more about their verisimilitude. It is, however, stimulating to continue to trace further interesting similarities between the two writers, both in the *Mémoires*, as well as the most famous works of the French poet, *Atala* and *René*, which are worthy of special consideration. In this direction we can accordingly follow the method used by Ronald Grimsley in his comparative study *Søren Kierkegaard and French Literature*[31]—in which we also find a chapter on the "Romantic Melancholy in Kierkegaard and Chateaubriand"—where the author at the beginning expressly states:

> Although the starting-point of these comparative studies will be...Kierkegaard's specific reactions to French authors, it should perhaps be made clear at once that they are not concerned primarily with investigating problems of "influence"; their aim, for the most part, is to determine Kierkegaard's fundamental attitude towards the questions raised rather then to examine the problem of any permanent influence they may have had upon his intellectual and religious development. By comparing two different views of a single cultural problem, I hope to bring out certain of its deeper implications more clearly than would have been possible through the examination of one author in isolation.[32]

---

[28]   Chateaubriand, *Lectures des "Mémoires" de M. de Chateaubriand, ou recueil d'articles publié sur ces "Mémoires," avec des fragments originaux*, pp. 5–14.

[29]   I take this information from Ronald Grimsley, *Søren Kierkegaard and French Literature*, Cardiff: University of Wales Press 1966, p. 3. He also mentions another library in Copenhagen known as the Athenaeum, to which Kierkegaard also belonged and from which he borrowed books on numerous occasions.

[30]   This information comes from Rohde, "Ørkenens sønner," pp. 74–5.

[31]   Grimsley, *Søren Kierkegaard and French Literature*.

[32]   Ibid., p. 1. However, from this perspective, one could ask why Grimsley did not take into account Chateaubriand's *Mémoires*, but only considered *Atala* and *René*. It is true that René is the prototype of the melancholic Romantic man, but it is also true that in the same direction Chateaubriand's autobiography too, plays a crucial role. This is the reason why I decided to start my analysis precisely here. On Grimsley's work, see also F.J. Billeskov Jansen's review "Søren Kierkegaard et la littérature française," in *Kierkegaardiana*, vol. 7, 1968, pp. 188–92.

In this sense it can be interesting to show some further stimulating points of contact between the two writers. I will continue by choosing some common themes used by the two authors in exactly the same way (at least apparently so, or from an "aesthetical" point of view, since we will subsequently also show some essential differences especially in their religious attitudes).

One of these similarities is, for example, the description of the father figure in both authors, in the first book of Chateaubriand's *Mémoires* and in several of Kierkegaard's writings. The two authors attribute their own melancholic temperament to paternal influence, their childhood seemingly having been oppressed by too severe an upbringing, but despite this, they both affirm how much they loved their father. This is Chateaubriand's text:

> My father's birth and the ordeals he endured in his early life, endowed him with one of the most somber characters there has ever been. This character influenced my ideas by terrifying my childhood, saddening my youth, and determining the nature of my upbringing....he had contracted, from habitual suffering, a rigidity of character which he retained all his life....Monsieur de Chateaubriand was tall and gaunt; he had an aquiline nose, thin pale lips, and small deep-set eyes, sea-green or glaucous, like those of lions or barbarians of old. I have never seen eyes like his: when anger filled them the glittering pupils seemed to detach themselves and issue forth to strike you like bullets... His habitual state was a profound sadness that age deepened, and a silence that he only emerged from to vent his anger.[33]

Also in his *Mémoires* Chateaubriand describes his childhood as follows:

> If only that peaceful *Star of the Seas* had been able to calm my life's disturbances! But I was to be troubled, even in childhood; like the Arab's date tree, my trunk had scarcely sprung from the rock before it was battered by the wind....Such is the picture of my childhood. I do not know if the harsh education I received is good in principle, but it was adopted by my family without design, and as a natural consequence of their temperaments. What is certain is that it made my ideas less like those of other men; what is even more certain is that it marked my sentiments with a melancholy character born in me from the habit of suffering at a tender age, heedlessness and joy. One might think that this manner of upbringing would lead to my detesting my parents. Not at all; the memory of their strictness is almost dear to me; I prize and honor their great qualities. When my father died, my comrades in the Navarre Regiment witnessed my grief.[34]

These remarks sound much like Kierkegaard's well-known words about his *alter ego* Johannes Climacus in *De Omnibus*:

> His home did not offer many diversions, and, since he practically never went out, he very early became accustomed to being occupied with himself and with his own thoughts. His father was a very strict man, seemingly dry and prosaic, but underneath this rough

---

[33]   Chateaubriand, *Mémoires*, vol. 1, Book I, Chapter I, p. 7.

[34]   Ibid., vol. 1, Book I, Chapter 5. See also ibid., vol. 1, Book III, Chapter I: "The bleak tranquility of the Château of Combourg was increased by my father's taciturn and unsociable nature."

homespun cloak he concealed a glowing imagination that not even his advanced age managed to dim.[35]

In his *Journal NB5* Kierkegaard writes the following about himself:

> Humanly speaking, I owe everything to my father. In every way he has made me as unhappy as possible, made my youth incomparable anguish...and yet my father was the most affectionate of fathers, and my longing for him was and is sincere, and no day goes by that I am not reminded of him morning and evening.[36]

So, this is actually another feature which connects Kierkegaard to Chateaubriand's attitude and personal experience, the fact that both locate the origin of their melancholy in their own father's temperament; moreover, both claim that their fathers represent a very particular figure: that of a man who is not simply a melancholic personality but a kind of strange mixture between an active and contemplative man, whose melancholy is in a certain sense his real essence, but kept hidden by an active and rigorous life. This real personal character seems to be wholly developed only in the second generation, that is, Kierkegaard and Chateaubriand.

Nevertheless, both authors, in spite of the suffering which marks their existence and their temperament from the first childhood on, at the same time love their sadness, in which they see a sign of their exceptional nature, called from God. Also in his *Mémoires* Chateaubriand writes, "It was in the woods of Combourg that I became what I am, that I began to feel the first assault of that *ennui* which I have dragged with me through life, of that sadness which has been my torment and my bliss."[37] He asks, "Why had God created a being destined only to suffer? What mysterious connection can there be between a tormented nature and an eternal principle?"[38] Kierkegaard continually stresses this point, to which he indeed returns several times. In *Either/Or* one reads, "I say of my sorrow what the Englishman says of his house: My sorrow is my castle. Many people look upon having sorrow as one of life's conveniences."[39] In the same text he writes, "I have only one friend, and that is echo. Why is it my friend? Because I love my sorrow, and echo does not take it away from me. I have only one confidant, and that is the silence of night. Why is it my

---

[35]   *Pap.* IV B 1, 106 / *JC*, 119–20.

[36]   *SKS* 20, 400–1, NB5:68 / *JP* 6, 6167. *SKS* 20, 400, NB5:67 / *JP* 6, 6166: "On someone else it may not have made so deep an impression, but my imagination—and especially at an early stage when it still had no tasks to apply itself to. A primitive depression like that, a huge dowry of distress, and in the profoundest sense the sad fact of being brought up as a child by a melancholy old man—and then with the native virtuosity of being able to deceive everyone into thinking me a jolly good fellow—and that God in heaven has helped me as he has."

[37]   Chateaubriand, *Mémoires*, vol. 1, Book III, Chapter 14, p. 105.

[38]   Ibid., vol. 1, Book XIII, Chapter 9, p. 457. See also vol. 2, Book XXV, Chapter 1, p. 4: "there is always a kind of primacy in individual human solitude." *Atala*, Epilogue: "man, you are nothing more than a rapid dream, a painful dream; only the sadness of your soul and the eternal melancholy of your thoughts make you someone."

[39]   *SKS* 2, 30 / *EO1*, 21.

confidant? Because it remains silent."[40] One finds similar remarks in his journals. For example in *NB5* we read, "Melancholy shadows everything in my life, but that, too, is an indescribable blessing."[41] This idea is continued a few entries further: "If I had not found my melancholy and depression to be nothing but a blessing, it would have been impossible to live without her [sc. Regine]."[42] In this way Kierkegaard twice describes his sorrow as a kind of castle, which, while it shuts him in, simultaneously also protects him, and, as from an eagle's nest, permits him to observe everything from the proper distance:

> *Bene vixit qui bene latuit* [Ovid, *Tristia*, III, 4, 25–26] then I have lived well, for my nook was well chosen. It certainly is true that the world and everything therein never look better than when seen from a nook and one must secretly contrive to see it; it is also true that everything heard and to be heard in the world sounds most delectable and enchanting heard from a nook when one must contrive to hear. Thus I have frequently visited my sequestered nook. I knew it before, long before; by now I have learned not to need night-time in order to find stillness, for here it is always still, always beautiful, but it seems most beautiful to me now when the autumn sun is having its mid-afternoon repast and the sky becomes a languorous blue when creation takes a deep breath after the heat, when the cooling starts and the meadow grass shivers voluptuously as the forest waves, when the sun is thinking of eventide and sinking into the ocean at eventide, when the earth is getting ready for rest and is thinking of giving thanks, when just before taking leave they have an understanding with one another in that tender melting together that darkens the forest and makes the meadow greener.[43]

That image of a solitary "nest" distant from the crowded common world is in fact one that Chateaubriand also uses when describing himself during his ocean passage, when in the spring of 1791 he decided to leave for the New World:

> My daily retreat, when I wished to evade the other passengers, was the maintop; I climbed to it....I sat there overlooking the waves....Descending from the mast's eyrie, as I once used to descend from my nest in the willow-tree, forever constrained to my solitary existence, I would eat a ship's biscuit, and a little sugar and lemon; then, I would lie down to sleep, on deck wrapped in my cloak, or below deck in my bunk: I had only to stretch my arm to reach from my bed to my coffin.[44]

---

[40]   *SKS* 2, 42 / *EO1*, 33. See also *SKS* 2, 51 / *EO1*, 42: "My sorrow is my baronial castle, which lies like an eagle's nest high up on the mountain peak among the clouds. No one can take it by storm. From it I swoop down into actuality and snatch my prey, but I do not stay down there. I bring my booty home, and this booty is a picture I weave into the tapestries at my castle. Then I live as one already dead."
[41]   *SKS* 20, 398 NB5:62 / *JP* 6, 6161.
[42]   *SKS* 20, 399, NB5:64 / *JP* 6, 6163.
[43]   *SKS* 6, 24 / *SLW*, p. 17.
[44]   Chateaubriand, *Mémoires*, vol. 1, Book VI, Chapter 5, p. 209. We could also notice that, strictly speaking, it would not be completely impossible to think that Kierkegaard might have read this chapter of Chateaubriand's autobiography, since it is precisely one of the few passages chosen to be read during the public readings in Madame Récamier's salon, and had been published in the above-mentioned collection of texts (passages from *Mémoires* and reviews of them) edited already in 1834 with the title of *Relache à l'île de Saint-Pierre de Terre-*

In a different passage in his *Mémoires*, he writes, "I retreated into my heart's depths, like a hare into its form: there I again set myself to contemplating the movement of a leaf or the angle of a blade of grass."[45] The detachment of the solitary, suffering man from the community seems to be possible, according to Kierkegaard, precisely due to this suffering itself, because, as the author states, a shirt woven with tears, protects more than a cuirass![46] This is indeed the paradox according to which—both in Kierkegaard and Chateaubriand, even with several differences—the deeper the inner suffering of the individual is, the stronger is this man in front of the adversities of the world, and the more independent towards other men,[47] since he is used to the much more difficult, exhausting and constant fight against himself.[48] Thus, the only power he can face, and the only power which can really comfort and help him, is the infinite power of God: "I fail badly when circulating as a piece of today's coinage; to protect myself I withdraw closer to God; a preoccupation sent from above isolates you, and makes everything around you die away."[49] In a different passage, he writes along the same lines, "Time is a veil interposed between God and ourselves, as our eyelid is between our eye and the light."[50] This passage could have been written by Kierkegaard.[51] The religious sphere ultimately remains the home of the work of both authors; nevertheless, this necessarily requires a careful consideration which we will postpone until the second section of this article.

Some further statements that can make us see Kierkegaard as close to Chateaubriand are those which describe the authors as looking for their solitude precisely in the middle of the crowd. Chateaubriand wrote:

> To find solitude, I fled to the theater: I settled into the depths of a box, and let my thoughts wander among Racine's verse, the music of Sacchini, or the ballet at the Opéra.

Neuve, in *Lectures des "Mémoires" de M. de Chateaubriand, ou recueil d'articles publié sur ces "Mémoires," avec des fragments originaux*, pp. 212–16. The fragment entitled *Traversé de l'Océan* (in *Mémoires*, vol. 1, Book VI, Chapter 2, pp. 198–203) was also published in the same volume.

45   Chateaubriand, *Mémoires*, vol. 1, Book XI, Chapter 1, pp. 380–1.

46   *SKS* 18, 33, EE:89 / *KJN* 2, 29: "There is a life-view that is acquired with tears but that is also stronger than iron, like the shirt: '*wenn sie ihn unter Thränen spinnt, mit Thränen bleicht, ein Hemde draus unter Thranen näht, schützt mich dis besser als alles Eisen, es ist undurchdringlich,*' but his life-view protects only the one who has himself prepared it, not like that shirt, which was for all. cf Magyarische Sagen by Graf Mailath. p. 152, bottom." (Kierkegaard refers here to Johann Garfen Mailáth, *Magyarische Sagen, und Mährchen*, Brünn: J.G. Trafsler 1825 (*ASKB* 1411).)

47   See, for example, Chateaubriand, *Mémoires*, vol. 1, Book XI, Chapter 2, p. 383: "My independence regarding diverse social attitudes has almost always wounded the men with whom I have been aligned."

48   See, for example, Kierkegaard: "I fear no one as I fear myself." *SKS* 6, 194 / *SLW*, 207.

49   Chateaubriand, *Mémoires*, vol. 2, Book XXV, Chapter 13, p. 33.

50   Ibid., vol. 1, Book X, Chapter 5, p. 356.

51   Among other things, the metaphor of the circulating coin is also used by Kierkegaard himself, when, in *The Sickness unto Death* (*SKS* 11, 150 / *SUD*, 34) he describes the ordinary man "as smooth as a rolling stone, as *courant* as a circulating coin."

I was forced to go barefacedly twenty times in succession to the Italiens, to *Barbe-bleue* and the *Sabot perdu*, boring myself in order to prevent boredom, like an owl in some hole in the wall.[52]

In his famous description in *Repetition* Kierkegaard states:

One enters the Königstädter Theater and gets a place in the first balcony, for relatively few sit there, and in seeing a farce, one must sit comfortably and in no way feel hampered by the exaltation of art that makes people jam a theater to see a play as if it were a matter of salvation. The air in the theater is also fairly pure, untainted by the sweat of a fervent empathizing audience or by the miasma of art enthusiasts. In the first balcony one can be quite sure of getting a box all to oneself. If not, however, may I recommend to the reader boxes five and six on the left so that he can still have some useful information from what I write. In a corner in the back there is a single seat where one has an unsurpassed position. So you are sitting alone in your box, and the theater is empty. The orchestra plays an overture, the music resounds in the hall a bit *unheimlich* simply because the place is so deserted. You have gone to the theater not as a tourist, not as an aesthete and critic but, if possible, as a nobody, and you are satisfied to sit as comfortably and well, almost as well, as in your own living room....As a rule, I sat far back in the box and therefore could not see the second balcony and gallery, which jutted out over my head like the visor of a cap. All the more magical is the effect of this noise. Everywhere I looked there was mainly emptiness. Before me the vast space of the theater changed into the belly of the whale in which Jonah sat; the noise in the gallery was like the motion of the monster's viscera....Thus did I lie in my theater box, discarded like a swimmer's clothing, stretched out by the stream of laughter and unrestraint and applause that ceaselessly foamed by me. I could see nothing but the expanse of theater, hear nothing but the noise in which I resided.[53]

The similarities between these two passages are striking, both in a rhetorical sense and in an existential one.

Moreover, both authors speak ironically about ordinary men, whom they describe as false heroes of their illusory world. We here also find a similar description of people returning together by carriage from some popular and busy place: Chateaubriand speaks, without hiding his contempt, about "those *heroes of domesticity*, returning from Verdun in their carriages,"[54] while Kierkegaard describes the crowd on "Strandveien on Sunday afternoon in the Deer Park season—they rush past one another, yell and shout, laugh and make fools of one another, drive their horses to death, tip over and are run over."[55] He is even more radical when, under the mask of A, the aesthete of *Either/Or*, he speaks of ordinary people in the following terms:

those who do not bore themselves are busy in the world in one way or another, but for that very reason they are, of all people, the most boring of all, the most unbearable. Certainly this class of animals is not the fruit of man's appetite and woman's desire. Like all lower classes of animals, it is distinguished by a high level of fecundity and propagates beyond

---

[52]   Chateaubriand, *Mémoires*, vol. 1, Book V, Chapter 15, p. 187.
[53]   *SKS* 4, 39–41 / *R*, 165–6.
[54]   Chateaubriand, *Mémoires*, vol. 1, Book X, Chapter 3, p. 344.
[55]   *SKS* 17, 23, AA:12 / *KJN* 1, 18.

belief. It is incomprehensible too, that nature should need nine months to produce such creatures, which presumably could rather be produced by the score.[56]

Nevertheless, despite their solitude, their detachment from the community and their intentional isolation, both the authors acknowledge their need to make their voices heard by the other: they ask themselves why they need this, but cannot answer; they simply recognize it, and can only poetically compare themselves to a strange breed of singing or crying birds. Chateaubriand says that "Poets are birds: any sound makes them sing,"[57] while Kierkegaard presents to us the following description of an excursion around Søborg, in the north of Zealand:

> reed growth, however, is as dense and thick as a forest, probably eight feet high. Concealed by it, one seems as if eternally lost to the world, forgotten in the stillness broken only by our struggling with the boat or when a bittern, that secret voice in the solitude, repeats its cry three times, and then repeats it again. *Strange bird, why do you wail and lament this way after all, you indeed wish only to remain in solitude!*[58]

Thus, as Chateaubriand states in the first book of his autobiography, it seems that the suffering poet sings merely in order to hear his own voice—as the echo does: "I am reciting the first couplets of a plaintive ballad which has charm only for myself; ask the goat-herd of the Tyrol why he loves the two or three notes he repeats to his flock, sounds of the mountain, throwing off echo after echo in order to resound from one side of a torrent to the other?"[59] This exclusive interest in oneself is common both to Chateaubriand and Kierkegaard's aesthetic pseudonymous authors—in particular A in *Either/Or*—as we will see later on. One cannot forget, however, that while as regards Chateaubriand one can assert with some certainty that his person coincides with the protagonists of his works—and *René* deliberately bears the name of his author—as he himself stated,[60] Kierkegaard, on the contrary—as is well known—conceals his identity with a multiplicity of masks, which, moreover, he pretended to consider as so many "poetically actual subjective thinkers."[61] They should only accentuate "a point, a stance, a position,"[62] but their role had to be only provisional,[63] since they had to be overcome by the higher religious point of view, which was the authentic position of the author. We will later see the real implications of this position, but if we look only at the movement drawn by Kierkegaard's whole authorship—the aesthetical works used as a kind of interesting bait in order to attract the attention of

---

[56]   *SKS* 2, 278 / *EO1*, 288–9.
[57]   Chateaubriand, *Mémoires*, vol. 1, Book XXII, Chapter 15, p. 874.
[58]   *SKS* 6, 176 / *SLW*, 188.
[59]   Chateaubriand, *Mémoires*, vol. 1, Book I, Chapter 7, p. 46.
[60]   "Of the modern French authors of my age, I am almost the only one whose life resembles his works: traveler, soldier, poet, publicist, it was in the forest that I sang of forests, aboard ship that I described the sea, in camp that I spoke of weapons, in exile that I learned about exile, at court, in assemblies, amongst public affairs, that I studied princes, politics, law and history," Chateaubriand, *Mémoires*, *Préface Testamentaire*.
[61]   *SKS* 7, 570 / *CUP1*, 626; see also *Pap.* VII–1 B 78.
[62]   *SKS* 22, 88, NB11:150 / *JP* 6, 6421.
[63]   See, for example, *SV1* XIII, 570 / *PV*, 86. *SV1* XIII, 498–9 / *PV*, 10.

the crowd and turn it toward the higher inner sphere of the religious—a similar one can be traced in Chateaubriand.

It is known, in fact, that he published *René* and *Atala* as two episodes of the wider religious essay, *Génie du christianisme, ou Beautés poétiques et morales de la religion chrétienne*, published in Paris in 1802.[64] *Atala* was nevertheless published beforehand in 1801 as a kind of appetizer for the work as a whole: its plot was the impossible love between Atala—the baptized daughter of a savage woman and a Catholic European—and the savage Chactas. The aim of the story was intended to be Chactas' conversion to Catholicism, thanks to Atala's sacrifice. The publication of the work was an extraordinary success, and Chateaubriand the following year also published the five volumes of the *Génie du christianisme*, which was similarly an enormous success, not least because it appeared to coincide with the solemn *Te Deum* which, during the Easter service of April 18, 1802, in the cathedral of Notre Dame in Paris, celebrated the restoration of the cult following the concordat established by Pope Pius VII and Napoleon. In a booklet written in 1803, which was intended to explain his position against the criticism of some journalists,[65] Chateaubriand emphasizes, precisely, that through the episodes of *Atala* and *René* he had intended to demonstrate, to prove, the things that in the theoretical part of the work he had merely illustrated through words, and that, at the same time, he had wanted to "prepare a bait" for those particular readers who only look for "impious" novels:

> the author had to fight the impious poems and novels through pious poems and novels; he has worn the same weapons which he saw the enemy has worn: it was the natural and necessary consequence of the type of apology he had chosen. He had tried to give the example through precepts. In the theoretical part of his work, the author had said that religion makes our existence beautiful, it corrects our passions without extinguishing them, it lends a singular interest to every subject in which it is used; he had said that its doctrine and its cult perfectly mix with emotions of heart and the scenes of nature; finally, it is the only resource in the great troubles of the life: it was not enough just to say all that, it was necessary to prove it. It is precisely what the author has tried to do in the two episodes of this book. These episodes were, moreover, a bait prepared especially for that type of readers for whom the work in particular was written. Thus, had the author investigated the human heart really so badly when he set that innocent trap for the unbelieving? Then, is it not probable that this kind of reader would have never opened the *Génie du christianisme*, if he would not have been looking for *René* and *Atala*?[66]

---

[64]   *Atala* had been conceived as an episode of *Génie du christianisme*, Paris: Migneret 1802, but it had also been edited beforehand in 1801: *Atala, ou les amours de deux sauvages dans le désert*, Paris: Migneret 1801. It was a tremendous success and was printed in five editions in only one year.

[65]   In particular against the hostile criticism of Pierre Louis Ginguené in three articles published in the review *Décade philosophique* (June 19, 29, and July 9, 1802); Alexandre-Louis de Villeterque in *Bibliothèque française* (July 1802).

[66]   See Chateaubriand, *Défense du Génie du Christianisme*, Paris: Migneret 1803 (see Chateaubriand, *Œuvres Complètes de M. le Vicomte de Chateaubriand*, vols. 1–28, Paris: Ladvocat 1826–31, vol. 6, pp. 161–2).

Several generations of fierce critics and reviewers—first and foremost Charles Augustin Sainte-Beuve[67]—have thrown themselves on the honesty of Chateaubriand's religious intentions, but this is not the proper place to discuss this point. Whatever interpretation is correct, suffice it to say here that this well-meant strategy of deception is the same in both authors, Kierkegaard and Chateaubriand. As the Danish thinker says:

> Do not be deceived by the word *deception*. One can deceive a person out of what is true, and—to recall old Socrates—one can deceive a person into what is true. Yes, in only this way can a deluded person actually be brought into what is true—by deceiving him. The one who is of another opinion thereby betrays that he simply is not much of a dialectician, which is precisely what is necessary in order to operate in this way. In other words there is a great difference, that is, the dialectical difference, or the difference of the dialectical, between these two situations: one who is ignorant and must be given some knowledge, and therefore he is like the empty vessel that must be filled or like the blank sheet of paper that must be written upon—and one who is under a delusion that must first be taken away. Likewise, there is also a difference between writing on a blank piece of paper and bringing out by means of chemicals some writing that is hidden under other writing....What, then, does it mean "to deceive"? It means that one does not begin directly with what one wishes to communicate but begins by taking the other's delusion at face value. Thus one does not begin (to hold to what essentially is the theme of this book) in this way: I am Christian, you are not a Christian—but this way: You are a Christian, I am not Christian. Or one does not begin in this way: It is Christianity that I am proclaiming, and you are living in purely aesthetic categories. No, one begins this way: Let us talk about the aesthetic. The deception consists in one's speaking this way precisely in order to arrive at the religious. But according to the assumption the other person is in fact under the delusion that the aesthetic is the essentially Christian, since he thinks he is a Christian and yet he is living in aesthetic categories.[68]

It should be specified that the real "deception" of Kierkegaard's strategy lay not in the use of pseudonymous authors—in fact everybody knew who was concealed under such odd and improbable names of Victor Eremita, Constantin Constantius, Frater Taciturnus. and so on—but precisely the way in which he intended to attract the "aesthetic" readers to the religious.

However, we find precisely here a fundamental difference between Kierkegaard and Chateaubriand, which we will be able to see still better below: it is, in fact, the final achievement of the religious point of view. While in Kierkegaard this involves an absolute detachment from every aesthetic aspect of life, in Chateaubriand the religious self is to be enveloped under the cloak of aesthetics: the subtitle of the major apologetic work of the French poet—the *Génie du christianisme*—is, indeed, as we

---

[67]   See, for instance, Charles-Augustin de Saint-Beuve, *Chateaubriand et son groupe littéraire sous l'Empire: cours professé à Liège en 1848–1849*, vols. 1–2, Paris: Garnier 1861, vol. 1, p. 379, where the critic speaks about "*une moralité plaquée*," a "stuck," false, morality.

[68]   *SV1* XIII, 541–2 / *PV*, 53–4.

said, "*The poetic and moral* Beauty *of the Christian Religion.*"[69] One might dare to say that Chateaubriand's religious sphere coincides with Kierkegaard's ethical sphere: and perhaps it is not so strange that Kierkegaard entitled the ethical answer to A's papers in *Either/Or* precisely "The *Esthetic* Validity of Marriage." The tenor of B's arguments against the aesthete A, indeed, echoes precisely father Aubry's arguments against the savage Chactas in *Atala*: and is it not true that precisely this second part of *Either/Or* is introduced by a motto taken exactly from *Atala*, precisely from Father Aubry's discourse? The role of B is thus also represented by the analogous character of Father Aubry in *René*, which is Father Souël. We see, in this way, in Chateaubriand's Catholic perspective, the fundamental and unavoidable role of the intermediary figures of faith, something that obviously is lacking in Kierkegaard, whereas the *ubique et nusquam* figure of God remains without face or words. One of the criticisms that Kierkegaard expressly presents against Chateaubriand, for instance, is that of the validity of the ecclesiastical *eloquence* of Christianity, as opposed to paganism. He states, indeed, that from a Christian point of view, eloquence is a mistake.[70] In a certain sense one could say that their similarity on this point is only formal, while the content is quite different.

---

69   This is the subtitle of *The Genius of Christianity*, i.e., *The Genius of Christianity or the Spirit and Beauty of the Christian Religion*.

70   See *SKS* 24, 122, NB22:34 / *JP* 1, 681: "In his *Spirit of Christianity* Chateaubriand speaks of Christian eloquence as something which distinguishes Christianity from paganism, something which paganism did not have—and Tzschirner in his *Letters to Ch.* (Leipzig: 1828) agrees. It must be said that this is an error. For, Christianly understood, the whole notion of Christian 'eloquence' is in many ways a mistake, an indirect proof that Christianity is set apart in the realm of practical activity; for eloquence increases in proportion [to decline]; all political analogies show that eloquence flourished at the time of the dissolution of states. To that extent it is perhaps rather a proof of paganism's greater proficiency in practical activity that it was ignorant of ecclesiastical eloquence." Tzchimer's book is *Briefe eines Deutschen an die Herren Chateaubriand, de la Mennais und Montlosier über Gegenstände der Religion und Politik* (ed. by T.W. Krug, Leipzig: Barth 1828), in French: *Lettres sur la religion et la politique, adressées à M. l'abbé de La Mennais, M. le Vte de Chateaubriand et M. le Cte de Montlosier par H. Th. Tzschirner*, Paris: Mesnier 1829, see here pp. 100–2, where we could read for example these interesting considerations: "*Première lettre à monsieur le vicomte de Chateaubriand: De l'esprit religieux du siècle et de la direction que M. de Chateaubriand cherche à lui donner*": "*Vous vous proposez d'établir, comme vous le dites dans votre chef-d'œuvre* [*Génie du christianisme*, 5 vol. Lyon, 1809, tom. Iᵉʳ, pp. 10 and 11]', '*que la religion chrétienne est la plus poétique, la plus humaine, la plus favorable à la liberté, aux arts et aux lettres de toutes les religions qui ont jamais existé; que le monde moderne lui doit tout, depuis l'agriculture jusqu'aux sciences abstraites, depuis les hôpitaux pour les malheureux jusqu'aux temples bâtis par Michel-Ange et décorés par Raphaël; qu'il n'y a rien de plus divin que sa morale, rien de plus aimable, de plus pompeux que ses dogmes, sa doctrine, son culte; qu'il favorise le génie, épure le goût, développe les passions vertueuses, donne de la vigueur à la pensée, offre des formes nobles à l'écrivain et des moules parfaites à l'architecte.' Quel texte plus digne de profonds développements, quel texte mieux approprié au but de ramener vos contemporains au christianisme! Car quoique vos arguments ne soient pas de nature à établir ni la vérité, ni la divine origine de la religion de Christ, c'et lui gagner les suffrages et la vénération des honnêtes gens, que de prouver qu'elle renferme*

Equally different was, among other things, the reaction the writers had to the extraordinary popular success that their works obtained. Chateaubriand declares that after the publication of *Atala*, he ceased to live alone by himself and that his public career began. He finally admits, "I became fashionable. My head was turned: I was unacquainted with the pleasures of self-importance, and I became drunk. I loved fame as one does a woman, like a first love."[71] This success marks for Chateaubriand his definitive entry into the world:

> from a private man I am about to become a public man; I am leaving the silent virginal sanctuary of solitude to enter the noisy, dusty cross-roads of the world; broad daylight will illuminate my life of dreams, light will penetrate the kingdom of shadows. I cast a tender glance over these books which enclose my unremembered hours; I seem to be saying a last goodbye to my paternal home; I take leave of the thoughts and chimeras of my youth as of sisters, as of sweethearts I am leaving by the family hearth, never to see them again.[72]

The same cannot be said for Kierkegaard, who, on the contrary, interpreted his success as a kind of guilty misunderstanding of his real intentions, since he could never have fallen victim to fame:

> I can attest that the author of *Either/Or* regularly and with monastic scrupulousness spent a certain period of each day reading devotional writings for his own sake, that in fear and much trembling he considered his responsibility. He particularly had in mind "The Seducer's Diary" (how strange!). And then what happened? The book was an enormous success, especially "The Seducer's Dairy" (how strange!). The world

---

les éléments d'une poésie sublime, qu'elle favorise la civilisation, les lettres et les arts.... Permettez-moi, cependant, de vous faire remarquer que vous auriez mieux atteint votre but, en donnant à votre sujet les développements dont il est susceptible, en distinguant la poésie de la mythologie du christianisme et en vous abstenant d'orner, certaines traditions, par le prestige de votre style. C'est néanmoins ce qui vous arrive assez souvent, et, pour ne citer qu'un seul exemple, je choisirai le passage suivant qui se rapporte à la mère du Sauveur. Vous dites [Génie du christianisme, tom. Ier, pp. 43 et 44]: 'Quoi de plus touchant que cette femme mortelle, devenue la mère immortelle d'un Dieu rédempteur, que cette Marie à la fois vierge et mère, les deux états les plus divins de la femme, que cette jeune fille de l'ancien Jacob qui vient au secours des misères humaines et sacrifie un fils pour sauver la race de ses pères. Cette tendre médiatrice entre nous et l'Éternel, ouvre, avec la douce vertu de son sexe, un cœur plein de pitié à nos tristes confidences et désarme un Dieu irrité. Dogme enchanté qui adoucit la terreur d'un Dieu, en interposant la beauté entre notre néant et la majesté divine.' Ce tableau très poétique, sans doute, n'appartient cependant pas à la poésie du christianisme. L'Évangile ne nous représente pas la vierge Marie comme un être divin régnant dans les cieux, exauçant nos prières, venant au secours des faibles mortels comme une médiatrice entre Dieu et les hommes." Then, from the "Deuxième lettre à monsieur le vicomte de Chateaubriand: Des essais de M. de Chateaubriand et de divers littérateurs allemands de donner le principe esthétique pour base au christianisme," ibid., p. 114: "J'appellerai donc votre principe le principe esthétique, et les développements que vous lui donnez la démonstration esthétique du christianisme."

71   Chateaubriand, *Mémoires*, vol. 1, Book XIII, Chapter 6, p. 445.
72   Ibid., vol. 1, Book XII, Chapter 6, p. 431.

opened up, even to a remarkable degree, to the admired author, who, however, was not "seduced" or changed by all this—for that he was an eternity too old. Then followed *Two Upbuilding Discourses*—what is most important often seems too insignificant. The big work, *Either/Or*, which was "much read and even more discussed"—and then *Two Upbuilding Discourses*, dedicated to my late father, published on my birthday (May 5), "a little flower under the cover of the great forest, sought neither for its splendor nor its fragrance nor its food value." There was no one who in the profounder sense paid any attention to or cared about the two discourses; indeed, I even recall that one of my acquaintances came to me and complained that he had in good faith gone and bought them, thinking that since they were by me they must be something rather witty and clever. I also recall that I promised him that he would have his money back if he so desired. With my left hand I passed *Either/Or* out into the world, with my right hand *Two Upbuilding Discourses*; but they all or almost all took the left hand with their right.[73]

The reading of these two passages is, perhaps, very useful in order to individuate an essential feature of Kierkegaard's attitude and activity as a writer that is the authentic and deep will of upbuilding, beyond the aesthetics and the public implication of his actions. While Chateaubriand just noticed with a kind of wonder that he became a public personality because of his success, Kierkegaard interprets it as a misunderstanding from a *personal* point of view, but he is willing to accept that it can be useful for the cause of upbuilding.

One final interesting point, in which we can see a similar situation in the writers' attitudes—before moving to the second part of this article—is the common fight against the "atheistic" philosophy of their respective times. Both writers saw in their authorship a kind of "providential" function that consisted in revaluating Christianity against the positions of those philosophers who subordinated religion to philosophy. The polemical reference for Chateaubriand was the point of view of the eighteenth-century materialist French *philosophes*:

> *Le Génie de christianisme* began the religious revolt against the philosophy of the eighteenth century....If the effect of *Le Génie du christianisme* had been no more than a reaction against the doctrines to which were attributed our revolutionary ills, that effect would have ceased when its cause vanished; it would not have lasted until this moment in which I write. But the effect of *Le Génie du christianisme* on opinion was not limited to a momentary resurrection of religion, as if it were on the point of death: a more lasting metamorphosis occurred. If there was stylistic innovation in the work, there was also a change of doctrine; the foundations were altered like the form; atheism and materialism were no longer the basis for belief or unbelief in young minds; the idea of God and the immortality of the soul reclaimed their empire: from then on, there was an alteration in that chain of ideas which linked one with another. One was not nailed in place by antireligious prejudice; one was no longer obliged to remain a mummy of non-existence, wound round by philosophical bindings; one allowed oneself to examine each system however absurd one might find it to be, even if it was a Christian one. Besides the faithful who returned to the voice of their Pastor, other faithful were formed *a priori*, by this right of free examination. Establish God as a principle, and the Word follows:

---

[73]   *SV1* XIII, 526–7 / *PV*, 35–6.

the Son is born inevitably of the Father. The various abstract schemes only serve to substitute more incomprehensible mysteries for the Christian ones.[74]

In Kierkegaard the polemic is directed against the Hegelian school of logical mediation, which is the main current of thought of his contemporaries. He writes:

> The fundamental derangement at the root of modern times (which branches out into logic, metaphysics, dogmatics, and the whole of modern life) consists in this: that the deep qualitative chasm in the difference between God and Man has been obliterated. Because of this there is in dogmatics (from logic and metaphysics) a depth of blasphemy which paganism never knew (for it knew what blasphemy against God is, but precisely this has been forgotten in our time, this theocentric age) and in ethics a brash unconcern or, more accurately, no ethics at all. The derangement has come about in many ways and has many forms, but mainly as follows. As the crowd intimidates the king, as the public intimidates counselors of state and authors, so the generation will ultimately want to intimidate God, constrain him to give in, become self-important before him, brazenly defiant in their numbers, etc. Thus what we have today, in modern times, is actually not doubt—it is insubordination. It is useless to want to bring religion to the front; it is not even possible to mount the machinery, for the soil is a swamp or a bog. "Of course, we will all be saved" etc. is more or less the refrain. This being the case, what is meant by all this about the consolation of religion!...I myself have had to learn as profoundly as anyone will come to learn arduously from me or through me: that a man is nothing before God. This is what I have to teach, not directly but indirectly.[75]

But even here, one notices that Kierkegaard had no intention—as, on the contrary, Chateaubriand did—to start a kind of new mass "revolt." Kierkegaard's objective was and remained only the singular inwardness, which was the only place in which, according to him, a real revolution could occur.

II. *"The Aesthetic Validity of Religion": Father Aubry, Father Souël, and "B" against the Young Chactas, René, and "A": Explicit Traces of Chateaubriand in Kierkegaard's Authorship*

As was pointed out above, the only explicit mention Kierkegaard makes of Chateaubriand's works in his own published writings is a motto taken from *Atala*, placed at the beginning of the second part of *Either/Or*, which contains B's papers and letters to the aesthete A: "*Les grandes passions sont solitaires, et les transporter au désert, c'est les rendre à leur empire*" [The great passions are hermits, and to transport them to the desert is to hand them over to their proper domain]."[76] In order

---

[74]   Chateaubriand, *Mémoires*, vol. 1, Book XIII, Chapters 9 and 10, p. 458 and p. 463. On this point see in particular A. Ages, "Chateaubriand and the Philosophes," in *Chateaubriand: actes du Congrès de Wisconsin pour le 200e anniversaire de la naissance de Chateaubriand, 1968. Proceedings of the Commemoration of the Bicentenary of the Birth of Chateaubriand, 1968*, ed. by Richard Switzer, Geneva: Droz 1970, pp. 273–81.

[75]   *SKS* 20, 250, NB3:14 / *JP* 5, 6075.

[76]   Chateaubriand, *Atala*, in *Œuvres Complètes de M. le Vicomte de Chateaubriand*, vol. 18, p. 41. Kierkegaard's quotation appears in *Either/Or*, Part II, see *SKS* 3, 9 / *EO2*, 2.

to understand the real meaning of this statement, it is necessary to place it in its proper context, that is, to determine the place where Chateaubriand put it and which character affirmed it and why.[77] Accordingly, we need to have a look at the story of the brief novel.

Chateaubriand tells us, in the first account of this work in 1801,[78] that it was an anecdote deriving directly from his own journey to the New World (1791), "written under the same huts of savages."[79] The story, in fact, is set in Louisiana[80]: the poet was still very young when he conceived of the idea to write a kind of epic of the natural man. As he put it in the preface to the first edition of the work, *Atala* is "a poem in part descriptive, in part dramatic: everything is brought back to the story of two lovers, who walk and talk in solitude; everything happens within the representation of love troubles, in the middle of the calm of the deserts and religion."[81]

The story is told by the old and blind Chactas ("harmonious voice"), a wise savage from the Indian nation of Natchez, with whom the first French missionaries to arrive in New Orleans had entered into an alliance. Chactas is described as an old patriarch "the favorite of the deserts, who, like everybody, had reached virtue through suffering."[82] In 1725 a young foreigner—a taciturn Frenchman called René—arrives in Louisiana and asks to be accepted by the Natchez as a warrior, for which reason the old Chactas decides to adopt him as son and give him a bride, the Indian Céluta. During the usual beaver shooting, one night Chactas and René remain alone, and the old man tells the young Frenchman the unlucky story of his life. When he was 17 he left with his father—the warrior Outalissi—to fight against the Muscogulges, the powerful nation of Florida. The Natchez were allied with the Spaniards, so that, accordingly, when they lost the war and Chactas' parents were killed, he was adopted by an old Castillian called Lopez in the Spanish city of Saint Augustine. Lopez was a very good father, but the young Chactas felt a strong homesickness for the desert, and so he decided to return to his savage life without embracing the Christian religion. Unfortunately, during the return journey to the Natchez, he is taken prisoner

---

[77]   A valuable analysis in this direction has been made by H.P. Rohde in his above-mentioned essay on Kierkegaard and Chateaubriand "Ørkenens sønner," which is at present the best research we have on the topic of Kierkegaard's use of *Atala*'s motto in *Either/Or.*

[78]   See the letter that he sent to the *Journal des Débats* (March 31, 1801) and to the *Publiciste* (April 1, 1801).

[79]   See *Journal des Débats*, March 31, 1801, p. 2.

[80]   Even if Chateaubriand did not visit Louisiana during his journey—as numerous critics pointed out in order to discredit the great success of *Atala*—he had, to give only one example, scrupulously studied the memoirs of the Jesuits explorers and missionaries Pierre-François-Xavier de Charlevoix (1682–1761)—who wrote, among other things, a *Histoire et description générale de la Nouvelle-France* (1744)—and Joseph-François Lafitau (1681–1746), who also wrote *Mœurs des sauvages américains* (1724). Further, he had also read the writings of the American naturalists and explorers William Bartram (1739–1823) and Jonathan Carver (1710–80), who wrote, for instance, *Travels Through the Interior Parts of North America in the Years 1766, 1767, and 1768*, first published in 1778.

[81]   These words stem from the *Preface* to the first edition of *Atala* in 1801.

[82]   Chateaubriand, *Atala*, in *Œuvres Complètes de M. le Vicomte de Chateaubriand*, vol. 18, p. 7.

by his enemies, who condemn him to the stake. But during the days preceding the execution, he began to admire the Muscogulges' habits, in particular those of their chief Simaghan, as well as the latter's daughter Atala, who tells him that while her father is a savage, her mother wanted her to be Christian. Chactas becomes friends with her, and, as a consequence, one night she releases him and they escape from the camp. Soon during their escape through the desert, they silently become aware of their love for each other, but they cannot express their feelings, because—as Chactas soon notices—Atala every day becomes sadder and more confused:

> sometimes I caught her looking at me passionately, but then she would suddenly look away with deep melancholy towards the sky. I was frightened by the idea of a kind of secret, a thought hidden in the depth of her soul and that I read in her eyes. She attracted and she repelled me, she gave me life and she destroyed my hopes; when I was sure I had got to her heart, I saw myself again at the same point. How many times she told me: "Oh young lover! I love you like the shadow of the woods in a sunny day! You are beautiful like the desert with all its flowers and all its breezes. When I bend over you, I tremble; when my hand touches yours, I feel I am going to die. Some days ago the wind tossed your hair on my face, while you rested on my bosom, and I believed I could feel the light touch of the invisible Spirits. Yes, I saw the children of the mountain of Occone; I heard the purposes of the men tired of this life; but the sweetness of the children and the wisdom of the elderly are less pleasant and less strong than your words. Well, I will never be your bride!"—The continuous contradictions of Atala's love and religion, her tender abandon and the chastity of her behavior, her pride and her deep delicacy, the lofty soul for the great things, the susceptibility for the lower things, all that made her incomprehensible to me.[83]

Atala becomes more depressed with every passing day; she prays to her mother but cannot give herself to her lover. At this point Chactas interrupts his story and warns René with precisely these words: "Oh René, if you fear the perturbation of your heart, beware of solitude: the great passions are hermits, and to transport them to the desert is to hand them over to their proper domain."[84] One day the two lovers are caught in a storm, from which they seek shelter inside a birch trunk, where the can talk to each other. Atala reveals to her lover that her mother, before being compelled to marry Simaghan, the chief of Muscogulges, had known a Spaniard and conceived a child. She told the good Simaghan, who nevertheless accepted her and adopted the baby, that her mother wanted to be Christian like her father, a Castillian called Lopez! In this way, they discover that Atala's father was the adoptive father of Chactas: they are, as it were, a kind of ideal brother and sister.

In fact, this theme of the "incestuous" love between brother and sister seems to be constant in Chateaubriand's works—even if in the case of Atala one cannot really speak of a real incest, but merely an ideal one. This will also be the topic of the novel *René*, which tells the story of the impossible love of Amélie for her melancholic brother René. The idea of a secret guilt as the hidden mechanism which animates

---

[83]   Ibid., pp. 36–7.
[84]   Ibid.

Chateaubriand's novels[85] has been taken into account by many critics, in our case especially by H.P. Rohde, who considers the hypothesis of a parallelism between the theme of the "secret" in Atala's family and in Kierkegaard's own family. Rohde, further, connects the theme of the "desert" in Atala's escape with the presence of the desolate Jutland heath in Kierkegaard's story of his father as a young and poor shepherd who cursed God because of his poverty.[86] Among other things, H.P. Rohde has focused his attention on the theme of the desert,[87] showing that Kierkegaard used the word "desert" (in Danish *ørken*) in a different sense in comparison with the ordinary meaning of the word. Kierkegaard, he claims, used it in a wider sense. Rohde compares the Danish word "*ørken*" with the Danish "*hede*" (heath); in this direction he associates the guilt of Kierkegaard's father as a young man with Chactas' word from *Atala*. So, *Atala*'s motto would be in certain way connected with the religious end of *Either/Or*. Rohde notices, indeed, that the image of the "*hede*" appears very often in the final part of *Either/Or*. He states that this connection between the desert and the peaceful emotional situation of the religious man, as it appears in the story of the pastor in the final pages of Kierkegaard's work of 1843, is taken from the Danish author Steen Steensen Blicher (1782–1848), who actually considered the image of the desert as a positive help in order to grow spiritually close to God. Concerning this, Rohde mentions as an example Kierkegaard's passage about Blicher in *From the Papers of One Still Living* (1838), where he says:

> In the wilderness, Steen Steensen Blicher, who, however, and this is precisely what is remarkable, transformed it into a friendly place of refuge for the imagination exiled in life. Admittedly, here we do not encounter a world-view tried out in so very many lives, not the life-gymnastic so characteristic of the aforementioned short novels, but a certain beginning from the beginning nevertheless takes place also here, undertaken, while the negative aspect is entirely latent, by virtue of a whole positivity that wakes up, so to speak, and makes itself heard and, youthfully fresh, renews and regenerates itself with autochthonic originality. Instead of the life-view contained in the short novels by the author of *En Hverdags-Historie*, which belongs to the individual who has finished the race and kept the faith, there here appears a deep poetic mood, shrouded in the mist veil of spontaneity, the unity of an individual-popular poetic keynote, echoing in the soul's

---

[85]   It actually seems to have a corresponding episode in Chateaubriand's own relationship with his beloved sister Lucile (1764–1804, four years older than him), who had a temperament very similar to Chateaubriand's. They spent some years of their childhood and youth together (from 1784 to 1786 at Combourg castle), sharing their common melancholy and love for literature. It was, in fact, Lucile who drove her brother to writing, as well as writing a lot herself. Lucile had taken vows—not as a resident—at the Largentière Chapter in 1783, as had Amélie in *René*. Chateaubriand also attempted to devote himself to an ecclesiastical career in 1783, and entered the College of Dinan, only to leave it definitively in the summer of 1784; for this, see Chateaubriand, *Mémoires*, vol. 1, Book III, Chapters 1–14, pp. 75–100. On this topic, see, for example, Marité Diniz, *Lucile ou la nostalgie du génie*, Paris: Presses de la Renaissance 1984; Jean-Claude Berchet, "Colloque de Cerisy," in his *Le frère d'Amélie ou la part du diable, Eros Philadelphe*, Paris: Editions du Félin 1992, pp. 107–34.

[86]   See *SKS* 18, 278, JJ:416 / *KJN* 2, 257.

[87]   Rohde, "Ørkenens sønner," pp. 70–1.

inner ear, and a popular-idyllic picture, spread out for the imagination, illuminated by mighty flashes of summer lightning.[88]

But let us continue now with the sequel of the *Atala* novel: While the storm increases, an old solitary missionary, Father Aubry, thanks to his dog's scent, finds the two lovers and saves them from danger, bringing them to his mission. There the tragedy finally finds it end: Atala's health rapidly grows worse, only to reveal to Chactas and Father Aubry prior to dying, that she in fact had poisoned herself in order not to break her mother's vow. She recounts that during her birth her life had been at risk, for which reason her mother took a vow for her daughter in order to save her: she consecrated Atala's virginity to the Virgin Mary. When the girl knew Chactas, she understood the danger this entailed for her promise, and, therefore, in the most difficult moment for her, the night in which Father Aubry found them together in the storm, she drank the poison she had brought with her before the escape. Having listened to this, Chactas begins to curse the Christian God who requires such inhuman sacrifices, and vigorously rails against Father Aubry: "Such is the religion you have praised to me so much! Death to the oath which takes Atala away from me! Death to the God who is against nature! Oh, priest, why did you come to these forests?"[89] To these words, the old missionary answers in a terrible voice:

I came to save you! For taming your passions and averting you, oh blasphemer, from attracting the divine wrath! It has not been difficult, oh young man, as soon as you entered into life, to start complaining over your sorrow! But where are the marks of your pain? Where are the injustices you had to bear? Where are those virtues which alone could allow you to complain? Which duty did you serve? Which good did you do? Ah, wretched boy, you have nothing to offer but passions and you dare to accuse God! When you will have spent, like father Aubry, thirty years of exile in the mountains, you will be no more ready to judge the plans of Providence. Then, you will understand that you do not know anything, you are nothing, and there does not exist a punishment so hard, nor a pain so terrible that the corrupted flesh cannot deserve to tolerate![90]

---

[88]   *SKS* 1, 24 / *EPW*, 69. These are Blicher's passages quoted by Kierkegaard in a footnote to this passage: "*Stille og mørkladen er vel min Hede; / Dog under Lyngtoppen Blomsteret staaer. / Lærken bag Gravhøie bygger sit Rede / Og sine Triller i Ørkenen slaaer* [Silent and dark-laden so is my heath, / Though under heather top flowers will spring. / Lark behind grave mound is building its nest / And in the wilderness warbles away]." These words appear as motto in Steen Steensen Blicher, *Samlede Digte*, 2nd ed., vols. 1–2, Copenhagen: C.A. Reitzel 1835–36 (*ASKB* U 23); see also *SKS* K1, 92. Blicher's image of the desert has been also taken into account by Nelly Viallaneix in her article "Kierkegaard romantique," *Romantisme*, no. 8, 1974, p. 69, see note 35, where the desert is a kind of symbol of the romantic absence of limits.

[89]   Chateaubriand, *Atala*, in *Œuvres Complètes de M. le Vicomte de Chateaubriand*, vol. 18, pp. 63–4.

[90]   Ibid., p. 64.

After this speech, Chactas is ashamed of himself, and Chateaubriand thinks that he has given the "*vague des passions*" of the young people of his century—as he says it in the *Génie du christianisme*—a serious dressing-down.[91]

The same can be applied to the novel *René*, where the main character is the young René, who had listened to the story of Chactas.[92] René will, indeed, become the prototype of the romantic melancholic young man.[93] As we saw, he also hides a cruel story—a sister who has fallen in love with him, and, in order to expiate her wrong feeling, withdrew to a monastery, where she will die as a saint—although in actual fact the main plot of his story is himself and his uncontrollable feelings devoid of any object.[94] It is precisely on this attitude of René and Chactas that we are now going to concentrate, drawing a comparison with Kierkegaard's aesthetic characters, in particular, A from *Either/Or*. As mentioned previously, the emotional situation that Chateaubriand attempts to represent in his novels *Atala* and *René* and to contend with in the *Génie du christianisme*, is that of the *diffuseness of passions*. As the writer also states, he intends to fight against

> that characteristic sickness of the young people of this century, a sickness that drives directly to suicide. J.-J. Rousseau has been the first to introduce us to these disastrously guilty reveries. By isolating himself from the community, abandoning himself to the reveries, he made a crowd of young men believe that it is nice to throw oneself into this diffuseness of life. Then the novel of *Werther* developed this poisonous seed. So, the author of the *Génie du christianisme* has been compelled to put within his apologetic

---

[91]   Chateaubriand, *Défense du Génie du Christianisme* (Part II, Book III, Chapter IX), in *Œuvres Complètes de M. le Vicomte de Chateaubriand*, op. cit., vol. 15, pp. 98 ff.

[92]   Subsequently, in the novel *René*, the old Chactas is, together with father Souël, one of the two confidants of the melancholic boy.

[93]   For Chateaubriand's *René* see, for example, Reinhard Kuhn, *The Demon of Noontide. Ennui in Western Literature*, Princeton: Princeton University Press 1976, especially pp. 199–213. Kuhn's research is also very interesting because it presents Chateaubriand's characters in the wider context of contemporary literature. The same also in Yves Chevrel, "De Werther à René: ébuche d'un mythe?," in *Dix-huitième siècle européen: en hommage à Jacques Lacant*, ed. by Claude De Grève, Paris: Aux Amateurs de Livres 1990, pp. 145–9. For René as the prototype of the "*mal du siècle*," see also James Hamilton, "The Anxious Hero in Chateaubriand's *René*," *Quarterly Review*, no. 34, 1987, pp. 415–24; Michèle Respaut, "*René*: Confession, Répétition, Révélation," *French Review*, October 1984, pp. 14–19; Nelly Viallaneix in her article "Kierkegaard romantique," *Romantisme*, vol. 8, 1974, p. 66, defines Kierkegaard as *le nouveau René*.

[94]   Concerning this question, see, for instance, Béatrice Didier, "La notion de personnage dans le roman ou la première personne au lendemain de la Révolution: 'René' et 'Atala,' " in *Personnages et histoire littéraire, Actes du Colloque International De Toulouse* (16–17–18 Mai 1990), Toulouse: Presses Universitaires du Mirail 1991, pp. 81–93; Isabelle Bernard, "Le mal de vivre de la première génération romantique. Chateaubriand: 'Génie du Christianisme' (1802), 'René' (1802)," *L'Ecole des Lettres*, January 15, 1990, pp. 21–33 and March 15, 1990, pp. 29–34; Eric Gans, "René and the Romantic Model of Self-Centralization," *Studies in Romanticism*, Fall 1984, pp. 421–35.

writing some descriptions fit for imagination; he wanted to denounce this kind of new vice and draw the fatal consequences of the excessive love for loneliness.[95]

As he had already written in the *Génie du christianisme*,[96] in the story of the young René—who was in his turn the former auditor of Chactas' story—Chateaubriand intends to show what kind of doom is provided for those young people "who guiltily shirk the duty of society by throwing themselves into meaningless reveries."[97] In this sense, as we said, the author follows the same strategy as Kierkegaard in *Either/Or*: in both cases we have two kinds of texts included in a unique book without any unifying plot. *Atala* and *René* are merely two separate episodes included in the wider apologetic work of the *Génie du christianisme*. If one disregarded the hidden global intention of the author, one could simply consider the two novels as separate texts— and, indeed, they would be published separately from 1805 onwards. The same thing happens in *Either/Or*, which is not a unified work, but contains different texts written at different moments, which can be separated into two large sections: the aesthetic and the ethical: that is A's paper and B's. The two sections, however, communicate with one another, or better, the second part is an answer to and a criticism of the first; moreover, the first part was written precisely so as to receive an answer from the second. In both writers, as we said, the first part is a bait to catch the readers who actually stand in greater need of reading the second part.

However, while Chateaubriand definitively stops at this second "stage," Kierkegaard proceeds on towards the "religious," which is the realm of an inner individual relationship between man and God, where every kind of "aesthetic" approach to the world is left behind. In this sense one could say that even the second section of the work contains a kind of bait, that of the "aesthetic taste" of social life and its institutions, *in primis* that of marriage. In this way, Chateaubriand's "religious stage" would seem to coincide with Kierkegaard's ethical sphere, which is the ideal sphere of duties,[98] and in which the final goal consists in the harmony of individual and society, based on religious duties.

Accordingly, a comparison of the two authors should stop at this ethical sphere, although this nevertheless remains a fruitful comparison, since numerous highly impressive points of overlap can be found there, both in the "aesthetic" realm[99] and in

---

[95]   Chateaubriand, *Défense du Génie du Christianisme*, in *Œuvres Complètes de M. le Vicomte de Chateaubriand*, vol. 15, pp. 162–3.

[96]   Ibid., pp. 98–9.

[97]   Ibid.

[98]   That is precisely the sphere of the "first" ethic, according to the categories of *The Concept of Anxiety*, see *SKS* 4, 328 and 323 / *CA*, 20 and 16.

[99]   With regard to this term, in Chateaubriand it does not have the negative meaning that it has in Kierkegaard when it is compared with the "religious." Actually one can say that this term obtains its highest meaning even within the religious ambit. If we would like to find a common terminological ground in order to indicate the content of A's papers and Chateaubriand's two brief novels, we could use the Kierkegaardian term *interessant*, the "interesting." Rohde, "Ørkenens sønner," p. 73, has especially focused on the topic of the aesthetical worth of religion in Chateaubriand.

the "ethical" one. In this way, one could say that Father Aubry's discourse could have been directed against A, and B's papers could be the adequate answer to René!

Let us start by showing the common themes to be found in A's papers and *Atala* and *René*. First, the most important common attitude is the exclusive interest in oneself: Kierkegaard's "Diapsalmata" are emblematically dedicated *Ad se ipsum*.[100] At times the author is even ironic concerning this point: "Time passes, life is a stream, etc., so people say. That is not what I find: time stands still, and so do I. All the plans I project fly straight back at me; when I want to spit, I spit in my own face."[101] This is precisely the situation of those men who seem to have a kind of imponderable atmosphere that separates them from the others, as Proust will say. A perfect example of this attitude is the figure of the Seducer in *Either/Or*, who clearly represents the impossibility of a proper distinction between the real world and the imaginary one. The description of the Seducer in "The Seducer's Diary" is in this sense truly a kind of manifesto for what Chateaubriand on numerous occasions calls the *mal du siècle*, for which reason it will be useful to quote the passage at length:

> his poetic nature...is not abundant enough or, if you please, not deficient enough to separate poetry and actuality from each other. The poetic was the plus he himself brought along. This plus was the poetic he enjoyed in the poetic situation of actuality; this he recaptured in the form of poetic reflection. This was the second enjoyment, and his whole life was intended for enjoyment. In the first case, he personally enjoyed the aesthetic; in the second case, he aesthetically enjoyed his personality. The point in the first case was that he egotistically enjoyed personally that which in part actuality has given to him and which in part he himself had used to fertilize actuality; in the second case, his personality was volatilized, and he then enjoyed the situation and himself in the situation. In the first case, he continually needed actuality as the occasion, as an element; in the second case, actuality was drowned in the poetic....Behind the world in which we live, far in the background, lies another world, and the two have about the same relation to each other as do the stage proper and the stage one sometimes sees behind it in the theater. Through a hanging of fine gauze, one sees, as it were, a world of gauze, lighter, more ethereal, with a quality different from that of the actual world. Many people who appear physically in the actual world are not at home in it but are at home in that other world. But a person's fading away in this manner, indeed, almost vanishing from actuality, can have its basis either in health or in sickness. The latter was the case with this man, whom I had once known without knowing him. He did not belong to the world of actuality, and yet he had very much to do with it. He continually ran lightly over it, but even when he most abandoned himself to it, he was beyond it. But it was not the good that beckoned him away, nor was it actually evil—even now at this moment I dare not say that of him. He had suffered from an *exacerbatio cerebri*, for which actuality did not have enough stimulation, at most only momentarily. He did not overstrain himself on actuality, he was not too weak to bear it; no, he was too strong, but this strength was a sickness. As soon as actuality had lost its significance as stimulation, he was disarmed, and the evil in him lay in this. He was conscious of this at the very moment of stimulation, and evil lay in this consciousness.[102]

---

100   *SKS* 2, 25 / *EO1*, 17.
101   *SKS* 2, 34 / *EO1*, 26.
102   *SKS* 2, 295f. / *EO1*, 305f.

It is also indicative of a common attitude that both in Kierkegaard's Seducer and in Chateaubriand's René, the two young romantic protagonists are themselves the *object* of love of a suffering girl, not the inverse, since they are too involved in the analysis of themselves, while reality (which is represented by the girl) merely has the function of a "stimulus." In this sense, the accusatory words of B against A in "The Esthetic Validity of Marriage" are emblematic:

> This is how it is with you, and you will also see how egotistical your enjoyment is, and that you never give of yourself, never let others enjoy you. To an extent, you are probably justified in ridiculing the people who are drained by every pleasure—for example, the infatuated people with shredded hearts—since you, on the contrary, understand superbly the art of falling in love in such a way that this love throws your own personality into relief.[103]

The same criticism could be well addressed to René!

As Vincent A. McCarthy suggests,[104] A's papers can be read through the perspective of the relationship between narcissism and desire. This leads him to draw a comparison with Chateaubriand's *René*.[105] For instance, he states about the Seducer that "his conquest of Cordelia is part of the fulfillment of his own ego-ideal as the reflective seducer. The essence of this conquest is that he has managed to become loved and desired without himself loving or desiring Cordelia."[106] The point is here again the "diffuseness of passions" about which Chateaubriand spoke. Without a *real* object,[107] these passions are destined continually to return to (or remain with) the subject like a kind of echo (here, in fact, the theme of Narcissus). It is not by accident that Kierkegaard, under the name of A, writes, as we quoted above: "I have only one friend, and that is *echo*. Why is it my friend? Because I love my sorrow, and echo does not take it away from me."[108] Similarly, we read in Chateaubriand: "I am reciting the first couplets of a plaintive ballad which has charm only for myself; ask the goatherd of the Tyrol why he loves the two or three notes he repeats to his flock, sounds of the mountain, throwing off *echo* after echo in order to resound from

---

[103]   *SKS* 3, 33 / *EO2*, 24–5.
[104]   Vincent A. McCarthy, "Narcissism and Desire in Kierkegaard's *Either/Or*, Part One," in *Either/Or, Part I*, ed. by Robert L. Perkins, Macon, Georgia: Mercer University Press 1995 (*International Kierkegaard Commentary*, vol. 3), pp. 51–71.
[105]   Ibid., pp. 59–60, note.
[106]   Ibid., p. 69.
[107]   McCarthy, among other things, mentions the psychoanalytical theory of the "lost object" elaborated by Lacan in order to explain the absence of the stage in which the desire can be satisfied; see McCarthy, "Narcissism and Desire in Kierkegaard's *Either/Or*, Part One," p. 70. A similar analysis with regards to the break between the relation of *désir* (desire) and *jouissance* (enjoyment, satisfaction)—which the eighteenth-century sensationalism had taken for granted—in the Romantic temperament, has been made by the Italian scholar Lionello Sozzi in "Desiderio senza oggetto: miti e motivi del romanticismo francese," in *Problemi del Romanticismo*, ed. by U. Cardinale, Milan: Shakespeare & Company 1983, p. 89, and "Malinconia dei tardi lumi," in *Lo "spleen" nella letteratura francese*, Fasano: Schena 1989, pp. 9–24.
[108]   *SKS* 2, 42 / *EO1*, 33.

one side of a torrent to the other?"[109] Moreover, he even comes to yearn for "an Eve created from myself,"[110] who is, in fact, the same "Phantom of love,"[111] an imaginary female prototype, described in the third book of *Mémoires*. The author recalls the vague desires of his youth: "Ignorant of all, knowing all, at once virgin and lover, innocent Eve, and fallen Eve, the enchantress through whom my madness arose was a blend of mysteries and passions: I set her on an altar and adored her."[112] Thus, this is Chateaubriand's description of the diffuseness of passion in *René*:

> I had an impetuous temperament, and an inconstant nature. Sometimes vehement and cheerful, sometimes silent and sad, I gathered around me young friends; then I suddenly abandoned them and went to sit to one side, and contemplated the fleeting cloud, heard the rain falling down on the leaves.[113]

He continues:

> I started to sound my heart, to ask myself what I really want. I did not know it....People accuse me of being inconstant, of not being content with the same chimera for long time, of being at the mercy of imagination, which hastens to consume pleasures through to the end, as though it were oppressed by their duration; they accuse me of always going beyond the goal I can reach: alas! I am only looking for an unknown good, pressed by instinct. Am I guilty if I find only limits everywhere, if the finite world is not worth it for me? Nevertheless I feel that I like the monotony of the feelings of life, and if I were so crazy as to believe in the possibility of joy, I would look for it in habit. The absolute loneliness, the spectacle of nature suddenly threw me into an indescribable state. Without any relatives, without friends, alone in the world, so to speak, without having loved anyone, I was oppressed by an exuberance of life. Sometimes I suddenly blushed, and I felt burning lava dripping on my heart; sometimes I involuntarily shouted, and the night was equally disturbed by waking and dreams. I needed something to fill the abyss of my existence.[114]

He exclaims:

> Alas, I was alone in the world! A secret languor took hold of my body. That disgust for life that I felt since my childhood returned with new force. Suddenly my heart did not feed my thought any more, and I perceived existence only because of tediousness. I fought for a time against my infirmity, but with apathy and without any steadfast conviction of beating it. Finally, since I could not find any remedy to that strange wound of my heart, which was everywhere and nowhere, I decided to abandon life.[115]

---

109   Chateaubriand, *Mémoires*, op. cit., vol. 1, Book I, Chapter 7, p. 46, quoted above.
110   Chateaubriand, *René*, in *Œuvres Complètes de M. le Vicomte de Chateaubriand*, vol. 18, p. 120.
111   Chateaubriand, *Mémoires*, vol. 1, Book III, Chapter 10, p. 93.
112   Ibid.
113   Chateaubriand, *René*, in *Œuvres Complètes de M. le Vicomte de Chateaubriand*, vol. 18, p. 104.
114   Ibid., pp. 116–18.
115   Ibid., p. 120.

The equivalent feeling is described by Kierkegaard in the "Diapsalmata" with the following words:

> No woman in maternity confinement can have stranger and more impatient wishes than I have. Sometimes these wishes involve the most insignificant things, sometimes the most sublime, but they all have to an equally high degree the momentary passion of the soul.[116]

He continues:

> How sterile my soul and my mind are, and yet constantly tormented by empty voluptuous and excruciating labor pains! Will the tongue ligament of my spirit never be loosened; will I always jabber? What I need is a voice as piercing as the glance of Lynceus, as terrifying as the groan of the giants, as sustained as a sound of nature, as mocking as an icy gust of wind, as malicious as echo's heartless taunting, extending in range from the deepest bass to the most melting high notes, and modulated from a solemn-silent whisper to the energy of rage. That is what I need in order to breathe, to give voice to what is on my mind, to have the viscera of both anger and sympathy shaken.—But my voice is only hoarse like the scream of a gull or moribund like the blessing on the lips of the mute.[117]

The major point of focus in the opponents' criticism, in both Kierkegaard's and Chateaubriand's texts, is the guilty loneliness of the individual who detaches himself from the community. The danger of this attitude—the voices of the two priests of Chateaubriand and that of B—belongs to both the community and to the individual himself: both to the girls who could fall in love with "a René," and to René himself, who actually reaches the point of planning to commit suicide. "Any man who has a conviction cannot at his pleasure turn himself and everything topsy-turvy in this way. Therefore, I do not warn you against the world but against yourself and the world against you."[118] Describing the dangers of loneliness, Chateaubriand even states:

> One has to fear the increase within the society of such a kind of solitary men, passionate and philosophical, who since they cannot renounce the vices of the century, nor can love it, will confuse hatred against men with the height of genius; they will renounce any

---

[116]   *SKS* 2, 35 / *EO1*, 26.

[117]   *SKS* 2, 32 / *EO1*, 24. See also *SKS* 2, 29 / *EO1*, 20: "In addition to my other numerous acquaintances, I have one more intimate confidant—my depression. In the midst of my joy, in the midst of my work, he beckons to me, calls me aside, even though physically I remain on the spot. My depression is the most faithful mistress I have known—no wonder, then, that I return the love." *SKS* 2, 32 / *EO1*, 23: "I have, I believe, the courage to doubt everything; I have, I believe, the courage to fight against everything; but I do not have the courage to acknowledge anything, the courage to possess, to own, anything. Most people complain that the world is so prosaic that things do not go in life as in the novel, where opportunity is always so favorable. I complain that in life it is not as in the novel, where one has hardhearted fathers and nisses and trolls to battle, and enchanted princesses to free. What are all such adversaries together compared with the pale, bloodless, tenacious-of-life nocturnal forms with which I battle and to which I myself give life and existence."

[118]   *SKS* 3, 25 / *EO2*, 16.

human and divine duties, they will feed aside on the most vain chimeras and, even more, they will sink into a proud misanthropy, which will drive them to madness or to death.[119]

Kierkegaard himself—it is important to notice—speaks about the melancholy and the diffuseness of passions, as a vice of the century: "is not depression[120] the defect of the age, is it not that which echoes even in its light-minded laughter; is it not depression that has robbed us of the courage to command, the courage to obey, the power to act, the confidence to hope?"[121] In this sense the only advice that the ethical (Kierkegaard) or the ethical/religious (Chateaubriand) opponent can give to the aesthete is to return to the ordinary people. As Father Souël says to the young René:

> I see only a young boy infatuated with chimeras, for whom everything is disgusting, and who escaped from the social duties in order to abandon himself to vain reveries. Sir, one is not a superior being just because one hates the world!...Presumptuous boy! You had thought that man could be self-sufficient! Loneliness harms he who does not live it with God! It doubles the faculties of the mind, but at the same time it takes away every object to which they could be applied. Whoever has received any resources, must put them at his fellows' service.[122]

To these words also the old Chactas adds the example of his own experience and concludes: "Yes, my dear, you must renounce this life outside the ordinary world; it is only full of sorrows. There is no joy outside of the common ways."[123] So, the two old confidants' discourses to René repeat what Amélie already wrote to her brother before dying as a victim of René's attitude:

> My dear brother, you have to escape the loneliness as long as it is possible, it is not for you. I suggest that you look for an ordinary employment. I know well that you sourly make fun of the necessity to *reach a good position* in France. Do not despise our fathers' experience and wisdom so much. My dear René, it is better to be more like ordinary men, but a little bit less unhappy.[124]

But, as we said before, Kierkegaard's position does not stop at this point: this point is just another stage on life's way, so that already in the work by that name, the philosopher seems to point to another—more distant—*way*. In the final letter addressed to the reader by Frater Taciturnus, Kierkegaard in fact seems to answer the false solution represented by Chateaubriand's "aesthetical validity of religion" with these words: "The religiousness that derives directly from actuality is a dubious

---

[119]   Chateaubriand, *Défense du Génie du Christianisme*, in *Œuvres Complètes de M. le Vicomte de Chateaubriand*, vol. 15, p. 163.
[120]   Actually the original Danish *Tungsind* corresponds in this case better to the English "melancholy."
[121]   *SKS* 3, 32 / *EO2*, 23–4. One could also define this kind of attitude with the words of *The Sickness unto Death*, see *SKS* 11, 146ff. / *SUD*, 30ff. where the author describes the "sickness unto death" as "*Infinitude's Despair*," which is actually "to lack finitude."
[122]   Chateaubriand, *René*, in *Œuvres Complètes de M. le Vicomte de Chateaubriand*, vol. 18, pp. 141–2.
[123]   Ibid.
[124]   Ibid., p. 126.

religiousness; it can very well be aesthetic categories that are used and worldly wisdom that is gained; but when actuality has not been capable of shattering and the individual succumbs by his own hand, then the religious is more distinct."[125]

---

[125]   *SKS* 6, 415 / *SLW*, 449.

Bibliography

I. Chateaubriand's Works in The Auction Catalogue *of Kierkegaard's Library*

Die Martyren oder der Triumph des Christenthums, vols. 1–2, trans. by T. von Haupt, Darmstadt: Leske 1810 (*ASKB* 465).

II. Works in The Auction Catalogue *of Kierkegaard's Library
that Discuss Chateaubriand*

Hase, Karl, *Kirkehistorie. Lærebog nærmest for akademiske Forelæsninger*, trans. by C. Winther and T. Schorn, Copenhagen: C.A. Reitzel 1837, p. 574; p. 591 (*ASKB* 160–166).

[Hegel, Georg Wilhelm Friedrich], *Georg Wilhelm Friedrich Hegel's Vorlesungen über die Aesthetik*, vols. 1–3, ed. by Heinrich Gustav Hotho, Berlin: Duncker und Humblot 1835–38 (vols. 10.1–10.3 in *Georg Wilhelm Friedrich Hegel's Werke. Vollständige Ausgabe*, vols. 1–18, ed. by Philipp Marheineke et al., Berlin: Duncker und Humblot 1832–45), vol. 2, p. 211 (*ASKB* 1384–1386).

Rosenkranz, Karl, *Psychologie oder die Wissenschaft vom subjectiven Geist*, Königsberg: Bornträger 1837, p. 42 (*ASKB* 744).

Steffens, Henrich, *Was ich erlebte. Aus der Erinnerung niedergeschrieben*, vols. 1–10, Breslau: Josef Max 1840–44, vol. 8, pp. 143–4 (*ASKB* 1834–1843).

Thomsen, Grimur, *Om den nyfranske Poesi, et Forsøg til Besvarelse af Universitetets æsthetiske Priisspørgsmaal for 1841: "Har Smag og Sands for Poesi gjort Frem- eller Tilbageskridt i Frankrig i de sidste Tider og hvilken er Aarsagen?,"* Copenhagen: Wahlske Boghandlings Forlag 1843, p. iii; p. xiv; p. xlvii; p. 26, note; pp. 47–52; pp 82–8 (*ASKB* 1390).

III. Secondary Literature on Kierkegaard's Relation to Chateaubriand

Grimsley, Ronald, "Romantic Melancholy in Chateaubriand and Kierkegaard," *Comparative Literature*, vol. 8, 1956, pp. 227–44 (republished in his *Søren Kierkegaard and French Literature. Eight Comparative Studies*, Cardiff: University of Wales Press 1966, pp. 45–64).

—— "Chateaubriand," in *Kierkegaard: Literary Miscellany*, ed. by Niels Thulstrup and Marie Mikulová Thulstrup, Copenhagen: C.A. Reitzel 1981 (*Bibliotheca Kierkegaardiana*, vol. 9), pp. 160–1.

McCarthy, Vincent A., "Narcissism and Desire in Kierkegaard's *Either/Or*, Part One," in *Either/Or, Part I*, ed. by Robert L. Perkins, Macon, Georgia: Mercer

University Press 1995 (*International Kierkegaard Commentary*, vol. 3), pp. 51–71, see pp. 59–60, note 15.

Rohde, Hermann Peter, "Ørkenens sønner," in his *Gaadefulde stadier paa Kierkegaards vej*, Copenhagen: Rosenkilde og Bagger 1974, pp. 64–80.

Viallaneix, Nelly, "Kierkegaard romantique," *Romantisme*, vol. 8, 1974, see p. 66; p. 69.

Johannes Ewald:

Poetic Fire

Kim Ravn

> One ought, I think, be somewhat cold to portray one's fire.
> Johannes Ewald[1]

I. Johannes Ewald: Short Biography

The Danish poet and playwright Johannes Ewald was born on November 18, 1743 and died on March 17, 1781. His father, dr. theol. Enevold Ewald (1696–1754) was one of Pietism's leading standard-bearers in Denmark, a solemn character and pastor at the orphans' home in Copenhagen. His mother, Marie Matthiasdatter Wulff (1715–91), who was far more lively and light-minded than her husband, came from a pronounced Moravian milieu. Ewald was thus stamped by the eighteenth century's Pietistic movements, a stamp which is also clearly visibly in his poetry.

His father died on November 11, 1754; on the same day he was sent away from home and enrolled in Slesvig's Grammar School (Latin school), where he lived in the home of the school's principal, Johan Friedrik Licht until 1758. It was here that Ewald received his first significant literary impulses; in the principal's well-stocked library he found, among other things, several works about journeys as well as the novelistic literature of the eighteenth century, including Daniel Defoe's *Robinson Crusoe* (1719). Ewald had an acute sense for how to shorten the distance between reading and action: he wrote in the preface to the first volume of his collected works edition, *Johannes Ewalds samtlige Skrifter*, regarding his reading of *Robinson Crusoe* that he had to be forcibly taken back "from the road to Holland, from where it was my intention to travel to Batavia, in the innocent hope that on the way I would be shipwrecked on some uninhabited island."[2] In addition, he also read extensively in Nordic mythology.

In 1758 he moved back to Copenhagen and began to study theology at the university. He lived with his mother's landlord Peder Huulegaard, and fell head over heels in love with his daughter, Arendse, who was one year older than he. At age 15, Ewald discontinued his study of theology; he would not have been able to apply for

---

[1]   *Johannes Ewalds samtlige Skrifter*, vols. 1–4, Copenhagen: Forlagt ved Christian Gottlob Prost 1780–91, vol. 1, p. XVII (*ASKB* 1533–1536).
[2]   Ibid., p. XIV.

positions until he was 25 in any case, and thus he had to seek his fortune elsewhere if he were to have any hopes of winning his Arendse. First he went to Hamburg in order to enlist in the Prussian army, but when this proved unsuccessful, he went to the Austrian army, where he was enrolled as a drummer.

On October 10, 1760 he returned home to Copenhagen, sick from the miserable conditions in the army, and with the first signs of the arthritis which was one of the few things he took home with him from the war and which would increasingly come to plague him for the rest of his life. After his return he resumed his theological studies at the university, which he completed in record time and with the best grades in the summer of 1761.[3]

Thereafter he received free lodging at Valkendorf Collegium, and to keep his right to this, he was obliged every year to write a treatise in Latin: *Pyrologia sacra* (The Sacred Fire) from 1763, *De paradiso* (On Paradise) from 1764, *De creatione* (On the Creation) from 1765 accompanied by a long introduction *Meletemata qvædam de pravis scriptoribus* (Some Exercises about Bad Writers) and *De poëseos natura et indole* (On the Nature and Function of Poetry) from 1767. In 1766 he received permission not to write a treatise, presumably because he had written the elegies for the funeral of Frederik V.

In the summer of 1764 the fate of Ewald's love for Arendse was finally sealed; she married the grocer Rasmus Riber, which caused Ewald to give up every hope of earthly happiness and, as he writes, to "drift through life as best I could."[4] Up until this point his poetry had consisted of scattered and sporadic attempts, but now it began to take on a more systematic form. In March of 1765 he submitted an ode or a didactic poem on God's benevolence. It was written as a response to a poetry competition issued by the newly established Danish Academy, the Society for the Advancement of the Beautiful and Useful Sciences. The Society refused to accept his response and indicated in its remarks where and how it could be improved.[5] Ewald's disappointment was so great that he chose to withdraw his response with the justification "when I could be the leading poet in my land of birth, I would not want to be anything else...."[6] The didactic poem was later, in 1769, reworked and made into the tragedy *Adam and Eve*.[7] Subsequently, he decided not to put pen to paper

---

[3]   See N.M. Petersen, *Bidrag til den danske Literaturs Historie*, vols. 1–5, 2nd ed., Copenhagen: Fr. Wøldikes Forlag 1870, where in vol. 5, *Oplysningens Tidsalder 1750–1800*, Første Afdeling, p. 259 one reads: "a little more than a year later he (in 1762) in his nineteenth year took his theological examination likewise with *laud*, a grade which was rare at the time since of the 27 candidates there was only one other one who received it." "*Laud.*" is of course the common abbreviation for "*laudabilis*" or praiseworthy.

[4]   *Johannes Ewalds samtlige Skrifter*, vol. 1, pp. XXII–XXIII.

[5]   For an account of the Society's treatment and evaluation of the works which Ewald submitted as response to the prize questions issued by the Society, see K.F. Plesner, *Det smagende Selskab. Selskabet til de skiønne og nyttige Videnskabers Forfremmelse 1759–1959*, Copenhagen: Gyldendal 1959, pp. 33–44. Here one learns, among other things, that Ewald had to wait 14 years to receive his honorarium for his allegorical piece *Lykkens Tempel* from 1764.

[6]   *Johannes Ewalds samtlige Skrifter*, vol. 1, p. XXVIII.

[7]   Johannes Ewald, *Adam og Eva*, in *Johannes Ewalds samtlige Skrifter*, vol. 1, pp. 35–235.

for the following two years, and instead of writing he began to read or reread the central parts of the canon of European literature. The only works which he published during this period were "Elegies for Frederik V,"[8] and "Cantata for Frederik V"[9] in connection with the King's funeral on March 18, 1766. It was also during this period that Ewald established connections with the German milieu in Copenhagen, and especially with the poet Friedrich Gottlieb Klopstock (1724–1803). Ewald lived in various places in Copenhagen and earned his living by writing occasional poems. He began to drink excessively and in December 1770 was admitted to Frederiks Hospital. After his stay in the hospital, he lived from 1771 to 1773 in the pension at Rygaard just outside Copenhagen, but he quickly fell back to his former lifestyle, which had landed him in the hospital.

From the fall of 1773 to the fall of 1775 Ewald lived at Rungsted Inn, far from Copenhagen. These two years were very productive for him. He wrote, among other things, his lyric masterpiece "The Happiness of Rungsted."[10] In the fall of 1775, he was moved to Søbækhus, when his landlord died, and his productivity almost came to a stop. He wrote a series of religious odes, made plans for a journal, and wrote a series of drafts of a novel. In August 1777 Ewald returned to Copenhagen and, although plagued by arthritis, lived his last years in relative peace, recognized as the nation's greatest poet. In 1775 "The Danish Literature Society" was established in his honor by young poets, and he became the first honorary member. He wrote the Singspiel *The Fishermen*,[11] which was performed with great success at the Royal Theater in January 1780. His funeral was a national event. According to the author Knud Lyhne Rahbek (1760–1830), he was carried to Trinitatis Cemetery behind the Round Tower on Denmark's shoulders. His grave can still be seen there to this day.

II. Ewald's Authorship

The poet Adam Oehlenschläger (1779–1850) in 1811–12 gave the first detailed account of Ewald's authorship in the lectures which he gave in 1811–13 as newly appointed professor of aesthetics at the University of Copenhagen. In 1831 the historian and philologist Christian Molbech (1783–1857), on occasion of the 50-year anniversary of Ewald's death, published the first biography of the poet, entitled *The Life of Johannes Ewald*.[12]

---

[8]   Johannes Ewald, "Klage-Sange over Frederik V," in *Johannes Ewalds samtlige Skrifter*, vol. 1, pp. 314–22.
[9]   Johannes Ewald, "Kantate over Frederik V," in *Johannes Ewalds samtlige Skrifter*, vol. 2, pp. 349–54.
[10]   Johannes Ewald, "Rungsteds Lyksaligheder," in *Johannes Ewalds samtlige Skrifter*, vol. 2, pp. 383–8 (written in 1773, printed in 1775).
[11]   Johannes Ewald, *Fiskerne*, in *Johannes Ewalds samtlige Skrifter*, vol. 3, pp. 125–261.
[12]   Christian Molbech, *Johannes Evalds Levnet, med Bidrag til hans Digterværkers Historie og Charakteristik*, Copenhagen: C.A. Reitzel 1831.

Oehlenschläger emphasized Ewald's odes, but found that his proclivity for pathos was "tasteless" and that it "seduced him to exaggerations."[13] Ewald did not correspond to Oehlenschläger's preferred ideal poet, the objective and naïve poet with a fresh and healthy spirit. He ascribes this to Ewald's fate, which led to an unhealthy mixture of melancholy and exaggerated narcissism. Molbech emphasizes Ewald as a break in Danish literature, and portrays him as an autonomous author who had writing as his sole goal: Ewald was first and foremost a poet for himself. According to Molbech, he was "the first one in Denmark, who dedicated himself completely to poetry, who was and became nothing except a poet, and who missed or lost almost everything that could be missed or lost in life—except a great name."[14] Molbech almost paints a picture of Ewald in the role of a mature author, where the poetry is slowly but surely detached from representing something outside itself, for example, power, morality or truth. Instead, poetry is made independent as such. This is evident from Ewald's elegy. To be sure, he describes the deceased's greatness and benevolence, but in a manner that even the poetic expression clearly comes forth in the poem, and thus shows the poetic or rhetorical work, which preceded the description of the grief. This is clear in "Tears at the Grave of Herr Frederik von Arnsbach."[15]

Prior to Oehlenschläger and Molbech, the most important detailed critical account of Ewald is found in the Society for the Promotion of the Beautiful and Useful Sciences. It is found in the members' correspondence, where the members' disagreement about the value of Ewald's work is expressed. Bolle Willum Luxdorph (1716–88) did not care for Ewald, while his loyal friend, Royal Advisor, Adolph Gotthard Carstens (1712–95), naturally defended his works. For the tragedy *Rolf Krage* (1770),[16] Ewald received 60 rix-dollars as an encouragement, although the piece "is not of the quality that in its present form it could be published in the Society's writings, indeed it could not even be recommended to be printed at all."[17] In November he submitted *The Death of Balder*,[18] and it was sent on with Carstens' recommendation to Luxdorph. He read it the same day he received it, and wrote the following clear judgment in his diary: "*Non sani hominis*" ("not the work of a sane man").[19]

In 1780 the first volume of Ewald's collected writings, entitled *Johannes Ewalds samtlige Skrifter*, was published, an edition which was completed with the fourth volume in 1791. It was Ewald himself who wrote the preface with the title "To the

---

[13]   Adam Oehlenschläger, *Om Evald og Schiller. Forelæsninger, holdte ved Kjøbenhavns Universitet i Aarene 1810 og 11*, vols. 1–2, Copenhagen: Lose & Delbanco 1854, vol. 1, pp. 48–9.

[14]   Molbech, *Johannes Evalds Levnet, med Bidrag til hans Digterværkers Historie og Charakteristik*, p. 46.

[15]   Johannes Ewald, "Taarer ved Herr Frederik von Arnsbachs Grav," in *Johannes Ewalds samtlige Skrifter*, vol. 3, pp. 292–6.

[16]   Johannes Ewald, *Rolf Krage*, in *Johannes Ewalds samtlige Skrifter*, vol. 2, pp. 1–185.

[17]   K.F. Plesner, *Det smagende Selskab*, p. 38.

[18]   Johannes Ewald, *Balders Død*, in *Johannes Ewalds samtlige Skrifter*, vol. 3, pp. 1–125.

[19]   K.F. Plesner, *Det smagende Selskab*, p. 40.

Reader," which introduced the first volume, and in it he gives his own account and evaluation of his authorship. "To the Reader" is dated "Copenhagen, February 14, 1780," and was thus completed a year before his death in March 1781, and thus at a time when the authorship, both quantitatively and qualitatively was finished. The edition was not complete since it did not include the unfinished prose works; but, moreover, it is not even complete with respect to the printed works. The preface is an ambiguous matter. On the one hand, it is the story of the poet's journey from confused youth, through industrious and goal-oriented journeyman years to a human and artistic maturity, which ends around 1770. The process is presented as a natural and harmonious growth, and in a sense it mirrors the edition itself, which in its organization of the authorship, attempts to tell the same story. All of Ewald's experiments, testing established conventions, are passed over in silence and given no significance in the authorship. To the degree to which the early and immature or incomplete works are discussed, this is done with reference to his lack of ability in contrast to his later declared maturity as a writer. The early texts, of course, cannot speak for themselves, but must be treated on the basis of their experimental character. But, on the other hand, the preface also tells another story, one which much more closely reflects the authorship, when the incomplete works are also taken into consideration. Ewald describes this himself as follows: "The smooth, noisy road has never been attractive to me. Its security, its comfort contained nothing amusing for my imagination, nothing, which could console my heart for the loss of the feelings which only unexpected events, difficulties and dangers can awaken."[20]

With the description of his life Ewald eliminates the basis for the bourgeois virtues, which he elsewhere in the preface makes into the basis for his successful and harmonious *Bildungsreise* from incomplete amateur to fully developed and fully mature professional poet. He describes here a poetry, where the sublime is the turning point of the text, and where the representation of literature's moral and edifying functions, in the best case, are on the surface, which makes it possible to read the text from within an officially accepted horizon of expectation. And since the king, the crown prince, the heir presumptive, and the queen were among the subscribers,[21] such a sublime aesthetics, for obvious reasons, had to be encapsulated and the results merely communicated indirectly; Ewald left it to the readers to draw their own conclusions.

A. Poems

Johannes Ewald's authorship covers the genres poetry, drama, and prose. And within these genres he was able to modify or change the limits and forms of expression. In his lifetime he founded his reputation as lyricist and dramatist, while the posthumously published works show that he unfolded the same genius in his often unfinished prose. He made his debut with "Elegres in Christiansborg's Castle Church on March 18,

---

[20]   Ewald, *Johannes Ewalds samtlige Skrifter*, vol. 1, pp. VIII–IX.
[21]   Ibid., p. XL.

1766, when King Frederik the Fifth Is to Brought to His Resting Place,"[22] written on
occasion of the death of Frederik V. His entire life he wrote occasional poems, but
without for this reason renouncing his higher artistic demand on himself. In "Tears
at the Grave of Mr. Frederik von Arnsbach"[23] he breaks with the genre's demand for
a distanced portrayal of the deceased, by also having the poem describe the lyric
I's personal grief. The best of his occasional pieces were, however, those written
without any official occasion, for example, "In Abrahamson's Album."[24]

    The main works in his lyric production were the odes, where Ewald combines
inspiration from ancient odes (Pindar and Horace) with neoclassical odes (Klopstock).
His most enduring odes are "Rungsted's Happiness: An Ode,"[25] which is a metaode,
where he praises the art's creative and liberating power. Alongside this stands "Hope
and Recollection" and "To the Soul: An Ode" as the absolute apex of Danish lyric.[26]
"Hope and Recollection" summarizes Ewald's feeling and philosophy since in the
poem itself he maintains the complexity which is introduced in the title: the now
can only be maintained in memory, that is, the present disappears immediately
into an absence. The goal of trying to hold onto the now is doomed to failure, but
the poem avoids this by nonetheless letting the reader experience the poem's long
chain of nows. The long poem "To the Soul: An Ode" describes the poet's (i.e.,
Ewald's) return to his original Pietistic view of man, where the self-glorifying and
sovereign poet is replaced by the penitent and repentant sinner. But also here there
are spots on the poem's appearance. In the poem's final verse the redeeming spirit is
invoked, "Great is the Spirit who raises the fallen." There are several elements in the
poem which point to the fact that this spirit can just as well be the spirit of the poet.
Although the poem deprives the soul of the last bit of self-movement and installs
it with a redeeming God, the poem also presents a picture of the soul which in fact
raises itself. And thus the poet's falling to his knees for the Pietistic Christianity of
his childhood appears in a far more ambiguous and problematic light.

B. Drama

Ewald achieved success as theater poet very late. It happened with the tragedy *The
Death of Balder*, which was performed at the Royal Theater in 1778, after the censor
had obliged Ewald to make several changes to the piece. On January 29, 1780, the
birthday of King Christian VI, the Singspiel *The Fishermen* was performed for the
first time at the theater. The piece is a large-scale tribute to the Danish people, the
nobility, and the Royal House. It is based on actual events. Five fishermen from

---

[22]   Johannes Ewald, "Sørge-Sange i Christiansborgs Slots-Kirke den 18de Martius 1766
da Kong Frederik den Femte skulde føres til sit Hvilested," in *Johannes Ewalds samtlige
Skrifter*, vol. 1, pp. 314–22.

[23]   Ewald, "Taarer ved Herr Frederik von Arnsbachs Grav."

[24]   Johannes Ewald, "I Abrahamsons Stambog," in *Johannes Ewalds samtlige Skrifter*,
vol. 4, pp. 355–7.

[25]   Ewald, "Rungsteds Lyksaligheder. En Ode."

[26]   Johannes Ewald, "Haab og Erindring," in *Johannes Ewalds samtlige Skrifter*,
vol. 4, pp. 347–55 and "Til Sielen. En Ode," in *Johannes Ewalds samtlige Skrifter*, vol. 1,
pp. 307–14.

the town of Hornbæk in North Zealand tried in vain to save the crew of an English ship in distress, ultimately only managing to save the captain. To the public's great admiration, the five fishermen were present at the premier near the front of the stage— a highly unusual theater audience but also entirely in line with Ewald's rebellious spirit. *The Fishermen* was both an artistic and financial success for Ewald. The piece also contains the best-known and most widely disseminated of all of Ewald's texts, namely, Denmark's royal anthem "King Christian Stood at the High Mast."

His first attempts in the dramatic genre were *Adam and Eve* followed by *Rolf Krage* and *The Violent Claqueurs*.[27] The earlier dramas reflect his belief in an individual humanism and an interest in what is universally human, which extends beyond the sharp social differences which divided contemporary class society. The fall of Struensee on January 17, 1772 led to marked limitations on the freedom of speech, which also included attempts directly or indirectly to say something about political matters in the theater.[28] For this reason Ewald abandoned his drafts of the political pieces *Frode* and *Helge* in accordance with a directive from above.[29] In this situation he wrote a comedy in Alexandrian verse, *Harlequin Patriot or The Inauthentic Patriotism. A Comic Comedy in Three Acts in Verse*,[30] which is a commentary on the prevailing conditions in the kingdom after the fall of Struensee. The piece *The Violent Claqueurs* should also be included in an account of Ewald's comic works.[31]

C. Prose

In the years 1771–73 Ewald wrote a special and idiosyncratic series of prose works. *Philet's Suggestion about the Bachelors* is a satire on the political audience under Struensee's rule.[32] *Master Sewing Needle's Story*[33] is modeled on Ludvig Holberg's

---

[27] Johannes Ewald, *De brutale Klappere*, in *Johannes Ewalds samtlige Skrifter*, vol. 4, pp. 191–341.

[28] Johann Friedrich Struensee (1737–72) was King Christian VII's personal physician. Due to his calming affect on the schizophrenic king's aggressive behavior and his relation to Queen Caroline Mathilde (1751–75), Struensee attained a decisive influence on Danish legislation. He was inspired by the Enlightenment's ideals of reason and rationality, and with this light he carried out a series of reforms of the central administration and society. On the night between January 16 and 17, 1772, he lost his position in a palace revolution and was executed on April 28, 1772. Ewald's benefactor J.H.E. Bernstorff (1712–72) was removed from the court by Struensee, and Ewald thus lost, among other things, all prospects of an educational trip to Scotland with public funds.

[29] Johannes Ewald, *Frode*, in *Johannes Ewalds samtlige Skrifter*, vol. 2, pp. 1–185; *Helge*, in *Johannes Ewalds samlede Skrifter*, vols. 1–6, ed. by Hans Brix, Victor Kuhr, Niels Møller and Svend Aage Pallis, Copenhagen: Gyldendal 1914–24, vol. 5, pp. 1–27.

[30] Johannes Ewald, *Harlequin Patriot eller Den uægte Patriotisme. En comisk Comoedie i tre Handlinger paa Vers*, in *Johannes Ewalds samtlige Skrifter*, vol. 4, pp. 1–163.

[31] See Ewald, *De brutale Klappere*.

[32] Johannes Ewald, *Philets Forslag om Pebersvendene*, in *Johannes Ewalds samtlige Skrifter*, vol. 2, pp. 237–349.

[33] Johannes Ewald, *Mester Synaals Fortelling*, in *Det almindelige Danske Bibliothek et Maaneds-Skrift*, Copenhagen: Christian Gottlob Prost 1780, vol. 1.2, pp. 113–53, and vol. 1.3, pp. 225–44.

Niels Klim,[34] but in contrast to Holberg's story, it lacks all trust in reason. *Hr. Panthakak's Story*, an unfinished draft of a novel, presumably written in 1771, represents another example of Ewald's manifold experiments with the form of the novel and prose in general in the 1770s.[35] The direct source is Voltaire's *Candide* (1759), which Ewald with *his* philosophical novel turns on its head. But the story can be regarded as belonging to a chain of pearls from the Enlightenment's main works of *belles lettres*: Montesquieu's *Persian Letters* (1721), Swift's *Gulliver's Travels* (1726), Holberg's *Niels Klim* (1741), and Diderot's *Jacques the Fatalist* (1773). Ewald's prose experiments are all marked by a critical skepticism as well as an ironic and playful relation to the Enlightenment's firm belief in reason. He, so to speak, turns the Enlightenment inside out, and shows how reason must limit and marginalize reason's respective oppositions, precisely in order that the Enlightenment can stand forth as grounded on reason.

Ewald's main work in the prose genre is the purportedly autobiographical novel fragment *Life and Opinions*, which he wrote between 1774 and 1778.[36] The models for this work are, among others, Cervantes' *Don Quixote* (1605, 1615) and Laurence Sterne's *Life and Opinions of Tristram Shandy, Gentleman* (1759-67).[37] But Daniel Defoe, Henry Fielding, and Voltaire are also among the threads that Ewald weaves into his literary autobiography. Ewald borrows in his *Life and Opinions* elements from genres such as confession of sins, the autobiography and the novel, but it is, first and foremost, the ironic, parodying elements which are predominant in his text. The narrative describes a novelistic life. The main character is a young man with a strong desire to break down and go beyond the safe and boring framework of bourgeois life. He tries everywhere to break with the existing norms. From the dreams of his youth the grown-up, insightful narrator weaves the work's refined text, knowing well that in the artwork the old dreams can shine with undiminished brilliance. The text steps in and takes the place of the life it portrays, and in a more undiminished and purer form than that life itself. The most famous scene in *Life and Opinions*, with the heading "Arendse," portrays a meeting of the narrator with the unattainable Arendse. And entirely in line with the novel's ironic and parodying character, the meeting is not about Arendse as a real possession. "Arendse" is first and foremost a picture in words, which should preserve the first surprising impression.

---

[34] Ludvig Holberg, *Nicolai Klimii iter subterraneum*, Copenhagen and Leipzig: Jacob Preuss 1741.

[35] Johannes Ewald, *Hr. Panthakaks Historie*, in *Ny Minerva*, ed. by Knud Lyhne Rahbek, July 1805, pp. 24–44, August 1805, pp. 129–62 and September 1805, pp. 233–74.

[36] Johannes Ewald, *Levnet og Meeninger*, in *Den danske Tilskuer*, ed. by K.L. Rahbek, vol. 2, 1804, pp. 809–24; vol. 1, 1805, pp. 1–8 and pp. 121–36 (also in *Ny Minerva*, ed. by K.L. Rahbek, May and June, 1808, pp. 151–68).

[37] For a detailed presentation and analysis of the extensive intertextual web which *Life and Opinions* is written in and out of, see Peer E. Sørensen, *Håb og erindring. Johannes Ewald i Oplysningen*, Copenhagen: Gyldendal 1989, pp. 169–313. This *Habilitation* thesis also shows how Ewald modifies all the genres, which he unfolds himself in, by means of a dialectical movement between affirmation and transgression. He changes, so to speak, the tradition with its own means; he opens up new possibilities precisely by his exact knowledge of the individual genres' possibilities of expression.

III. Kierkegaard's Editions of Ewald

In *The Auction Catalogue* of Søren Kierkegaard's library, Ewald is represented with two editions of his collected works, both called *Johannes Ewalds samtlige Skrifter*. The first edition from 1780–91 is not a critical edition but rather a popular one.[38] As already mentioned, it is organized in order to illustrate a quite determined and preconceived picture of the authorship. This edition is illustrated by Nicolai Abildgaard (1743–1809) and Daniel Nicolaus Chodowiecki (1726–1801).

The second edition of Ewald's collected works, edited by F.L. Liebenberg (1767–1828), was the first critical edition of Ewald's authorship.[39] The edition includes his poems, theater pieces, as well as a large part of Ewald's unfinished works, among others, his masterpiece, *Life and Opinions*. One can also find in Liebenberg's edition several of Ewald's Latin treatises, written while he lived at Valkendorf Collegium. In addition to the fact that this edition is more comprehensive than the first one, it is accompanied with verbal and personal commentaries; Liebenberg also gives an account of the changes in the text, just as he suggests alternative readings if he does not find it necessary to make a correction.

IV. Ewald in Kierkegaard's Writings

A. The Published Works

The first time that Ewald appears in Kierkegaard's published authorship is in his debut work, *From the Papers of One Still Living*. Towards the end of the preface Kierkegaard discusses how the treatise is a fixing of the idea's many forms in one determinate form. The many possible forms are compared, via a quotation from *The Fishermen*, with a landscape, which alternately appears and disappears in the fog; the idea's manifold "Shows itself and smiles and disappears / Like the point of the desired headland in fog."[40]

In the second part of *Either/Or* Judge Wilhelm discusses "the first love," and says that it is "humble and is therefore happy that there is an authority higher than itself, if for no other reason, then at least in order to have someone to thank."[41] After this he says that the same thing can be seen in the person Wilhelm is addressing; in other words, he too seeks "a higher point of departure" for his love, namely, by "beseech[ing] all the powers in heaven and on earth."[42] This is an allusion to the

---

[38]   Ewald, *Johannes Ewalds samtlige Skrifter*, vols. 1–4.
[39]   Johannes Ewald, *Johannes Ewalds samtlige Skrifter*, vols. 1–8, Copenhagen: E.L. Thaarup 1850–55 (*ASKB* 1537–1544).
[40]   *SKS* 1, 11 / *EPW*, 57: "*viser sig og smiler, og undviger / Som Pynten af et ønsket Næs i Taage.*" Kierkegaard is here in line with the essential elements of Ewald's poetry; on the one hand, the quotation thematizes the testing of the forms' many possibilities, and on the other hand, it witnesses an awareness of the fact that writing cannot always only be held in one form at a time.
[41]   *SKS* 3, 60 / *EO2*, 54.
[42]   Ibid.

myth of the death of Balder, which is also the title of Ewald's drama, written in 1773 and first published in 1775.[43]

In *Repetition* there is a direct reference to Ewald. It appears near the end of the first part of the work, where the narrator, after a sleepless night, sits in his usual café and drinks coffee. The evening before he investigated whether repetition was possible by visiting the theater which he visited the first time he was in Berlin. The result was disappointing. At the café he now makes the same experiment as in the theater. And just before he tastes the coffee he quotes a verse from Ewald's two-line poem, "Label on a Coffee Pot,"[44] "pure and hot and strong and not misused,"[45] where Ewald draws a parallel between friendship and coffee. The narrator in *Repetition* chooses coffee over friendship and is disappointed in the same manner as in the theater. Likewise, coffee cannot be repeated—in contrast with the first time, it now tastes bad.

In the discourse "Love Will Hide a Multitude of Sins" from *Three Upbuilding Discourses* (1843) Kierkegaard describes at the beginning of the discourse the love of the heathen: "his love could turn into something else that he extolled almost more. Love was beautiful, more beautiful than everything; but revenge was sweet, sweeter than everything."[46] The expression "revenge is sweet" presumably plays on Ewald's *Adam and Eve or The Unhappy Trial*, where the angel of peace and Adam's friend Irmiel say "I know you base creature, that man's broken heart / alone satisfies you. Revenge alone cools your pain."[47] The answer comes in a dialogue with Satan about God's justice.

In "Caput II" of *The Concept of Anxiety* toward the end of the section "A. The Consequence of the Relationship of Generation," Kierkegaard uses an expression from Ewald's *The Fishermen* to describe the presence of anxiety in the erotic. The presence of anxiety in the erotic is due to the fact that it does not express itself in the erotic and is therefore foreign to the erotic. Anxiety hides itself and in this manner is related to chastity. For this reason Kierkegaard can say, "when the erotic is pure, innocent, and beautiful, this anxiety is friendly and gentle. Therefore the poet is correct in speaking of a sweet anxiousness."[48] The expression "sweet anxiousness" presumably comes, as noted, from *The Fishermen*. In the fifth act Adam attempts to prevent Eve from eating the forbidden fruit from the tree of knowledge, to which he remarks: "The uncertain tempt; / My secure safety confirms my thoughts. / I—see

---

43   According to Nordic mythology, Frigg (the goddess of love and marriage), swore Balder's mother, and the entire world to an oath that no one would harm him. But she forgot to have the mistletoe take the oath. For this reason, Loke (a giant and an ambiguous figure in Nordic mythology) can induce the blind Høder to murder his brother with an arrow made of mistletoe.

44   Johannes Ewald, "Paaskrift paa en Kaffekande," in *Johannes Ewalds samtlige Skrifter*, vol. 4, p. 365.

45   *SKS* 4, 43 / *R*, 170: "*reen og varm og stærk og umisbrugt.*"

46   *SKS* 5, 66 / *EUD*, 55.

47   Ewald, *Johannes Ewalds samtlige Skrifter*, vol. 1, p. 208: "*Jeg veed det, Nedrige, at Mandens knuste Hierte / Alene mætter dig. Hevn kiøler kun din Smerte.*"

48   *SKS* 4, 376 / *CA*, 71–2, translation slightly modified.

now it is done."[49] In the accompanying remarks for the staging one reads: "She has really tasted it; and she says this with a voice which already seems to disclose her fear."[50]

In a draft to the discourse "On the Occasion of a Confession" from *Three Discourses on Imagined Occasions* Kierkegaard adds in the margin a remark which once again alludes to Ewald's *The Fishermen*. The addition comes toward the end of the discourse where he is speaking of sincerity toward God not being grounded in extensive knowledge but in being faithful to what is small. Addressing the reader, he writes, "you still would rather be faithful over little than faithless over much.... you still would rather be true as gold."[51] It is from the draft to this passage that Kierkegaard adds a direct reference to Ewald and *The Fishermen*. He writes, "A poet has so beautifully said of a girl: Her young soul was tested gold...."[52] The situation referred to is from Act 3, Scene 4, where the fisherman's daughter Lise sings a romance about "Little Gunver" for the fisherman Knud: "Little Gunver prefers to walk in the evening, / So thoughtful. / Her heart was malleable like wax, her young soul / Was tested gold."[53] The addition did not, however, find its way to the fair copy and thus the published version of "On the Occasion of a Confession."

B. Journals and Papers

The first references to Ewald in Kierkegaard's journals and papers, which are also the first references to Ewald in the authorship generally, are indirect. The references appear in the *Journal BB* and *Notebook 3*, where Kierkegaard excerpts parts of Christian Molbech's *Lectures on More Recent Danish Poetry, Especially on the Poets Ewald, Baggesen and Oehlenschläger's Works*.[54] Both excerpts are dated March 1836. Molbech's lectures treat "Danish poetry from our age, with that immediately preceding it, regarded partly from a historical and partly from an aesthetic-critical standpoint."[55] In lectures 9 and 10 he reached Ewald, who is treated in a summary fashion.

In the entry Not3:18 Kierkegaard comments on a passage from the first lecture, which treats "the universal," and lectures 9 and 10, which treat Ewald, and lecture 11, which is dedicated to Jens Baggesen. Molbech writes of "the universal," that the work of art is equally accessible to everyone regardless of "whether the beholder is a Spaniard or an Englishman."[56] Kierkegaard objects that there will always be a distance

---

[49]   Ewald, *Johannes Ewalds samtlige Skrifter* vols. 1–4, vol. 1, p. 202: "*Den uvisse vanker; / Min trygge Sikkerhed bekræfter mine Tanker. / Jeg – see nu er det gjort.*"

[50]   Ibid.

[51]   *SKS* 5, 415 / *TD*, 37.

[52]   *Pap.* VI B 108, 10 / *TD*, Supplement, p. 137.

[53]   Ewald, *Johannes Ewalds samtlige Skrifter*, vol. 1, p. 233: "*Liden Gunver vandrer som helst i Qvel, / Saa tankefuld. / Hendes Hierte var Vox, hendes unge Siel / Var prøvet Guld.*"

[54]   Christian Molbech, *Forelæsninger over den nyere danske Poesie, særdeles efter Digterne Ewald, Baggesen og Oehlenschlägers Værker*, vols. 1–2, Copenhagen: C.A. Reitzel 1832.

[55]   Ibid., vol. 1, p. VII.

[56]   *SKS* 19, 119, Not3:18 / *JP* 5, 5134. Molbech's lectures are quoted here from Kierkegaard's excerpt in *Notebook 3*.

or gap between the observer and the work of art, namely, "the national individuality [*det folkelige-Individuelle*] by which the poet was essentially nurtured." Moreover, "a certain historical aspect is more prominent—which consists in contemplating that such and such was the case with that people."[57] Literature is thus no guarantee for an intimacy between the text and the reader: the reader will always be at a distance from the text.

The next commentary to Molbech concerns his description of the relation between form and content in Ewald's *Singspiel, The Fishermen*, a description which apparently meets with Kierkegaard's approbation. According to Molbech, the Singspiel is not about a realistic description of the fishermen. Ewald's intent was quite different; the work had "a poetic aim which could not but raise Evald's spirit, inflamed by love of the fatherland, to a more lofty lyrical enthusiasm than that required by a merely idyllic-emotional subject."[58]

The entry 133 from the *Journal FF* is comprised of four verses from the choir in Act 2, Scene 9 of *The Fishermen*: "Equal strokes, / Don't pause long. / Hold on strong, / Danish blokes."[59] The entry was presumably written between September 1836 and October 1837. This journal entry has a special history. Although the entries in *FF* were written between September 1836 and September 1838, they were presumably not put in the journal itself during this period. The assumption is based on the fact that there are several chronological breaks in the journal, for example, the entry FF:156 from December 30, 1837 appears immediately after FF:155, which is dated July 18, 1838.

According to their dating, the entries fall into four groups: FF:1–106 are from September 1836 to October 1837; FF:107–55 are from April to July 1838; FF:156–84 are from December 1837 to February 1838; and finally, FF:185–215 are from the period from August to September 1838. Seen chronologically, it is clear that the entries in group three, FF:156–84, according to their dating, ought to precede the entries in group two, FF:107–55. The entries in FF were thus not written in the journal in the same sequence that Kierkegaard thought them.

The explanation for this might be that the *Journal FF* consists of older entries, which presumably were written on loose pieces of paper and thereafter collected and written into *FF*. This assumption is supported by the fact that the writing is everywhere neat and regular, written with straight margins and few corrections. In addition to this, there are only two marginal additions in the entire journal. The chronological break can be explained by the fact that Kierkegaard had organized the old entries perhaps into groups and while writing them into the *Journal FF* unintentionally confused the groups, since the chronological break between FF:106 and 107, between FF:155 and 156 as well as that between FF:184 and 185 all take place on the same pages in the journal, respectively, pp. 63, [80], and 93.

---

[57]   *SKS* 19, 119, Not3:18 / *JP* 5, 5134.

[58]   *SKS* 17, 12, FF:133 / *KJN* 2, 93.

[59]   *SKS* 18, 101: "*Lige Slag / Dvæl ei længe / Seie Tag / Danske Drenge.*" Kierkegaard omits Ewald's punctuation in FF:133; the four verses in Ewald are as follows: "*Lige Slag! / Dvæl ei længe! / Seie Tag, / Danske Drenge!*"; see *Johannes Ewalds samtlige Skrifter*, vol. 3, p. 213.

The quotation from *The Fishermen* does not stand in a context which immediately makes clear why Kierkegaard quotes Ewald at just that place in the journal. The surrounding entries contain, for example, an idea for a novella (FF:129), references to a book (FF:134), experiences from a walk (FF:137), remarks on Don Juan (FF:130), and two entries with theological content (FF:127–8). The patchwork character of the journal means that no thematic thread runs through it. The entry FF:133 *might* thus come from a context in which it was meaningfully connected with the surrounding context.

In the *Journal JJ*, which Kierkegaard wrote between 1842 and 1846, he quotes in an entry from 1843 three verses from Ewald's poem from 1779 with the long title, "A New Spiritual Song, in which is introduced the Savior Jesus Christ's dear Warning to those who are tempted by evil and unholy Thoughts to shorten their own Lives." [60] The poem was published as a street-song with the following warning from Ewald: "When suicide seemed to be common among the humblest people, I sought to compose this song and even its title in according with the simple people's capacities and demands." [61] The poem contains in all 32 stanzas each consisting of six verses, and Kierkegaard quotes the first three verses of stanza 25: "Do the ocean waves obliterate? / Does poison corrode the stamp of God? / Can the dagger kill thoughts?" [62] The thought in the three verses is that a human being does not escape the wrath of the judge, either by drowning himself or by killing his soul with poison or dagger. As was seen earlier, the entry JJ:59 does not appear in any context which immediately explains why Kierkegaard chose to quote Ewald just here, just as the entry's theme does not seem to have left any traces in the entries in the journal which immediately follow it.

Ewald does not occupy much space in Kierkegaard's authorship. Either the connection is indirect, for example, via the excerpts from Molbech's lectures on Danish literature, or direct, as, for example, when a quotation finds its way into the preface of *From the Papers of One Still Living* or a short quotation constitutes an entry in a journal. The indirect connection has an occasion outside itself (for example, Molbech), while in the few cases where Ewald is used directly it has an illustrative function. Although there is not much of Ewald in Kierkegaard, what is there bears witness to the fact that the two authors are in many ways poetically related.

Translated by Jon Stewart

---

[60]   "*En nye aandelig Sang, hvori indføres Forsonerens Jesu Christi kierlige Advarsel til dem som fristes af de onde og ulyksalige Tanker at ville forkorte deres eget Liv.*"

[61]   *Johannes Ewalds samlede Skrifter*, vols. 1–6, vol. 6, p. 257.

[62]   *SKS* 18, 159, JJ:59 / *KJN* 2, 147: "*Mon Havets Bølger slette ud? / Mon Gift fortærer Præg af Gud? / Kan Dolken dræbe Tanker?*" The three last verses in strophe 25 are as follows: "*Kan Aander døe? Kan Mennesket / Undflye sin Siel, sig selv saa let / Som Støv, hvorpaa det anker?*"; see Ewald, *Johannes Ewalds samtlige Skrifter*, vol. 1, p. 299.

Bibliography

I. Ewald's Works in The Auction Catalogue *of Kierkegaard's Library*

Johannes Ewalds samtlige Skrifter, vols. 1–4, Copenhagen: Christian Gottlob Prost 1780–91 (*ASKB* 1533–1536).
Johannes Ewalds samtlige Skrifter, vols. 1–8, 2nd ed., Copenhagen: E.L. Thaarup 1850–55 (*ASKB* 1537–1544).

II. Works in The Auction Catalogue *of Kierkegaard's Library that Discuss Ewald*

Heiberg, Johan Ludvig, "Lyrisk Poesie," in *Intelligensblade*, vol. 3, nos. 25–6, 1843, pp. 25–72, see pp. 45–6; p. 55 (*ASKB* U 56).
—— *Prosaiske Skrifter*, vol. 3, Copenhagen: J.H. Schubothe 1843 (vol. 3, in Johan Ludvig Heiberg, *Prosaiske Skrifter*, vols. 1–3, Copenhagen: J.H. Schubothe 1841–43 which is part of *Johan Ludvig Heiberg's Samlede Skrifter* consisting of *Skuespil*, vols. 1–7, Copenhagen: J.H. Schubothe 1833–41 and *Digte og Fortællinger*, vols. 1–2, Copenhagen: J.H. Schubothe 1834–35), p. 379 (*ASKB* 1560).
Mynster, Jakob Peter, *Blandede Skrivter*, vols. 1–3, Copenhagen: Gyldendal 1852–53 [vols. 4–6, Copenhagen: Gyldendal 1855–57], vol. 2, p. 366; vol. 3, p. 154; p. 174 (*ASKB* 358–363).
Steffens, Henrich, *Was ich erlebte. Aus der Erinnerung niedergeschrieben*, vols. 1–10, Breslau: Josef Max und Comp. 1840–44, vol. 2, pp. 112–16 (*ASKB* 1834–1843).
Thortsen, Carl Adolph, *Historisk Udsigt over den danske Litteratur indtil Aar 1814*, Copenhagen: C.A. Reitzel 1839, p. 70; p. 102; p. 108 (*ASKB* 970).

III. Secondary Literature on Kierkegaard's Relation to Ewald

None.

Ludvig Holberg:
Kierkegaard's Unacknowledged Mentor

Julie K. Allen

One of the brightest stars in Denmark's literary firmament, during Kierkegaard's lifetime as now, is the eighteenth-century Norwegian-born Enlightenment scholar and dramatist Ludvig Baron Holberg. He is frequently dubbed the father of Danish literature, due to the seminal impact of his dramas on the development of Danish letters and culture. F.J. Billeskov Jansen suggests that "scarcely any Dane, whether of the common people or not, is unaffected by the spriteliness and thoughtfulness that Holberg's comedies have been spreading since 1722, when, for the first time, a regular, Danish-language, popular theater was established in Copenhagen."[1] Holberg's comedies formed the basis of the repertoire of the Royal Danish Theater from its establishment in 1749; between 1722 and 1752, he wrote 33 plays, several of which have been performed consistently in Denmark ever since. Consequently, many of Holberg's characters, in particular the drunken peasant Jeppe of the Hill and the arrogant scholar Erasmus Montanus, have assumed iconic status within Danish culture.

Yet while Holberg's importance for Danish culture in general is indisputable, his specific significance for Kierkegaard is more tenuous. There are relatively few scholarly treatments of the connections between these two larger-than-life Danish thinkers,[2] perhaps because Kierkegaard himself did not acknowledge any particular stylistic or philosophical debt to Holberg, aside from making several casual allusions to various Holberg comedies in his private writings. In various works, Kierkegaard quotes from a total of 18 of Holberg's comedies, testifying to a thorough familiarity with Holberg's work. F.J. Billeskov Jansen points out that Holberg is the author most frequently quoted in Kierkegaard's writings, but cautions that Kierkegaard was generally more interested in adapting motifs and tropes from Holberg's texts than in engaging with Holberg's ideological opinions:

> The matter that Holberg provides for SK is fairly uniform: words, situations, characters of comic content and shape. But we shall see now how SK can use this material for

---

[1]   F.J. Billeskov Jansen, "Holberg," in *Kierkegaard Literary Miscellany*, ed. by Niels Thulstrup and Marie Mikulová Thulstrup, Copenhagen: C.A. Reitzel 1981 (*Bibliotheca Kierkegaardiana*, vol. 9), p. 65.

[2]   The most notable of these are Billeskov Jansen's "Holberg" and Birgit Bertung's essay "Kierkegaard og Holberg—i meddelelsesdialektisk perspektiv," *Kierkegaards inspiration. En antologi*, ed. by Birgit Bertung, Paul Müller, Fritz Norman, and Julia Watkin, Copenhagen: C.A. Reitzel 1991 (*Søren Kierkegaard Selskabets Populære Skrifter*, vol. 20), pp. 26–34.

very varied purposes: to characterize fictional characters; in philosophical argument; in aesthetic definitions; to caricature J.L. Heiberg; as well as in religious polemic.[3]

The irrelevance suggested by this paucity of textual connections is reinforced by the dissimilarities in their lifestyles and personalities. Both men were just a generation or two removed from the peasant class, but their situations in life were marked by very disparate personal and professional circumstances. While Holberg was plagued with financial difficulties during much of his life, Kierkegaard lived comfortably, primarily through the largesse of his father and, later, his inheritance. They had very different temperaments as well, which affected both their personal and professional lives. Holberg traveled incessantly in his youth, to Germany, France, England, and Italy, whereas Kierkegaard confined himself largely to Copenhagen, aside from a few journeys to Berlin and Jutland. Holberg was upwardly mobile, climbing the academic and social ladders, currying favor with kings, and basking in the adulation of theater-goers; Kierkegaard was a highly private person who never held an academic post and reaped little praise along with a great deal of criticism and mockery for his literary efforts during his lifetime.

When their respective oeuvres and legacies are viewed from a more holistic perspective, however, Holberg appears to have functioned as a kind of mentor for Kierkegaard, albeit unacknowledged. Their relationship goes beyond simple allusions and moves into the realm of similar communicative strategies, thematic interests, and common didactic aims, many of which Holberg modeled for Kierkegaard. These similarities may be circumstantial, but provide nonetheless compelling grounds for considering the possibility of their interconnectedness. Both men's interest in literature encompassed both the aesthetic and the moral/ethical, and their works demonstrate the power of satire, irony, dialectical thinking, and Socratic-inspired indirect communication.[4] Despite their use of different genres and their focus on period-specific concerns, Holberg and Kierkegaard play a similar role in Danish intellectual history, namely, that of Denmark's itchy conscience, pointing out social problems that required public attention. They were both conservative in their views of the democratization of the political process, but not in their faith in the power of the individual to change himself and the world around him. They used their literary texts as tools for educating their countrymen and empowering them to pursue social and philosophical self-determination. Though Kierkegaard arrived at his Socratic style independently of Holberg, they were nevertheless fellow-travelers on the path of motivating their readers to take responsibility for their own lives and destinies.

I. Holberg's Biography and Significance

Born in Bergen, Norway presumably on December 3, 1684, Ludvig Holberg was destined to travel far from his origins, both social and geographic, in pursuit of the professional and artistic success he craved. He lived in a tumultuous time, marked by political and religious upheaval as well as increasing social mobility. Although

---

[3]   Billeskov Jansen, "Holberg," p. 71.
[4]   Bertung, "Kierkegaard og Holberg," p. 26.

his youth coincided with bitter battles between Sweden and Denmark over Norway, Holberg was a staunch supporter of the absolutist Danish crown throughout his life, in part because of the opportunities for advancement for the middle class that followed from absolutism's displacement of the old aristocracy. His parents were members of the bureaucratic middle class created by absolutism and upon which the dual monarchy of Denmark-Norway depended. His father, Christian Nielsen Holberg (1620–86), was a career civil servant with origins in the peasantry, while his mother, Karen Lem (1647–95), came from a long line of clergymen, being the granddaughter of a former bishop of Bergen, Ludvig Munthe (1597–1649). In his memoirs, Holberg points out both the noble rank of his great-grandfather as well as his father's more democratic origins: "My father, of blessed memory, rose from the ranks to the command of a regiment; and it may be inferred from this circumstance, that he was rather indebted to his personal merit than to his ancestry for his promotion."[5]

Despite the early death of his parents, Holberg was able to obtain a reasonably good education. At the age of ten, he became a scholarship student of the Upland regiment, for, as he states, "it was at the time the practice in Norway to give pay to the children of officers, and to initiate them almost from the cradle in military tactics."[6] Given his early inclination toward literature, this was not to Holberg's liking and, after a brief but disastrous interlude with private tutors in the homes of relatives, his wealthy uncle, Peder Lem, became his guardian and sent him to the Bergen Cathedral Latin School, which he attended until a fire in 1702 destroyed the school and his uncle's home. Even before the fire, Bergen's educational system was far from ideal, however, since the curriculum for the Norwegian Latin schools was outmoded and would not be reformed until 1739, when the focus was shifted from teaching Greek and Latin to more practical subjects, such as religion, reading, writing, and mathematics.[7] However, although educational reforms lagged during Holberg's youth, one educational innovation proved to be decisively important for Holberg's writings: namely, the rise of Danish as a literary language. The first Danish grammar was published in 1646 and some of its most important literary texts, along with the religious poetry of Thomas Kingo (1643–1703), would be written by Holberg himself.

Supplementing Holberg's formal education, the cosmopolitan hustle and bustle of the Hanseatic port city of Bergen offered a tantalizing introduction to other European cultures. With 15,000 inhabitants in 1700, Bergen was considerably smaller than the next-largest city in the kingdom, Copenhagen, with its 70,000 inhabitants, but it was the center of the kingdom's foreign maritime trade.[8] In his memoirs, Holberg described

---

[5]   *Ludvig Holberg's Memoirs. An Eighteenth Century Danish Contribution to International Understanding*, ed. by Stewart E. Fraser, Leiden: Brill 1970, p. 24. The memoirs consist of three fictitious letters, originally published in Latin under the titles *Ad virum perillustrem. Epistola prima* (1728), *Epistola secunda* (1737), and *Epistola tertia* (1743). The standard Danish edition is the bilingual *Ludvig Holbergs tre levnedsbreve 1728–1743,* ed. and trans. by A. Kragelund, Copenhagen: Gad 1965.

[6]   *Ludvig Holberg's Memoirs*, p. 24.

[7]   Sven H. Rossel, "Ludvig Holberg: The Cosmopolitan. A Monographic Sketch," in *Ludvig Holberg. A European Writer*, ed. by Sven H. Rossel, Amsterdam: Rodopi 1994, p. 7.

[8]   Rossel, "Ludvig Holberg," p. 6.

the city as being, "like Noah's ark, the receptacle of all living creatures. Thither, as to common country, people of all nations, neighboring and remote, are constantly repairing."[9] This international exposure seems to have kindled Holberg's lifelong interest in travel, which took him throughout Europe and the British Isles, despite recurrent pecuniary difficulties. His travels brought their own reward, however, in broadening his intellectual and artistic horizons and providing him with material for his later work. Sven H. Rossel postulates that Holberg's travels, in particular his extended visits to England, were a major influence on the development of his literary abilities: "With Ludvig Holberg we encounter a figure who displays an insatiable appetite as a traveler, who 'does' almost all of Europe's cultural centers, and who *returns home* with an enormous intellectual enrichment."[10] Holberg summarized his *wanderlust* with the laconic remark, "The renowned author has led a stormy life. He has undertaken several journeys abroad even though he was without money."[11]

The position of penniless traveler was familiar to Holberg from his first major journey to Copenhagen to complete his studies at the university. Because of financial constraints, he completed his studies in about six months, then returned to Bergen to work as a private tutor. The work did not suit him, and so he returned to Copenhagen in the fall of 1703 for another few months of university study, earning degrees in philosophy and theology in April 1704 "with a good character, but an empty purse."[12] After another brief stint as a tutor in Bergen, Holberg began a period of extensive travel throughout Europe. To finance his initial journey to Holland, he explained, "I proceeded to turn everything I could collect into money. All my goods, chattels, and hereditaments, all my convertible property, in short, of what description soever, was sold, ceded, and alienated without remorse; like the alchemists, I endeavored to make gold from every thing."[13] Thus outfitted with 60 rix-dollars, Holberg bid farewell to Bergen for the last time and spent the next seven years primarily in the Netherlands, England, and Germany, before settling in Copenhagen in 1709.

Holberg's benefactors in Copenhagen sustained him financially as he embarked on his writing career. He became friends with several university professors, including Poul Vinding (1658–1712), professor of Greek, Christian Reitzer (1665–1736), professor of law, and Johann Burkhard Mencke (1674–1732), professor of history, all of whom helped to direct Holberg's nascent literary efforts.[14] While living at no cost in Borchs Collegium in Copenhagen, thanks to Vinding, Holberg published his first book, *Introduction to the History of the Leading European Countries*.[15] A generous scholarship to study theology allowed him to spend the years 1714 to 1716 in France and Italy. This journey, in particular with the exposure to modern French, Spanish, and Italian literature, proved to be decisive in shaping his literary style, as

---

9   *Ludvig Holberg's Memoirs*, p. 23.

10   Rossel, "Ludvig Holberg," p. 9.

11   Ibid., p. 9.

12   *Ludvig Holberg's Memoirs*, p. 30.

13   Ibid., p. 30.

14   Rossel, "Ludvig Holberg," p. 12–13.

15   Ludvig Holberg, *Ludvig Holbergs Introduction til de fornemste Europæiske Rigers Historier, Forstat Indtil disse sidste Tider, Med Et tilstræckeligt Register*, vols. 1–2, Copenhagen: Bornheinrich 1711–13.

he acknowledged in his memoirs: "I confess that I owe everything to French books; for by reading these I acquired the literary taste for which my works have obtained some character."[16] Nevertheless, his next book, published in 1715, was non-fiction, an *Introduction to the Science of Natural Law and the Law of Nations*,[17] dedicated to King Frederik IV, whereas his first book had been dedicated to the crown prince, the future King Christian VI. His first major literary work, the heroic-comic epic poem *Peder Paars*, appeared pseudonymously in 1719–20 and showcased not only many of the attributes that would become hallmarks of Holberg's literary style, in particular a satirical tone, classical allusions, and slapstick-style comedy, but also many of the characters who would later secure his legacy.[18]

Over the next several decades, Holberg achieved both an academic career and prolific literary output. Two years after his return to Copenhagen, Holberg finally received the professorship at the University of Copenhagen long promised him. Since professorships were awarded by seniority rather than academic qualifications, he had to content himself with a professorship in metaphysics, which he despised, before moving up to a position in Latin poetry in 1720 and finally history in 1730, where he at last felt competent and well-situated. In later years, he played a central role in university administration, serving as rector from 1735 to 1736 and as university bursar from 1737 to 1751. His writing falls into roughly three periods: historical and scientific writings during the 1710s, dramas during the 1720s, and then a return to historical and, increasingly, philosophical texts between 1730 and 1750. Some of his most notable works from the two later periods include *Jeppe of the Hill*,[19] *The Political Tinker*,[20] *Gert the Westphaler*,[21] *The Lying-In Room*,[22] *Jacob von Thybo or the Braggart Soldier*,[23] and *Erasmus Montanus or Rasmus Berg*,[24] as well as the prose texts *Niels Klim's Underground Journey*,[25] *Epistles*,[26] and *Moral Thoughts*.[27]

---

[16]   *Ludvig Holberg's Memoirs*, p. 216.

[17]   Ludvig Holberg, *Introduction til Naturens og Folke-rettens Kundskab*, Parts 1–2 in 1 volume, Copenhagen: Johan Kruse 1715.

[18]   Rossel, "Ludvig Holberg," p. 21.

[19]   Ludvig Holberg, *Jeppe paa Bjerget eller den forvandlede Bonde. Komedie i 5 Akter*, Copenhagen: Jul. Strandberg 1722.

[20]   Ludvig Holberg, *Den politiske Kandestøber*, Copenhagen: J.J. Høpffner 1722.

[21]   Ludvig Holberg, *Mester Gert Westphaler* (1722), vol. 1 in *Comoedier, sammenskrevne for den nye oprettede Danske Skue-Plads ved Hans Mickelsen, Borger og Indvaaner i Callundborg. Med Just Justesens Fortale*, vols. 1–2, Copenhagen: Trykt paa Autors Bekostning i Aarene 1723–24.

[22]   Ludvig Holberg, *Barselstuen* (1723), vol. 2 in *Comoedier, sammenskrevne for den nye oprettede Danske Skue-Plads ved Hans Mickelsen, Borger og Indvaaner i Callundborg. Med Just Justesens Fortale*.

[23]   Ludvig Holberg, *Jakob von Tyboe eller den stortalende Soldat*, Copenhagen 1723.

[24]   Ludvig Holberg, *Erasmus Montanus*, Copenhagen 1723.

[25]   Ludvig Holberg, *Nicolai Klimii iter subterraneum*, Copenhagen and Leipzig: Sumptibus Iacobi Preussii 1741.

[26]   Ludvig Holberg, *Epistler*, Copenhagen: Trykt paa Autors Bekostning 1748–54.

[27]   Ludvig Holberg, *Moralske Tanker*, Copenhagen: E.H. Berling 1744.

Holberg's continued involvement with academia alongside his dramatic writing was a wise choice, given the shifting winds of royal opinion toward the theater. When Holberg began writing dramas, the state of the Danish national theater was dire, relying primarily on traveling professional companies from abroad who performed highly dramatic historical events in a grotesque style that relied heavily on "outward, exaggerated effects, farcical elements, loud noises, and crude gestures,"[28] or French dramas in the original. While Holberg almost single-handedly accumulated a repertoire of Danish dramas for the new Danish theater, run by a Frenchman, in Lille Grønnegade during the 1720s, the royal court was one of the primary patrons, but this support varied according to the religious fervor of the individual monarch. Under King Frederik IV, the theater flourished but the great Copenhagen fire of 1728, which many people viewed as "God's punishment of a sinful city,"[29] helped to popularize pietistic religious views at court, which fostered correspondingly repressive policies toward public entertainment. In the mid-1730s, King Christian VI banned theater performances on holidays and Sundays; by 1738, actors and entertainers were not allowed to enter the country.[30] Under his son, Frederik V, however, whose regime Holberg described in a dedication to the king as "a life-loving regimen,"[31] theater performances were reinstated and Danish drama received a new lease on life when a new national theater was inaugurated in 1748.

It was neither in academia, however, nor on the stage that Holberg made either his fortune or his title. Having struggled for financial stability all of his life, he knew well the value of each coin. He lived frugally and stretched his university salary quite far, but he was also entrepreneurial in the marketing and sale of his own books and was able to amass a small fortune in this manner. His financial situation improved rapidly after 1730, when he began speculating on the stock market and in real estate. After buying two country estates, Brorupgård by Slagelse in 1740 and Tersløsegård near Sorø in 1745, he found himself not only the holder of a title, a position he had ridiculed in many of his comedies, but also a landlord, a role that he played conscientiously, implementing reforms for the benefit of his tenant farmers which also served his own ends. As he explained in his memoirs, "a prosperous peasant is generally also an industrious and competent householder, while a poor one is usually nothing more than a slothful and neglectful tenant."[32] The revenue from these estates qualified Holberg for a barony, which he obtained from the king in 1747. In 1737 he had announced his intention of "donating his fortune to the public for the advancement of the Danish language, which he did by agreeing to will his lands to historic Sorø Academy for its reestablishment as a center of Danish learning. Holberg died in Copenhagen on January 28, 1754 and was buried in the monastery chapel at Sorø, alongside several Danish kings.

---

28   Rossel, "Ludvig Holberg," p. 23.
29   Ibid., p. 8.
30   Ibid.
31   Quoted in ibid.
32   Ludvig Holberg, *Epistler*, vols. 1–8, ed. by F.J. Billeskov Jansen, Copenhagen: Hagerup 1944–55, vol. 1, p. 329.

Holberg's significance for Danish culture is difficult to overstate, particularly when one looks deeper than just at his popular dramas. For, in addition to providing centuries' worth of entertaining comedies and laying the foundation for Denmark's impressive theatrical tradition, Holberg demonstrated how literature could be used as a tool both to enhance international opinion of Dano-Norwegian culture and to shape the mentality of the citizens of the Dano-Norwegian kingdom. Rossel argues for Holberg's unprecedented achievements with regard to improving the quality and status of Danish literature:

> With his writings Holberg in fact raised a backward and provincial Dano-Norwegian culture with an almost nonexistent dramatic literature to a contemporary and international level. Holberg should rightly be seen, as he always has been, as the father of Danish and Norwegian literature, instrumental in opening the door for Denmark and Norway onto the rest of Europe.[33]

Holberg himself focused more on the domestic impact of his writings, congratulating himself that "our Danish plays have remoulded the common people of these kingdoms into another form and taught them to reason upon vices and virtues, about which many had previously very little idea."[34] His writings often aroused controversy, but always provoked critical thinking about social conditions. For example, his satirical text *Zille Hans-daughter's Gynaicologia or Defense of Womankind*[35] offered a "radical assertion for its time of women's equality not only with regard to education, but also in filling public office."[36] For centuries, scholars have struggled to categorize his ideological position. His fierce attacks on what he perceived as "affected" and "unnatural" ideas, including Catholicism, have led some scholars to characterize him as "radical," "anti-authoritarian," "progressive," and "democratic," while others point to his insistence on a centralized, rational form of government such as absolutism as evidence that he was, in fact, more "conservative," "reactionary," and "paternalistic."[37] Overarching these disagreements, however, is widespread consensus that Holberg was a highly critical thinker whose contributions to Danish intellectual life consist of more than just his comedic dramas.

Despite the popular acclaim that Holberg enjoys today, the reception of his works and ideas in Golden Age Copenhagen is more problematic and undoubtedly contributed to Kierkegaard's conscious opinion of Holberg. In a survey of Holberg's shifting reception and interpretation in Scandinavia across the centuries, Bent Holm notes that even though Holberg's comedies remained popular among the peasantry in the early nineteenth century, the Copenhagen elite either regarded him as an author for the lower classes or whitewashed his satirical and socially critical stances,

---

[33]   Rossel, "Ludvig Holberg," p. 39.
[34]   Quoted in Billeskov Jansen, "Holberg," p. 65.
[35]   Ludvig Holberg, *Zille Hans Dotters Gynaicologia eller Forsvars Skrift for Qvinde-Kiønnet*, Copenhagen: Joachim Wielandt 1720.
[36]   Rossel, "Ludvig Holberg," p. 22.
[37]   Bent Holm, "Ludvig Holberg and His Double: Holberg in Scandinavia," *Ludvig Holberg: A European Writer,* ed. by Sven H. Rossel, Amsterdam: Rodopi 1994, pp. 191–2.

transforming him into "a purely historical figure."[38] Holberg's down-to-earth attitude and earthy humor clashed with the idealistic, sanitized values of national Romanticism and his direct engagement with questions of political and social power struggles appeared vulgar and coarse in light of the Golden Age distaste for political involvement. Yet it is precisely this willingness to engage with unpopular but indispensable topics that Holberg had in common with that most prominent Golden Age misfit, Kierkegaard himself.

II. Kierkegaard's Indebtedness to Holberg

It is unclear exactly when Kierkegaard first encountered Holberg's works, possibly while a pupil at "Borgerdydskolen," but most certainly at the Royal Theater while a student at the University of Copenhagen in the late 1820s and 1830s. In his journal for the year 1834, he refers to several pieces by Holberg which were performed at the Royal Theater that spring, including *Jacob von Thyboe*, performed on April 23, 1834, and *The Fussy Man*, performed on March 14 and October 12, 1834.[39] In both a lengthy footnote in *Concluding Unscientific Postscript* and a journal entry from 1843, he mentions "Holberg's Ulysses, who was also the man of the hour," in reference to Holberg's comedy *Ulysses von Ithacia* (1725), which had not been performed at the Royal Theater since March 1835 but was included in the seven-volume collection of Holberg's comedies, *The Danish Theater*,[40] that Kierkegaard owned, along with copies of *Peder Paars* and *Niels Klim*,[41] as well as several biographical and reference works that discuss Holberg's life.

Kierkegaard readily acknowledged Holberg's foundational position in the Danish literary canon, in particular as a source of ideas for contemporary writers. In *Stages on Life's Way*, he cites Holberg, along with Holy Writ, as an impeccable reference for linguistic tradition, arguing, "When there is need, one should not shy away from using the descriptive terms that both the Bible and Holberg use."[42] In his journal in 1837, he describes Holberg as "our literary fountainhead,"[43] the source of Danish literature, and proposes conducting an experiment to determine, based on Holberg's comedic works, what people in different age groups find amusing. He reiterates this view in the reply he composed—but never published—to an attack on him in the *Humoristiske Intelligentsblade* in May 1836, in which he accuses Johannes Hage (1800–37), the editor of the newspaper *Fædrelandet,* of borrowing ideas from Holberg, among others, in an attempt to maintain the creativity of his work: "It isn't just at Holberg's much frequented pawnshop that he borrows on credit. It isn't just among well-known and unknown authors, no, it's even with friends and

---

38   Ibid., p. 203.
39   Billeskov Jansen, "Holberg," pp. 67–8.
40   Ludvig Holberg, *Den danske Skue-Plads, deelt Udi 7 Tomer*, Parts 1–7 in vols. 1–2, Copenhagen: J.J. Høpffner [1788] (*ASKB* 1566–1567).
41   Billeskov Jansen, "Holberg," p. 79.
42   *SKS* 6, 272 / *SLW*, 293.
43   *SKS* 17, 240, DD:55 / *KJN* 1, 231.

acquaintances!"[44] Yet Kierkegaard also found inspiration in Holberg's work for his own on at least one occasion. In his notebook from 1849, Kierkegaard explored the idea of writing a parody of a scene from Holberg's drama *The Happy Shipwreck*,[45] tentatively entitled "A Strange Encounter," in which two servants meet to discuss the curious discrepancy between the courage of the apostle Paul in the year 48 and the accolades accorded priests in 1848 for just talking about Paul's bravery.[46]

Kierkegaard occasionally used phrases and words from Holberg's works as well. In *The Concept of Anxiety*, Kierkegaard uses the term "Projektmagere," i.e., project makers,[47] a derogatory term often used by Holberg in the novel *Niels Klim* to denote individuals who consistently conceive of useless or impossible projects.[48] Aimed at a European audience, Holberg's novel appeared originally in Latin under the title *Nicolai Klimii Iter subterraneum* in 1741, but Kierkegaard, despite his fabled competency in Latin, apparently read it in Danish in Jens Baggesen's lively translation from 1789.[49] In his notebook in 1849, Kierkegaard refers to the pastry Niels Klim lost as he fell toward the center of the earth,[50] which is consistent with the Baggesen translation, although the original, and N.V. Dorph's 1841 translation, uses the word "*panem*" or "bread." In *Stages on Life's Way*, Kierkegaard uses the Latin expression "*lectori benevolo*" [to the willing reader], that Holberg used in the introduction to *Peder Paars* (1719–20).[51] Kierkegaard also uses the phrase "*mundus vult decipi*" on several occasions in his notebooks,[52] an expression about which Holberg recounted a historical anecdote in his *Several Comparative Histories and Deeds of Various Great Heroes*.[53] In the *Concluding Unscientific Postscript,* Kierkegaard uses the phrase "the world will not last until Easter," an expression which Holberg often used.[54]

In general, however, Kierkegaard's published works offer little material for an investigation of his indebtedness to Holberg, since most of Kierkegaard's explicit references to Holberg and his works occur in his journals, private correspondence, or footnotes to his published and unpublished works. These references range from brief, general asides, such as the comment in a journal entry from 1837, "This is something Holberg has so excellently perceived,"[55] to more detailed allusions to

---

44   *SKS* 17, 38, AA:21 / *KJN* 1, 33

45   Ludvig Holberg, *Det lykkelige Skibbrud*, Copenhagen 1724.

46   SKS 22, 176, NB12:60.a.

47   *SKS* 4, 230 / *PF*, 21.

48   Ludvig Holberg, *Niels Klims Underjordiske Reise. Efter Holbergs latinske Original*, trans. by Jens Baggesen, in *Jens Baggesens danske Værker*, vols. 1–12, ed. by the sons of the author and C.J. Boye, Copenhagen: Andreas Seidelin 1827–32, vol. 12, pp. 165–524, see pp. 387ff.

49   Billeskov Jansen, "Holberg," p. 80.

50   SKS 20, 418, NB14:128.

51   *SKS* 6, 11 / *SLW*, 4.

52   *SKS* 20, 40, NB:36. *SKS* 20, 47, NB:47.

53   See *Ludvig Holbergs udvalgte Skrifter*, vols. 1–21, ed. by Knud Lyhne Rahbek, Copenhagen: J.F. Schultz 1804–14, vol. 9, p. 86 (first edition, see Ludvig Holberg, *Adskillige store Heltes...sammenlignede Historier og Bedrifter*, Copenhagen: E.H. Berling 1739).

54   See *SKS* 7, 330 / *CUP1*, 362.

55   *SKS* 17, 47, AA:32 / *KJN* 1, 40.

specific characters in individual works, including a wide range of characters from the comedies as well as figures that appear in Holberg's historical works. On the basis of these entries, Billeskov Jansen asserts that Kierkegaard's relation to Holberg gradually transforms from identification with Holberg's characters, in particular the misunderstood protagonist of *The Fussy Man*, to appreciation for Holberg's ability to balance pathos and comedy through wit. After the *Corsair* affair, however, when Kierkegaard found himself the butt of the kind of jokes that pervade Holberg's comedies, he became more critical of Holberg's humor, noting in his journal in 1849: "Really, though, there is something low, simple-minded in most of Holberg's comedy...for it depends on the quite ordinary, human, teasing and guffawing malice."[56]

In the most significant instances where he refers to Holberg's works, Kierkegaard draws on Holberg's plays for examples to illustrate concepts with which he was currently grappling. One of the thematic areas in which Kierkegaard found Holberg most relevant regarded the relation between the comic and the tragic in drama. In his journal Kierkegaard speculated about the aesthetic paradox that might be created by the unexpected death of a ridiculous character, such as Jacob von Thyboe in Holberg's comedy of the same name: "Would Jacob von Thyboe, if we were to think of him dying by tripping over his spurs in the fifth act...become [a] traged[y]?"[57] The possibility of the tragic existing within comedy fascinated Kierkegaard and drew him to Holberg's plays, in particular *Erasmus Montanus.* On January 19, 1835, Kierkegaard noted in his journal, "The proximity of the tragic to the comic (an observation particularly attributable to Holberg's use of comedy—for example his *Jeppe paa Bjerget* [Jeppe of the Hill], *Erasmus Montanus*, *Den Stundesløse* [The Fussy Man], etc.)—seems to account also for the fact that a person can *laugh until he begins to cry.*"[58] Despite or perhaps precisely because of Kierkegaard's failure to master the genre of dramatic comedy, he looked to Holberg for the incarnation of his own theoretical ideas. Self-reflection is another area where Holberg's characters provided the framework for Kierkegaard's thoughts. In connection with his examination of himself as a philosopher in the *Concluding Unscientific Postscript*, Kierkegaard muses: "Thus abstract thinking helps me with my immortality by killing me as a particular existing individual and then making me immortal and therefore helps somewhat as in Holberg the doctor took the patient's life with his medicine—but also drove out the fever."[59]

Yet the key to the mentoring relationship between Holberg and Kierkegaard can perhaps best be found in Kierkegaard's attitude toward Holberg himself, as revealed in textual references which confirm his respect for Holberg's rhetorical acumen and suggest that he was not unaware of the similarities between them and their self-selected tasks of showing society the error of its ways. In the journal entry "Something about Hamann" from 1837, Kierkegaard notes:

---

[56]   *SKS* 22, 416, NB14:126; Billeskov Jansen, "Holberg," p. 81.
[57]   *Pap.* I A 25 / *JP* 4, 4822. See also *Pap.* I A 209 / *JP* 4, 4824 for a similar comment.
[58]   *Pap.* I A 34 / *JP* 4, 4823.
[59]   *SKS* 7, 275 / *CUP1*, 302.

> I hope furthermore that it will be abundantly evident that every man who in the real sense is to fulfill an historical epoch must always begin polemically, precisely because a subsequent stage is not the pure and simple consequences of what has gone before. Wasn't this the case with Holberg? with Goethe? with Kant, etc. etc.?[60]

Kierkegaard's categorization of Holberg, together with Goethe and Kant, as a "man who is...to fulfill an historical epoch" conveys his admiration for Holberg's abilities and significance, as well as his familiarity with Holberg's biography and writings outside of his comedies. The public display of Holberg's polemical skills to which Kierkegaard is most likely referring in this passage occurred in 1719, at the beginning of Holberg's career, when he was accused of having plagiarized his first book, *Introduction to the History of the Leading European Countries*, by Andreas Hojer (1690–1739), a doctor, lawyer, and historian in Schleswig and author of *A Brief History of Denmark*.[61] Over the course of the exchange of accusations and polemical arguments, Holberg discovered his gift for writing satire. In his memoirs, he explains, "In replying to a satirical production, I became a satirist myself,"[62] a skill which would serve him well in his dramatic and poetic writing. Kierkegaard may have identified with Holberg's sentiment, as he too discovered his polemical talent in the exercise of it, though his satirical works, unlike Holberg's, did not generally take the form of comedic dramas and poems, but rather essays.

Holberg and Kierkegaard shared not only a fondness for satire and a keen recognition of its effectiveness, but also a deep investment in empowering their audiences, even at their own expense. Like Kierkegaard, Holberg used pseudonyms on several occasions, not because he could really expect to conceal his authorship of particular texts from the tight-knit intellectual circles in Copenhagen, but because of the rhetorical possibilities such a move made possible, in particular the opportunity of discussing his own works from the perspective of an observer and thus reaching his audience on a different level than in the work itself. Holberg's first major literary works, *Peder Paars*[63] and *Four Satirical Poems* with *Two Prefaces* as well as *Zille Hans-Daughter's Defense of Womankind*[64] were published under the pseudonym Hans Mikkelsen and struck a deliberately provocative tone. *Peder Paars* is both a parody of Virgil's *Aeneid* and a satire of Danish society, as seen in microcosmic form on the island of Anholt, while the *Four Satirical Poems* includes a *Critique of Peder Paars*,[65] in which Holberg defends his own satirical poem "by stressing, in perfect

---

[60]   *SKS* 17, 209, CC:25 / *KJN* 1, 200.
[61]   [Andreas Hojer], *Andreæ Hojern Kurtzgefasste Dännemärckische Geschichte: Vom Anfang dieses mächtigen Reichs Bis zum Ausgang des XVII. Seculi; Aus den bewährtesten Scribenten zu mehrerer Deutlichkeit in Fragen und Antworten verfasset, Und mit nöthigen Allegationibus versehen*, Flensburg: Bosseck 1719.
[62]   *Ludvig Holberg's Memoirs*, p. 99.
[63]   Ludvig Holberg, *Peder Pars: poema heroica-comicum*, Copenhagen: P.J. Phoenixberg 1720.
[64]   Ludvig Holberg, *Hans Mikkelsens fire Skiemte-Digte med Tvende Fortaler, samt Sille Hans Dotters Forsvars-Skrift for Qvinde-Kiønned*, Copenhagen: Joachim Wielandt 1722.
[65]   Ibid.

accordance with rationalism, its usefulness."[66] In the resulting uproar, Holberg drew intense criticism and alienated some of his friends,[67] an experience that Kierkegaard would repeat to his own chagrin during the *Corsair* affair.

Perhaps as a result of such personal experiences with public scorn and humiliation, both Kierkegaard and Holberg were, understandably, skeptical about the wholesale democratization of political power, though not of the necessary intellectual emancipation of the common man. Holberg was a staunch supporter of Denmark's absolutist political system, but his comedies exhibit distinctly anti-aristocratic leanings as well, suggesting that his support of the privileged elite was neither unqualified nor uncritical. He believed in the necessity of a firm hand at the helm of the ship of state, but with the support of the people, not at their expense. Holberg's enthusiasm for a rational, paternalistic government was moderated by his basic trust in human nature, a conviction that Kierkegaard shared, though Kierkegaard's trust in the individual was tempered by his fear of the undifferentiated crowd. Billeskov Jansen draws attention to Kierkegaard's journal entry about *Erasmus Montanus* on December 2, 1837 where he laments, "I weep when I see or read Erasmus Montanus; he is right and is subdued by *the mass*. Yes, that is the point. When every confirmed glutton is given the franchise, when plurality of votes decides the issues—is not one then subdued by the mass, by fatheads?"[68] However, this fear of mob rule did not dissuade either Kierkegaard or Holberg from investing himself in bringing about the intellectual and philosophical empowerment of the common man in Denmark. On the contrary, they regarded their efforts as integral to the liberation of the individual from the unthinking masses.

Both Kierkegaard and Holberg were educated in the classical tradition and drew on antiquity for inspiration, but they were also instrumental in the modernization of Danish literature and intellectual culture. Their works are replete with references to biblical and classical literature, but they are also, with a few strategic exceptions on Holberg's part, written in Danish, which, despite the century separating Holberg's dramas and Kierkegaard's doctoral dissertation, was still revolutionary. Holberg helped to establish Danish as a literary language and, in turn, Kierkegaard built on this foundation to make Danish capable of conveying complex philosophical concepts, in particular Socratic irony and dialectical thinking, of which Holberg had also made use, though not as systematically.

Socrates thus represents one of the most compelling links between Holberg and Kierkegaard, guiding them both to develop methods of indirect communication that would motivate their listeners to reach their own conclusions and act on them. Each was attracted to indirect communication for different reasons, as Birgit Bertung explains, "Kierkegaard because he believed that existential truths could not be transmitted to others directly, and Holberg because he believed that 'the moral is the most effective thing and has the greatest effect.' "[69] Yet they shared the conviction that it is the philosopher's task to function as a teacher; Holberg explained, "it is in this regard

---

[66]   Rossel, "Ludvig Holberg," p. 22.
[67]   *Ludvig Holberg's Memoirs*, p. 100.
[68]   Billeskov Jansen, "Holberg," p. 70.
[69]   Bertung, "Kierkegaard og Holberg," p. 26, my translation.

that I recommend paradoxical opinions."[70] To this end, both employed a wide range of genres and narrative styles to get their message across to the common man. For example, although Holberg relied heavily on comedies to demonstrate the follies and virtues he wanted to make his audience aware of, he also tried his hand at fables and parables, much like those Kierkegaard made use of in his attack on Christendom.

Although Holberg's name is rarely mentioned in connection with Kierkegaard's religious writings, religion was in fact one of the areas where their interests overlapped, though there are few indications of Kierkegaard having studied Holberg's theological writings. Billeskov Jansen attempts to explain this gap by suggesting that Kierkegaard was simply unfamiliar with Holberg's philosophical and historical works, particularly *Moral Thoughts* and *Epistles*.[71] However, there are still several points at which Kierkegaard draws on Holberg to legitimize his own struggle against the Danish State Church, suggesting that Kierkegaard regarded Holberg as a compatriot in his struggle to facilitate the emancipation of the minds and souls of the Danish people. In " 'Guilty?'/'Not Guilty?' " in *Stages on Life's Way,* for example, Kierkegaard refers to both Holberg's *General History of the Church*[72] and his *Several Comparative Histories and Deeds of Various Great Heroes*.[73] In both cases, Kierkegaard selects examples of pagans whose relationship to Christianity is strained by the excesses of Christendom. From the former, Kierkegaard cites the story of King Radbodus of the Goths (died 719) who decided against being baptized by the missionary Wulfranus in order to be together with his pagan, and hence damned, forefathers in the afterlife. From the latter work, he recounts the fear of Spanish brutality among the native peoples of Mexico that led them to reject the Christian heaven if Spaniards would be there as well.[74] Although the theological content of these examples is vanishingly small, the consistency is clear between Holberg's critical account of Europe's checkered religious history and Kierkegaard's desperate determination to challenge the hegemony of the ecclesiastical culture rooted in that history.

In 1851, Kierkegaard wrote that "we Danes live approximately in such a way that Holberg is the wisdom we live by."[75] However tongue-in-cheek this comment might have been intended, it brings into focus the fact that Kierkegaard's indebtedness to Holberg is twofold: first, as a member of the Danish culture to which Holberg contributed so much; and second, as an author trying to shape his own ideas and looking to his predecessors for inspiration. The multiplicity of ways and contexts in which Kierkegaard encountered Holberg testifies to the enduring effectiveness of Holberg's strategy of indirect communication, which Kierkegaard perfected. It would be impossible to unravel the knot of allusions and affinities between Kierkegaard

---

[70]   Ludvig Holberg, *Moralske Tanker*, ed. by F.J. Billeskov Jansen, Copenhagen: H. Hagerup 1943, p. 24.

[71]   Billeskov Jansen, "Holberg," p. 76.

[72]   Ludvig Holberg, *Almindelig Kirke-Historie. Fra Christendomens første Begyndelse, Til Lutheri Reformation, Med nogle Anmærkninger Over de udi Historien omtalte Cyclis og Aars-Beregninger*, vols. 1–2, Copenhagen: Trykt udi Hans Kongel. Majestaets og Universitets Bogtrykkerie, af Johann Georg Høpffner 1738.

[73]   *SKS* 6, 241 / *SLW*, 259.

[74]   Ibid.

[75]   Billeskov Jansen, "Holberg," p. 81.

and Holberg in such a way as to determine precisely how and when Holberg's works might have influenced Kierkegaard, but such an exercise is unnecessary, for the deed is done either way. Holberg and Kierkegaard shared enough values, ideas, techniques, and opinions to complement each other well, regardless of whether Holberg's mentoring role in Kierkegaard's development is explicitly acknowledged or merely implied.

Bibliography

I. Holberg's Works in The Auction Catalogue *of Kierkegaard's Library*

Den danske Skue-Plads, deelt Udi 7 Tomer, tomes 1–7 in vols. 1–2, Copenhagen: J.J. Høpffner [1788] (*ASKB* 1566–1567).

II. Works in The Auction Catalogue *of Kierkegaard's Library that Discuss Holberg*

[Becker, Karl Friedrich], *Karl Friedrich Beckers Verdenshistorie, omarbeidet af Johan Gottfried Woltmann*, vols. 1–12, trans. by J. Riise, Copenhagen: Fr. Brummer 1822–29, vol. 10, p. 76 (*ASKB* 1972–1983).

Flögel, Karl Friedrich, *Geschichte der komischen Litteratur*, vols. 1–4, Liegnitz and Leipzig: David Siegert 1784–87, vol. 3, pp. 593–8; vol. 4, pp. 346–7 (*ASKB* 1396–1399).

Heiberg, Johan Ludvig, "Lyrisk Poesie," in *Intelligensblade*, vol. 3, nos. 25–6, 1843, pp. 25–72, see pp. 44–5 (*ASKB* U 56).

—— *Prosaiske Skrifter*, vol. 3, Copenhagen: J.H. Schubothes Boghandling 1843 (vol. 3, in Johan Ludvig Heiberg, *Prosaiske Skrifter*, vols. 1–3, Copenhagen: J.H. Schubothe 1841–43 which is part of *Johan Ludvig Heiberg's Samlede Skrifter* consisting of *Skuespil*, vols. 1–7, Copenhagen: J.H. Schubothe 1833–41 and *Digte og Fortællinger*, vols. 1–2, Copenhagen: J.H. Schubothe 1834–35), pp. 306–7; pp. 380–1 (*ASKB* 1560).

Møller, Jens, "Holbergs Selvbekjendelse om Dobbelthed i hans Stiil og Charakteer, mon grundet?," *Nyt theologisk Bibliothek*, vols. 1–20, ed. by Jens Møller, Copenhagen: Andreas Seidelin 1821–32, vol. 11, 1827, pp. 284–9 (*ASKB* 336–345).

Munthe, Eiler Chr. K., *De vigtigste indenlandske Tildragelser og de mærkeligste danske og norske Personers Levnetsbeskrivelser, fra de ældste Tider til vore Dage. En Læse- og Lærebog i Fædrelandets Historie for Begyndere og Ustuderede*, 5th revised ed., Copenhagen: Andreas Seidelin 1837, pp. 300–6 (*ASKB* 2012).

Overskou, Thomas, *Den danske Skueplads, i dens Historie, fra de første Spor af danske Skuespil indtil vor Tid*, vols. 1–7, Copenhagen: Samfundet til den danske Literaturs Fremme 1854–76, vol. 1, 1854, p. 140 [Kierkegaard owned only vol. 1; vols. 6–7 were entitled *Den kongelig danske Skuepladses Historie, fra dens Overdragelse til Staten i 1849 indtil 1874. Efter Forfatterens Død fuldført af Edgar Collin*, 1874–76] (*ASKB* 1395).

[Richter, Johann Paul Friedrich], Jean Paul, *Vorschule der Aesthetik nebst einigen Vorlesungen in Leipzig über die Parteien der Zeit*, vols. 1–3, 2nd revised ed., Stuttgart and Tübingen: J.G. Cotta 1813, vol. 1, p. 699 (*ASKB* 1381–1383).

Schlegel, August Wilhelm, *Ueber dramatische Kunst und Litteratur. Vorlesungen*, vols. 1–2 [vol. 2 in 2 Parts], Heidelberg: Mohr und Zimmer 1809–11, vol. 2.2, p. 384 (*ASKB* 1392–1394).

Steffens, Henrich, *Was ich erlebte. Aus der Erinnerung niedergeschrieben*, vols. 1–10, Breslau: Josef Max und Comp. 1840–44, vol. 2, pp. 65–8; pp. 73–6; vol. 4, p. 196; vol. 5, pp. 63–4; pp. 97–8 (*ASKB* 1834–1843).

Thomsen, Grimur, *Om den nyfranske Poesi, et Forsøg til Besvarelse af Universitetets æsthetiske Priisspørgsmaal for 1841: "Har Smag og Sands for Poesi gjort Frem- eller Tilbageskridt i Frankrig i de sidste Tider og hvilken er Aarsagen?,"* Copenhagen: Wahlske Boghandlings Forlag 1843, p. 5 (*ASKB* 1390).

Thortsen, Carl Adolph, *Historisk Udsigt over den danske Litteratur indtil Aar 1814*, Copenhagen: C.A. Reitzel 1839, pp. 42–55 (*ASKB* 970).

III. Secondary Literature on Kierkegaard's Relation to Holberg

Bertung, Birgit, "Kierkegaard og Holberg—i meddelelsesdialektisk perspektiv," in *Kierkegaard inspiration. En antologi*, ed. by Birgit Bertung, Paul Müller, Fritz Norman, and Julia Watkin, Copenhagen: C.A. Reitzel 1991 (*Søren Kierkegaard Selskabets Populære Skrifter*, vol. 20), pp. 26–34.

Billeskov Jansen, F.J., "Holberg," in *Kierkegaard Literary Miscellany*, ed. by Niels Thulstrup and Marie Mikulová Thulstrup, Copenhagen: C.A. Reitzel 1981 (*Bibliotheca Kierkegaardiana*, vol. 9), pp. 65–82.

Henningsen, Bernd, *Die Politik des Einzelnen. Studien zur Genese der skandinavischen Ziviltheologie. Ludvig Holberg, Søren Kierkegaard, N.F.S. Grundtvig*, Göttingen: Vandenhoeck & Ruprecht 1977.

Holm, Søren, "Holberg, Grundtvig, Kierkegaard, drei dänische Denker," *Neue Zeitschrift für systematische Theologie*, vol. 7, 1965, pp. 49–61.

Lippitt, John, *Humour and Irony in Kierkegaard's Thought*, London: Macmillan 2000, pp. 128–30; p. 133.

Alphonse de Lamartine:

The Movement *"en masse"* versus the Individual Choice

Ingrid Basso

When on September 30, 1832, during Lamartine's *voyage en Orient*, Lady Stanhope asked the poet-diplomat and politician whether he was an aristocrat,[1] the latter replied that he was neither an aristocrat nor a democrat:

> I am neither on the side of the lower class nor on the side of the upper class, but am simply for the whole of humanity. I think that the virtue of perfecting humanity is exclusive neither to the aristocratic institutions nor to the democratic ones. This virtue lies simply in a divine morality, fruit of a perfect religion.[2]

The issue at stake here is what the poet might have meant by "perfect religion," and, concomitantly, what relationship between politics and religion this notion might have, or should have, implied. It is essential to consider this point if one is to grasp, in all its profundity, the fundamental connection between the three inseparable aspects that constitute the figure of Lamartine: poetry, religion, and politics. These are, indeed, the three sides of a unique spiritual project.

Once one has properly understood the theoretical outlines of this idea, it will also be possible to appreciate and assess accurately the few words that Kierkegaard dedicated to this contemporary, whose authorship he seems to have known only through the latter's historical-political work of 1849,[3] the *Histoire de la Révolution*

---

[1]   Lady Hester Lucy Stanhope (1776–1839) was the eccentric niece and confidante of William Pitt. After growing increasingly intolerant of the restrictions of ordinary society, she left England definitively for the Levant in 1810, where she settled down in the village of Djouni, on the slopes of Mount Lebanon, among the Druze. Because of her fearlessness and her remarkable insight into human character, she soon became the point of reference for the Europeans traveling through the East. She was held to be a clairvoyant.

[2]   Alphonse de Lamartine, *Voyage en Orient*, in *Oeuvres Complètes de Lamartine. Édition complète en un volume*, Brussels: Wahlen 1836, p. 69.

[3]   As Nelly Viallaneix points out in her article "Kierkegaard, juge de Lamartine," in *Lamartine. Le Livre du Centenaire*, ed. by Paul Viallaneix, Paris: Flammarion 1971, pp. 281–8. This seems to be the only work that specifically examines the relationship between these two authors. Kierkegaard only considered Lamartine as a historian and politician, completely ignoring the poet (p. 284). This is true, although one could add that, in some way, it is possible to grasp the deep meaning of his poetics through the reading of Lamartine's

de 1848.[4] This book was most famous and much discussed by the intellectuals of
Europe in those hard times when France held the stage. The work was also translated
and published in the same year in Danish as a *feuilleton* in the newspaper *Berlingske
Tidende.*[5]

I. Lamartine's Ideal-Real Project

The political "mission" of Lamartine reached its peak, and then its end, with the
French Revolution of 1848, when, during the so-called Second Republic, Lamartine
took active part in the government as Minister for Foreign Affairs—shortly before
the President of the Republic, the prince Louis Napoleon, re-established the empire
(the "Second Empire") in a *coup d'état*, and assumed the name Napoleon III.

In an age in which "the only omnipotent conspirator in modern States is public
opinion,"[6] the poet understood well what great power words could wield if they
were strongly connected with precise ideas and a grand project. Lamartine had such
a project in mind, and—in line with the legendary Romantic figure of the *poète
législateur*—he also chose to become just such a compound being: to connect the
ideal power of the word with the real results of actions. In this way, the aristocratic, ex-
monarchic poet began working to realize his idea of a "conservative and progressive
Republic, the only one durable, the only one possible, —may it cause to bloom forth
what is germinant in this kind of institution—the morality of the people and the
realm of God."[7] This apparent self-contradiction, the "conservative and progressive
Republic," must be explained in terms of a specific point of view, which is that of
"harmony": a fundamental principle that governs both Lamartine's poetry and his

---

historical-political works. One can also say that if Kierkegaard did not consider Lamartine
from an aesthetic point of view, this was merely for contingent reasons: one might indeed
notice that the success of Lamartine's poetical works occurred very early and was almost
exclusively limited to his *Méditations Poétiques*, edited in 1820, a work which was greeted
in a triumphal way, but which also remained an isolated instance, a kind of miracle which
did not repeat itself. Marius-François Guyard, the editor of the first edition of Lamartine's
poetical works in the well-known and prestigious French library editions of *Bibliothèque de
La Pléiade* by Gallimard (*Lamartine. Oeuvres poétiques complètes*, ed. by Marius-François
Guyard, Paris: Gallimard 1963), even states that after 1832, when Lamartine's poetical vein
was already exhausted, he fell into financial straits and in addition lost his beloved ten-
year-old daughter Julie; he threw himself into politics, which represented for him a kind of
divertissement (p. XIII).

[4]   Alphonse de Lamartine, *Histoire de la Révolution de 1848*, vols. 1–2, Brussels and
Leipzig: Charles Muquardt 1849.

[5]   See Alphonse de Lamartine, *Den franske Revolutions Historie i 1848*, vols. 1–2,
Copenhagen 1850–51. (Originally published in *Berlingske Tidende* from the July 27 to
September 20 (nos. 176–223) and from October 16 (no. 245) onward.)

[6]   Lamartine, *Histoire de la Révolution de 1848*, Tome 1, Book II, Chapter VII, p. 46.
(English translation: *History of the French Revolution of 1848*, trans. by Francis A. Durivage
and William S. Chase, Boston: Phillips Sampson & Company 1854, p. 36.)

[7]   Lamartine, *Histoire de la Révolution de 1848*, Tome II, Book XV, Chapter XXII,
p. 345. (*History of the French Revolution of 1848*, p. 270.)

political ideas,[8] and which is connected to a religious conception. In this sense, it is possible to speak of Lamartine's political action in terms of a "mission," for this is precisely how he intended it.

This can already be seen in 1831, in a brochure titled *Sur la politique rationelle*.[9] Here Lamartine's title already expresses his program:

> Humanity is young, its social form is old, and it is falling to pieces; immortal chrysalis, it laboriously goes out from its primitive covering, to wear its virile clothes, the form of its maturity. Here is the truth! We live in one of the strongest ages that humanity has to pass through in order to advance towards the aim of its divine destination, to an epoch of renewal and social transformation like, maybe, the evangelical one.[10]

With these words the poet did not mean to declare "theocratic rule" to be necessary. On the contrary, Lamartine was an absolute supporter of the firm and definitive separation of church and state, in order to obtain the emancipation of the conscience of the human race by the complete liberty of religious creeds.[11] What is meant, rather, is that the state is a kind of unnecessary and bad intermediary between God and human consciousness. Moreover, Lamartine also saw Catholic institutions as obstacles interposed between human beings and God, in a particular sense: "I would like to see religion simply between God and men. The governments profane it when they use it like an instrument."[12]

What Lamartine could not accept, and what he saw as an obstacle, was not the church in the sense of a community (which, from a Kierkegaardian point of view—where the single individual is the protagonist of the religious life—could have represented a weakening of the particular relationship between man and God), but rather the rules of the Catholic Church, which, in his opinion, had no rational foundation, for example, priestly celibacy,[13] monastic life, or the *amulettes catholiques*, such as votive altars, clerical dresses, and other holy objects, all of

---

[8]   On the fundamental importance of this concept see, for example, Aurélie Loiseleur, *L'harmonie selon Lamartine. Utopie d'un lieu commun*, Paris: Honoré Champion Éditeur 2005, where the principle of harmony is viewed especially from the poetical-religious point of view. *Harmonies poétiques et religieuse* was indeed also the title of Lamartine's collected poems of 1830, Paris: Gosselin. As we will show, the same principle governs the *three* connected aspects of poetry, religion and politics, connecting them in a project, which actually dates back to 1830.

[9]   See Alphonse de Lamartine, *Sur la politique rationelle*, Paris: Gosselin 1831, a work which takes the form of a letter to the director of the *Revue europénne*.

[10]   Ibid., p. 19.

[11]   See, for example, Lamartine, *Histoire de la Révolution de 1848*, Tome I, Book II, Chapter XIII, pp. 55–6. (*History of the French Revolution of 1848*, p. 43.)

[12]   Letter to de Fontenay (April 20, 1826), in *Correspondance de Lamartine*, vols. 1–4, ed. by Valentine de Lamartine, Paris: Hachette 1881–82, vol. 2, p. 336; quoted by Paul Bénichou, "Lamartine," in his *Les mages romantiques*, Paris: Gallimard 1988, p. 24.

[13]   On the criticism of this point see especially the poem *Jocelyn: Episode*, Paris: Gosselin et Furne 1836.

which Lamartine deemed repugnant to reason because they were contrary to nature.[14] Reason is the principle that, in Lamartine's view, binds humanity and God; and it is through the faculty of reason that a political-religious project must be elaborated. In Lamartine's words, reason is indeed "the reflection of God upon the human race," so that "the sovereignty of reason was the sovereignty of God,"[15] because God gave to all men of goodwill the same language of reason.[16] On this view, liberty is not a goal in its own right, but is the condition for exercising reason in order to reach a higher destination, namely, the realization of a particular kind of Republic. In his 1849 work on the 1848 Revolution in France, Lamartine describes this Republic as one in which the maturity of all humanity is embodied in a democracy that is only *gradually* reached. For Lamartine feared the sudden movements of the masses without a common program, venturing into the unknown, while governed only by irrational principles.[17] The danger of a blind movement, first and foremost, is that the idea of a republic could degrade into that of a mere and futile utopia. In Lamartine's opinion, indeed, this was the lot of all extreme democratic theories that pretend to reach social equality immediately by abolishing private property, as, for example, in Louis Blanc's (1811–82) movement.[18] Lamartine defines himself as "sensible of the advantage of property," since this is "the true civic right of modern times": in this sense he argues for the respect of the proprietors, merchants and working men, who are "elevated by labor and inheritance to dignity and prosperity,"[19] and he strongly criticizes the excesses of these ideological positions which would pretend to dispossess some in order to enrich others. One can now understand better what Lamartine meant when he wrote of a "conservative and progressive Republic":

---

[14]   On this point see, for example, Henri Guillemin, *Le "Jocelyn" de Lamartine*, Paris: Boivin 1936, p. 219, and in general also Guillemin, *Lamartine et le Catholicisme*, n.p. 1934. On the affinity between Lamartine's point of view on religion and Protestantism one can see Marguerite Maurice, "Lamartine et le protestantisme," in *Actes du cinquantième Congrès de l'A.B.S.S.*, Tome I: *Quatrièmes journées d'études Lamartiniennes, 25 au 27 mai 1979)*, Mâcon: Association Bourguignonne des Sociétés Savantes 1979, pp. 43–52. Among other things it is interesting to notice—as M. Maurice informs (ibid., p. 48)—that Lamartine's writings had been translated into German by two famous personalities of the protestant bourgeoisie of Württemberg, educated at the seminary of Liberal Theology of Tübingen: Georges Herwegh (1817–55) and Gustav Swab (1792–1850). The first translated a complete edition of Lamartine's works, the second published between 1836 and 1840 some detailed analysis of Lamartine's *Jocelyn* and *Chute d'un ange* (Brussels: Mary-Müller 1838), writings which were put on the Index in Rome respectively in 1836 and 1838.
[15]   Lamartine, *Histoire de la Révolution de 1848*, Tome I, Book. II, Chapter XII, p. 55. (*History of the French Revolution of 1848*, p. 41.)
[16]   See, for example, Lamartine, *Histoire de la Révolution de 1848*, Tome I, Book II, Chapter XII, pp. 52–3. (*History of the French Revolution of 1848*, p. 41.)
[17]   See Lamartine, *Histoire de la Révolution de 1848*, Tome I, Book I, Chapter I, pp. 1ff. (*History of the French Revolution of 1848*, pp. 1ff.)
[18]   Lamartine, *Histoire de la Révolution de 1848*, Tome I, Book II, Chapter XVI, p. 62. (*History of the French Revolution of 1848*, p. 48.)
[19]   Lamartine, *Histoire de la Révolution de 1848*, Tome I, Book II, Chapter XII, p. 54. (*History of the French Revolution of 1848*, p. 42.)

The political principles of Lamartine[20] were those of the eternal truth of which the gospel is a page, the equality of men in the eyes of God, realized on earth by those laws and forms of government which give to the greatest number, and presently to all citizens, the most equal share of personal participation in the government, and thence eventually in the moral and material benefits of human society.[21]

So, these laws and the forms of government should be suggested by that universal reason which is superior to the brutal sovereignty of numbers: the reason is the reflection of God upon the human race that means "the sovereignty of reason is the sovereignty of God."[22] In this sense Lamartine points out as chimerical the violent equalization of social conditions.

In this view, one must note certain theoretical assumptions: in order to reach its maturity, the development of society should follow a gradual process, which is that of the maturation of *universal* (divine) reason,[23] and this reason is embodied both in the entire community and in the single individual, to different degrees. This means that this process of development is *single*: it can slow down in its course, or endure an arbitrary acceleration—which is precisely, in Lamartine's view, what constitutes

---

[20]   Lamartine writes about his own opinions using the third person: Kierkegaard in a passage of his journals (in 1849) in fact criticizes this style, accusing the poet of affectation and, moreover, of childishness. Then, he also states that the final result of this style is comical. See *SKS* 22, 279, NB13:12 / *JP* 1, 72: "We cannot find a better parody of antiquity and its use of the third person than Lamartine's speech in the third person about himself. It is completely improper. Stimulated to the point of lyrical reflection, Lamartine takes up all these things— and yet talks in the third person. This is affectation. Yes, he goes so far—and this has a kind of esthetic worth—as to engage in mimicry. He declares: Thereupon Lamartine said with a look of...etc. Here Lamartine has really made a kind of discovery; he has discovered what is absolutely impossible to say in the third person, for one himself cannot possibly know it. It becomes altogether comic and reminds us of Charles in *The First Love*, who also narrates his life in the third person. To use the third person is either—at a certain age a child talks in the third person, simply because the child is still not a person—or it is an eminence which is more than a person, a person who himself is the event. Anything between the two becomes comic if the third person is used."

[21]   Lamartine, *Histoire de la Révolution de 1848*, Tome I, Book II, Chapter XII, pp. 52–3. (*History of the French Revolution of 1848*, p. 41.)

[22]   Ibid.

[23]   Lamartine frequently compares the development of the spiritual growth of the community with the organic development of the life in the vegetable realm as well as the physical life of human beings; see, for example, the very beginning of his *Histoire de la Révolution de 1848*, Tome I, Book I, Chapter I, p. 1. (*History of the French Revolution of 1848*, p. 1.): "The revolutions of the human mind are slow, like the eras of the life of nations. They resemble the phenomena of vegetation, which enlarges the plant without the naked eye being able to measure its growth during its development. God has proportioned this period of growth, in all beings, to the period of duration which he assigns them. Men, who are to live a hundred years, continue growing till the age of twenty-five, and even upwards. Nations, which are to live two or three thousand years, have revolutions of development, of infancy, youth, manhood, and lastly old age, which do not embrace fewer than two or three centuries. The difficulty with the vulgar, in respect to these convulsive phenomena of popular revolutions, is to distinguish crises of growth from crises of decadence, youth from old age, life from death."

revolutions—all of which define the particular history of different peoples. Only a gradual development of institutions, through a "rational" politics, towards an equilibrated democracy can ensure the stability of the institutions themselves; every sudden "speeding up" will only lead to an equally strong sudden shift. Lamartine, indeed, defines the political reaction metaphorically, as an "irregular ballistic regression," which is to say the recoil of a gun:

> Political reactions are nothing but this recoil of guns in artillery. Reactions are the recoil of ideas. It seems as if the human mind, stunned, as it were, by the new truths which revolutions, accomplished in its name, have launched upon the world, falls back and retires basely from the ground which it has conquered....[24]

Thus, beyond the inconstant movement of history, beyond the unconscious, fickle wishes of the crowds, Lamartine believes that he can nevertheless catch sight of Intelligence, the Reason that is hidden from most people. Accordingly—because of this faculty—he imagines himself as a kind of educator of the people. Lamartine considers himself a special man, chosen by Divine Providence; in this sense, his political role is simply a "mission." Likewise, his poetical talent, his ability to use words well, is similarly a sign that God has decided to make him into an instrument of his Word on earth. That is why he claims about himself that he has "the instinct of the masses,"[25] which is in his mind his only political virtue: he can feel what the masses feel and what they wish to do, even if they keep silent. He even compares the law of the sociability to the law that Newton found in the spheres, "the law of unity and power," so he can easily conclude as a Romantic physicist of society:

---

[24]   Lamartine, *Histoire de la Révolution de 1848*, Tome I, Book I, Chapter XVI, p. 25. (*History of the French Revolution of 1848*, p. 20.)

[25]   Letter to his friend Aymon de Virieu (April 1, 1828), in *Correspondance de Lamartine*, vol. 3, p. 89. The poet wrote the same—"*Croyez-moi bien, j'ai l'instinct des masses*"—in a letter to his father in 1834 (January 9 and 17), in *Correspondance générale de 1830 à 1848*, vols. 1–2, ed. by Maurice Levaillant, Paris: Droz and Lille-Geneva: Giard 1943–48, vol. 2, pp. 5–12. About this point see also *Jocelyn*, page of his diary dated February 28, 1793, in *Œuvres poétiques complètes*, ed. by M.-F. Guyard, pp. 596–7, where the object of author's consideration is now the French Revolution of 1789: "I pass my sleepless nights thinking, trying to decipher the abyss of the revolutions: remedy or evil for human society; they destroy or consolidate the social machine....In order to deeply examine this upheaval is necessary to hush our feelings when they are born from passion or cold egoism. For people who want to judge them without realism or too closely, their hands tremble, just as for the people who belong to a very low level in the human training, the goal is too often hidden. But me, I contemplate all in the light of God, so maybe I judge in a better way that eternal process of the time always at war, at war with itself....Who can plumb God's boundless mind? Who can say where his work ends?...God never revealed his Word to anybody: only to time and to nature, he just talked with them. And if something of his knowledge leaks out, it is just there in the time and nature, it is there we have to search....In the labor [of history] which generates, which kills, there is in the universe a fermenting leaven, which impregnates God himself, God eternally working, because eternal is the course of the Eternal."

"Shake the nations as much as you want, they will always and necessarily restore the balance."[26]

When Lamartine began his journey towards the Levant in 1832, it was indeed, as he stated, because he was interested in analyzing "the history of the divine spirit in the different stages of humanity, the history of the divine within the human being."[27]

As the Lamartine scholar Louis de Ronchaud wrote in 1870 in his Introduction to a selection of political discourses and writings by the poet, "He lived in front of God; he saw everything from the point of view of Providence....In other times, and under different skies, Lamartine would have been a prophet like Mohammed; legislator, warrior, and poet, he would have stirred up the world in the name of a religious idea."[28] In Lamartine's "rational politics," God would act by means of human reason,[29] and the final realm of Christianity would be nothing but "the rational age, the realm of reason, because reason is divine too."[30] In this sense, "rational politics has to be intended as simultaneously secular and transcendent."[31] Within this horizon, poetry will be *raison chantée*; it will be at the same time philosophical, political, and social poetry, matching the stages that human reason must go through.[32]

---

[26]   Letter to his friend Aymon de Virieu (April 1, 1828), in *Correspondance de Lamartine*, vol. 3, p. 89.

[27]   Lamartine, *Voyage en Orient*, p. 145. See also what Agnès Antoine writes about this in "Le voyage en Orient de Lamartine: du poète au prophète," in *Relire Lamartine aujourd'hui, "Actes du Colloque International, Macon, juin 1990,"* ed. by Simone Bernard-Griffiths, Christian Croisille, et al., Paris: Librairie Nizet 1993, p. 194: "For the '*lumières*' brought by the progress of the sciences and the arts in civilization, Lamartine substitutes '*la lumière*' divine, for the spirit, he substitutes the Holy Spirit. He wants to show that the progress of mankind has not simply arrived with Christianity and, moreover, due to it, but by means of it."

[28]   Louis De Ronchaud, "Introduction" to *La Politique de Lamartine, choix de discours et écrits politiques*, vols. 1–2, Paris: Hachette 1878, vol. 1, p. XXVI, quoted by Bénichou, "Lamartine," p. 29, who also goes over the various moments of Lamartine's authorship in order to show the testimonies of this conviction.

[29]   See also *Jocelyn*, in *Oeuvres poétiques complètes*, pp. 598–9: "God, the Eternal is always working by means of mortals—his blind instrument; He gave as life to the human thought this eternal flow, which drags him....But if God always uses us, he condemns humanity to those hard proofs, and why does he mark with the blood of the pure victims every revolution, solstice of dirtiness? Why does he—who is love, justice, peace, serve the iniquity and the most grasping hatred? Because in his working God acts together with man; the latter would like the good, but evil reduces him to slavery. The worker is divine, but the instrument is human."

[30]   Lamartine: *Sur la politique rationelle*, p. 111.

[31]   Bénichou, "Lamartine," p. 44. As the poet wrote to Aymon de Virieu (September 12, 1838), "Your system reduces to individualism, the least patriotic and the least *human* thing. My system reduces to collectivity and unity that give to human actions the intensity and the irresistibility of a divine action. You forget the great utility of governments: it is necessary to obtain not only liberty, law, security, but also the social force to realize what God wants to manage for man and by means of man," in *Correspondance de Lamartine*, vol. 4, p. 470.

[32]   See for instance Lamartine, "Des Destinées de la poésie," in *Oeuvres complètes de Lamartine. Édition complète en un volume*, p. 370.

II. The *"enormous skepticism" of European Development:*
Kierkegaard's Unpolitical Christianity

What I have so often said jokingly—that it does not make any difference what government I live under just so I get to know who it is, who is *Imprimatur*—it now occurs to me that this is really Christianity. For in the story about the tax coin Christ asks: Whose likeness is this, who is *Imprimatur*? Christ clearly means this: If you want to be a Christian, then snap your fingers first and foremost and above all at politics; whether the picture you see on the coin is named Peter or Paul, is a native or an alien—forget it—give him the tax and do not waste a single moment on such squabbling, you who as a Christian have enough to do giving God what is his due, for the emperor's image is on the tax coin, but the Christian bears God's image and therefore does with his whole person what he is commanded to do with the coin—gives himself wholly to the one whose image he bears.[33]

In this passage from Kierkegaard, dated precisely to the revolutionary year 1848, a view can be detected that is opposite to that of Lamartine. In fact, the gap between Kierkegaard and Lamartine is even wider than it might appear; its roots are deeper than Kierkegaard's mere disregard for political movements. In what follows, we will analyze how the differences between these two authors manifest themselves in relation to a variety of particular issues (their respective views on crowds, and on the validity of the crowd's passions and opinions; on the principle of human equality; on the conditions for the possibility of realizing this principle concretely; and so on). At the end of our analysis, however, what will emerge will be a fundamental *metaphysical* gap between two theories whose political "applications"—though undeniably important—can be defined simply as "epiphenomena."

Let us start by comparing Kierkegaard's and Lamartine's respective views of crowds. For Lamartine, crowds are entities with two faces: one positive (or real) face, and one negative. The latter face is simply the immediate deformation of the former; with adequate education, its real essence can be restored. The "good" face of the masses consists in the fact that, in Lamartine's opinion, one can speak of a "national soul" [*l'âme du pays*],[34] whose wishes and needs—beyond transitory excesses of passion—embody the eternal Intelligence of God. As we remarked above, the special faculty that Lamartine claimed to possess, and which he considered a gift from God, was *l'instinct des masses*, which is, in the final analysis, the masses' faculty for understanding God's will.

In Kierkegaard's view, by contrast, such a "collective soul" simply cannot exist. It is merely the result of a pure abstraction; the only true reality is that of the singular existence. One text in which Kierkegaard specifically considers this topic is his 1846 *A Literary Review*, his review of Thomasine Gyllembourg's (1773–1856) 1845 novel *Two Ages*, where he analyzes the transition from the age of revolution to the present age. In this review, Kierkegaard details his criticism of modern leveling and

---

[33]   *SKS* 21, 126, NB7:94 / *JP* 4, 4151.
[34]   See Lamartine, *Histoire de la Révolution de 1848*, Tome I, Book I, Chapter XVII, p. 28. (*History of the French Revolution of 1848*, p. 22.)

its destruction of the single individual, and states explicitly that this leveling means the negation of the sole truth of singularity[35]:

> It is very doubtful, then, that the age will be saved by the ideal of sociality, of association. On the contrary, this idea is the skepticism necessary for the proper development of individuality, inasmuch as every individual either is lost or, disciplined by the abstraction, finds himself religiously. In our age the principle of association (which at best can have validity with respect to material interest) is not affirmative but negative; it is an evasion, a dissipation, an illusion, whose dialectic is as follows: as it strengthens individuals, it vitiates them; it strengthens by numbers, by sticking together, but from the ethical point of view this is a weakening. Not until the single individual has established an ethical stance despite the whole world, not until then can there by any question of genuinely uniting; otherwise it gets to be a union of people who separately are weak, a union as unbeautiful and depraved as a child-marriage.[36]

In this way, the immediate result of the abstraction of an imaginary collective body bound by the same convictions, the so-called "socialized reflecting,"[37] is the idea of the "public." This is the crowd that holds an *opinion*, and whose specific organ is the press. Kierkegaard defines the "public" as a mirage, a phantom, because it is actually something not existing, that is, a "monstrous nonentity."[38] This position is actually the very opposite of that of Lamartine, who, on the contrary, describes the "sovereignty of ideas," *opinion* as that "modern power whose very name was unknown to antiquity."[39] In this sense he can state that the public opinion, as "circulating" discussion of intelligences "was really born on the very day when Gutenberg, whom I have styled *the artificer of a new world*, invented, by printing, the multiplication and indefinite communication of thought and human reason."[40] This was in fact what Lamartine called—as though in ideal contrast to Kierkegaard's words—the "prophetic cry of the national soul."[41]

If both authors consider their own perspective to be the authentic religious point of view, it is clear that the gap between them must be situated in the ground of their theories. Consider, for example, the idea of equality among men. What does this mean for Lamartine and Kierkegaard, respectively? Apart from the material conditions of such equality (which is, from a logical point of view, simply a "consequence" of our discourse), let us here consider precisely in which sense it is possible to speak of

---

[35]   Salvatore Spera has profoundly analyzed this topic in his work *Kierkegaard politico*, Rome, Istituto di Studi Filosofici 1978; see in particular Chapter II, "Kierkegaard e la crisi europea del 1848," pp. 37–59. He shows that in Kierkegaard the "socialization" has the specific meaning of "collective alienation" (p. 46), an expression that seems emblematically to contrast with Lamartine's idea of a "collective soul."

[36]   *SKS* 8, 100–1 / *TA*, 106.

[37]   See Spera, *Kierkegaard politico*, p. 47.

[38]   *SKS* 8, 86 / *TA*, 90f.

[39]   Lamartine, *Histoire de la Révolution de 1848*, Tome I, Book I, Chapter XVI, p. 27. (*History of the French Revolution of 1848*, p. 21.)

[40]   Ibid.

[41]   Lamartine, *Histoire de la Révolution de 1848*, Tome I, Book I, Chapter XVII, p. 28. (*History of the French Revolution of 1848*, p. 22.)

"equality" among men, and what this means for the two authors. We saw above that, according to Lamartine, the real value of democracy consists in the fact that divine reason is embodied in the entire collectivity, whose liberty is simply the precondition to act; and so the republican form of government has the aim of allowing the soul of the collectivity to develop towards its divine perfection. One can say that the equality of men is due to their equal participation in divine reason, which is in fact embodied in the soul of the collectivity. One could speak of (divine) reason as an *immanent* principle,[42] even if Lamartine is not a philosopher and never expresses himself in these terms. But what, then, is the equality among men preached by the Gospel, in Kierkegaard's view? Talking precisely about the irrelevance of politics for actualizing this equality, in the writing which became a final "note" added to *The Point of View for My Work as an Author*, entitled "The Single Individual," Kierkegaard stated:

> No politics has been able, no politics is able, no worldliness has been able, no worldliness is able to think through or to actualize to the ultimate consequences this idea: human-equality, human likeness [*Menneske-Lighed*]. To achieve perfect equality in the medium of *world-likeness* [*Verds-Lighed*], that is, in the medium that by nature is dissimilarity, and to achieve it in a *world-like* [*verds-ligt*], that is differentiating way, is eternally impossible, as one can see by the categories. If perfect equality, likeness, should be achieved, then *worldliness* would have to be completely eradicated, and when perfect equality, likeness, is achieved, *worldliness* [*Verdslighed*] ceases to be. But is it not, then like an obsession, that worldliness has gotten the idea of wanting to force perfect

---

[42]   In a certain way, we could also compare Lamartine's view on politics (which consistently places its foundation on the Romantic current) with that of Hans Christian Ørsted on nature, when he says that "the laws of Nature are Divine thoughts" (*Hele Tilværelsen eet Fornuftrige*), in *Aanden i Naturen*, vols. 1–2, Copenhagen: Andr. Fred. Høst 1850, p. 154 (*ASKB* 945). (English translation: *The Soul in Nature*, trans. by Leonora and Joanna B. Horner, London: Dawsons of Pall Mall 1966 [1852], p. 115.) In this sense he also states that there cannot be a conflict between religion and science/reason: the harmony that exists between religion and science is indeed due to the fact that the essence of religion is the love of God, from whom the truth comes forth. Therefore this love originates in the wish to know this truth in all its forms. If someone would ask where the constant in the continuous changes of natural life is—Ørsted states—he would answer that it is in the forces that produce all things, and in the laws by means of which these forces operate. These forces/laws coincide with the unique power of Reason, which permeates the whole of nature. In this sense, the scientist should devote himself to his researches as to a religious exercise (*Videnskabsdyrkningen, betragtet som Religionsudøvelse*). This is a different field, but it is clear that it is the same attitude that Lamartine had of his political "mission." Kierkegaard, indeed, with a particular vehemence, also refused Ørsted's position in a passage of his journals, after *Berlingske Tidende* in 1849 (no. 303, December 22) praised Ørsted's work: "The *Berlingske Tidende* trumpets Ørsted's book (*Aanden i Naturen*) as a work which will clear up the relations between faith and science, a work which 'even when it is polemical always uses the finest phrases of the cultured urbanite.' One is tempted to answer: The whole book from first to last is scientifically—that is, philosophically-scientifically—insignificant, and even when it tries to be most significant it always moves in the direction of the most insignificant phrases of triviality." *SKS* 22, 415–6. NB14:124/*JP* 6, 6564. It is clear that Kierkegaard could not accept every attempt to make earth closer to heaven!

equality, likeness, and to force it in a worldly way—in worldliness, world-likeness! Ultimately only the essentially religious can with help of eternity effect human equality [*Menneske-Lighed*], the godly, the essential, the not-worldly, the true, the only possible human equality; and this is also why—be it said to its glorification—the essentially religious is the true humanity [*Menneskelighed*].[43]

Here we see that the author plays with the double meanings of *Menneskelighed* (humanity) and *Menneske-Lighed* (equality among men), *Verdslighed* (worldliness) and *Verds-Lighed* (the equality among men in that medium which is the world). Kierkegaard's claim about this equality and its incompatibility with a worldly-political perspective becomes clearer when we consider another passage from the same work, in which Kierkegaard specifies that in modern times "everything is politics."[44] But the viewpoint of the religious is worlds apart from this: thus, while the political begins on earth in order to remain on earth, the religious, "taking its beginning from above, wants to transfigure and then to lift the earthly to heaven."[45]

There is still another work, however, which can help us to understand better these last words: namely, *Works of Love* (1847), where Kierkegaard shows what the ground of equality really is. Kierkegaard speaks, indeed, of an equality only "at the very top,"[46] which is to say that real equality can only be achieved by men when they look at their neighbors through God's love. This is so because Christianity does not concern itself at all with earthly distinctions; its eyes are turned towards the equality of eternity. Accordingly, Kierkegaard tries to explain his point by contrasting the Christian and the temporal view on earthly/social diversities. He argues that Christianity and the so-called "humanitarian doctrines" simply belong to two qualitatively different spheres: all the worldly dissimilarities do not preoccupy Christianity at all, such a preoccupation and concern is nothing but worldliness, and "Christianity and worldliness will never come to a mutual understanding."[47] As Kierkegaard states, worldly similarity, if it were possible, is simply not Christian equality, and moreover to bring about worldly similarity perfectly is an impossibility, and that is why the world lives in a perpetual fruitless struggle. It is not the same in Christianity, which is—aided by the shortcut of eternity—immediately at the goal: "it allows all the dissimilarities to stand but teaches the equality of eternity."[48]

The Kierkegaardian movement of love among men can be represented as a kind of triangle, whose apex is situated at the top, which is, so to speak, in heaven, not on earth. This is precisely the "metaphysical" gap mentioned earlier. Kierkegaard, then, places the ground of his view outside the world, in the "Archimedean point," that is, the transcendent God. In this sense, "pantheism is an acoustical illusion that

---

43   *SV1* XIII, 589–90 / *PV*, Supplement, pp. 103–4.

44   *SV1* XIII, 589 / *PV*, Supplement, p. 103.

45   Ibid.

46   *SKS* 9, 79 / *WL*, 72.

47   *SKS* 9, 78 / *WL*, 71. On this point it is interesting to notice that Gregor Malantschuk in his *Den kontroversielle Kierkegaard*, Copenhagen: Vinten 1976 (it is Spera, *Kierkegaard politico*, p. 88 who reminds us of this) in fact claimed that Kierkegaard's first "anti-Communist manifesto" was *Works of Love*, more than *A Literary Review*.

48   Ibid.

confuses the *vox populi* and the *vox dei*, an optical illusion, a vaporous image formed out of the fog of temporality, a mirage formed by its reflection, which claims to be eternal."[49] Here again Kierkegaard stresses that it is an illusion to believe that something like a "soul of the collectivity" could really exist, while the only reality that "humanity" has is that of the concept, which is an abstraction. Humanity is indeed, according to Kierkegaard, a *fantastical social determination*,

> ...a confusion that wants to teach an ungodly contempt for what is the first condition of all religiousness; to be an individual human being. This confusion can be opposed, if possible, only by getting hold of people individually—but every human being is indeed an individual human being!...It is impossible to build up or to be built up *en masse*, even more impossible than to "fall in love *en quatre*" or *en masse*—upbuilding, even more decisively than erotic love pertains to the single individual.[50]

In this manner, Kierkegaard closes by characterizing the entire political question related to the French Revolution of 1848 as an "enormous skepticism," or as "a vortex"[51] which lacks "a fixed point."[52] It is precisely on the occasion of this great European event that Kierkegaard expresses his opinion about Lamartine's position on the revolution and on politics in general, and therefore also takes the opportunity to show his apolitical religious point of view concerning that matter.

The writings in which Kierkegaard considers Lamartine's view are not published works. They are a series of letters to a special friend, the conservative professor of jurisprudence at Copenhagen University, Janus Lauritz Andreas Kolderup-Rosenvinge (1792–1850),[53] with whom the philosopher used to promenade, discussing a wide

---

[49]   *SV1* XIII, 609 / *PV*, Supplement, p. 123.

[50]   *SV1* XIII, 603 / *PV*, Supplement, p. 117.

[51]   *B&A*, vol. 1, p. 206 / *LD*, Letter 186, p. 260.

[52]   Ibid. A similar position in this sense seems to have been that of Pascal, when he criticized the groundless arbitrariness of the human rules which inevitably should bring one to skepticism: see, for example, the fragment no. 294 of his *Pensées* (in *Oeuvres*, ed. by Léon Brunschvicg, Paris: Hachette 1906, pp. 214–16. (English translation: *Pensées*, trans. by Alban J. Krailsheimer, London: Penguin Book 1995, p. 16: "What basis will he take for the economy of the world he wants to rule? Will it be the whim of each individual? What confusion! Will it be justice? He does not know what it is. If he did know he would certainly never have laid down this most commonly received of all human maxims: that each man should follow the customs of his own country. True equity would have enthralled all the peoples of the world with its splendour, and lawgivers would not have taken as their model the whims and fancies of Persians and Germans in place of this consistent justice. We should see it planted in every country of the world, in every age, whereas what we do see is that there is nothing just or unjust but it changes colour as it changes climate. Three degrees of latitude upset the whole of jurisprudence and one meridian determines what is true. Basic laws change when they have been in force only a few years, law has its periods, the entry of Saturn into the house of the Lion marks the origin of a given crime. It is a funny sort of justice whose limits are marked by a river; true on this side of the Pyrenees, false on the other."

[53]   On this special friend of Kierkegaard we have a testimony by Hans Brøchner in his memoirs on the philosopher: "A man with whom I often saw K. walking in those years was Prof. Kolderup-Rosenvinge. They had most likely been brought together by their common interest in aesthetics. K.-R. was a cultivated man who was interested in the literature of

variety of subjects including—unusually for Kierkegaard—politics, to such a degree that the professor remarked upon it when they failed to do so! "We have not spoken about politics," he wrote in July 1848, almost ironically.[54] And Kierkegaard soon answered:

> "We did not get around to talking about politics," you remark. No wonder!...No, politics is not for me. To follow politics, even if only domestic politics, is nowadays an impossibility, for me, at any rate. Whenever anything happens very quickly—well, then one attempts to follow it; whenever anything goes very slowly—well, then one attempts to put up with the boredom of following it. But whenever something fluctuates back and forth, up and down and down and up, and then comes to a halt, and around and up and down and back again, then I am incapable of voluntarily following. If necessary I should prefer going to war as "coerced volunteer" to sitting at home—following it.[55]

Kierkegaard's claim is that a "fixed point" outside of movement itself is needed in order to stop the enormous vortex that is politics.[56] This claim is directed precisely against Lamartine,[57] who sought to arrest the movement of revolution by means of another movement, namely, the Republic. In reply to this, Kierkegaard remarks that it is the law of confusion that governs recent European events: he ironically describes the French, who wish to stop by means of a revolution and to stop a revolution by means of a counter-revolution, that is actually another revolution. Then he compares the revolution to a gadfly, which is both an exiguous and inadequate instrument and points out to his friend that he should consider the whole development in Europe as an "enormous skepticism or as a vortex" lacking

> a fixed point where it can stop. (Therefore, you see, I seek—said *in parenthesi*—"that single individual.") We all seem to agree that a stop is necessary. But that person who, while wishing to stop, fails to find a fixed point—that person who in other words wants to stop by means of the moved or the moving only enlarges the vortex....Lamartine wanted to stop corruption etc. by means of—a gadfly, alas, and so, just like the carpenter,

---

southern Europe and has translated a play by Calderón. On the other hand, he was already rather lethargic and in many ways extremely narrow-minded at that point. Once, when I expressed my surprise to S.K. that he could find it interesting to talk with Rosenvinge, he emphasized the man's general cultivation. He set great store by people from the older generation who had retained the humane interest of earlier times and the refined bearing that was so sorely lacking in the younger generation." (*Encounters with Kierkegaard: A Life as Seen by his Contemporaries*, ed. and trans. by Bruce H. Kirmmse and Virginia R. Laursen, Princeton: Princeton University Press 1996, pp. 241–2)

[54]   *B&A*, vol. 1, p. 198 / *LD*, Letter 181, p. 249.

[55]   *B&A*, vol. 1, pp. 200–1 / *LD*, Letter 184, pp. 252–3.

[56]   On this we might refer to what we said above on the immanent (Lamartine) or the transcendent (Kierkegaard) point of view on religion and Providence.

[57]   It is interesting to note that even Ibsen 20 years later will express a similar opinion about Lamartine's "weak political attitude." See his letter to Magdalene Thoresen from Dresden in 1870 (June 5th): "Such kinds of things [he is referring to some difficulties in the administration of the theatre of Kristiania. *Editor's note*] cause just chaos, rumor and confusion, like when Lamartine tried to govern France"; Cf. *Breve fra Henrik Ibsen*, vols. 1–2, ed. by Halvdan Koht and Julius Elias, Copenhagen and Kristiania: Gyldendal 1904, vol. 1, p. 205.

he was run over. Citizens had been shot at—still, the Republic was also bought at that price, so probably the defense could be made that they caused the shooting. Therefore, they wanted to stop by means of a law, the first one decreed by the Republic, which abolishes capital punishment for political crimes. But alas, the Republic itself was not an established order, it was a gadfly—and so they wanted to stop by means of a gadfly.[58]

Kierkegaard then begins to expound his own kind of "theory of movement," according to which most people believe that as long as one has a fixed point *to which* one wants to get, then motion is no vortex, but this is a misunderstanding, because "it all depends on having a fixed point *from which to set out.*" Kierkegaard indicates that stopping is only possible at a point *behind*, not at a point *ahead*. This is actually the difference between a political movement and a religious one: any purely political movement, which accordingly lacks the religious element is a vortex that cannot be stopped by finding a fixed point ahead, so, Kierkegaard concludes:

> My opinion about the whole European confusion is that it cannot be stopped except by religion, and I am convinced that—as so strangely happened once with the Reformation, which appeared to be a religious movement but turned out to be a political one—in the same way, the movement of our time, which appears to be purely political, will turn out suddenly to be religious or the need for religion.[59]

Among Kierkegaard scholars, Nelly Viallaneix has analyzed Kierkegaard's "theory."[60] She has shown that the perspective that Kierkegaard describes—which conceives of a fixed point *behind* itself—presupposes a view of time in which the past has to be found in the midst of the present in order to explain the future. As Kierkegaard had already written in his journals in 1839:

> Premonition does not lie in the direction, the path of the eye being pointed in the direction of existence and its future, but in the reflection of the eye's direction [toward] the past, so that by staring at what lies behind (in another sense, what lies in front) the eye develops a disposition to see what lies in front (in another sense, what lies behind). If A is thus the present time, the time in which we are living, and B its future, then I do not see B by standing at A and turning my face toward B; for if I turn that way I don't see anything at all, but if C is the past, then it is by turning toward C that I see B.[61]

This movement is, in fact, the same as the so-called existential "repetition," or "recollecting forward."[62] And for this reason, Viallaneix continues, Kierkegaard did not consider Lamartine a real historian. Indeed, as we read in Kierkegaard's ironical letter to his friend the jurist, he agrees completely with "Professor Lamartine," who is "engaged in cutting up and preparing for history" that remarkable year that was 1848.[63] Then he continues by saying that Lamartine could have done with the

---

[58]   *B&A*, vol. 1, pp. 206–7 / *LD*, Letter 186, pp. 260–1.
[59]   *B&A*, vol. 1, p. 207 / *LD*, Letter 186, pp. 260–2.
[60]   Viallaneix, "Kierkegaard, juge de Lamartine," p. 286.
[61]   *SKS* 18, 60–1, EE:178 / *KJN* 2, 55–6.
[62]   See *SKS* 4, 9 / *R*, 131.
[63]   *B&A*, vol. 1, p. 235 / *LD*, Letter 214, p. 299.

history the same that happens to New Year's gift books, which usually make their appearance the preceding year. That is why "Professor Lamartine" already considered himself as an historical subject and talked about himself in the third person.[64] From Kierkegaard's perspective, this remark has an even deeper meaning, since it alludes once more to that essential Christian category, the "individual," which is the furthest thing from the false abstraction of the "crowd" or "humanity." Much as Kierkegaard criticized idealism by insisting that the sole consistent existential consequence of pure thought is suicide,[65] he similarly infers that, because Lamartine reasons about himself as though he were outside himself (i.e., as if he were dead), his thought is thus founded on contradiction or falsehood, and as such is affectation.

For Kierkegaard, the category of the *concrete individual* is the unique way to find the "fixed point" that is needed to stop the vortex of European politics. What is needed, in particular, is not a man of iron, a despot or a tyrant—as the conservative Kolderup-Rosenvinge argued—but rather a *martyr*,[66] who is in fact a real single individual, willing to sacrifice his life for God. But this is not politics:

> *The single individual* is the category of spirit, of spiritual awakening, as diametrically opposite to politics as possible....*The single individual*—from the Christian point of view, this is the decisive category, and it will also become decisive for the future of Christianity....The single individual—with this category the cause of Christianity stands or falls, now that the world-development has gone as far as it has in reflection. Without this category pantheism would be unconditionally victorious. [67]

And this latter definition—the category of *pantheism*—can be actually seen by Kierkegaard as the real metaphysical ground of the Romantic Lamartine's political thought, which is something that Kierkegaard could never accept.

---

[64]   *B&A*, vol. 1, pp. 235–6 / *LD*, Letter 214, pp. 299–300.
[65]   See *SKS* 7, 281 / *CUP1*, 308.
[66]   Letter to J.L.A. Kolderup Rosenvinge (August 1848), see *B&A*, vol. 1, pp. 213–14 / *LD*, Letter 188, pp. 270–1.
[67]   *SV1* XIII, 607–8 / *PV*, Supplement, pp. 121–2.

Bibliography

I. Lamartine's Works in The Auction Catalogue *of Kierkegaard's Library*

None.

II. Works in The Auction Catalogue *of Kierkegaard's Library*
that Discuss Lamartine

None.

III. Secondary Literature on Kierkegaard's Relation to Lamartine

Loiseleur, Aurélie, *L'harmonie selon Lamartine. Utopie d'un lieu commun*, Paris: Honoré Champion Éditeur 2005, see p. 12; p. 273.

Viallaneix, Nelly, "Kierkegaard, juge de Lamartine," in *Lamartine. Le Livre du Centenaire*, ed. by Paul Viallaneix, Paris: Flammarion 1971, pp. 281–8.

Prosper Mérimée:
A New Don Juan

Nataliya Vorobyova

Kierkegaard clearly had some interest in French literature and drama, as is evinced by his references to writers such as Michel de Montaigne (1533–92), Blaise Pascal (1623–62), Jean-Jacques Rousseau (1712–78), and Eugène Scribe (1791–1861). However, his use of Prosper Mérimée remains a wholly unexplored topic in the secondary literature. Indeed, even Grimsley's standard study, *Søren Kierkegaard and French Literature*, refers to Mérimée only once.[1] This neglect is somewhat odd when one considers that some of Mérimée's innovations in authorial deception might well have served as models for Kierkegaard's use of pseudonyms, as well as for the polyphony of voices that Kierkegaard lets speak in his works. In the present article I will explore Kierkegaard's use of Mérimée as exhaustively as possible. In the first part, I will provide a brief overview of Mérimée's life and works; in the second, I will explore Kierkegaard's relation to him. I will argue that although no direct relationship can be established unambiguously, there is nonetheless good reason to suspect a deeper influence.

I. Mérimée's Life

Prosper Mérimée (1803–70) was born in Paris in an artistic, free-thinking, cultivated Anglophile family. His father, Jean-François-Léonor Mérimée (1757–1836), was not only a painter but also an aficionado of the arts, remembered mostly for his lifelong work, *History of Oil Painting from Van Eyck to Our Own Days*.[2] Mérimée's mother, Anne Moreau, was also a painter, chiefly of portraits and pictures of small children, and a great storyteller, a quality which she passed on to her son. It would be very difficult to understand the world of Mérimée and the specificity of his writing style without knowing what kind of development he went through.

Mérimée developed an interest in independent creative writing rather early in life: in his early twenties, while still a student at law school. (He graduated from the

---

[1]   Ronald Grimsley, *Søren Kierkegaard and French Literature*, Cardiff: University of Wales Press 1966, p. 7.
[2]   Jean-François-Léonor Mérimée, *De la Peinture à l'huile, ou des procédés matériels employés dans ce genre de peinture, depuis Hubert et Jean Van-Eyck jusqu'à nos jours*, Paris: Mme Huzard 1830.

faculty of law of the University of Paris in 1823). Originally, Mérimée's aesthetic predilections had an explicitly Romantic character. From his parents he acquired a passion for English literature, which led to his great fascination with Walter Scott's (1771–1832) historical narrative and Lord Byron's (1788–1824) poetry. However, the most crucial role in the shaping of Mérimée's creativity was played by his close friendship with Stendhal, whom the young writer met during the summer of 1822, while still in law school. Twenty years his senior, Marie-Henri Beyle—that is, Stendhal (1783–1842)—had just returned from Italy, where he had spent six years, and was full of stories and impressions about a country that would later become one of Mérimée's passions. It was Stendhal who introduced Mérimée to the bohemian society of the day and to many people who would later become his close friends. And it was Mérimée who acquired and used, in his dramatic works, the artistic program that had been put forward by Stendhal in the literary manifesto *Racine and Shakespeare*.[3] This is what Mérimée wrote himself about his relationship with Stendhal in *Notes et Souvenirs*: "except for a few preferences and a few literary aversions we did not perhaps have one idea in common, and there were few subjects on which we were in agreement."[4] In one of the letters to his friend Jenny Dacquin he wrote: "we spent our time arguing with each other, with the best faith in the world, each accusing the other of stubbornness and paradox."[5]

The same year saw Mérimée's literary debut with a tragedy entitled *Cromwell*, which was in no way successful and remained unpublished. Shortly after that literary fiasco, Mérimée turned his attention to the subject that has always attracted him, Spain and Spanish literature. He began by publishing four reviews on the dramas of the Golden Age of Spanish literature. This allowed him to prepare the ground for the first book that brought him popularity and fame. In 1825, a collection of six plays appeared entitled *Théâtre de Clara Gazul*.[6] This was Mérimée's first deception, and it was successful: the young author hid behind the mask of an imaginary Spanish actress Clara Gazul. The hoax was raised to perfection by the production of a portrait of Clara, for which Mérimée posed wearing a dress, mantilla, and a necklace! To make the deception more convincing, in the introduction to the book its imaginary translator Joseph L'Estrange tells the story of Clara's biography. Mérimée did not make a secret of his authorship, and this is how, at the age of 22, he found an appreciation for his talent. The most famous of the plays from this collection is *Les Espagnols en Danemarck*, which describes the events of the still-recent Napoleonic war. In 1808 a Spanish division that was then stationed in Denmark, under the general La Romana, was secretly shipped back to Spain by the English when the news broke that Napoleon wanted to install his brother on the Spanish throne. The modernity of this subject matter ran contrary to the classical theory of drama and was more in line with Stendhal's manifesto. The same is true of Mérimée's rejection of the unity of time and space (since there are ten scene changes in the play).

---

3   Stendhal, *Racine et Shakespeare*, Paris: Bossange 1823.

4   Quoted from Maxwell A. Smith, *Prosper Mérimée*, New York: Twayne Publishers 1972, p. 17.

5   Ibid., p. 18.

6   Prosper Mérimée, *Théâtre de Clara Gazul*, Paris: A. Lautelet 1825.

The second deception was planned with more care and kept in greater secrecy than the first one. *La Guzla*, subtitled *Choice of Illyrian Poems Collected in Dalmatia, Bosnia, Croatia and Herzegovina* was a collection of fictitious folk ballads[7] which purported to be translated by an Italian and written by a Dalmatian bard, Hyacinthe Maglanovich, whose biography was also included in the volume to increase its credibility. The book was published in 1827 and favorably received as a collection of Serbian folklore. The disguise was so successful that the book was taken as genuine Slavic folk poetry even by Alexander Pushkin (1799–1837) and Adam Mickiewicz (1798–1855), who both admired its "local color" and even translated some of the ballads into Russian and Polish respectively. There also appeared translations into English and German.[8] Only two people were not taken in, namely, Johann Wolfgang von Goethe (1749–1832) and Victor Hugo (1802–85).[9]

Next Mérimée turned his interest to the historical narratives. A great admirer of Walter Scott and an appreciator of Shakespeare's historical plays, he began writing "historical scenes," a genre which was a "hybrid form consist[ing] of historical subjects treated in sequences of dialogue, but much more episodically than in a regular drama, and without any thought of stage performance."[10] *La Jaquerie*, published in 1828,[11] was devoted to the peasant uprising that took place in Northern France in the fourteenth century.

After this he moved to the more ambitious genre of the historical novel. Here is how he commented on his *The Chronicle of Reign of Charles IX* in a letter to his friend Albert Stapfer on December 16, 1828: "a bad novel that bores me stiff, but I want to finish it because I have a lot of other ideas in my head."[12] *The Chronicle* can be regarded as a vivid example of Mérimée's lively interest in a historical problematic: in the study and evaluation of the national past. The piece required a lot of detailed research, for it was devoted to the sixteenth century, which was his favorite. In *The Chronicle*, Mérimée turned to the events of 1572, when on August 24, on St. Bartholomew's Night, the Catholics slaughtered several thousand Huguenots. Raitt mentions that the choice of the topic is not surprising, for "it was a favorite topic for liberal and anti-Catholic authors under the rule of Charles X."[13] And even though the novel was not intended as a political pamphlet, it is quite clear that Mérimée attempted, using the similarities between the Guises and the Ligue, to remind his contemporaries about the consequences of the civil war: religious fanaticism and persecution. Yet even though he wrote with compassion, being himself an agnostic,

---

[7]   Prosper Mérimée, *La Guzla, ou Choix de poésies illyriques, recueillies dans la Dalmatie, la Bosnie, la Croatie et l'Herzégovine*, Paris: F.-G. Levrault 1827.

[8]   Wilhelm Gerhardt included all the ballads from *La Guzla* in his two-volume edition of Serbian Folk song under the title *Wila*.

[9]   Alan William Raitt, *Prosper Mérimée*, New York: Scribner 1970, p. 43.

[10]   Ibid., p. 72.

[11]   Prosper Mérimée, *1572. Chronique du temps de Charles IX*, Paris: A. Mesnier 1829.

[12]   Quoted in English by Raitt in *Prosper Mérimée*, p. 73 (originally in Prosper Merimee, *Correspondance generale*, ed. by M. Parturier, P. Josserand and J.Mallion, vols. 1–4, Paris: Le Divan 1941–47, vol. 1, p. 33).

[13]   Raitt, *Prosper Mérimée*, p. 89: "one of the most controversial pieces of legislation enacted under Charles X provided that anyone guilty of sacrilege might have his hand cut off."

Mérimée failed to present the motives and experiences of those who were strong believers, and was unable to evaluate the intensity of the religious feeling of those days. For him the strong religious convictions on both sides remained an expression of fanaticism. Mérimée's sympathy lies with the persecuted, most likely because the persecutors constituted the most powerful religious group even in his own times, which made them more dangerous.

Raitt suggests that one of the characters of the *Chronicle*, George de Mergy, represents the views of Mérimée himself, which can be summarized in the following statement: "I couldn't believe and I still can't. Belief is a precious gift which has been withheld from me, but I would never dream of trying to deprive others of it."[14] Belief is one thing and being a fanatic another, and here a red flag is raised against the latter. Raitt quotes what Mérimée wrote on this subject in his later article on Henry de Guise:

> I am on the whole inclined to think that the sum total of vice and virtue has always been the same; consequently I do not believe we are any better than our forefathers, though we murder less. Murder was one of their passions; their passions are still ours, but they have different forms; but I think we must congratulate ourselves on living in a time when these forms have become appreciably less harsh.[15]

The characters of *The Chronicle* are not very complex; some are mere sketches and designed strictly to recreate the peculiarities of life of the sixteenth century. The same can be said with regard to the plot: "Simple in outline and episodic in nature, its function is to provide a pretext for a series of brilliant *tableaux de genre*, not all of which are even strictly necessary."[16]

In the introduction to the novel Mérimée explains his aspiration to remain objective: to be able to present an unbiased image of the historical past. Here he engages, to some extent, in polemics with the Romantics' concept of the historical novel, for it seemed to him that the way the Romantics treated history was excessively simplified and tendentious. Rather, Mérimée believed that if one wishes to find the true reasons for historical shifts in the country's moral development, then one must analyze the moods of various layers of society. This is why in *The Chronicle* Mérimée describes in detail the customs of the nobility at court, of the representatives of the Catholic Church, the leaders of Huguenot camp and its clerics, the habits of the German cavalry, the thoughts of the simple soldiers, and the destiny of the common citizens.

The four early works devoted to historical themes showed the natural interest of the young French writer in historical narrative. His research on these subjects was much more thorough than that of any of his contemporary colleagues like Alexandre Dumas, père (1802–70) or Alfred de Vigny (1797–1863). And it is in these early years that we see how Mérimée developed his interest in history, which would later slowly win out at the expense of fiction.

---

[14]   Ibid., p. 92, quoted and translated by Raitt from Mérimée, *Romans et nouvelles*, vols. 1–2, ed. by Maurice Parturier, Paris: Garnier 1967, vol. 1, p. 62.
[15]   Raitt, *Prosper Mérimée*, p. 90.
[16]   Ibid., p. 93.

As for his private life: in the late 1820s Mérimée was rarely seen without Stendhal. They spent most of their time in *salons*, having private meetings, arguing about literature, or dining with a fixed group of friends.[17] It is from these early years that Mérimée showed himself to be a great womanizer, "addicted to the company of *grisettes*, *rats* and other varieties of easy-living ladies."[18]

The young writer's love for English culture resulted in a great friendship with Sutton Sharp (1797–1843), a brilliant English lawyer, who was to visit Mérimée frequently in Paris and entertain him in London. Even in Paris Mérimée preferred not to lose contact with English-speaking society; he was a frequent visitor to several *salons* hosted by prominent Irish, English, and American families. In one of these he met Mary Wollstonecraft (1759–97), the widow of Percy Bysshe Shelley (1792–1822), whom he courted and about whom had matrimonial hopes, which were delicately declined. It is there as well that he met Emilie Lacoste (1798–ca.1864), the mistress of Napoleon's elder brother, Joseph-Napoléon Bonaparte (1768–1844), who in 1827 returned with her husband from America. Mérimée's affair with Madame Lacoste is significant for two reasons. Emilie was a devoted Catholic and spent quite a lot of time trying to convert Mérimée: "echoes of this are perceptible in the relationship between Mergy and the pious but sensual Diane de Turgis in Mérimée's historical novel *Chronique du regne de Charles IX*."[19] In addition, this relationship cost the writer a duel with Felix Lacoste, Emilie's husband. But this only strengthened Mérimée's Don-Juanesque reputation. Mérimée was wounded in his left arm, and when people inquired about the cause of the injury he would reply that it was caused "by a gentleman who didn't like my prose."[20] This remark was even more sardonic since the reason why Felix challenged him was because of a love letter Mérimée had written to Emilie.

In 1830 Mérimée undertook his first trip to Spain, sponsored by his father, the purpose of which was to investigate Spanish museums (specifically, it was supposed to aid his father's research on paintings). But he was much more interested in the local customs, traditions, and landscapes than in classical art. Later, many of the incidents and observations which he had made during this trip would find their reflection in a collection of short stories entitled *Mosaïque*, published in 1833.[21] It was on this trip that he became acquainted with Don Cipriano Guzman Palafoz y Portpcarrero (1784–1839), Count of Teba (later the Count of Montijo), his wife Manuela (1794–1879), and their daughters, Paca and Eugenia. This was the beginning of a long friendship that would one day change Mérimée's life. A couple of years later Countess de Teba and her daughters stayed in Paris. During this time Mérimée grew very close to the girls and in letters mentioned these children with affection.

---

[17]   This group consisted of Eugene Delacroix, Alfred de Musset, Baron Adolphe de Mareste, Horace de Viel-Castel, David Ferdinand Koreff, and Edouard Grasset, all of whom were very prominent young men.

[18]   Raitt, *Prosper Mérimée*, p. 64.

[19]   Ibid., p. 68.

[20]   Ibid.

[21]   Prosper Mérimée, *Mosaïque*, Paris: H. Fournier 1833.

After six months in Spain, in 1830, Mérimée "was immediately drafted into the National Guard, the middle-class militia which was called out in civil emergencies."[22] Duing this period he would spend a lot of time with Dumas, discussing literature and enjoying intellectual debate. Later, he would once again join these forces after the abdication of Louis-Philippe. Guided by his deep patriotism, Mérimée felt an urge to join the Guard to preserve law and order. Then he would witness all the horrors of civil war, which he had described so vividly much earlier in his *Chronicle*.

Although he was a successful writer from the very start, Mérimée always treated writing as a vocation and never as a profession or a way to earn a living. Like his father, he preferred not to cut himself off from a stable income offered by a regular job. That is why he accepted a post as a private secretary to the Minister of Navy, a position which was relatively easy to get after the July Revolution. This appointment laid the foundation for Mérimée's career as a civil servant (at that time he was 27 years old). Mérimée's biographers note that even though the early period of his life was professionally quite successful, the writer was in a depression which began before his trip to Spain and was caused by unsuccessful love affairs. To lighten up his mood, he did not have anything better to do but to plunge into the world of pleasure. As Raitt comments on Mérimée's correspondence from that period: in his letters "he seems to want to exaggerate the obscenity of his stories in order to forget that anything nobler existed."[23] Shortly after his appointment as a private assistant, he was sent to England as an observer of the 1832 elections, an experience which only increased his disappointment with parliamentary democracy. In the meantime Mérimée was finishing writing the aforementioned collection of short narrative fiction, *Mosaïque*.

In 1834, after a series of changes in the government, Mérimée was offered the post of Inspector General of Historic Monuments. As he wrote in one of his letters: "it's just the thing for my tastes, my indolence and my desire to travel."[24] He did not have a lot of experience in archeology; however, at that time this was not the most significant factor in the choice of candidate, since in general an interest in the preservation of ancient and outstanding buildings was somewhat of a novelty: "What mattered most was that Mérimée had a keen sense for historical research, a real if unostentatious love of beauty, and a proven ability to master quickly the intricacies of any subject which might be thrust upon him."[25] For the next 18 years he spent every summer traveling in different parts of France in order to identify valuable buildings and supervise their reconstruction. Within a few years he managed to get more funds from the government to establish a stable budget for his projects. This was also a post which required negotiating numerous complicated intergovernmental relationships. His achievements in this field were quite remarkable. Besides restoring several dilapidated buildings, he worked out a system for the prioritization of the restoration of buildings and the distribution of the funds. This appointment changed his way of life and character. Apparently, Mérimée enjoyed being a public figure.

---

22   Raitt, *Prosper Mérimée*, p. 98.
23   Ibid., p. 102.
24   Ibid., p. 137.
25   Ibid., p. 139.

"So when he went on tour, he was careful to impress his provincial hosts with his icily correct behavior, even when his one desire was to discover the whereabouts of the local brothel."[26] His life in Paris had also become calmer, and even though he continued to meet with his old friends,

> increasingly he frequented men of learning, partly because his new occupation brought him inevitably into contact with them, partly because he was anxious to consolidate his qualifications as Inspector General by learning from them, but most of all because his own tastes were undoubtedly developing in that direction.[27]

Obviously Mérimée's life became busier and busier. Nevertheless, in the period between 1834 and 1840 he still managed to write and publish three fictional narratives: "Les âmes du purgatoire" (1834), "La Venus d'Ille" (1837), and "Colomba" (1840).[28] Yet, most of his writings from this period were devoted to history and archeological discoveries from his trips as Inspector General. They were designed to help the author to become accepted and recognized by academic society. For it was another of Mérimée's ambitions, which he tried to pursue from the moment he became an Inspector General, to be elected to either the Academy of Inscriptions or the French Academy. The publication of *Essai sur la guerre sociale* was meant to make his name known in the circles of historians and archeologists.[29] In 1844 he was finally elected a member of the first Academy, but still felt rather uncomfortable about the situation since "it was most paradoxical for a man like himself, who prided himself on frank speaking and disdain for shams, to lend himself to so much hypocritical presence."[30]

To complete the picture of Mérimée's private life, it is worth mentioning his relationship with two more women: Jenny Darquine and Valentine Delessert. It was in 1831 that Mérimée received the first letter supposedly from Lady Algernon Seymour, with a request for the author's autograph. This is how a long friendship and correspondence that lasted 37 years began. Lady Seymour turned out to be a young, smart and witty Frenchwoman Jenny Darquine. Their relationship has always been a matter of discussion, for it has never been clear whether it remained purely platonic. Jenny never married, and Raitt suggests that when she came to Paris in 1842, she could have had hopes that their relationship would result in something more serious, but at that time Mérimée had a mistress, Valentine Delessert, the greatest love and passion of his life. Mérimée first met Valentine in 1830 and was so fascinated by her beauty and wit that unexpectedly for a Don Juan such as himself he began a six-year courtship. On February 16, 1836 she finally became his mistress, and their liaison lasted until the final break-up in 1853. But this was not a stable relationship, for

---

26   Ibid., p. 155.
27   Ibid., p. 158.
28   The novella "Colomba" was first published in *Revue des Deux Mondes* on July 1, 1840. The three stories were collected in Prosper Mérimée, *Colomba*, Paris: Magen et Comon 1841; for the story "Colomba" see pp. 1–280; for "La Venus d'Ille" see pp. 281–340; and for "Les âmes du purgatoire," see pp. 341–463.
29   Prosper Mérimée, *Essai sur la guerre sociale*, Paris: Firmin-Didot frères 1841.
30   Raitt, *Prosper Mérimée*, p. 209.

Valentine was very demanding and loved to feel power over men. In 1844, apparently bored by Mérimée's complete devotion, she found a new lover. Mérimée tried to win her back by taking her now grown-up children under his wing, but this made very little impression on her. In 1848, after the abdication of Louis-Philippe, Valentine's husband, the chief of the royal police, had to go into exile to England. With Valentine in England, and sensing obvious coldness from her rare letters, Mérimée lost his peace of mind, realizing how deep his feelings were for her and his inability to return her love. This feeling only increased with years and was finally transformed into depression—to which the writer was generally rather susceptible.

Mérimée had an extraordinarily warm relationship with his parents. A devoted son, upon the death of his father in 1836, he decided to move and live with his mother. He remained with her until her death in 1852, which came abruptly and was a great blow to him.

The post of Inspector General permitted Mérimée to enjoy semi-official trips not only around France, but also to Corsica, Italy, and Spain. His trip to Corsica in 1840 influenced the setting and subjects of his fiction, and most of his impressions were transformed and used in his "Colomba." In 1841 he undertook an archeological trip to Greece, which stimulated two new interests: one in mythology (later he would write: "I wanted to find the law of the human mind which makes it invent religious myths"[31]). The other interest was to learn Russian (this was inspired by the Russian wife of the French ambassador, Mme Barbe de Lagrené née Doubenski (1806–1901), who would later become Mérimée's instructor).

The longer he remained a public figure, the more he stopped enjoying soirées and social gatherings. He plunged himself into work, writing essays on Julius Caesar. From the beginning of the 1840s he so completely devoted himself to the historical studies and writings that he not only had little time left for fiction, but also changed his attitude towards it. For now fiction became a relaxation from serious research. In addition, he developed a feeling that he was growing old that only increased when, within a period of two months in 1842–43, two of his closest friends, Sutton Sharpe and Stendhal died. He was left with only a memory of the eight friends who used to dine at Véry together—at the time he was only 39. This is the mood in which he writes *Carmen*,[32] and the novellas "L'Abbe Aubain" and "Il Viccolo di Madama Lucrezia,"[33] given as a present to Valentine's sister. On top of all these occupations, Mérimée continued as Inspector General, undertaking regular annual trips around France. He seemed to be able to work with little sleep and, due to his efficiency, even had time to pursue a small hobby of studying a gypsy dialect. Never short of money, he could spend substantial sums on servants, and, having the luxury of his mother running the household, he led a comfortable life. When the new stormy times of the French Revolution came, Mérimée decided to distract himself from

---

[31]   Ibid., p. 201.

[32]   Prosper Mérimée, *Carmen*, Paris: Michel Lévy frères 1846.

[33]   The novella "L'Abbe Aubain" was published in the *Constitutionnel* on February 24, 1846. The novella "Il Viccolo di Madama Lucrezia" was dated by the author April 27, 1846 and published posthumously in Prosper Mérimée, *Derniéres Nouvelles*, Paris: Michel-Lévy frères 1873.

gloomy thoughts by challenging his mind with a new intellectual occupation: he began Russian studies. He started his lessons in the late 1847, and by the summer 1848 he moved on to the translation of Pushkin's *The Queen of Spades*. The political upheavals were also the reason that in 1848 the publication of *Histoire de Don Pédre*,[34] a history of a fourteenth-century Castilian king, went almost unnoticed. However, the book was warmly received abroad, due to translations into Spanish (1848), English (1849), and German (1852).

His last years were closely connected with the Empire. In 1853 Eugenia Montijo, the daughter of the Countess de Teba, married the emperor Louis Napoleon, and from the moment she became Empress she was determined to find a high office for Mérimée. This is how he became a senator with an annual salary of 30,000 francs, which removed all his financial worries. But he still continued to perform the duties of the Inspector General until 1860. Mérimée died in September 1870. In his will he asked to be buried by a Protestant minister.

II. Kierkegaard and Mérimée

In Kierkegaard's *Journal AA*, there is what some commentators assume to be a fictitious letter, which is supposed to be a part of series of "Faustian letters."[35] Here the philosopher makes several comments about what it means to be young and to mature. Kierkegaard suggests that there are two types of young people. One of them, to whom he would never like to belong, represents those "others who let themselves be so completely directed by their surroundings that they never become clear about what they are really after."[36] But the first type which captivates the philosopher's attention represents young men who are "fortunate temperaments so decisively inclined in a particular direction that they faithfully follow the path once assigned to them, undeterred for a moment by the thought that perhaps they should really be treading another."[37] He compares those who realize their destiny with the figure of Faust:

> Just as our forefathers had a goddess of longing so, in my opinion, is Faust the personification of doubt. More than that he should not be; and it is surely as much a sin against the idea when Goethe lets Faust be converted as it is when Mérimée allows Don Juan to convert.[38]

As Kierkegaard explains, Faust could not possibly turn to God instead of the devil, because if he did, he would have found out that the true knowledge and enlightenment is on God's side and this "would have denied his character as a doubter."[39] Unfortunately, Kierkegaard does not develop his train of thought about

34   Prosper Mérimée, *Histoire de don Pèdre Ier, roi de Castille*, Paris: Charpentier 1848.
35   Cf. *EO1*, Notes, p. 662, note 1.
36   *SKS* 17, 19, AA:12 / *KJN* 1, 14.
37   Ibid.
38   Ibid.
39   *SKS* 17, 19, AA:12 / *KJN* 1, 15.

Mérimée's Don Juan, but his opinion about this particular story did not seem to be favorable.

For, in fact, the character produced by Mérimée is quite remarkable. Mérimée himself had Don-Juanian inclinations. A confirmed bachelor, he was never fastidious about the company of *grisettes* or chorus-girls, nor did he have any restraints with regard to the marital ties that bound some of his mistresses. In the above mentioned "Les âmes du purgatoire," he reveals an obvious change in his perception of such a lifestyle. The novella, although set in seventeenth-century Spain, is thematically closely connected with Mérimée's "reactions to the life he was leading in the Parisian society of the 1830s."[40] It became a critique of the Don Juan figure and "a compassionate recognition of the ravages his selfishness can cause."[41] In addition, this is probably the only work from which humor is entirely banished. According to Mérimée, while writing this novella he intended to separate the legends which portrayed two different Spanish womanizers: Don Juan de Mañara[42] and Don Juan Tenorio.[43] He also uses this opportunity to evoke the fantastic and the supernatural in order to bring the story to an unconventional conclusion.

Don Juan was the only male child and heir of his father Don Carlos de Maraña. Spoiled by his parents from early childhood, he was raised as a God-fearing Catholic by his mother and a fearless fighter by his father. In his mother's private chapel there was a picture that depicted the punishments and sufferings of Purgatory. The condemned souls were placed in a cave at the top of which stood an angel holding out his hand for those who could be saved. Captivated and terrified, the boy spent hours looking at the picture. He was especially impressed by one scene in which a sinner was hanging from hooks stuck in his ribs and with a snake eating his internal organs (his mother explained that this was a punishment for those who did not pay attention during the sermon and disrespected priests).

When Don Juan turned 18, his father sent him to study at the University of Salamanca. It is there that Don Juan met Don Garcia Navarro, an idler, brawler, and famous seducer. There was a rumor according to which, when Don Garcia was a child, his father made a pact with the devil to save his son from a severe illness, for since the day of his recovery, the boy had been uncontrollable. Naive Don Juan accepted Garcia's offer of friendship from his very first day in Salamanca—and this is the start of his adventure.

Don Garcia is courting a noble young lady Fausta. He suggests that Don Juan should try his luck with her younger sister Teresa. After a month of serenades under the windows of the sisters, both meet with great success, but one evening they are

---

[40]   Raitt, *Prosper Mérimée*, p. 172

[41]   Ibid., p. 176.

[42]   Another set of Spanish legends concerned Don Migel de Mañara (1626–79), whom Mérimée persistently calls de Maraña: a nobleman who spent most of his life in dissipation, but towards its end repented, becoming a monk.

[43]   Don Juan Tenorio is a personage of a number of legends, which were given literary form for the first time by the Spanish playwright Tirso de Molina (1571–1648), in a play entitled *El Burlador de Sevilla y convidado de piedra*. The same prototype was used to create the character of Don Juan by Molière in his eponymous comedy, by Mozart in his eponymous opera, and by Pushkin in his tragedy *The Stone Guest*.

interrupted by a rival, Don Cristoval, who has arrived at the house with a group of friends and musicians. The friends refuse to leave, and a duel results in which Don Juan kills Cristoval and loses his sword during the escape. To ensure Don Juan's alibi, Don Garcia stops in one of the churches and presents a version of the story to a priest. He asks the father to advise him on this matter of conscience: whether Don Juan should consider himself an accomplice if someone borrows his sword and kills a man in a duel. But they do not have to worry about the consequences since Teresa finds and hides the broken sword, bringing it back to Don Juan the next morning. After some months of genuine happiness, Don Juan becomes bored with Teresa, and Garcia suggests that they swap mistresses. Garcia writes a letter in which he offers Fausta to his friend, who goes to see the girl the same evening. Fausta is furious and raises the household against the intruder. As Don Juan tries to escape, the father of the family shoots from a harquebus accidentally and instantaneously kills Fausta, while Don Juan stabs the man in the confusion. In this situation, the only way for Don Juan to avoid punishment is to flee. Don Juan and Don Garcia decide to join the Spanish army, which is fighting near Brussels against the Dutch. The friends join the regiment of Captain Manuel Gomare. Things return to normal again: parties and seduction continue, and Don Juan even receives forgiveness from his father for the murders.

One day Gomare is mortally wounded in a battle, and Don Juan is the first officer to find him. The Captain bequeaths Don Juan his entire fortune, 60 pieces of gold, with the request to spend them on prayers for the Captain's soul. But the very same night Juan loses all the money in a card game, quickly forgetting about the promise that he has given.

Next, when Don Garcia and Don Juan are sitting on guard duty in a trench, with Garcia expressing his atheistic views challenging both God and the devil as a scourge of God, a shot from the Spanish side abruptly hits Garcia. Some see this as a sign of Providence; but others see it as a murder, and suspect a soldier nicknamed Modesto, who coincidentally disappeared from the regiment after this accident. Nevertheless, as Don Garcia had many enemies, revenge from a cuckolded husband would not surprise anyone. Shortly after the loss of his friend, Don Juan learns of his parents' death and decides to return to Spain to claim his inheritance.

Upon his return, Don Juan continues to enjoy all the pleasures of life; not even a serious illness, nor the picture of Purgatory in his mother's chapel, encourages him to repent. During his recovery, Don Juan makes a list of all the women he has seduced and the men he has betrayed. When he shows the list to friends, one of them remarks that it is incomplete, for it does not include God himself. This comment inspires Don Juan to seduce a nun. He thus embarks on a new adventure, and soon finds a victim, the beautiful nun Augusta. But the more he looks at her, the more familiar she seems. One day he receives a letter from Sister Augusta in which she asks him to stop pursuing her. The letter is signed "Teresa." The knowledge that it was his old love only encourages Don Juan; and after some time, Teresa agrees to run away with him. But during the night for which the escape is planned, Juan sees a vision of his own funeral, after which two ghosts, Don Garcia and Captain Gomare, pay him a visit. Don Juan is so terrified that he forgets to signal Teresa—and faints on the pavement in the middle of Seville.

After returning to his senses, Don Juan calls a confessor, gives half of his possessions to the poor relatives, donates the other half for a new hospital, finally keeps his promise to Gomare and orders prayers for his soul, and in the end decides to become a monk. But before he leaves for the monastery, he writes a letter of apology to Teresa confessing his ill intentions. The girl is so shocked by his cruelty that she dies shortly after receiving the letter.

Don Juan's repentance is so frank that, even in the eyes of the public, his image changes from that of a seducer to almost that of a saint. But one day, in the garden of the monastery, Modesto appears—and challenges Juan to a duel. Modesto, or Don Pedro, turns out to be the brother of Teresa and Fausta. He confesses that the shot that killed Don Garcia was intended to hit Don Juan. Juan refuses to fight, but explodes when Pedro slaps him in the face. Modesto is dead within a minute.

No one finds out about this murder. Nevertheless, until the end of his days, Don Juan keeps the bloody sword that killed Pedro in his bed; and every day, he goes to the monastery's cook, whose slaps in the face teach Don Juan to accept humiliation, and remind him that modesty and forgiveness are among the highest virtues. Juan's last wish is to be buried in the church entrance, and to have an engraving on his tomb which says: "*Aqui yace el peor hombre que fue en el mundo*" or "Here lies the worst man who was ever in the world." But his first wish is not granted. Don Juan is buried near the altar in the chapel that he himself founded.

The story is unusually serious; yet it does not contain even a tiny bit of moralizing. In fact, the parts that describe the supernatural experience are so gloomy that the story begins to sound like a warning. Raitt explains the author's sober sincerity as a product of his unreasonable and superstitious personal nature: "Though Mérimée was an irreligious man, he could never rid himself of uneasy and irrational attachment to talismans, magic formulae, fetishist precautions and the like."[44]

Mérimée's presentation of the Don Juan myth may strike the reader as cold, enigmatic, and impersonal. The events and incidents are related as though they occur with great speed—as if to stress the transience and irreversibility of the human life. Mérimée's critics do not speak highly about this novella, for it cannot compare to Byron's or Mozart's interpretation of Don Juan's archetype. But it does present an interesting story of repentance.

We do not know whether Kierkegaard had ever read "Les âmes du purgatoire,"[45] or whether he knew of it only through hearsay. Grimsley is almost certain that Kierkegaard read a *review* of the novella—a suggestion that could explain the vagueness of his remark. Nevertheless, it is quite remarkable that Kierkegaard mentions the novella in his writings a little less than a year after its publication in France. The novella did not appear in Danish until 1899, when Carl Michelsen translated it with the title *Don Juan*, reflecting its main theme.[46] In any case, there is no doubt that this story would

---

[44]   Raitt, *Prosper Mérimée*, p. 177.

[45]   Some commentators (see *KJN* 1, Notes, p. 320) suggest that Kierkegaard could have read the review in *Revue des Deux Mondes*, vol. 3, August 15, 1834, pp. 377–434; see also Grimsley, *Søren Kierkegaard and French Literature*, p. 7.

[46]   Prosper Mérimée, *Don Juan*, trans. by Carl Michelsen, Copenhagen: A. Christiansen 1899.

have been interesting to Kierkegaard. For it treats—albeit in a manner that he does not admire—one of his favorite fictitious characters.

If one takes a closer look at the two authors, it is possible to find more similarities than appear at a first glance. The most striking of these is the fact that both began their authorship by publishing works that are not exclusively signed by pseudonyms; moreover, both tell the whole story behind the pseudonymous authors that they introduce. In a sense, Kierkegaard went even further: for he allows several of his pseudonymous personages to appear as characters on their own texts. *Either/Or*, for example, purports to have been assembled by a fictitious editor, Victor Emerita, who decided to publish works by various authors: author A, Judge Wilhelm or author B, and Johannes the Seducer. Kierkegaard's pseudonymous authorship is definitely much more complex than Mérimée's hoax, even though both of them were executed with proficiency, and even though both made a bit of a stir, In both cases there were those who swallowed the hook of mystification, believing every single word written by the imaginary editors and translators; and there were also those who saw through the pseudonymous masks to the real genius underneath.

In Mérimée's case, in retrospect, both mystifications are much more than an extravagant whim or a boyish joke. *Le Théâtre de Clara Gazul* is the writer's attempt to join the campaign in favor of the radical reformation of the classical theater, as is stated in Stendhal's aforementioned essay *Racine et Shakespeare*. In the prologue, Clara boldly discards the classical unities of time, place and action, and advocates recent history instead as the more appropriate subject for tragedies. It was risky to make such an open attempt to revolutionize the conservative perception of drama that dominated French theater at that time. For this reason, "the pretext that the plays are the work of a Spanish actress is a mischievously cunning device: if the public of the time accepts that a Spaniard has a right to his own dramatic system, why should it object when it discovers that the Spaniard is a Frenchman?"[47] Even after the disclosure of the true author, Mérimée did not change his perception of the art of drama. The later editions of the volume include three new plays; and one of these, *L'Occasion* (1829), was translated into Danish by Johan Ludvig Heiberg (1791–1860) and published in "The Royal Theater Repertoire" in 1830.[48]

It might seem more difficult to justify the second mystification, since some biographers believe that *La Guzla* was written only to earn money for a trip to Illyria. On the other hand, Mérimée's initial fascination with primitive poetry and local color inspired him to master those arts. The process of writing the ballads "had revealed to him that local color was a simple trick,"[49] and was apparently a very picturesque addition to any literary work, for the writer would rely on this feature in his later works, such as *Carmen* and *Colombo*. As for folk poetry, Mérimée believed that it was the only real form of this genre. Much later, in an article on "Rumanian

---

[47]   Raitt, *Prosper Mérimée*, p. 48.

[48]   Henning Fenger, *The Heibergs*, trans. by Frederick J. Marker, New York: Twayne Publishers 1971, p. 79. (In Danish as *Familien Heiberg*, Copenhagen: Museum Tusculanum Press 1992.)

[49]   Raitt, *Prosper Mérimée*, p. 59.

Folk-songs and Ballads," he would write: "It is only in that blessed state that the poet can be naïve without being silly and natural without being trivial."[50]

For Kierkegaard, each pseudonym is carefully chosen and has an idea to bear. All of them are designed to be in a dialogue with each other: when one is praised, another is condemned. A broad look at the pseudonymous works would reveal that in each of them ideas, questions, or doubts are not only developed but are constantly challenged from other angles. Literary masks allow the philosopher to describe a dialectically complex philosophical system without being accused of inconsistency. And there is no doubt that if Kierkegaard would have been able to develop a familiarity with Mérimée's masks, he would have embraced the Frenchman's ingenuity.

While there is little to say about direct references to Mérimée in Kierkegaard's works, the author's significance for the Danish literature of that period should not be disregarded. It was the Heibergs who introduced a number of French writers, Mérimée among them, onto the Danish scene. Fenger reminds us that J.L. Heiberg dismissed English literature with the claim that the greatness of the English was already over; and as for German literature, Heiberg remarked that their poetry "is so deeply asleep that one fears it may sleep forever."[51] Instead, Heiberg believed that "there is at the moment no country in which literature is undergoing a fresher and more youthful development than in France."[52]

It seems that Heiberg's project of bringing French literature to Denmark was completed in the year 1830, a year marked by Heiberg's translation of *L'Occasion* and translations of *Mateo Falcone* and *Tamango* by Fru Gyllembourg (1773–1856), J.L. Heiberg's mother. Fru Gyllembourg, in particular, valued Mérimée highly. In a preface to her novel *Two Ages*, she calls him "the pearl in modern French literature,"[53] and cites one of his observations in the *Chronicle* on the features by which one epoch differs from another.

It might seem surprising that, despite Heiberg's high regard for Mérimée's dramatic art, he did not attempt to adapt any of his plays for the Danish stage. Heiberg instead preferred to introduce his audience to Eugène Scribe (1791–1861), who was frequently staged at The Royal Theater of Copenhagen. Fenger suggests that "as a practical matter...Heiberg realized that Mérimée was too advanced, too daring."[54] This can only be partly true. Mérimée was indeed an innovative playwright; yet neither his critics nor he himself believed that his works were never intended to be performed. For Mérimée, *Le Théâtre de Clara Gazul* was a provocative experiment; but he refused to develop his career in that direction for two reasons: "1) Guessing

---

[50]   Quoted from Raitt, *Prosper Mérimée*, p. 60 ("Ballades et chants populaires de la Roumanie," *Le Moniteur universel*, January 17, 1856).

[51]   Quoted from Fenger, *The Heibergs*, p. 80. (In Heiberg's translation as "Leiligheden. Af Mérimée (Oversat af J.L.H.). I. Oversætterens Forerindring," *Kjøbenhavns flyvende Post*, vol. 1, no. 14 (February 1), 1830 [p. 62]. (Reprinted in *Poetiske Skrifter*, vols. 1–11, Copenhagen: C.A. Reitzel 1862, vol. 5, p. 205.) (The page numbers in square brackets refer to the photomechanical reproduction of *Kjøbenhavns flyvende Post*, vols. 1–4, ed. by Uffe Andreasen, Copenhagen: Det Danske Sprog- og Litteraturselskab 1980–84.)

[52]   Fenger, *The Heibergs*, p. 81.

[53]   *TA*, Supplement, p. 153.

[54]   Fenger, *The Heibergs*, p. 82.

the tastes and susceptibilities of the public, what are called stage effects, 2) Having inexhaustible patience, firmness and resignation to get the actors to do what you want. Even if I had No. 1, which I completely lack, I know that I could never stand the boredom of a rehearsal."[55] Being a playwright himself, Heiberg felt that the narrative of *Le Théâtre de Clara Gazul* was of different nature, for this is what he asked his reader to think about the play he translated. It should be read as "a novel with such dramatic vigor that its form automatically becomes dramatic."[56]

Unfortunately, very little is known about the reception of Mérimée's works in Denmark in general, and about Kierkegaard's knowledge of the author and his specific works in particular. Nevertheless, it is easy to assume that Kierkegaard could have had an interest in at least some of the Frenchman's published pieces, had they been available to him.

---

[55] Raitt, *Prosper Mérimée*, p. 58.
[56] Fenger, *The Heibergs*, p. 63.

Bibliography

I. Mérimée's Works in The Auction Catalogue *of Kierkegaard's Library*

None.

II. Works in The Auction Catalogue *of Kierkegaard's Library that Discuss Mérimée*

[Gyllembourg, Thomasine], *To Tidsaldre. Novelle af Forfatteren til "En Hverdags-Historie,"* ed. by Johan Ludvig Heiberg, Copenhagen: C.A. Reitzel 1845, p. vi (*ASKB* 1563).

Thomsen, Grimur, *Om den nyfranske Poesi, et Forsøg til Besvarelse af Universitetets æsthetiske Priisspørgsmaal for 1841: "Har Smag og Sands for Poesi gjort Frem- eller Tilbageskridt i Frankrig i de sidste Tider og hvilken er Aarsagen?,"* Copenhagen: Wahlske Boghandling 1843, p. lxv; p. 129 (*ASKB* 1390).

Heiberg, Johan Ludvig, "Leiligheden. Af Mérimée (Oversat af J.L.H.). I. Oversætterens Forerindring," *Kjøbenhavns flyvende Post*, vol. 1, no. 14, February 1, 1830 [p. 62] (see *ASKB* 1606–1607; U55).

III. Secondary Literature on Kierkegaard's Relation to Mérimée

Fenger, Henning, *Kierkegaard, The Myths and Their Origins. Studies in the Kierkegaardian Papers and Letters*, trans. by George C. Schoolfield, New Haven and London: Yale University Press 1980, pp. 92–3; p. 125; p. 175.

— "Kierkegaard: A Literary Approach," in *Kierkegaard and His Contemporaries. The Culture of Golden Age Denmark*, ed. by Jon Stewart, Berlin and New York: Walter de Gruyter 2003 (*Kierkegaard Studies. Monograph Series*, vol. 10), pp. 301–18, see p. 313.

Grimsley, Ronald, *Søren Kierkegaard and French Literature*, Cardiff: University of Wales Press 1966, p. 7.

Hertel, Hans, "P.L. Møller and Romanticism in Danish Literature," in *Kierkegaard and His Contemporaries. The Culture of Golden Age Denmark*, ed. by Jon Stewart, Berlin and New York: Walter de Gruyter 2003 (*Kierkegaard Studies. Monograph Series*, vol. 10), pp. 356–72, see p. 364; p. 366.

Molière:

An Existential Vision of Authenticity in Man Across Time

Jeanette Bresson Ladegaard Knox

In early seventeenth-century France it was the strict and forceful governance of Cardinal Richelieu (1585–1642) that led to the creation of an absolute monarchy. The Cardinal had a defining influence on French political and intellectual life; he founded the French Academy and organized the French political structure. Almost single-handedly Richelieu paved the way for the exorbitant throne of Louis XIV whose enormous court at the Louvre and in Versaille set the stage for an affected tone of the aristocracy, while the church remained Pietistic, dogmatic, and dominant. But French theater is also indebted to the Cardinal since he helped transform the Parisian stage from leading a dilettante and pitiful existence (as well as being a literary disaster) to being a rich, innovative, and talented artistic environment of which Molière is a glorious example.[1]

Molière was born Jean-Baptiste Poquelin in 1622 in rue Saint Honoré near the Pont Neuf bridge in Paris at the time of Pierre Corneille (1606–84), Jean Racine (1639–99), Pascal (1623–62), Descartes (1596–1650), and Hobbes (1588–1679).[2] In 1644 Poquelin signed a contract *Jean Baptiste Poquelin, dit Molière* thereby creating one of the most famous literary stage names, or pseudonyms, in the world.

---

[1]   Cardinal Richelieu had a state of the art theater, Hôtel de Richelieu, built in his palace which 20 years after his death in 1642, was renamed Palais Royal and handed over to Molière by his protegé the king, Louis XIV.

[2]   Descartes' revolutionary books *Discours de la Méthode* (1637) and *Meditationes de Prima Philosophia* (1641) had already been published when he visited Paris and his friend Pierre Gassendi in 1642. Molière had attended some of Gassendi's lectures around the same time, giving him good opportunity to have encountered Descartes or at least to have been introduced to the new thinking. Descartes brought the age of reason to France and a focus on the individual's free will with his famous remark "*Cogito ergo sum.*" One can easily imagine the appeal of such thinking for a free spirit like Molière. One of his most fascinating characters is that of the *raisonneur*, who is a man of reason offering a contrast to the protagonists' extremism as wonderfully illustrated by Philinte in the *Misanthrope* or Cléante in *Tartuffe*. The *raisonneur*, is the voice of common sense, wisdom, nature, and moderation, inviting the fanatics to self-examination and confrontation of the evil in the self. Molière could also have met both Pascal and Hobbes who lived in Paris from 1640 to 1651 and whose friends included Marsenne and Gassendi.

To both friends and future admirers of Molière, his choice of this name is an enigma. He never explained why he chose the name or its origin. In fact, Molière's life is in large part covered by a veil. Unlike the case with Kierkegaard, we are not in possession of Molière's original papers and manuscripts or his library. Posterity is left with a couple of dedications and prefaces of the first editions of his plays, 3 *placets* (pleadings) to the king, Louis XIV, in connection with the *Tartuffe* affair and a handful of poems, and, due to contemporary publication and attentive colleagues, all of Molière's 31 comedies have been preserved.

Molière's theater company, *L'Illustre Théâtre*, had a rough start, having young and inexperienced actors and traditional material to perform. The troupe decided to leave the capital and perform around the country. It was during these formative years that Molière started to write. After having toured the provinces with the troupe for 12 years, Molière returned to Paris in 1658 where the standard repertoire was tragedy. Tragedy was viewed as a more sophisticated and refined form of artistic expression than comedy. Corneille was the hero on the Parisian stage, a master of the grand theatrical style. He was the epitome of the French classic heroic tragedies and enjoyed the honor and respect of his colleagues and the aristocratic audience.

Molière, however, found this traditional style to be majestic, pompous, monotonous, and ridiculous. He wanted real people on stage who talked and walked like real people, characters who did not declaim their lines while facing the audience in an extravagant manner that sought their applause. Where the traditional style hid reality behind a mask of bombastic, idealized, and eccentric playwriting and acting, Molière wanted to peal off all abstract layers of his characters in order to expose the natural and naked aspects of human existence in all its glory or horror. Kierkegaard's decision to have various pseudonyms do his analysis of human existence, instead of doing a more traditional abstract analysis *à la* Hegel or Sibbern, mirrors Molière's wish to depict human dilemmas, choices, and situations through characters that the audience could relate to or identify with, while laughing at them. Both authors use their characters as a channel for exploring the human spirit and human judgment, and for emphasizing the concrete nature of man's task in life; they avoid juxtaposing one's social role and status with one's identity with the aim of becoming who one already is (Kierkegaard) or bringing out one's natural character and to live and act without pretense (Molière).

Seventeenth-century French society was becoming increasingly aware of the philosophy of reason as the individual was becoming more important and less dependent upon God. On the threshold to the period of Enlightenment and long before Kierkegaard, Molière defended the refusal to be subjected to the social and religious doctrines of others without having been given the chance to relate to them first in order to personally digest them. Though it is certainly an exaggeration to interpret Molière as an early example of existential thinking in the Kierkegaardian sense, much in his plays does defend the quest for individual authenticity, liberation from exterior and interior tyranny, and confrontation with the major questions in any individual's life: death, identity, despair, responsibility, freedom, and love.

Molière lived in an era where the aristocracy glorified a snobbish and grandiose behavior, a time for marquis, barons, and dukes with names such as the Marquis de Sablé and the Duke de La Feuillade (who is said to have been the real life version of the ridiculous marquis in *La critique de l'Ecole des femmes* (1663)). It was a time interested in flamboyant living. Molière stood in opposition as the critical watchdog of his time, as an incisive social critic, ridiculing institutions from organized religion to medicine. His polemical opposition would put him on the lips of priests and aristocrats, pious and poor people.

Molière was loved and hated all at the same time, and in this way both Molière and Kierkegaard enjoyed similar notoriety. Situated in two different centuries, they became the talk of the town. Everybody but the aristocracy and the church welcomed both Molière's sharp parody of the elite that took itself too seriously, and his bold attempts to expose the prejudices, moods, and caprices of his time and protect the vulnerable and tortuous search for the natural self. One of these attempts is wonderfully portrayed in *L'Ecole des femmes* (1662). The chief personage in the play is the middle-aged egomaniac, Arnolphe, who seeks to correct and control existence to an extreme extent. He is utterly convinced that the perfect solution for safeguarding a marriage and keeping a wife chaste and devoted is by keeping her in ignorance. One should not cultivate the intellect of a girl but rather arrange for her to grow up a fool, which Arnolphe desperately tries with Agnes, his ward and future wife. However, from being an ignorant young girl, who asks about whether children are born out of the ear, she gradually matures and reveals a confident personality of her own, due in large part to the man, Horace, whom she is in love with.

Molière's implicit encouragement to fight against being manipulated by others and against being robbed of one's voice, one's identity and personality, echoes Kierkegaard's critique of the philistine and Kierkegaard's quest for an individual to become what he already is. Arnolphe is somewhat of a philistine; he is a product of his society, making decisions that he thinks are his own but that are basically the work of anonymous forces around him. He is in self-betrayal; if anybody loses their identity in the play, it is certainly Arnolphe, not Agnes. Agnes expresses both the importance of personal appropriation in the journey to selfhood (in Kierkegaard's terminology) and portrays the interplay and interdependence of love and identity which can be said to be the overall message of Kierkegaard's *Works of Love* (1847).

People cherished Molière's reading of human existence with its focus on common sense, self-examination, individual decision-making, and responsibility, while a large part of the literary circle, the aristocratic milieu and the Catholic Church saw him as a menace to their world-view and view of human nature. Molière favored, explored, and developed a revolutionary style for the stage that changed French theater and French comic drama; he emphasized that a play is a team effort and that the characters should be three-dimensional.[3] He depicted all facets of human character, creating the *comédie de caractére* (character plays).[4] Just as Kierkegaard carefully

---

[3]   Molière introduced stage directing as one of the first in the history of theater. See his fantastic *L'impromptu de Versaille* (1663) in which we gain considerable insight into Molière as a theater director and actor but most interestingly as a stage director.

[4]   Though Molière definitely made the *comédie de caractére* his own, his plays are generally characterized by his mixing intrigue, virtue, and character comedy, just as it is not entirely true to state that his plays are strictly comedies since some of them delicately balance between tragedy and comedy, for instance, *Le Misanthrope* and *Tartuffe*.

and meticulously created many human types that exhibited great psychological realism and satirical wit, for instance, Johannes the Seducer or Judge William, so also Molière was a master at capturing the universally true in the individual. He created a gallery of archetypes: Argan (from *Le Malade imaginaire*) is a representation of hypochondria, Tartuffe of hypocrisy, Alceste (of *Le Misanthrope*) of rigid idealism and so forth. We will never meet the corrupt and ice-cold Johannes the Seducer (from *Either/Or*) or the equally corrupt and ice-cold Don Juan (from *Don Juan ou le festin de pierre*) in flesh and blood, though they still represent a mirror of the human character; they express a personified concept that the author wishes to clarify. Molière's plays are a study of human nature in its most delightful and most devious dimensions. They portray in a sharply focused way existential themes and ethical dilemmas that Kierkegaard two centuries later would expose in an unprecedented manner, with conciseness and subtlety.

Molière's enemies preferred to label him a simple (but nonetheless dangerous) author of farces. Throughout his life he was, indeed, greatly influenced by the Italian genre *commedia dell'arte*, and though he created human types and not individual persons both in his *comédie de caractére* and in his farces just like the Italian mime tradition, it is just as wrong to interpret Molière this way as it is to view Charlie Chaplin or Dario Fo as simple comics with no depth, or to read Kierkegaard merely as a poetic spin-doctor. Molière added an openhearted humanity, original profundity, and audacious sincerity to the genre which is obvious in the outrageously absurd yet eternally true plays *Les Précieuses Ridicules* (1659) or *Le Medicin malgré lui* (1666). In this latter, just as in *Le Malade imaginaire* (1673) which was to be Molière's last play, he pokes fun at the medical profession and its gullible clientele. While the former is more of a nonsensical farce, a farce primarily for entertainment value, the latter shows considerable substance dealing with issues such as death versus life and mind versus body. Both plays, on different levels, are a celebration of human folly and about self-deception to which we can easily imagine the amusement and attention of Kierkegaard, himself a gifted creator of fugitives of reality.

Both Molière and Kierkegaard were publicly humiliated. Kierkegaard suffered humiliation in the streets and in newspapers. Molière suffered maybe even more than Kierkegaard since he became the victim of vicious intrigues, slanderous gossip, and outright lies that were all a conscious attempt to silence him. In no other incident was this so flagrant as the *Tartuffe* affair. If Kierkegaard believed that he went through a rough time during his attack on the church, he would surely revise his opinion if he had to live through the nightmare that Molière was dragged through after having performed *Le Tartuffe ou l'imposteur* (1664–69).

Tartuffe was, one can argue, Molière's attack on the Church, though unlike Kierkegaard, Molière did not consciously stage or encourage any public attack.[5]

---

[5]   *Tartuffe* created a huge controversy right from the beginning. Molière performed the play for the first time on May 12, 1664 for the royal court in Versailles. Pressured by religious groups, in particular the Compagny of the Holy Sacrament supported by the Queen Mother, Louis XIV had to ban any public showing of the play. Due to several critical pamphlets published by priests, Molière sent the king a letter (*placet*) where he defended himself and his play. When the king allowed the play to be played two years later, it was immediately shut

Molière rigorously attacked religious fanatism, religious hypocrisy and the abandonment of individual reason in *Tartuffe*. He did not claim the falsification of religion *per se*, rather he criticized the use of religion for egoistic purposes, for turning it into an apparatus for power over people that would rob them of their individual freedom. Implicitly and almost involuntarily, Molière came to argue for uprightness and authenticity, be it in religious faith or in a more secular existence, though in his terminology it would be called "naturalness." He loathed simulation, the *brouhaha* of people.[6] He praised integrity and honesty. One cannot but wonder why Kierkegaard in his writings did not refer to *Tartuffe*, which had been translated into Danish as early as 1724, since this play beautifully captures both the quest for individual appropriation of truth and the coming to terms with who we are. One reason could be that Kierkegaard did not have access to the play. Did Kierkegaard, in fact, have access to the writings of Molière, including *Tartuffe*?

We know that Kierkegaard owned a copy of *L'Ecole des femmes* and *Le Malade imaginaire* since they are listed in the catalogue of the all books sold at the auction following his death in 1855.[7] But looking at the register of the book collection of the Athenæum reading society,[8] to which Kierkegaard had access, we find listed the collected works of Molière. However, the works were in French, a language that Kierkegaard spoke and read very poorly, if at all. In 1813, the year of Kierkegaard's birth, Knud Lyhne Rahbek's (1760–1830) translation of selected Molière plays came out in Denmark, and he did have these at his disposal since this edition is registered in the auction catalogue.[9] The translation consists of four Molière plays: *Le Malade imaginaire*, *L'École des Mariés* (1661), *Don Juan* and, finally, *Le Misanthrope*.

We may never know if Kierkegaard ever read *Le Misanthrope*, which was translated into Danish in 1724 as was *Tartuffe*, though it is highly unlikely that he was unaware of the play since it is among Molière's masterpieces. He could not have seen *Le Misanthrope* on stage since the records show that it was performed between 1751 and 1756, that is, before Kierkegaard's birth, and again in 1880, that is, after

---

down by the police commissioner. The king was away in Flanders and yet another letter was sent by Molière. Shortly after the situation worsened as the archbishop of Paris threatened to excommunicate everyone who read, performed or heard the play. Molière was forced to shut down his theater for a couple of weeks at great financial losses. Not until February 5, 1669 was Molière finally allowed to play *Tartuffe* at Palais Royal. It became an instant and immense success.

[6]   *Brouhaha* comes from scene 9 of *Les Précieuses ridicules* (1659); this beautifully written ironic farce about the ridiculous manner of speaking, behaving and posing of the court is also a hilarious mime of the royal actors who, without any consideration for the text, would roar out the last verse to gain the appraisal of the audience.

[7]   See *Fruentimmer-Skolen. Komedie i 5 Acter*, trans. by Thomas Overskou, Copenhagen n. p. 1847 (*ASKB* U 82); *Den indbildte Syge: Komedie i 3 Acter*, trans. by Thomas Overskou, Copenhagen n. p. 1849 (*ASKB* U 83).

[8]   See *Fortegnelse over Selskabet Athenæums Bogsamling*, vols. 1–2, Copenhagen: Bianco Luno 1847–57, vol. 1, p. 345.

[9]   See *Molieres udvalgte Skuespil*, new trans. by Knud Lyhne Rahbek, Copenhagen: G. Bonnier 1813 (*ASKB* 1921).

his death, nor is it likely that he saw *Tartuffe* since he was only 14 years old when the Royal Theater played it in September 1827.[10]

Both *Tartuffe* and *Le Misanthrope* present a candid commentary on a decadent, hypocritical environment that smothers the individual, regardless of whether this infectious environment is manifested through religion, literature, or science. Both plays courageously and brilliantly illustrate the importance of having a critical stance, the invaluable guidance of conscience, and the danger of bigotry, all of which cannot but have interested Kierkegaard's sharp mind and concern for the individual's self-relation.

It is one thing to read plays, another to see them on stage. Kierkegaard and Molière shared their love for the theater. For Molière, it was his life. He was linked to the theater like letters to a book: he was an actor, a theater director, a stage director, and playwright all in one. For Kierkegaard, it was a passion that he would never give up on; a passion that represented a source of relaxation and reflection. But did Kierkegaard ever see any plays by Molière? And if he did, which ones?

No one can say for certain that Kierkegaard saw any Molière plays since we are not in possession of any of his individual theater tickets—though we do know that he had a subscription to the Royal Theater. Similarly, he makes no references to actual performances of Molière plays that he saw. However, we do know what was performed at the Royal Theater at this time. The records show that several Molière plays were performed in Kierkegaard's lifetime which made it possible for him to have seen numerous plays by the French writer.[11] *Le Medicin malgré lui* was performed between June 17, 1842 and May 13, 1850. The play *L'Ecole des femmes* was put on stage several times between February 19, 1847 and May 4, 1848. *Le Malade imaginaire* was performed occasionally between November 15, 1849 and December 6, 1851. Finally, Kierkegaard could have seen *L'Avare* since it played a couple of times between October 14, 1850 and January 23, 1850.

Thus Kierkegaard could have seen two plays of which he also had the book. Although we can only speculate about Kierkegaard actually going to the theater to see Molière plays, the fact that he owned two plays by Molière makes the case at least plausible. This becomes particularly plausible when we compare the year that he purchased *L'Ecole des femmes* and *Le Malade imaginaire* with the year that the plays were performed at the Royal Theater. The auction catalogue indicates that Kierkegaard bought *L'Ecole des femmes* the same year as it was put on stage and the same applies for *Le Malade imaginaire*. There is a logical explanation for this since the publications Kierkegaard bought were publications of plays that the theater was playing that particular season, and it would thus be plausible to assume that he bought these works after having seen them performed.

---

[10]   This information comes from Arthur Aumont and Edgar Collin, *Det danske Nationalteater 1748–1889*, vols. 1–3 [in 5 sections], [Copenhagen]: J. Jørgensen 1896–99, vol. 3, section 5.2, pp. 324–6.

[11]   See the overview in ibid., vol. 1, section 2 ("Tabellarisk Repertoire-Oversigt"), see "Udenlandske Forfattere og Komponister," pp. 41–2.

The only explicit reference to Molière is in Kierkegaard's papers,[12] where on October 29, 1836 he enters a line referring to Molière's humorous perception of Don Juan, and in the subchapter "Other Versions of Don Juan Considered in Relation to the Musical Interpretation" in *Either/Or* (1843), where Kierkegaard reflects on Molière's *Don Juan ou le festin de pierre*. As noted, Molière's *Don Juan* had first been translated into Danish in 1813 by Knud Lyhne Rahbek, a book in Kierkegaard's possession, and since Kierkegaard devotes considerable attention to Molière's play by comparing it to Mozart's *Don Juan*, it is safe to say that he had carefully read it. Kierkegaard could also have seen Molière's *Don Juan* on stage. However, he would have seen *Don Juan* performed after he wrote his reflections on it since the records show that *Don Juan* was performed several times between June 15, 1844 and May 5, 1850.[13] It is a known fact that Kierkegaard went to see and hear Mozart's *Don Juan* at the Royal Theater numerous times.

Molière and Kierkegaard shared a great interest in the character of Don Juan which has also caught the attention of Mozart, Byron, and even Heiberg. But Kierkegaard's reflective analysis is rather critical towards Molière's treatment of the Spanish womanizer. Their portrayal of this fascinating mind of a seducer reveals fundamental differences in the understanding of the character. The major discrepancy lies in how Molière incorporates a religious and more reflective dimension to the character where Kierkegaard insists on a Don Juan of purity (pure pleasure, pure narcissism) and above all of non-reflection: "The turning point in the interpretation of Don Juan has been designated above in this way: as soon as he is given spoken lines, everything is changed. That is, the reflection that motivates the lines reflects him out of the vagueness in which he is only musically audible."[14] Thus, it is music, as expressed in Mozart's opera *Don Juan*, that best captures this abstract, elusive character that never becomes an "individual" [*hiin Enkelte*], but who exists in the bizarre intersection between pure idea and sensual reality. His existence is as incoherent and fragmented as the pearls on a string without the string. He is obscure, intangible, and fluid.

Molière's Don Juan is more than (but also) just a Kierkegaardian aesthete obsessed with his scrupulous search for immediate pleasure, buried in his own sensuality and stripped of any conscience, self-reflection, guilt, and remorse. He is a free thinker who takes much pleasure in criticizing God and the church. He is confronted with the paradoxical reality and the monotony of life like the rest of us.

Kierkegaard views Don Juan as a principle, a category; Molière views him as an individual, a man. Though the Don Juan of both Molière and Kierkegaard expounds the slavery of the moment, it is Kierkegaard's conviction that, by making Don Juan an individual, Molière makes him a comic figure stripped of his aesthetic stance to life: "he promptly loses the ideality he has in the opera, and the effect becomes comic."[15] It makes the audience focus more on Don Juan's interests and the conflicts

---

[12]   *Pap.* I C 109 / *JP* 5, 5170.
[13]   Aumont and Collin, *Det danske Nationalteater 1748–1889*, vol. 2, section 5.1, pp. 146–8.
[14]   *SKS* 2, 109 / *EO1*, 106.
[15]   *SKS* 2, 112 / *EO1*, 109.

he creates, on the psychology and morality of the personality, than on his ideality or purity as a category:

> Don Juan's desire is aroused because he sees a girl happy in her relation to the one she loves....This is an interest that in the opera would not occupy us at all, simply because Don Juan is not a reflective individual. As soon as Don Juan is interpreted as a reflective individual, an ideality corresponding to the musical ideality can be attained only when the matter is shifted into the psychological realm.[16]

By borrowing from the tradition of the Middle Ages, where Don Juan is the ideal seducer (as shown by Mozart), Kierkegaard believes that Molière betrays the original character.

At the heart of Kierkegaard's writings lies the spirit of the theater: drama, dialogue, and dilemma. At times this spirit comes to the forefront like the prosceniums on a stage, and at other times it lurks in the wings, waiting to jump out on stage. Kierkegaard's style of writing is known for its use of dialogue, but it is, obviously, a different kind of dialogue to the one playwrights use. Molière's use of dialogue is a kind of ping-pong, an implicitly reflective dialogue between actual individuals (the dialogue of exposure), whereas Kierkegaard's use of dialogue is of a more explicitly reflective and analytical nature (the dialogue of introspection). Kierkegaard stages a theme within a concrete context and puts individuals across from each other in an often passionate and elaborate debate. We see the debate between the aesthete and Judge William of *Either/Or*, the debate between Climacus and his critic in *Philosophical Fragments* or the exchanges between the young man, the fashion dealer, Victor Eremita, Constantin Constantius, and Johannes the Seducer in *Stages on Life's Way*.

A play needs to expose the intrinsic conflict of particular situations thus creating dilemmas for the lives of its characters. Without the conflict and dilemma, the play looses its dramatic punch and becomes uninteresting. Dilemma is what keeps the motor of the play running, sustaining suspense and curiosity. It is the substance that creates the drama. As a playwright, Molière was of course very conscious of the practical and indispensable tools for creating a drama. In *Tartuffe*, for example, the audience witnesses the intense conflict that the presence of Tartuffe and the talk of the blinded Orgon create within the family. Implicitly Orgon is faced early on with the dilemma of choice, responsibility, and faith: to go with Tartuffe or with his family. The characters of the household of Orgon are all entangled in an increasingly frantic and melodramatic situation, culminating in the scene where Damis, the son of Orgon, exposes Tartuffe's, the imposter's, morally despicable behavior and artificial piety. But we find a similar use of conflict, drama, and dilemma in Kierkegaard's writings. Johannes the Seducer of *Either/Or* carefully paves the way for the dramatic play with Cordelia abandoning her in the end with a multitude of conflicts and questions. This reflective seducer takes pleasure in the diabolic pursuit, in the creation of a fake but enchanting and mesmerizing reality, and in the cynical rejection. Johannes' scheme is highly dramatic, leaving the readers sitting at the edge of their seats dreading his next devious move.

---

[16]   *SKS* 2, 111 / *EO1*, 108.

Kierkegaard did not meticulously study Molière's work though he had ample opportunity to both read and see his plays. It is surprising that he did not engage in a more elaborate study of Molière given that their existential gaze on life, their sense of biting humor, and sensibility towards language seem very close. Thus, one can conclude, that, although Kierkegaard does not allude frequently to Molière in his writings there is sufficient evidence to justify a more elaborate and comparative study of the significant and similar existential messages of these two brilliant writers.

Bibliography

I. Molière's Works in The Auction Catalogue *of Kierkegaard's Library*

Molieres udvalgte Skuespil, new trans. by Knud Lyhne Rahbek, Copenhagen: G. Bonnier 1813 (*ASKB* 1921).
Fruentimmer-Skolen. Komedie i 5 Acter, trans. by Thomas Overskou, Copenhagen n.p. 1847 (*ASKB* U 82).
Den indbildte Syge: Komedie i 3 Acter, trans. by Thomas Overskou, Copenhagen n.p. 1849 (*ASKB* U 83).

II. Works in The Auction Catalogue *of Kierkegaard's Library that Discuss Molière*

[Becker, Karl Friedrich], *Karl Friedrich Beckers Verdenshistorie, omarbeidet af Johan Gottfried Woltmann*, vols. 1–12, trans. by J. Riise, Copenhagen: Fr. Brummers Forlag 1822–29, vol. 8, p. 402 (*ASKB* 1972–1983).
Flögel, Karl Friedrich, *Geschichte der komischen Litteratur*, vols. 1–4, Liegnitz and Leipzig: David Siegert 1784–87, vol. 1, p. 243; p. 307; vol. 4, p. 215; pp. 264–6 (*ASKB* 1396–1399).
[Hegel, Georg Wilhelm Friedrich], *Georg Wilhelm Friedrich Hegel's Vorlesungen über die Aesthetik*, vols. 1–3, ed. by von Heinrich Gustav Hotho, Berlin: Verlag von Duncker und Humblot 1835–38 (vols. 10.1–10.3 in *Georg Wilhelm Friedrich Hegel's Werke. Vollständige Ausgabe*, vols. 1–18, ed. by Philipp Marheineke et al., Berlin: Verlag von Duncker und Humblot 1832–45), vol. 3, p. 577 (*ASKB* 1384–1386).
[Richter, Johann Paul Friedrich], Jean Paul, *Vorschule der Aesthetik nebst einigen Vorlesungen in Leipzig über die Parteien der Zeit*, vols. 1–3, 2nd revised ed., Stuttgart and Tübingen: J.G. Cotta 1813, vol. 1, p. 292 (*ASKB* 1381–1383).
Schlegel, August Wilhelm, *Ueber dramatische Kunst und Litteratur. Vorlesungen*, vols. 1–2 [vol. 2 in 2 Parts], Heidelberg: Mohr und Zimmer 1809–11, vol. 2.1, pp. 226–55 (*ASKB* 1392–1394).
Steffens, Henrich, *Was ich erlebte. Aus der Erinnerung niedergeschrieben*, vols. 1–10, Breslau: Josef Max 1840–44, vol. 9, p. 9; p. 351; vol. 10, p. 9 (*ASKB* 1834–1843).
Sulzer, Johann Georg, *Allgemeine Theorie der Schönen Künste, in einzeln, nach alphabetischer Ordnung der Kunstwörter auf einander folgenden, Artikeln abgehandelt*, vols. 1–4 and a register volume, 2nd revised ed., Leipzig: Weidmann 1792–99, vol. 2, p. 75 (*ASKB* 1365–1369).
Thomsen, Grimur, *Om den nyfranske Poesi, et Forsøg til Besvarelse af Universitetets æsthetiske Priisspørgsmaal for 1841: "Har Smag og Sands for Poesi gjort*

Frem- eller Tilbageskridt i Frankrig i de sidste Tider og hvilken er Aarsagen?,"
Copenhagen: Wahlske Boghandlings Forlag 1843, p. 5; p. 7; p. 57; p. 134 (*ASKB* 1390).

III. Secondary Literature on Kierkegaard's Relation to Molière

Grimsley, Ronald, "The Don Juan Theme in Molière and Kierkegaard," *Comparative Literature*, vol. 6, no. 4, 1954, pp. 316–34.
—— "Kierkegaard and the Don Juan Legend. 1. Kierkegaard as a Critic of Molière," in his *Søren Kierkegaard and French Literature. Eight Comparative Studies*, Cardiff: University of Wales Press 1966, pp. 11–25.
—— "Kierkegaard and the Don Juan Legend. 2. Kierkegaard and Laclos," in his *Søren Kierkegaard and French Literature. Eight Comparative Studies*, Cardiff: University of Wales Press 1966, pp. 26–45.

Wolfgang Amadeus Mozart:
The Love for Music and the Music of Love

Elisabete M. de Sousa

I. Mozart in Golden Age Denmark

At an early age, Wolfgang Amadeus Mozart (1756–91) witnessed the celebration of his musical genius, though he had to strive during his lifetime in order to get the chance and the occasion to create many of his works, which eventually outdid all that his contemporaries might have expected from a child prodigy. Soon after his death, the growing demand for his scores prompted the first editions in Germany; by 1806, Breitkopf and Härtel had already published 17 volumes, including piano compositions (solo and duet), piano concertos, string quartets, a few masses, the complete *Don Giovanni*, and many concert arias, and by 1807–08 a large number of orchestral works had also been published.[1] During the next two decades, over a hundred music publishers from many European cities, Copenhagen included, published roughly two-thirds of Mozart's production, comprising symphonies, *divertimenti*, variations, concerts, chamber music, and operas, in order to meet the demand for scores for professional use as well as domestic, since Mozart's music was already being widely used as teaching material. By then, Mozart was indeed ranked in importance with Joseph Haydn (1732–1809) and was accepted as a forerunner of Ludwig van Beethoven (1770–1827). He was on his way to gaining the middle position in the triad of composers (Bach, Mozart, Beethoven) who would later be acknowledged as the great tradition and recognized as masters by the Romantic school. Although later in the second half of the nineteenth century, Mozart's star would fall into oblivion to rise again after the first centenary of his death, until the mid-century he was first acclaimed as a forerunner of the Romantics and then as an epitome of classicism. Mozart would then be often praised in the terms used to describe the idea of what the poetic in Beethoven stands for, which meant that many statements ended up by saying that "music has reached the level of the poetic by manifesting form as expression, and expression as form," as Carl

---

[1]   See John Daverio, "Mozart in the Nineteenth Century," in *The Cambridge Companion to Mozart*, ed. by Simon P. Keefe, Cambridge: Cambridge University Press 2003, pp. 171–84, see p. 172 for the present reference. The Copenhagen musical circles were also current subscribers of German editions of Mozart's scores, see p. 172, note 12.

Dahlhaus eloquently observed.[2] On the other hand, he would also be praised in the style used by Johann Joachim Winckelmann (1717–68) to pay tribute to Greek art, as Robert Schumann (1810–56) did in 1834: "Serenity, repose, grace—these are the characteristics of ancient works of art, to be found in Mozart's school as well. Just as the Greek pictured his thundering Jupiter with a serene expression, so Mozart withholds his bolts of lightning."[3] Meanwhile, the operas of his later period, the three Mozart-Da Ponte ones, *Le Nozze di Figaro* (1786), *Don Giovanni* (1787) and *Così fan tutte* (1790), together with *Die Zauberflöte* (1791), assured him fame and popularity all over Europe; nevertheless, these early productions were far from being faithful to the works originally created and, consequently, had little in common with what modern audiences were familiar with, namely, because there remained few vestiges of the original librettos by Lorenzo Da Ponte (1749–1838) and Emanuel Schikaneder (1751–1812), as we shall see.

What is more, one wonders how these operas managed to contribute to Mozart's status as classic, due to all the cuts, arrangements and re-arrangements of arias, duets and sometimes of complete acts, which engendered eccentricities, such as *Les Mystères d'Isis*, a puzzling version of *Die Zauberflöte* staged in Paris in 1801, composed of extracts taken from *La Clemenza di Tito*, *Le Nozze di Figaro* and *Don Giovanni*,[4] an opera that would have a similar destiny. In 1834 it was produced by the Académie Royale, at a time when it was already labeled as a canonical work, though with the required changes to transform the original *dramma giocoso* into a romantic *grand opéra* comprehending five acts, ballets, a redistribution of the voices and a new libretto in French. This meant that new scenes and *entr'actes* were introduced in order to create a romantic image of the hero, deeply influenced by E.T.A. Hoffmann (1776–1822) and his novella *Don Juan* (1813),[5] as well as by some poems of Alfred de Musset (1810–57). As a result, the public saw new scenes with Don Juan having a premonitory dream of his downfall in the churchyard scene and Donna Anna committing suicide and being buried in the last act, whereas the role of Donna Elvira was effaced; moreover, the relation between Leporello and his master lost loyalty and gained sarcasm.[6] In Germany, the original *Don Giovanni* was also

---

[2]   See Carl Dahlhaus, *Nineteenth-Century Music*, trans. by J. Bradford Robinson, Berkeley and Los Angeles: University of California Press 1989, pp. 32–3; p. 85.

[3]   Robert Schumann, *Gesammelte Schriften über Musik und Musiker*, vols. 1–4, Wiesband: Breitkopf & Härtel 1985 (photomechanical reprint of the edition, Leipzig: Wiegand 1854), vol. 1, p. 12. See also Leon B. Plantinga, *Schumann as Critic*, New Haven and London: Yale University Press 1967, pp. 92–4.

[4]   Arranged by Christian Kalkbrenner (1755–1806), the father of Friedrich Kalkbrenner (1785–1849), who would be a famous virtuoso pianist and teacher, among others of the young Friedrich Chopin (1810–49).

[5]   See E.T.A. Hoffmann, "Don Juan," in E.T.A. Hoffmann, *Sämtliche Werke in sechs Bänden*, vols. 1–6, ed. by Wulf Segebrecht and Hartmut Steinecke, Frankfurt am Main: Deutscher Klassiker Verlag 1985–2004, vol. 2.1, pp. 83–97.

[6]   For a detailed account of this production, see Katharine Ellis, "Rewriting 'Don Giovanni,' or 'The Thieving Magpies,' " *Journal of the Royal Musical Association*, vol. 119, no. 2, 1994, pp. 212–50. For a full analysis of German production, see Christof Bitter, *Wandlungen in der Inszzenierungsformen des "Don Giovanni" von 1787 bis 1928*,

quickly dropped, and before Mozart's death there had already been performances in sixteen cities using seven versions of the libretto, all of them substituting spoken dialogue for the recitatives, generally farcical in tone, since the opera was presented as a *Singspiel*, a sub-genre that would soon become extinct, although it still proved to be popular at the time[7] The first translation by Friedrich Rochlitz (1769–1842) was published in 1801, and it remained in use until the mid-century; it included previous material from the 1789 versions by Christian Gottlob Neefe (1748–98) and Heinrich Gottlieb Schmieder (1763–1811), as well as the 1790 version by Friedrich Ludwig Schröder (1744–1816); all of them borrowed material from Molière's *Don Juan* and the German popular tradition, and they were performed so many times and with such success that the ideas incorporated into the work became accepted as being the original ones by Mozart and Da Ponte[8] Rochlitz's division into four acts, with one of the new acts beginning with the entrance of Massetto and Zerlina and the other with the churchyard scene, quickly became standard, as well as the omission of the *scena ultima*. With this omission, the public no longer joined the remaining characters to ponder the consequences of sinning and not repenting and was thus deprived of any references to a deserved punishment at the end of the opera or at the beginning, since *Il dissoluto punito ossia il Don Giovanni* would make his fame under the original Spanish name, *Don Juan*.

This pattern of modifications, even if it was not thoroughly copied in other productions elsewhere in Europe, set the example for the continual shaping of Don Juan, precisely because it departed from Da Ponte's version, and inevitably gained a strongly romantic contour. The character of Don Juan often became less of a libertine whose misconduct ought to be punished simply by abiding religious and social conventions, and more of a hero whose (dis)grace lagged behind an unusual erotic strength, but who was still capable of determining the behavior of all the other characters in the opera and of outdoing any ordinary human being, nonetheless falling tragically in the end. In the meantime, Hoffmann's *Don Juan* had underlined the aura of mystery and fantasy that surrounded Mozart and his masterpiece, while it exalted the part of Donna Anna, in those days considered to be the dominant feminine role in the opera, whereas it tinged Don Juan with Faustian colors, as a character disputed by God and Satan.[9] In Daverio's opinion,[10] the Rochlitz version should even be regarded as the main source of Hoffmann's *Don Juan*, and later of *Mozart auf der Reise nach Prag* (1856) by Eduard Mörike (1804–75), as well as of

---

Regensburg: Bosse 1961. For an overall view, see James Parakilas, "The Afterlife of Don Giovanni: Turning Production History into Criticism," *The Journal of Musicology*, vol. 8, no. 2, 1990, pp. 251–65.

[7]   On its place in the eighteenth and nineteenth century's operatic productions, see *The Oxford History of Opera*, ed. by Roger Parker, Oxford: Oxford University Press 1996, pp. 67–9; p. 139; p. 160.

[8]   See Julian Rushton, "Don Giovanni in the Theater," in *W.A. Mozart: Don Giovanni*, ed. by Julian Rushton, Cambridge: Cambridge University Press 1994, pp. 68–9.

[9]   For a brief accurate account of the novel, its reception and especially its importance for the shaping of the Don Juan myth see Pierre Brunel, "E.T.A. Hoffmann," in *Dictionnaire de Don Juan*, ed. by Pierre Brunel, Paris: Robert Laffont 1999, pp. 468–72.

[10]   See Daverio, "Mozart in the Nineteenth Century," p. 175.

the operatic fantasy, *Réminiscences de Don Juan* (1841) by Franz Liszt (1811–86), which is itself one of the musical sources for Kierkegaard's portrait of the seducer, as I have previously argued.[11]

In reality, the idea that an opera was a set of exchangeable numbers would only very slowly give way to the concept of opera as an unchanging dramatic and musical work; at least until the mid nineteenth century, it sounded only natural that the libretto should be rendered into the native language of the audiences, mostly in a rather free translation; the internal changes in the musical and dramatic structure preferably occurred in the recitatives, borrowing material from other Don Juan sources, and for that reason a new division of acts often became unavoidable. Copenhagen was no exception to this state of affairs; therefore, the first point to be taken into consideration is that Kierkegaard attended performances of Mozart's operas that reproduced this common pattern of free arrangement of the original work, a circumstance which deeply destabilized the character of Don Giovanni (and the whole opera), as we tend to see it either today or as it was premiered in Prague in 1787. It suffices to say that, although *Così fan tutte* was popular in musical circles,[12] Kierkegaard could only have heard its music as the musical accompaniment to *Flugten af Klosteret* (which premiered on December 19, 1826) by Adam Oehlenschläger (1779–1850), who was by no means the only author to make use of Mozart's music for the pursuit of his own artistic purposes. Eugène Scribe (1791–1861) and the different musicians he wrote librettos to followed exactly the same practice, and due to the popularity of the plays and operas, their dramatic and musical solutions would be imitated. As for Johan Ludvig Heiberg (1791–1860), he believed that music played its proper role in the vaudeville and not in opera, be it *seria* or *buffa*; loyal to the principles he had set out in *On Vaudeville as a Form of Dramatic Poetry and its Significance in the Danish Theater*,[13] he borrowed Mozart's music and dramatic solutions for his vaudevilles. Among these, the idea of the letter duet (*Che soave zeffiretto*, *Le Nozze di Figaro*) for *Aprilsnarrene* (1826) probably cost him a parody by Kierkegaard in the character

---

[11]   See Elisabete M. de Sousa, "Kierkegaard's Musical Recollections," *Kierkegaard Studies. Yearbook*, 2008, pp. 85–108.

[12]   It was actually first performed with a libretto translated by A.G. Thoroup (1751–1804) with the title *Elskernes Skole* eller *Væddemaalet* (which premiered on October 19, 1798). From the 1886–87 season onwards it was staged in a translation by Erik Bøgh (1822–99), this time in four acts, entitled *Elskernes Skole* eller *Det gjør de alle!*. However, C.E. Hatting mentions that excerpts were played in concerts, and there is notice of the existence of 96 scores of the opera in Copenhagen in the first half of the nineteenth century, according to the books of the German publisher G.M. Meyer (Braunschweig). See Carsten E. Hatting, *Mozart og Danmark*, Copenhagen: Engstrøm & Sødring Musikforlag 1991, p. 108.

[13]   Johan Ludvig Heiberg, *Om Vaudevillen som dramatisk Digtart, og dens Betydning paa den danske Skueplads*, Copenhagen: Jens Hostrup Schultz 1826. For a detailed account of Heiberg's criticism on opera, see Gerhard Schepelern, "Den nyere italienske Opera, dens Modtagelse i København og Kampen imod den," in his *Italienerne paa Hofteateret*, Copenhagen: Selskabet For Dansk Teaterhistorie og Rhodos 1976, pp. 128–63, especially pp. 153–8. Schepelern discusses extensively Heiberg's views, his role in the production of operas and in the choice of singers.

of Willibald in the *Soap-Cellars* drama,[14] which did not stop him from using music from *Don Giovanni* and *Die Zauberflöte* in *De Uadskillelige* (1857).[15] Moreover, as official playwright and translator (from 1828 onwards) and later as Director of the Royal Theater (1849–56), he continued to supervise opera productions of Mozart and other musicians, which had often undergone such profound changes in their dramaturgy that the translation of the libretto into Danish would definitely sound like a minor issue.

Another point, not to be underestimated, is the fact that it was in Kierkegaard's time, or shortly before, that Mozart's operas were premiered in Copenhagen. This meant that subsequent performances of an opera were more liable to suffer the impact of a number of indiscriminate factors, besides the word or whims of the Theater Director. One can count a disparate number of them, such as the popularity of the singers chosen for the production, the favorable reception of the original scenario of the opera once it was compared to another opera based on the same theme or literary source, or merely the success of other theatrical or musical events which were held in the same season. Accordingly, the positive reception of any other theatrical event might provide the occasion to reassess the number of performances previously scheduled for another production. Since the Royal Theater staged all kinds of theatrical productions, the triumph of a play in the season, be it tragedy or comedy, contemporary or not, by Oehlenschläger or Scribe, Heiberg or Shakespeare, depended to a considerable extent not only on the quality of the play or the current popularity of the author, but also on the successful outcome of at least a few of the above-mentioned factors.

Given that Kierkegaard would presumably have attended Mozart productions from his mid-teens until the early 1850s, only the years between 1831–32 and 1844–45 will be here examined more attentively, since they are the crucial times for his reception of Mozart. For that reason, the second obvious conclusion to keep in mind is that Kierkegaard did not have the opportunity to watch or hear the majority of Mozart's operas, simply because they were not performed at the Royal Theater, the Court Theater, or even at the Vesterbro Theater during that period. On the other hand, the simultaneity of different kinds of opera performances in these three theaters was far from being a bewildering drawback; on the contrary, the fact that the Court Theater and the Vesterbro Theater offered a wide choice of operas by contemporary composers provided the occasion for a close scrutiny of different operatic patterns. Mozart was indeed presented side by side with a group of composers born around the time of his death, who were true representatives either of the triumph of Italian Romantic opera and *belcanto*, or of the French pattern of opera genres, namely, *comique*, *lyrique* or *tragique*, and especially of *grand opéra*, dominated by arias supported by grand choruses and ensembles in tableaux full of local color fitting the

---

[14]   In a note of the manuscript of *The Battle between the Old and the New Soap Cellars*, Willibald is made to sing to the music of *Notte e giorno fatticar*. See Peter Tudvad, "Dyrehavsbakken og det Kgl. Teater," in *Kierkegaards København*, Copenhagen: Politikens Forlag 2004, p. 249.

[15]   See *Om Mozarts Don Juan*, introduced by Carl Johan Elmquist, Copenhagen: Jespersen og Pio 1968, p. 8.

religious, political, and historical context. In the first group, one may count Gaetano Donizetti (1797–1848), Gioacchino Rossini (1792–1868), Vincenzo Bellini (1801–35) and the rising star Giuseppe Verdi (1813–1901),[16] and in the second Giacomo Meyerbeer (1791–1864) and Jacques François Halévy (1799–1862), whose operas created a vivid contrast to the emotionalism and the gothic atmosphere of the Italian ones. These sub-genres showed a striking dissimilarity to Mozart's works, because these, as *Singspiele*, had to rely more heavily on the acting skills of the singers, who also had to be technically apt to meet the highly demanding vocal scores of Mozart's dramatic music. Moreover, in the case of Mozart, his works were originally conceived as operas of numbers (the radically opposite model of the thoroughly composed operas) where full emphasis on the expression of feelings or passions is concentrated in the singing parts, whereas the intrigue is developed in the recitatives which, more than reproducing the development of a plot, often just aim at supplying the necessary clues to allow for the dramaturgy of a scene to be understood or for a sequence of scenes to be coherently articulated. Once they were transformed into *Singspiele*, the spoken dialogue would increase the amount of dramaturgical information, thus widening the gap between the aesthetic impact of the singing moments, be it arias, duets or ensembles, and the actual theatrical interaction, a new situation which might have contributed to drawing attention to the expressive qualities of music.

An overview of the productions of Mozart's operas staged in Copenhagen leaves little doubt, firstly, about the small number of those Kierkegaard must have attended and consequently the ones he was actually acquainted with and, secondly, about the unique position they occupied among the diversity of the representatives of emerging operatic sub-genres. *Don Giovanni*, *Le Nozze di Figaro*, and *Die Zauberflöte* are indeed the only Mozart operas to have been performed not only several times during the same season but also in continuous seasons during the time period in question.[17] Together with *Così fan tutte*, the chances of Kierkegaard having seen *La Clemenza di Tito* (1791) should also be discarded, since *Titus eller Fyrste-Mildhed* had only five performances in the 1822–23 season.[18] Most likely, the same applies to *Die Entführung aus dem Serail* (1782), which was presented as *Bortførelsen fra Seraillet eller Constance og Belmonte*[19] only seven times between 1829 and 1837. Mozart was also popular at other theaters, and the Vesterbro Theater staged four Mozart operas in 1834 and 1835: *Bortførelsen fra Seraillet, Figaros*

---

[16]   Donizetti, Rossini, and Bellini were also produced at the Royal Theater in Kierkegaard's time.
[17]   The data concerning performances of Mozart's operas presented in this article result from information provided by Tudvad, *Kierkegaards København*, pp. 208–91, and by Schepelern, *Italierne paa Hofteateret*.
[18]   The premiere was on January 29, 1823 with the libretto translated by Niels Thoroup Bruun. It was staged with no recitatives, which would be introduced much later (ca. 1860), in a translation by H.H. Nyegaard (1824–93).
[19]   The premiere was on April 1, 1813, and N.T. Bruun was once again responsible for the translation, keeping the original three acts. Bruun would also translate *Die Zauberflöte* with the title *Tryllefløjten*, presenting four acts instead of the original two, following the dramatic pattern imposed by Charles Nuitter (1828–99) and Alexandre Beaume (known as Beaumont, 1827–1909) for *La Flûte enchantée*.

Bryllup, *Don Juan*, and *Tryllefløjten*.[20] The few performances of *Don Giovanni* at the Court Theater deserve to be singled out, since the opera was sung in Italian with the original recitatives, conveying a completely different tone from the *Don Juan* at the Royal Theater, whose dramaturgy closely followed the adaptation introduced in the German theaters; though the five performances of March 1844 were not warmly welcomed because of a heterogeneous casting, the single performance of March 1850 was roundly applauded by a full house.[21]

Le Nozze di Figaro was first performed in the 1820–21 season as *Figaros Givtermaal eller Den gale Dag* (which premiered on January 9, 1821), a translation by Niels Thorup Bruun (1778–1823), which would be used until the 1837–38 season. It was extremely popular and saw an average of almost four performances per season in the nineteenth century;[22] in fact, the 1842–43 season at the Royal Theater was the only one in Kierkegaard's time without a single Mozart opera. Acting as solace, a major event took place at the Court Theater in the spring of 1842; with the support of the guitar musician and composer Henrik Rung (1807–71), who held the post of director of the opera singers at the Royal Theater, the ballet master and choreographer August Bournonville (1805–79) was responsible for the *mise-en-scène* and the choreography of a *Fandango* in two performances of *Le Nozze di Figaro*, in Italian and with recitatives, a much more satisfactory version than the ones at the Royal Theater, although the role of Cherubino was sung by a tenor.[23] This event and the success of the Italian repertoire sung at the Court Theater would eventually set a new pace in opera production at the Royal Theater, with Bournonville taking a more active part in the staging of operas, by putting an end to their customary transformation into *Singspiele*. Together with the already mentioned *Don Giovanni* performances at the Court Theater, the 1842 Bournonville production was the only opportunity to listen to *Le Nozze di Figaro* sung in the original libretto in Kierkegaard's day, since the new 1844 Royal Theater production of this opera by Bournonville would continue to make use of a new translation of the Da Ponte libretto by Nicolai Christian Levin Abrahams (1798–1870), *Figaros Bryllup* staged until 1872.[24]

As Daniel Heartz observes, *Le Nozze di Figaro* benefited from being based on a very well-known play by Beaumarchais that actually served as a subtext,[25] thus

---

[20]   See Schepelerne, *Italienerne paa Hofteateret*, pp. 460–1.

[21]   Ibid., pp. 189–90 and p. 306.

[22]   There were 32 performances between 1821 and 1825, 34 between 1826 and 1838 and 17 between 1844 and 1850.

[23]   At the time, Rung was a member of the *Musikforening* in Copenhagen; he admired Renaissance Italian music and founded the *Cæciliaforening* in 1851, after Niels W. Gade (1817–90) became the leader of the *Musikforening*. See Hatting, *Mozart og Danmark*, p. 114 and p. 86 for the score used at the 1842 Court Theater performances.

[24]   See Knud Arne Jürgensen, *The Bournonville Tradition: The First Fifty Years, 1829–1879*, vols. 1–2, London: Dance Books 1997, vol. 2, *An Annotated Bibliography of the Choreography and the Music, the Chronology, the Performing History, and the Sources*, pp. 74–5; pp. 83–4; p. 126.

[25]   Pierre-Augustin Caron de Beaumarchais (1732–99) published *La Folle journée ou le Mariage de Figaro* in 1778, the comedy used by da Ponte for *Le Nozze di Figaro*; based on his *Le Barbier de Séville ou la Précaution inutile* (1775), Cesare Sterbini (1784–1831) wrote the

making it easier for the audiences to supply any information they might find omitted in the libretto or in a version in a new language.[26] Much in the same line of thought, Julian Rushton points out that a *Singspiel* version of *Le Nozze di Figaro* could not depart significantly from the original plot, whereas the *Singspiel* versions of *Don Giovanni* could incorporate other sources of the myth of Don Juan more easily, namely, German ones, which had had no influence whatsoever on Da Ponte, who had followed the Italian operatic tradition.[27] For this set of reasons, Rushton believes that the general tendency for a popular moralizing tone, condemning the excesses of Don Juan, the weakness of Don Ottavio, and the passionate character of Donna Elvira, is due to this blend of sources. Besides the optional division into four acts and the omission of the *scena ultima*, which would become a regular feature at the Royal Theater, the prominence of Donna Anna dates from this time, as well as the characterization of the Commendatore as an instrument of vengeance instead of a messenger of repentance.

By far, *Don Giovanni* was the opera that saw the most adaptations and translations in Kierkegaard's time. Although the scenes were rearranged, the first translation by Laurids Kruse (1778–1839) from 1807 kept the original two acts, and it reached 70 performances between 1827 and 1845. It was replaced by a more faithful translation, still keeping the two acts, by N.C.L. Abrahams, who did not borrow so extensively from Molière's *Don Juan*, as Kruse had done, though he continued to suppress recitatives.[28] Kruse followed the Rochlitz version, but also took into account the musical mainstream, which disapproved of the use of recitatives and looked suspiciously on opera as a dramatic genre, on ethical and on aesthetical grounds. As previously stated, opera was considered to be an unnatural and even immoral form of art, whereas the vaudeville was seen as a more appropriate genre to give musical expression to the Danish dramatic meter and stanza. The Kruse version is the one Kierkegaard watched over and over again, and, as a result, Kierkegaard's reception of Mozart's *Don Giovanni* assimilated the modifications introduced in the German-speaking countries immediately after Mozart's death. Besides adding dramatic material borrowed from Molière, Kruse not only suppressed all recitatives in favor of spoken dialogue, but altered the structural development of the scenes and omitted the *scena ultima*, the whole following the structural pattern of the *Singspiel*.

---

libretto for Rossini's *Le Barbier de Séville* (1816), which was performed at the Royal Theater every season between 1822 and 1835, and then again between 1845 and 1851 (except for the 1850 season).

[26]   See Daniel Heartz, "From Beaumarchais to Da Ponte," in *Mozart's Operas*, ed. by Thomas Bauman (with contributing essays), Berkeley and Los Angeles: University of California Press 1990, p. 111.

[27]   For an account of Da Ponte's Italian sources, see Daniela Goldin Folena, "L'art du librettiste, Da Ponte et la tradition italienne," *Don Giovanni—Mozart, L'Avant-Scène Opéra, No. 172*, Paris: Éditions Premières Loges 1996, pp. 141–9.

[28]   Until the end of the nineteenth century this version would be performed another 160 times. From 1899 onwards, a new translation by Erik Bøgh (1822–99) was used, also with two acts. There is also notice of a four-act version in a translation by August Zinck (1831–85); no. 229 in The Royal Danish Theater's Repertoire, with three editions available: 1874, 1884, and 1888, according to the catalogues of the Danish Royal Library.

This state of affairs secured its stronghold well into the late 1830s, which might also explain why Mozart's operas continued to be produced as *Singspiele* at the Royal Theater,[29] a fact that was common knowledge in Copenhagen's musical milieu, as the review of the 1836 production clearly reveals. The review begins by making no objection against the use of spoken dialogue instead of the original recitatives, besides the need for a good diction in all singers, a quality lacked by Giovanni Battista Cetti (1794–1858) who sang Don Juan's part. In his analysis of Kruse's version and the singers' performances, the reviewer states that the role of Donna Anna was weakened by a pale, though musically accurate, performance of Eleonora Christine Zrza (1797–1862), which totally ran against customary practices and Hoffmann's depiction of this character. He adds that Donna Elvira, instead, gained significance, brought to light by an outstanding performance by Anna Nielsen (1803–56), who portrayed Donna Elvira's grief over herself and over Don Juan's conduct, because, in the reviewer's opinion, she tried to convince him of the possibility of repentance, thus ranking with the Commendatore in giving voice to his conscience.[30] Another reminder of the German tradition is the weight given to the role of Leporello, who is seen as a double nature, either scorning his master, or passing as faithful servant, rendered more cynical by the performance of Joachim Ludvig Phister (1807–96), who obliterated Leporello's better side.[31] The reading of the whole piece allows us to believe that this production was relatively judicious in the modifications introduced, since the reviewer in reality managed to point out the structural differences between the original work and Kruse's version, which would be impracticable in the case of profound changes. Yet, the next point to note is that the *Don Juan* performances attended by Kierkegaard undoubtedly showed striking vestiges of what modern criticism labels as the romanticizing of the main character, with Don Juan becoming a superhuman individual who defies contingency, by underestimating the cosmic and social order and by overestimating his erotic impulse as the core of his vitality.[32]

As Daverio points out, the romanticizing of Don Juan by uniting bizarrerie and gloom, affectation and murkiness, is epitomized in Hoffmann's *Don Juan* and may be associated with the idea of the characteristic, as developed by Friedrich Schlegel (1772–1829).[33] This trend faded out gradually, to see the rise of an image of Mozart as the representative of classical art and the quintessence of the beautiful and the graceful. However, both views co-existed during the 1820s and the 1830s in a number of critical pieces by influential critics, composers, and biographers. Furthermore, the growing interest for Mozart's music fostered the appearance of several biographies of the musician in Germany, France, and Italy, which were

[29]   For a detailed account of this debate, which involved the public and the critics, see Schepelern, *Italienerne paa Hofteateret*, pp. 22–31.
[30]   Don Juan was sung by Giovanni Battista Cetti from 1822 until 1837 and by Jørgen Christian Hansen (1812–80) from 1839 onwards.
[31]   See A.B. Bergreen, "Theateret: Don Juan, Opera i 4 Acter, bearbeidet til Mozarts Musik af Hr. Professor Kruse," *Musikalsk Tidende*, no 14, (April 10) 1836, pp. 218–23. The review also analyzes the overture.
[32]   On this topic, see Bernard Williams, "Don Giovanni as an Idea," in *W.A. Mozart, Don Giovanni*, ed. by Julian Rushton, Cambridge: Cambridge University Press 1994, pp. 81–91.
[33]   See Daverio, "Mozart in the Nineteenth Century," pp. 176–7.

chiefly collections of biographical sketches or scattered episodes concerning the performance of his works. The ones here mentioned may have been read or heard of by Kierkegaard, specifically, Mozart's obituary by Friedrich Schlichtegroll (1765–1822), his first biography by Franz Xaver Niemetschek (1766–1849), and an extended biographical note by Johann Friedrich Rochlitz (1769–1842), who is taken to be responsible for having forged stories about Mozart's creative genius which would eventually reach mythical proportions. This is echoed in *Musikalsk Tiderne* which features a full column dedicated to these stories in 1835.[34] Schlichtegroll had already set the tone in 1793,[35] by inaugurating the celebration of Mozart as an eternal child prodigy with a Janus-faced personality in his mature years, divided between a Papageno and a Tamino double personality. If Schlichtegroll had relied on the sources provided by Maria Anna Mozart (1751–1829), the composer's sister, Niemetschek chose Constanze Mozart (1762–1842), the widow, who would later be the key element for the first full biography of the composer, which was published by Breitkopf in 1828. This biography is of special interest, not only for the information contained in its 965 pages, but mainly because it used the most reliable documentary sources, provided by Constanze to her second husband and author, the Danish diplomat Georg Nikolaus von Nissen (1761–1826). The couple lived in Copenhagen for ten years, until 1820, and Constanze attended performances of *Don Juan* in 1811, which seem to have been to her satisfaction in what concerns the rendering of the music.[36] Nissen's study is a quite chaotic amount of musical and strictly biographical facts, but it would serve as second source for Alexandre Oulibicheff (1794–1878), who published in French the first reliable biography of the composer in Moscow in 1843,[37] a date which rules out any possibility that Kierkegaard could have read it before the writing of *Either/Or*.

---

[34]   Berggreen, "Theateret: Don Juan, Opera i 4 Acter, bearbeidet til Mozarts Musik af Hr. Professor Kruse," pp. 223–4. Among them, one counts the composing of the overture during the night before the Prague premiere.

[35]   Friedrich Schlichtegroll, "Johannes Chrysostomos Wolfgang Gottlieb Mozart," in *Nekrolog auf das Jahr 1791*, 1793, pp. 82–112; Franz Xaver Niemetschek, *Leben des K.K. Kapellmeisters Wolfgang Gottlieb Mozart, nach Originalquellen beschrieben* (Prague 1798); Friedrich Rochlitz, "Anekdoten aus W.G. Mozarts Leben," *Allgemeine musikalische Zeitung*, published in different numbers between 1798 and 1801. For a detailed account, see Maynard Solomon, "The Rochlitz Anecdotes," in *Mozart Studies*, ed. by Cliff Eisen, Oxford: Clarendon Press 1991, pp. 1–59.

[36]   See *Om Mozarts Don Juan*, p. 10. For an account of a few contacts between Constanze Mozart Nissen and three Danish musicians and composers—F.L.Æ. Kunzen (1761–1817), C.E.F. Weyse (1774–1842), and Claus Schall (1757–1835)—see Anne Ørbæk Jensen, Claus Røllum-Larsen, and Inger Sørensen, *Wahlverwandtschaften, Zwei Jahrhunderte musikalischer Wechselwirkungen zwischen Dänemark und Deutschland*, Copenhagen: Det kongelige Bibliotek 2004, pp. 26–8.

[37]   Alexandre Oulibicheff, *Nouvelle Biographie de Mozart: suivie d'un aperçu sur l'histoire générale de la musique et de l'analyse des principales oeuvres de Mozart*, Moscow: Semen 1843. Sometimes the author is also mentioned by his Russian name, Alexander Ulïbïshev. The first German translation dates from 1847, and there is a Swedish translation from 1850 or 1851.

Nevertheless, some of the information concerning *Don Giovanni* in Kierkegaard and Oulibicheff is coincident, which may lead us to sources read by both of them, namely, the two well-known periodicals, *Revue musicale* and *Gazette musicale* (from 1839 onwards, they were united and published as *Revue et gazette musicale de Paris*), which were read in Copenhagen in private and public reading circles.[38] Within the decades of 1830 and 1840, François Fétis (1784–1871), Hector Berlioz (1806–69), and Richard Wagner (1813–83) contributed to the celebration of Mozart as a classical composer, and at the same time as a forerunner of the then modern Romantic composers, in articles whose main points I pass over here, though I shall return to some of them in the second part of the present essay. In Katherine Ellis' opinion, Fétis was a confessed admirer of Mozart to whom he attributed the creation of a new and universal language, and he analyzed Mozart's music according to the principles established in his music treatises where he correlated the vagueness of music to its expressiveness and pathos.[39] As for Berlioz, he praised Mozart as a classic composer and *Don Giovanni* as a perfect opera in form and style and pronounced its immortality; moreover, he highlighted the dramatic nature of the music and its thoughtfulness and expressiveness, qualities which brought it closer to modern Romantic music.[40] As for Wagner, during his stay in Paris in the early stages of his career (September 1841–April 1842), he wrote ten articles for the Parisian press, one of them being "De l'ouverture,"[41] where he defends the idea that the overture should

---

[38]   See *Fortegnelse over Selskabet Athenæums Bogsamling*, vols. 1–2, Copenhagen: Bianco Luno 1847–57, vol. 1, p. 407. It is also in the catalogue of the Danish Royal Library.

[39]   Katherine Ellis, *Music Criticism in Nineteenth-Century France: La Revue et gazette musicale de Paris*, Cambridge: Cambridge University Press 1999, especially pp. 89–92. Fétis' original quotation reads: "*Si Mozart n'emprunta rien à la nouvelle déclamation musicale, c'est qu'elle n'était point l'art nouveau qu'il concevait tout entier et dont la manifestation n'attendait qu'une occasion favorable. Lors donc qu'il alla deux ans après inventer une autre musique dans l'Idoménée, toute la musique de l'Italie, de l'Allemagne et de la France s'anéantit devant lui pour faire place à une immense création, celle de la musique actuelle.*" (*Revue et Gazette musicale*, vol. 6, no. 49, September 20, 1839, p. 388). Quoted by Ellis, in ibid., p. 90. François Fétis' treatises are *Esquisse de l'histoire de l'harmonie* (Paris 1840) and *Traité complet de la pratique et de la théorie de l'harmonie* (Paris: M. Schlesinger 1844). Fétis was also widely known for his *La Musique mise à la portée de tout le monde* (Paris: Alexandre Mesnier 1830), which is registered in *Fortegnelse over Selskabet Athenæums Bogsamling*, vol. 2, p. 532. The book became extremely popular and was translated into German in 1830 and into English in 1831.

[40]   See Sousa, "Kierkegaard's Musical Recollections," and the following articles by Berlioz, collected in Hector Berlioz, *Critique Musicale*, vols. 1–5, ed. by Anne Bongrain and Marie-Hélène Coudroy-Saghaï, Paris: Buchet-Chastel 1996–2004; article published on January 5, 1834 in *Le Rénovateur*, reprinted in *Critique Musicale*, vol. 1, p. 129; article published on January 12, 1834 in *Le Rénovateur*, reprinted in *Critique Musicale*, vol. 1, 135; article published on June 8, 1834 in *Le Rénovateur*, reprinted in *Critique Musicale*, vol. 1, p. 271; and article published on November 15, 1835 in *Journal des Débats*, reprinted in *Critique Musicale*, vol. 2, pp. 345–6.

[41]   See *Revue et Gazette musicale de Paris*, January 8, 1841, pp. 17–19 and January 10–17, 1841, pp. 28–9 and pp. 33–5 (published also as *Dix écrits de Richard Wagner*, Paris: Fischbacher 1898, see pp. 92–100).

announce the dramatic content of the opera in the form of a struggle between two forces represented by two musical themes based on different musical material from the rest of the opera. What is more, he divided the history of the overture into three periods—a first one, where the overture is defined as a kind of musical prologue to the opera, a middle one when overtures followed the three-movement pattern of the symphony, with the Baroque and G.F. Handel (1685–1759) given as examples, and a third one which reached perfection with C.W. Gluck (1714–87) and Mozart, precisely because their overtures to *Iphigénie en Aulide* (1774) and *Don Giovanni* developed the main dramatic ideas of the opera by using distinctive musical material, that is, without mingling the musical themes used in the singing parts into "pot-pourris," as Rossini and Hérold (1791–1833) did.

To sum up, Kierkegaard's reception of Mozart took place at the first turning point of Mozart's reception in the nineteenth century, that is, when his operatic works were going through deep structural changes, in order to fit in the different stage and operatic traditions where they were performed. The outpouring of praise for his dramatic work was not immediately followed by the attribution of a classical status to his instrumental or religious works, which would reach the canon as masterpieces around the mid century and then again later in the Mozart revival of the first centenary. Therefore, Mozart's fame in Kierkegaard's time resulted mainly from the huge success of his late operas, and, to my knowledge, concerts featuring his symphonies and other instrumental music were held in Copenhagen only after 1850, which implies that Kierkegaard may not have had any occasion to listen to masses or oratorios, even less to his *Requiem*. In addition, Kierkegaard's reception of Mozart occurred when the ideas on music as musical language and, generally speaking, on musical expression, were building up very quickly, often taking Mozart's dramatic works as examples, and the amount of contemporary literature on the operas themselves sheds light on Kierkegaard's writings on his music and particularly on *Don Giovanni*, as I shall survey in the next section.

II. Kierkegaard in Mozart's World

Regardless of how much one may fail to appreciate Kierkegaard's aesthetic standpoint, it must be acknowledged that his love for music and his reflections on Mozart's music as the music of love, *par excellence*, set up a level of awareness in his reader which endows him with enough guidelines to make his way amid the divergent paths of Kierkegaard's thought on love and of its place in his authorship. His relationship to music stands as much more than the enthusiasm he describes as a young girl's infatuation or than the reverence and admiration that A demonstrates in the opening paragraph of the chapter on the musical-erotic,[42] which is later repeated in "In Vino Veritas" by Victor Eremita at the beginning of the banquet, where Don Giovanni plays the role of an absent character or of silent music.[43] The first fact to be acknowledged is that, both in the journals and in his major works, there are

---

[42]   *SKS* 2, 55–6 / *EO1*, 47–8.
[43]   *SKS* 6, 26 / *SLW*, 28.

a considerable number of references or allusions to Mozart's music and to many characters of *Don Juan*, *Figaros Givtermaal eller Den gale Dag*, and *Tryllefløjten*, with a diverse distribution and a different emphasis. In the case of allusions, Mozart or one of the characters from these three operas are often used as a term of comparison, inasmuch as other philosophers, poets, writers, and their works actually serve the same purpose. The discussion of the Mozartian characters used for the immediate erotic stages is a recurrent issue in the journals until 1842, and the nature of Don Juan is also considered in the many commentaries on Faust, especially in the early journals. Yet, most significantly, the idea of a three-stage partition for the erotic stages dates back to 1837,[44] thus leaving a long period of time for this idea to mature until it reached its definite form in the chapter on the musical-erotic.

The chapter, often read as a self-contained essay on Mozart and specifically on *Don Giovanni*, belongs to *Either/Or*, and it acts as an opening gate to the double series of works, placed, as it is, right after Victor Eremita's preface and the introductory collection of aphorisms contained in "Diapsalmata." "The Immediate Erotic Stages or the Musical-Erotic"[45] is also one of the longest and most complete analyses of *Don Giovanni* to be published in the first half of the nineteenth century and in the whole authorship; only Hans Christian Andersen (1805–75) and Scribe would deserve the same kind of attention.[46] Mozart, however, is the only artist to be worthy of a comprehensive analysis that takes into account all the dramatic works Kierkegaard could actually become acquainted with and its comparison to works by other authors, as well as the correlation of this analysis with the interpretation of Mozart's condition as genius. The commentaries on *Don Juan*, *Figaros Givtermaal* and *Tryllefløjten* are thus many-sided and extensive,[47] and, with regard to musical analysis, they operate as a framework for Kierkegaard's own theories about musical language and expression, the act of musical creation and its relation to the role of the artist, and the classic status of the artwork and its author. In addition to this, much of the content of this chapter is fully articulated with the thematic development of the two volumes of *Either/Or* and of the rest of the authorship, since they introduce concepts which are subsequently developed in later works. Taking into consideration the observations on *Don Giovanni* contained in the chapter, one notes that Don Juan's and Donna Elvira's dramatic interaction present the concepts of erotic love, despair and love, and immediacy and reflection, to say the least. One should also mention the contrast between the significance given to Donna Elvira's awareness of the Don's misconduct (the unavoidable consequence of having been seduced and neglected) and the interpretation of the catalogue aria as a symbol of the power and of the victory of the seducer, taking the seduced part as a universal category, which announces the discussion of the complexity of Donna Elvira in "Silhouettes." Here,

---

[44]   *SKS* 17, 113ff., BB:24 / *KJN* 1, 107ff.

[45]   *SKS* 2, 53–136 / *EO1*, 45–135.

[46]   *SKS* 1, 5–57 / *EPW*, 61–102. *SKS* 2, 225–70 / *EO1*, 231–79.

[47]   For the sake of clarity, when I refer to A/Kierkegaard's view on Mozart's works, I use the Danish title and subsume all that I have already said about their versions as *Singspiele*. I use the original name of the operas when I introduce my own commentary or other scholarly opinions.

Donna Elvira is described as a case of reflective sorrow, although she is unable to reach reflective grief, seeing that she is dominated by love-hate feelings towards her seducer. Similarly, in the "The Seducer's Diary," Johannes joins Don Juan so as to embody further modalities of erotic love and of living poetically which are developed antithetically by B in the first two chapters of *Either/Or*, Part II.[48] More than a straightforward essay on Mozart or *Don Giovanni*, the chapter on the musical-erotic has thus a decisive role in a comprehensive reading of *Either/Or*. A's criticism of the dramaturgical content of the opera and even the comparative analysis with Molière's *Don Juan*, though full of insight on these works, aims at more than a systematic overview of the opera, as it succeeds in instilling in the reader the adequate critical mood for a reading of *Either/Or*, Part I, which should take the volume both as a set of accounts of A's aesthetic experiences and of his experiments on art criticism. The reading of this chapter is quite distinct from the impression one gets, for example, from the 1845 article "A Cursory Observation Concerning a Detail in *Don Giovanni*."[49] There the interpretation of the roles of Don Giovanni and Zerlina is commented on in the style of a regular opera review, that is, giving attention to the work of the singers, especially voice delivery, poise, and acting skills, in order to assess if they have respected the score and the dramaturgy, and only afterwards criticizing the effect produced according to the reviewer's own point of view on the matter. This is a pattern of reviewing regularly used by Kierkegaard and, incidentally, typical of Berlioz in his copious critical pieces.[50] Kierkegaard's article goes into so much detail concerning the right poise and delivery to represent Don Juan's non-reflective nature that it actually stands as an essential documentary source for the reception of the opera at the Royal Theater, together with the already mentioned 1836 review, all the more so because their main points are absolutely complementary, since Kierkegaard's article focuses on the duet *Là ci darem la mano*, whereas the *Musikalsk Tidende* review examines other characters, especially Donna Anna, Donna Elvira, and Leporello.

This state of affairs has generated two trends in the criticism on the chapter on the musical-erotic: one that may generally be described as a mere reproduction of its content on music and Mozart, attempting to build a Kierkegaardian systematic musical theory out of its content, and another that aims at contextualizing some aspects of Kierkegaard's views on music in his work, especially in his concept of the aesthetic. There have also been a growing number of Mozart scholars and other musicologists who have relied on Kierkegaard's conception of the musical-erotic for their understanding of *Don Giovanni*, taking it as a major landmark in the reception

[48]   See "Silhouettes," *SKS* 2, 163–209 / *EOI*, 165–215. "Diary of the Seducer," *SKS* 2, 291–431 / *EOI*, 301–445. "The Esthetic Validity of Marriage" and "The Balance between the Esthetic and the Ethical in the Development of the Personality," *SKS* 3, 13–314 / *EO2*, 3–333.
[49]   See "En flygtig Bemærkning betræffende en Enkelthed i Don Juan," *Fædrelandet*, nos. 1890–91, May 19–20, 1845, see *SV1* XIII, 447–56 / *COR*, 28–37.
[50]   For an annotated overview of the articles on acting, see Janne Risum, "Towards Transparency. Søren Kierkegaard on Danish Actresses," trans. by Annette Mester, in *Kierkegaard and His Contemporaries, The Culture of Golden Age Denmark*, ed. by Jon Stewart, Berlin and New York: Walter de Gruyter 2003, pp. 330–42.

of the opera in the first half of the nineteenth century. I believe that this chapter is also one of the richest sources for grasping the debate surrounding the expressiveness of musical language. Moreover, it is of extreme value in order to realize how and why musical language confronts itself with verbal language during the same period, since, to my knowledge, it is the only text to develop at length the controversy by means of arguments that are as rooted both in philosophy and in contemporary musical criticism. Taking this into consideration, in my analysis of Kierkegaard's ideas concerning the musical-erotic, I first comment on the section on the three stages of the musical-erotic as a wise collection of musical evidence for the defense of the autonomy of musical language and as a construct based on Mozart's artistic quality and his *Don Giovanni*, but firmly structured based on a deep critical insight into Mozart's late dramatic works. Secondly, I provide some of the missing links between contemporary musical theories authored by musicians and philosophers, in the hope of illuminating the origin of a few puzzling inconsistencies concerning key issues in Kierkegaard's discussion of the essence of musical language and that of a classical work of art, among others, the classification of "poor" and "abstract" to the idea and the medium. Thirdly, I demonstrate how A's observations on the overture of *Don Giovanni* reveal more than an attentive reading of musical criticism on the topic, since in certain instances it may be seen virtually as a case of plagiarism.

In *Either/Or*, Part I, A is not the only narrator to claim that erotic love and music belong to each other, since later in the volume Johannes, the true seducer, the representative of psychic love, states that Eros expresses itself by a kind of symbolic music associated with motion. This music replaces verbal language when the latter becomes inappropriate, a music that may be "silent," that is to say, speechless, and yet "eloquent," which means that it is capable of making itself perfectly understood due to its expressive quality:

> Erotic love is much too substantial to be satisfied with chatter, the erotic situations much too significant to be filled with chatter. They are silent, still, definitely outlined, and yet eloquent, like the music of Memnon's statue. Eros gesticulates, does not speak; or if he does, it is an enigmatic intimidation, symbolic music. The erotic situations are always either sculptural or pictorial, but two people speaking together about their love is neither sculptural nor pictorial.[51]

The music of Eros is here associated with an inner music, and its expressiveness dispenses with speech, an association of ideas quite similar to the qualification of elemental sensuality as an idea that may be rendered immediately by a musical Don Juan. In fact, the seducer as impostor, the embodiment of sensual love is defined as permanently moving in search of fulfilling his desire, a definition of the Don that resounds in the whole chapter and that may be described as a musical-dramatic idea. The above quotation might have been found in the introductory remarks to the section on the three stages of the musical-erotic, where, in my opinion, the genius of Kierkegaard as a critic of art is revealed, since not only do the three stages provide a convincing framework for the argument that reflection and sensuality are unable to coexist in Don Juan, but they also confirm Kierkegaard's knowledge and expertise

---

51   *SKS* 2, 404 / *EO1*, 418.

on the three operas in question. As we shall see, A/Kierkegaard is cautious enough to choose Cherubino, Papageno, and Don Giovanni as characters whose ability to reflect is gradually overshadowed by desire, thus allowing A to establish a relation of inverse proportion between the ability to reflect and the fulfillment of "desiring desire."

For A, an excess of erotic love that is unconsummated (and for that reason, forced to remain latent) accounts for Cherubino's melancholy and the page's two arias of exquisite gracefulness and beauty provide him with enough substance for the definition of his first erotic stage. In *Non son più cosa so, cosa faccio* one hears mainly Cherubino's lament—the page feels desire, but cannot find a way out, and complains that his real life shares the unreality of his dreams because his dreams never actually come true. However, one also hears in the final line, *Parlo d'amore con me*, a euphemistic confession of Cherubino's ventures in self-pleasure, later confirmed by Figaro in *Non più andrai* when he names Cherubino as *Narcisetto, adoncino d'amor*. A leaves out any reference to this point and restricts his commentary to the classification of this stage as the realm of "dreaming desire," but Cherubino's self-contemplation actually confirms that desire as elemental sensuality is already present, although in a narcissistic manner. The second aria, *Voi che sapete*, underlines the effects of this unconsummated desire and shows a powerless but reflective Cherubino who voices the result of his introspection, thus confessing that he is aware of the reason for his torments, and also of the absolutely helpless condition that leaves him dependent on external advice. In *Le Nozze di Figaro*, Cherubino stands as the perfect example of the early stages of the conflict between one's eroticism and moral and social norms; to be exact, in this opera, desire can be found at various levels in all the characters, male or female, who all reflect on which steps should be taken to fulfill their erotic desire, while all along managing to limit the consequences of their impulses. The coexistence of erotic love and marriage is seen as a possibility in the case of Susanna and Figaro, although one is left with the suspicion that in such a world they may end up like the Countess and the Count, since the validity of marriage is far from being taken for granted. Therefore, the latency of Cherubino's desire and his inconclusive reflections on his own attitudes are part of a *modus vivendi* that is left out with no further commentaries, probably to B's discontentment, but to A's great relief. Had A/Kierkegaard taken his analysis further, he would have had to distinguish at least two axes of male eroticism, one defined by Figaro and the Count, and another defined by Cherubino and Figaro, which would obviously tinge A's idea of "dreaming desire" and Cherubino as representative of the first stage. As for female eroticism, not even *Così fan tutti* may rival *Le Nozze di Figaro* as a school for lovers; Susanna and the Countess, for example, are as aware of their charms as Fiordiligi and Dorabella, but are as cunning as Despina and as intelligent as Don Alfonso. Once we recall that Cherubino is a role for *contralto* or *mezzo-soprano*, a situation acknowledged by A, a new conflict would arise, seeing that A's praise of this trace of female eroticism in Cherubino's character has very little to do with female eroticism as it is represented in *Le Nozze di Figaro*.[52]

---

[52]   I owe much of my understanding of the treatment of eroticism and sex in Mozart's operas to Jean H. Hagstrum, *Sex and Sensibility, Ideal and Erotic Love from Milton to Mozart*,

Papageno offers a new set of dense problems to A's theory on the musical expression of desire, especially because of the complex dramaturgical context and the genuine conception of the work as *Singspiel*. For A's purposes, *The Magic Flute* presented too many mingled nuances of what Kierkegaard tried to represent separately as *Elskov* and *Kjœrlighed* in the two volumes of *Either/Or*. The whole deals with the seeking and finding (and not only with "seeking" or "discovering," as A claims) of the ideal partner for marriage, or better said, of gaining the ideal partner, since both Papageno and Tamino, and their future spouses, overcome all sorts of obstacles. Papageno and Papagena represent a fairly straightforward fulfillment of their erotic impulse, as they anticipate their offspring in the repeated *pa-pa-pa-pa* of their final duet, the moment they are reunited and in the best of spirits. As for Tamino and Pamina, they aim at representing the perfect union, a love conquered by merit, by the recognition of the natural good qualities of the lovers, which renders practicable a marriage commanded by ethical principles and norms, as a reward for a love born out of physical attraction, an issue that is fully discussed in the many dialogues of the *Singspiel*, but promptly dismissed as "lunatic and foolish" by A. This dramaturgical context obviously serves neither A's nor B's intents, as they become evident in the structural organization of the two parts of *Either/Or*; moreover, the idea of elemental sensuality is very well represented by Monostatos in *Alles fühlt der Liebe Freuden*, an aria very similar in duration and tempo to *Fin ch'han del vino*,[53] where Monostatos shows that he has absolute conscience of his desire, that he has reflected on it and reached a conclusion—his skin color is the unsurmounting obstacle for the fulfillment of his erotic impulse. Under these circumstances, it is no wonder that A finds the opera "un-musical" and Tamino "completely beyond the musical" and openly states that he is only concerned with showing how the awakening of desire in Papageno sets him moving, actually looking for an object to fulfill such desire. Therefore, A emphasizes the expressiveness of musical language and really proves his point; his claim that "seeking desire" is already expressed by the *Glockenspiel* phrase is a major step for the recognition of the existence of a musical-dramatic idea as a basis for a musical phrase, something that is wholly corroborated by the attitude and the words of Papageno. It suffices to recall that, from Papageno's entrance in his first aria onwards, the continuous repetition of the *Glockenspiel* throughout the work represents the re-awakening of desire at each new encounter of this character with a potential partner, which becomes an identifying tag for the character, much in the manner of the Wagnerian *Leitmotiv*. At the same time, the repeated *Glockenspiel* phrase reminds us of the advancement of desire over reflection—as his desire grows, Papageno looks ready to accept any woman, old or young. When Papagena, now the object of his desire, disappears from his sight, he wants to put an end to his life, only to be saved by the *Glockenspiel* phrase once again, which successfully summons both his sensuality and Papagena. Thus, Papageno is accurately described when A

Chicago and London: University of Chicago Press 1980, especially pp. 316–32, and to Brigid Brophy, *Mozart the Dramatist, The Value of His Operas to Him, to His Age and to Us*, London: Libris 2006 [1964].

[53]   *Alles fühlt der Liebe Freuden* is marked *allegro* and *Fin ch'han del vino*, *accelerando*.

takes him to represent an extreme modality of "seeking desire," still reflecting on the object of his desire, precisely because it is taken individually, but once it has been found, desire overcomes him, and he is unable to reflect.

This remark on the expressiveness of musical language and the statement that "Papageno selects, Don Giovanni enjoys, Leporello reviews"[54] are further developed in the considerations on the third stage. In A's terms, Don Giovanni is dominated by desire, like Cherubino, and actively seeks to fulfill it, like Papageno. But the third stage is a metamorphosis of the first and the second stages, and, consequently, Don Giovanni represents a step further in elemental sensuality and a step back in self-awareness. He does not stop to reflect on his own desire and even less on who exactly is the object of his desire, like Cherubino does. In addition, neither does he attempt to discover the perfect match, nor does he lose nerve when faced with the urge to possess the object of his desire, like Papageno does. In Don Giovanni, the narcissistic self-contemplation of Cherubino is canceled by the intensity of a desire that will, at the end of the opera, annihilate the Don's physical image when he utters his final words, the only moment in the opera where he stops to reflect on his impending destruction.[55] Until then, the seducer as deceiver or impostor moves continually from scene to scene, seeking not the perfect match that might please him, had he been individuated, like Papageno, but in the pursuit of the multiple objects of his desire, anonymously listed in the catalogue aria, the necessary condition for him to represent desire as a universal category and to be defined as "genuine, victorious, triumphant, irresistible and demonic"[56] and the embodiment of elemental sensuality. Once the reasons for the omissions are taken into account, Kierkegaard's real knowledge of these operas materializes, his views lose bias and gain in critical stance, leaving behind the idea of mere youthful enthusiasm that the reader had previously taken as explanation for A's piece.

Although the sections on the three stages are designed to serve the main purpose of the chapter, the views on the dramaturgy of the operas illustrate the depth of Kierkegaard's critical genius, as if he himself could challenge what is claimed for Mozart. The main argument of the chapter on the musical-erotic is composite, since it associates the genius of the artist, the genius of his creation, and the double nature of the artwork. A describes the genius of the artist as a consequence of an act of creation, which, by fortune and by accident, managed to match to perfection a subject matter and a medium in order to produce an artwork that may be considered classical. In the case of Mozart's *Don Giovanni*, sensuality in its pristine essence is the most abstract subject matter, posited outside the spirit, although capable of being represented by an individual character, whereas music is the most abstract medium and cannot be posited within historical time or space, standing in opposition to verbal language, which is taken as the most concrete medium conceivable. We are left to presume that Mozart's fortune must have resided in his immense talent and *technê* and that the

---

[54]   *SKS* 2, 86 / *EO1*, 81.

[55]   "*Da qual tremore insolito / Sento assalir gli spiriti? / Donde escono quei vortici / Di foco pien d'orror?*" and shortly afterwards "*Chi l'anima mi lacera? / Chi m'agita le viscere? / Che stazio, ohimè, che samnia! / Ah! / Che inferno! / che terror!*"

[56]   *SKS* 2, 121 / *EO1*, 118.

accidental circumstances might include the commission of the opera for the Prague Theater, after the success of *Le Nozze di Figaro*, and the existence of such a strong operatic tradition of Don Juan operas that Da Ponte could not resist creating a libretto of his own.[57] When compared to the practical reasons evoked for the canonization of Mozart and *Don Giovanni*, which I have put forward in the first part of this article, it may seem that A's standpoint shows little evidence of common features in Mozart's reception at the time; it is my conviction, though, that A's formulations may be rooted in the philosophical discussion on the essence of music, but they are much more intertwined in the musical criticism of Kierkegaard's day.

Hegel's approach to music is confronted straightaway by A's definition of a classic author and of a canonical artwork,[58] since A's definition bypasses the possibility of a fully rational explanation for creation, by excluding the possibility of any formula or method for success. A's formalism is apparently solved by his statement that form and content are so permeated that it is useless to distinguish between the two, whereas for Hegel the outer and the inner are laboriously interrelated by means of correspondences between form and content, and made dependent on dichotomies between space and time and subject and object. Moreover, Hegel places musical expression in the realm of the spirit, and, as a result, music can be based on any subject matter, as long as it is entirely subjective, which is then rendered as feeling and emotion, once it is put into music. Therefore, the existence of a spiritual content stipulates the essence of music as a work of art, and is already expressed on the score by musical notation. For Hegel, music cancels space, and its time corresponds to the time of the subject, since it exists within each and everyone who listens to it. This means that more than a mere case of subjective interaction between the listener and sound, "music is spirit, or the soul which resounds directly on its own account and feels satisfaction in its perception of itself."[59] Jacques Colette claims that A is following Hegel's theory in his remarks on the champagne aria (*Fin ch'han dal vino*),[60] because music is here the expression of the self as characterized by A, who classifies the aria as one of the most intense lyrical moments of the opera, since it conveys the joy of living and the idea of seduction as victory, in other words, the essence of the libertine, a remark that is similar to Schumann's and Berlioz's comments, as I have observed before.[61] However, A's analysis of the champagne aria does not aim at demonstrating that the outer has a corresponding inner; on the contrary, he demonstrates that form and content are fully permeated. For A, Don Juan is not an individual, but he rather substantiates a universal idea that can only be represented by music; accordingly, the Don lacks the power of words and dispenses with self-awareness. Furthermore, Don

---

[57]   For a deeply interesting analysis of Da Ponte's stance as librettist, see Heartz, "The Poet as Stage Director: Metastasio, Goldoni and Da Ponte," *Mozart's Operas*, pp. 89–106.

[58]   G.W.F. Hegel, *Aesthetics*, vols. 1–2, trans. by T.M. Knox, Oxford: Oxford University Press 1998 [1975], vol. 2, pp. 888–958.

[59]   Ibid., vol. 2, p. 939.

[60]   See Jacques Colette, "Le medium musical," in *Kierkegaard et la non-philosophie*, Paris: Gallimard 1994, pp. 171–86. See Friedrich Schlegel, *Kritische Schriften und Fragmente (1798–1801)*, vols. 1–6, ed. by Ernst Behler and Hans Eichner, Paderborn: Schöningh 1988, vol. 2, p. 114 for Fragment 116.

[61]   See Sousa, "Kierkegaard's Musical Recollections."

Juan is defined as an impulsive character always moving in search of the fulfillment of his desire because he *is* the embodiment of desire; this means that the time of musical sound is coincident with the intensity of the Don's desire, not with the time of the self, as it should be according to Hegel's theory. For that reason, it is elemental sensuality that resounds in the champagne aria, which Berlioz described as "that libertine laughter that condenses the character of Don Juan,"[62] and not the spirit of a particular sensuous individual, who for Hegel would eventually see his soul rising above his feelings, moved by the power of music. Likewise, since A's Don Juan need not be reflective, he is incapable of returning into inwardness "along with a pure sense of the self," as Hegel proposes.[63]

The representation of sensuousness by Don Juan incorporates an intriguing suggestion, that of an opera limiting itself to the immediate representation of one elemental idea and even so, being described as a "poor" medium, although A fully acknowledges the complexity of the genre when he comments that *Don Giovanni*'s uniqueness relies on the circumstance that it combines lyrical, epic, and tragic elements. Moreover, any opera-goer knows that no musical genre endures more mediations than opera, whose effect depends precisely on the successful input of an intricate combination of arts, crafts, and skills. Nevertheless, the qualification of "poor" as applied to the medium and the subject matter by A becomes clearer, once we recall other operas, as successful as *Don Juan* during Kierkegaard's time, whose productions demanded elaborate imaginary scenery and large choirs to support the fate of heroines and heroes, who were helplessly in love but destined to succumb to great national causes, divine commandment, family authority, or a combination of the three. Two of the most popular five-act *grands opéras* in that period, which saw as many performances as *Don Juan*, were *La Muette de Portici* by Daniel François Auber (1782–1871) and *Robert le Diable* by Giacomo Meyerbeer (1791–1864), both with librettos by Scribe,[64] which included spectacular scenery and frantic scenes, such as the suicide of the dumb Fiorella who plunges herself into a volcano in eruption or Robert who summons a number of nuns from their graves in a ruined convent, with their subsequent on-stage cortege as dead living creatures. All things considered, the idea that the opera and Don Juan share some poverty of means and content, exactly because the elemental idea of sensuality is so overwhelmingly present in the dramatic action and in the music, sounds quite reasonable. Additionally, the libretto follows the classical rule of unity of action, place, and time, thus allowing the audience to concentrate without any strain on the Don's endeavor; and also, conceived as it was for the limited scenic resources of the

---

[62]   Berlioz's article was published on May 1, 1836 in *Journal des Débats* and reprinted in *Critique Musicale*, vol. 2, p. 459 (the quotation in French: "*cet éclat de verve libertine où se résume le caractère de Don Juan*").

[63]   Hegel, *Aesthetics*, vol. 2, p. 940.

[64]   *La Muette de Portici* was translated by Heiberg as *Den Stumme i Portici* (which premiered on May 22, 1830) and was performed every season since the premiere until 1842–43, except for the 1837–38 season; *Robert le Diable* was translated by Thomas Overskou (1798–1873) as *Robert af Normandiet* (which premiered on October 28, 1833) and was performed every season between 1837 and 1843, except for the two seasons of 1839–40 and 1841–42.

small opera houses of the eighteenth century, *Don Giovanni* requires no exceptional scenery or scenic effects, apart from the speaking statue of the Commendatore.

As for the qualification of "abstract" applied to the medium and to the subject matter, a decisive factor for A to canonize Don Juan, it is more clearly rooted in the debate around the expressiveness of musical language. As is known, the justification of music as an abstract art was currently in use in the Baroque, when taking the imitation of feelings or passions, as universals, not particulars, was correlated to the mathematical basic principles of the art. The debate about the supremacy of instrumental music and the long controversy on the primacy of the word versus the music in vocal music is originally linked, as Dahlhaus points out, to the tripartite Platonic division of music into *harmonia*, *rhythmos*, and *logos*, a conception which presupposed that music and verbal language were irrevocably associated, and which thus generated some instability in the quest either for expressiveness in musical language and for absolute music, from the Baroque until late Romanticism.[65] Although during the Classical and Romantic periods, musical language would progressively be endowed with the capacity of expressing actions and feelings, the idea of abstraction in music survived well into the nineteenth century either in musical analysis, as in the case of Anton Reicha (1770–1836) in his *Traité de mélodie* (1814),[66] or towards the end of the century in the concept of absolute music, a reaction to program music which, as is known, stands as the furthest vindication of content and denotation for musical language in purely instrumental music.

A's definition of a classical artwork in music, as the perfect match between the most abstract subject matter to be conceived and the most abstract medium to be imagined, may be seen as Kierkegaard's ambiguous reaction to this state of affairs, in the sense that it proclaims the superiority of dramatic music (after all, it is *Don Giovanni* that enters the canon), as long as its subject matter limits itself to an abstract idea, a connection that is more commonly made for instrumental music. According to Theodor Adorno, Kierkegaard is here reading "eighteenth-century theses out of Hegel,"[67] which is correct once we keep in mind that A neither proceeds to discuss the relation between words and music, as Hegel does extensively,[68] nor concludes that they are complementary. A's idea of abstraction, and of a musical language based on the expression of universals, bears more resemblance to the theory of Arthur Schopenhauer (1788–1860) on musical language and its components.[69] Although Hegel, like Schopenhauer, grants to scales, modes, and intervals the power

---

[65]   See Carl Dahlhaus, "Absolute Music as an Esthetic Paradigm," in *The Idea of Absolute Music*, trans. by Roger Lustig, Chicago and London: University of Chicago Press 1991 [1978], pp. 1–17.

[66]   For examples and commentaries on Reicha's influential treatise, see Scott Burnham, "Anton Reicha, Form," in *The Cambridge History of Western Music Theory*, ed. by Thomas Christensen, Cambridge: Cambridge University Press 2002, pp. 884–7.

[67]   See Theodor Adorno, *Kierkegaard, Construction of the Aesthetic*, trans. and ed. by Robert Hullot-Kentor, Minneapolis: University of Minnesota Press 1989 [1933], p. 19.

[68]   See Hegel, *Aesthetics*, vol. 2, pp. 943–9.

[69]   See Arthur Schopenhauer, *Die Welt als Wille und Vorstellung*, vols. 1–4 in Arthur Schopenhauer, *Zürcher Ausgabe: Werke in zehn Bänden*, vols. 1–10, ed. by Claudia Schmölders et al., Zürich: Diogenes Verlag 1977, vol. 3, § 52, pp. 321–35.

of denoting feelings and temperament, he continually correlates the meanings they convey to the aims of melody and harmony, whereas for Schopenhauer, the nature of music allows it to denote directly universals, not particulars. He claims that music needs no mediation from verbal language, lying at a higher level than ideas, and its object is the direct and immediate reproduction of the will; accordingly, he produces a long series of analogies in order to demonstrate that music establishes a direct relation to the world and its objects, in opposition to what Platonic ideas do. For example, the dominant note is for harmony what non-organic matter is for nature, and the range of fixed intervals is shown as being equivalent to a sequence of degrees of the objectification of the will, taken in this case as different natural species—for instance, dissonance corresponds to monstrous beings. Melody, at the highest level of objectification of the will, represents human life and ambition, thus becoming the language of reason, feeling, and passion; as for musical time, the faster a *tempo* is, the more intense the joy it expresses, whereas an abrupt change in tonality denotes death. A's argument about music is much more restrictive than Schopenhauer's, since he confines musical expression to elemental sensuality, but they both share the conviction that music has an absolute expressive power, as well as the idea that musical perception is purely temporal, completely undetermined by reason or causality, and that musical language is not only meaningful, but truthful and accurate.

According to A's proposal, had Mozart composed no other work than *Don Giovanni*, he would nonetheless be a classic musician, as if the fortune of the act of creation, of the creator and of the created artwork were one and the same. That such was the case was also the firm conviction of Schumann, who expressed this in his pseudonymous criticism in the many articles published in the *Neue Zeitschrift für Musik*, perhaps the most read musical periodical in Copenhagen in Kierkegaard's day.[70] One of his best-known articles from 1835 is the review on the *Symphonie Fantastique* by Berlioz,[71] himself a champion of musical expressiveness, not only in his musical compositions, but also in his critical columns in the Parisian press, having published a treatise in 16 feuilletons in 1841–42.[72] Schumann begins by

---

[70]   For its impact on the Copenhagen Musical Society and its forerunners, see Sousa, "Kierkegaard's Musical Recollections," and Anna Harwell Celenza, "Imagined Communities Made Real: The Impact of Robert Schumann's *Neue Zeitschrift für Musik* on the Formation of Music Communities in the Mid-Nineteenth Century," *Journal of Musicological Research*, vol. 24, no. 1, 2005, pp. 1–26, see especially pp. 8–14.

[71]   Hegel, *Aesthetics*, vol. 1, p. 48.

[72]   Published between November 21, 1841 and November 17, 1842 in the *Revue et Gazette musicale de Paris*. Berlioz demonstrates how musical language (either instrumental or vocal) expresses feelings and actions that are perceived by the listener as sound images of dramatic action, giving examples from different kinds of musical compositions, especially from operas, by various musicians. See also Hector Berlioz, *De l'instrumentation*, Paris: Le Castor Astral 1994, the edition that follows the feuilletons. The standard edition follows the text revised by Berlioz in 1855; see *Grand Traité d'Instrumentation et d'Orchestration Modernes*, ed. by Peter Bloom, Kassel et al.: Bärenreiter 2003 (vol. 24 in Hector Berlioz, *Benvenuto Cellini* (i.e., *New edition of the Complete Works*), vols. 1–4, ed. by Hugh Macdonald, Kassel et al.: Bärenreiter 1994–2005).

explaining the audacity revealed in Berlioz's five-movement symphony by a set of two epigrams, "Form is the vessel of the spirit" and "Greater spaces require greater minds to fill them," and from here proceeds to analyze the work. The opening paragraph is of special interest, since Schumann's words evoke the same notion of unity between the act of creation, of the creator and of the created artwork which pervades A's criticism of Mozart and *Don Giovanni*:

> The various matters that this symphony offers for reflection could easily then become too entangled during the following [review]; therefore I prefer to analyze them under separate parts, though often borrowing from one to explain another, namely, according to the four points of view from which a work of musical art can be surveyed, i.e., according to form (the whole, the separate movements, the section, the phrase); according to musical composition (harmony, melody, phrase, workmanship, style); according to the special idea which the artist intended to represent, and according to the spirit, which governs form, idea, material.[73]

These final lines clearly point to a duality of skills and tasks that may be correlated to another long-lived duality, that of the musician taken as *faber*, who would here oversee form and musical composition itself, and of the musician as *artifex*, who would be concerned with the subject matter and the idea, which naturally cannot exist by themselves without taking musical form. It is the spirit of the artist that overcomes the tension between the musician as *faber* and as *artifex*, the same spirit whose greatness is revealed by the dimension of the work of art he creates. The tripartite division in the creativeness of the musician sheds a new light on the so-called formalism of A's analysis of the musical artwork, which, once considered as an analysis made from the point of view of the creator, becomes less inquisitive about the nature of form and content, thus losing a strictly formalist angle, while leaving to the spirit the possibility of revealing its genius. Schumann claimed to have divided his review of the *Symphonie fantastique* not into parts to be taken as constituent elements of Berlioz's symphony or of its creative process, but into parts to be taken as points of view from which the work can be commented upon, while keeping in mind all along that the symphony as work of art is one indivisible piece and its creator, a great spirit. A very similar point of view is expressed by A right after his initial criticism of Heinrich Gustav Hotho's (1802–73) analysis of *Don Giovanni*,[74] which he finds to be too fragmentary and failing to reproduce the "absolute validity" of the opera, when he firmly states:

> This acknowledgment is what I am striving for, because this acknowledgment is identical with the proper insight into what constitutes the subject of my investigation. Therefore, my aim is to make the subject of consideration not the whole opera but the opera in its

73   See Schumann, *Gesammelte Schriften über Musik und Musiker*, vol. 3, p. 118.
74   See Niels Barfoed, "Hotho und Kierkegaard, Eine literarische Quelle zur Don Juan-Auffassung des Ästhetikers A," *Orbis Litterarum*, vol. 22, no. 1, 1988, pp. 378–86, and Joachim Grage, "Hotho: A Dialogue on Romantic Irony and the Fascination with Mozart's *Don Giovanni*," *Kierkegaard and His German Contemporaries*, Tome III, *Literature and Aesthetics*, ed. by Jon Stewart, Aldershot: Ashgate 2008 (*Kierkegaard Research: Sources, Reception and Resources*, vol. 6), pp. 139–53.

totality, not to discuss the individual parts separately but as far as possible to incorporate them into the whole, to see them as detached from the whole but integrated in it.[75]

Without further delay, A develops his argument about the predominant role played by mood in the opera, a crucial feature to maintain its unity and to keep the immediacy of action.[76] Accordingly, A argues that mood is "the absolute centrality"[77] of the main character and demonstrates how Don Juan's mood resounds in all the other characters. This mood is also present in the overture, described vividly as a piece of tone-painting music, in an often-quoted paragraph where A attributes to the overture a powerful foresight into the unfolding drama. It is written in a strikingly dramatic style, as an attempt to reproduce the pathos induced by Mozart's overture, which we already know impressed Kierkegaard so indelibly that it was enough for him to listen to the overture in order to feel the emotion of a whole performance.[78] I here quote only the parts that will be put side by side with the source text:

> This overture is no mingling together of themes; it is not a labyrinthian interlacing of associations of ideas, it is concise, defined, strongly structured, and, above all, impregnated with the essence of the whole opera....And this it has not attained by sucking the blood of the opera, on the contrary, it is rather a prophecy in relation to the opera. In the overture, the music unfurls its total range; with a few powerful wing beats it soars above itself, as it were, it floats above the place where it will descend. It is a struggle, but a struggle in the higher atmosphere. To anyone hearing the overture after he has become more familiar with the opera, it may seem as if he had penetrated the hidden workshop where the forces he has learned to identify in the opera move with a primitive power, where they wrestle with one another with all their might....Therefore, although in one sense the overture is independent, in the other sense it is to be regarded as a running start to the opera....But if, as has been observed above, the overture can be regarded as a running start to the opera, if in the overture one descends from that higher atmosphere, then the question is: at what point is it best for one to land in the opera, or how is the beginning of the opera achieved?...But there is a vast difference [from Molière], and here again one has occasion to admire Mozart's mastery. He has placed the first servant-aria in immediate connection with the overture.[79]

Moreover, this paragraph is preceded by general considerations on how an overture should be composed, with A firmly claiming that it must not be composed, and subsequently heard, as a collection of motifs from the opera, but should rather consist of its proper musical material which naturally ought to reflect the content of the

---

[75]   *SKS* 2, 119–20 / *EO1*, 116–17.
[76]   *SKS* 2, 121 / *EO1*, 118: "The mood is not sublimated in character and action. Consequently, the action in an opera can be only immediate action."
[77]   *SKS* 2, 121 / *EO1*, 118.
[78]   Richard Eldrige suggests that this is a fictional construct, having Hoffmann's narrator as model, revealing what he names as the narrator's "sexual spectatorhood" in both authors. See Richard Eldrige, "Hidden Secrets of the Self," in *The Don Giovanni Moment, Essays on the Legacy of an Opera*, ed. by Lydia Goehr and Daniel Herwitz, New York: Columbia University Press 2006, pp. 33–46.
[79]   *SKS* 2, 128–34 / *EO1*, 126–30.

work, but "in another way," quite an imprecise assertion that contrasts unexpectedly with his beautifully styled paraphrase of the overture:

> Although it is obvious that the overture should not have the same content as the opera, it of course should not contain something altogether different, indeed, it should have the same content as the opera, but in another way; it should contain it in a central way, and with the full power of what is central it should grip the listener.[80]

It is only natural that A/Kierkegaard found some difficulty in describing methods of composition; after all, he was a music lover, not a musician, and in spite of his fondness for reading what musicians had to say about composing overtures, he was vigilant enough not to overdo his zeal. Schumann has another excellent article from 1839 on Berlioz's overture *Waverley* (H. 26) commenting on the expressiveness of the musical language,[81] and the 1836 review in the *Musikalsk Tidende* also offers a good analysis of *Don Giovanni*'s overture that must have been the basis for Kierkegaard's remarks on the effect of the violins.[82] This time, though, the main inspiring source is to be found in Wagner's seminal article "De l'ouverture" from 1841, with his words on the overture of *Don Giovanni* resounding in A's piece. Since the article is quite long and the information gathered by A is scattered in different parts, I shall here quote and briefly comment on a few excerpts, arranged in a set sequence so that Wagner's words may match, as far as possible, the order of A's sentences in the extracts quoted above.

Wagner argues in his essay that opera overtures fall into two compositional patterns, one which is to be condemned as a mere rearrangement of themes of the opera, and another one which stands as a true introduction to the dramatic content of the opera, choosing *Don Giovanni*'s as an example. About the first type of overture, Wagner claims that "the overture conceived that way falls thus more and more in the category of pieces that deserve less the name of overture than that of pot-pourri,"[83] whereas about the second type, he plainly points out that "no matter how precise, clear and understandable this overture is at least for its poetical organization, that main tragic idea of the opera, there is not a single passage that refers immediately to the dramatic course of the action."[84] This statement concludes Wagner's description of an apt overture as one where "the main idea, the dominating idea in the drama may be designated by two main traits and takes what is complementary of a real, incontestable life in the movement of the musical work" and where "human passion is agitated in a conflict against the infernal power under which it seems destined to succumb."[85] He proceeds to

---

[80]   *SKS* 2, 128–29 / *EO1*, 126.

[81]   See Schumann, *Gesammelte Schriften über Musik und Musiker*, vol. 3, pp. 129–32.

[82]   See ibid., pp. 221–2.

[83]   See Richard Wagner, "De l'ouverture," in *Dix écrits de Richard Wagner*, Paris: Fischbacher 1898, pp. 92–112, see p. 99, my translation. The original German text would only be published in the second German edition, see Richard Wagner, *Gesammelte Schriften und Dichtungen*, vols. 1–10, Leipzig: Fritzsch 1871–83, vol. 1, pp. 194–207.

[84]   Ibid., p. 101, my translation.

[85]   Ibid., p. 100, my translation.

state that "the composer abandons to presentiment the outcome of that fight that his overture embodies" and mentions explicitly the effects on the audience by claiming that "the listener is gripped by the alternatives of a brutal fight, but he hardly knows it will become a drama."[86] For Wagner, Mozart effectively passes to the audience what A designated as mood, and he celebrates the dramatic importance of the immediate transition between the end of the overture and Leporello's aria in the first scene of *Don Giovanni*:

> Without attempting painstakingly to express and to put [musically] what music, by its nature, never can do, and to express the details and the twists of the action, like the ancient prologues rendered them, he [Mozart] seized the guiding idea of the drama, took the element that belonged by essence to music, that is, passion, and thus made a poetic counterpart of the drama itself, a picture which had enough independent value to be seen on its own, but which took its intrinsic necessity out of the drama that it was serving. This way, the overture became a piece of music that stood on its own, and that consequently was perfectly finished, while all along its context was linking it to the first scene of the opera…one had otherwise to agree that the prodigious transition from the last sentences of the overture to the first scene of the opera is a feat of genius.…[87]

Toward the end of the essay, Wagner reaffirms the independent dramatic nature of the overture, enhancing its intrinsic abstract value, in a commentary which implicitly compares the task of a composer like Mozart (and Wagner himself) to the task of the philosopher:

> The overture, as soon as it has presented its main thoughts and its performing means in a strictly musical sense, may always develop the constituent principles of the drama, but has nothing to do with the individual fate of the characters. The composer should only solve the superior philosophical issue of the work, and express immediately the feeling that stretches itself and runs through it all like a guiding thread.[88]

Though it is evident that many of A's ideas on the overture are borrowed directly from Wagner, they are further expanded and beautifully styled to fit the general aim of the chapter. A keeps firmly anchored to the original definition of a classical artwork in music, as one that matches the most abstract subject matter to be conceived and the most abstract medium to be imagined, and his observations on the overture are perfectly intertwined in the main argument.

Yet, such a close reading of Wagner, and of Schumann, makes Kierkegaard more than a music lover and a theater lover who developed the ear and the eye by his frequent visits to the theater and the opera. Together with his recollection of Liszt,[89] the depth of his study and research on Mozart provides evidence for the time consumed in reading musical periodicals and most likely in occasional conversation

---

86   Ibid., p. 101, my translation.
87   Ibid., pp. 96–7, my translation.
88   Ibid., p. 110, my translation.
89   Cf. Sousa, "Kierkegaard's Musical Recollections."

with members of the Copenhagen *Davidsbund*,[90] themselves actors, singers, and musicians at the Royal Theater. It also makes Kierkegaard more than an attentive listener, since he puts forward a critical stance that converts the critic into a creator, a master of forgetting and recollecting, standing on equal footing with the author or artist he analyzes. Just as Mozart and Da Ponte had forgotten and recollected the musical and literary tradition on *Don Juan* and created an immortal work of art, so would Kierkegaard forget and recollect all that he had heard or read on *Don Giovanni* to create the inimitable essay on Mozart's masterpiece. Kierkegaard's fortune lies where Mozart's recollection accidentally joins Molière's, Hoffmann's, Hegel's, Schopenhauer's, and that of many others, who give him a hand in the creation of an essay that reaches matchless perfection and shall be as immortal and unrepeatable as Mozart's Don Giovanni singing *Là ci darem la mano*, the famous duet whose lines are left unmentioned, although they resound throughout Kierkegaard's experiment on the poetic recollection of Mozart's music of love.

---

[90]   Founded in 1834; the members were, among others, Niels W. Gade (1817–90), the brothers Carl Helsted (1818–1904), Edvard Helsted (1816–1900), H.C. Andersen, as well as the actors Nicolai Peter Nielsen (1795–1860) and his wife, Anna Nielsen (1803–1856); cf. Celenza, "Imagined Communities Made Real," pp. 1–26.

Bibliography

I. Mozart's Works in The Auction Catalogue *of Kierkegaard's Library*

None.

II. Works in The Auction Catalogue *of Kierkegaard's Library that Discuss Mozart*

Hegel, Georg Wilhelm Friedrich, Georg *Wilhelm Friedrich Hegel's Vorlesungen über die Aesthetik*, vols. 1–3, ed. by Heinrich Gustav Hotho, Berlin: Verlag von Duncker und Humblot 1835–38 (vols. 10.1–10.3 in *Georg Wilhelm Friedrich Hegel's Werke. Vollständige Ausgabe*, vols. 1–18, ed. by Philipp Marheineke et al., Berlin: Verlag von Duncker und Humblot 1832–45), vol. 1, p. 360; vol. 3, p. 171; p. 194; p. 203; p. 524 (*ASKB* 1384–1386).

[Hoffmann, Ernst Theodor Amadeus], *E.T.A. Hoffmann's ausgewählte Schriften*, vols. 1–10, Berlin: G. Reimer 1827–28 (*ASKB* 1712–1716; for vols. 11–15 see *ASKB* 1717–1721).

—— *E.T.A. Hoffmann's ausgewählte Schriften*, vols. 11–15 [i.e., *E.T.A. Hoffmann's Erzählungen aus seinen letzten Lebensjahren, sein Leben und Nachlaß. In fünf Bänden*], ed. by Micheline Hoffmann, geb. Rorer, Stuttgart: Fr. Brodhag'sche Buchhandlung 1839 (*ASKB* 1717–1721; for vols. 1–10 see *ASKB* 1712–1716).

Hotho, Heinrich Gustav, *Vorstudien für Leben und Kunst*, Stuttgart and Tübingen: J.G. Cotta 1835 (*ASKB* 580).

Schopenhauer, Arthur, *Die Welt als Wille und Vorstellung*, vols. 1–2, 2nd revised and enlarged ed., Leipzig: F.A. Brockhaus 1844 [1819], vol. 2, p. 165; p. 396; p. 409; p. 452; p. 523 (*ASKB* 773–773a).

III. Secondary Literature on Kierkegaard's Relation to Mozart

Adorno, Theodor, *Kierkegaard, Construction of the Aesthetic*, trans. and ed. by Robert Hullot-Kentor, Minneapolis: University of Minnesota Press 1989, p. 17; pp. 21–2; p. 54; p. 116.

Barfoed, Niels, *Don Juan: En studie i dansk litteratur*, Copenhagen: Gyldendal 1978, pp. 193–247.

—— "Hotho und Kierkegaard, Eine literarische Quelle zur Don Juan-Auffassung des Ästhetikers A," *Orbis Litterarum*, vol. 22, no. 1, 1988, pp. 378–86.

Brunel, Pierre, "Kierkegaard, Søren," in *Dictionnaire de Don Juan*, ed. by Pierre Brunel, Paris: Robert Laffont 1999, pp. 530–4.

Celenza, Anna Harwell, "Imagined Communities Made Real: The Impact of Robert Schumann's *Neue Zeitschrift für Musik* on the Formation of Music Communities in the Mid-Nineteenth Century," *Journal of Musicological Research*, vol. 24, no. 1, pp. 1–26.

Clive, Geoffrey, "The Demonic in Music," *Music and Letters*, vol. 37, no. 1, 1956, pp. 1–13.

Cochrane, Arthur C., "On the Anniversaries of Mozart, Kierkegaard and Barth," *Scottish Journal of Theology*, vol. 9, 1956, pp. 251–63.

Colette, Jacques, "Musique et Sensualité, Kierkegaard et le Don Juan de Mozart," *La Vie Spirituelle*, vol. 126, no. 588, 1972, pp. 33–45.

—— "Musique et érotisme," in *Kierkegaard ou le Don Juan Chrétien*, Monaco: Editions du Rocher 1989, pp. 117–34.

Croxhall, Thomas H., *Kierkegaard Commentary*, London: James Nisbet 1956, especially Chapter V ("Music"), pp. 47–125.

Curi, Humberto, "Il mancato pentimento di Don Giovanni," in *Kierkegaard Contemporaneo, Riprese, pentimento, perdono*, ed. by Humberto Regina and Ettore Rocca, Brescia: Morcelliana 2007, pp. 175–96.

Davini, Simonella, *Arte e critica nell'estetica di Kierkegaard*, Palermo: Centro Internazionale Studi di Estetica 2003 (*Aesthetica Preprint*, vol. 69).

Dolar, Mladen, "The Opera and Philosophy: Mozart and Kierkegaard," in *Opera's Second Death*, ed. by Mladen Dolar and Slavoj Žižek, New York and London: Routledge 2002, pp. 50–8.

Eldrige, Richard, "Hidden Secrets of the Self," in *The Don Giovanni Moment, Essays on the Legacy of an Opera*, ed. by Lydia Goehr and Daniel Herwitz, New York: Columbia University Press 2006, pp. 33–46.

Garrera, Gianni, "Musicalità dell'intelligenza demoniaca: Kierkegaard interprete di Mozart," *Leggere oggi Kierkegaard*, ed. by Isabella Adinolfi, *Nota bene, Quaderni di studi Kierkegaardiani*, Roma: Città nuova 2000, pp. 87–100.

Görner, Rüdiger, "Zu Kierkegaards Verständnis der Zauberflöte," *Mitteilungen der Internationalen Stiftung Mozarteum*, vol. 28, 1980, pp. 25–31.

Gouwens, David J., "Mozart among the Theologians," *Modern Theology*, vol. 16, no. 4, 2000, pp. 461–74.

Grage, Joachim, "Durch Musik zur Erkenntnis kommen?," *Kierkegaard Studies Yearbook*, 2005, pp. 418–39.

—— "Hotho: A Dialogue on Romantic Irony and the Fascination with Mozart's *Don Giovanni*," *Kierkegaard and His German Contemporaries*, Tome III, *Literature and Aesthetics*, ed. by Jon Stewart, Aldershot: Ashgate 2008 (*Kierkegaard Research: Sources, Reception and Resources*, vol. 6), pp. 139–53.

Grey, Thomas S., "The Gothic Libertine: The Shadow of Don Giovanni in Romantic Music and Culture," in *The Don Giovanni Moment, Essays on the Legacy of an Opera*, ed. by Lydia Goehr and Daniel Herwitz, New York: Columbia University Press 2006, pp. 75–106.

Hall, Ronald L., "*Don Giovanni*, Music and the Demonic Immediacy of Sensuality," in his *Word and Spirit, A Kierkegaardian Critique of the Modern Age*, Indiana University Press, Bloomington and Indianapolis 1993, pp. 90–117.

Harbsmeier, Götz, *Unmittelbares Leben: Mozart und Kierkegaard*, Göttingen: Vandenhoeck & Ruprecht 1980.

Hatting, Carsten E., *Mozart og Danmark*, Copenhagen: Engstrøm & Sødring Musikforlag 1991, pp. 81–94.

Herwitz, Daniel, "Kierkegaard Writes His Opera" in *The Don Giovanni Moment, Essays on the Legacy of an Opera*, ed. by Lydia Goehr and Daniel Herwitz, New York: Columbia University Press 2006, pp. 119–36.

Hoffmann-Axthelm, Moritz, "Kierkegaards Verhältnis zur Musik," *Kierkegaardiana*, vol. 21, 2000, pp. 78–91.

Jacobs, Rolf, "Søren Kierkegaard und das Don Juan-Thema bei Wolfgang Amadé Mozart," *Mitteilungen der Internationalen Stiftung Mozarteum*, vol. 22, nos. 3–4, 1974, pp. 7–15.

Janz, Curt Paul, "Kierkegaard und das Musikalische, dargestellt an seiner Auffassung von Mozarts Don Juan," *Die Musikforschung*, vol. 10, no. 3, 1957, pp. 364–81.

Jensen, Anne Ørbæk, Claus Røllum-Larsen, and Inger Sørensen, *Wahlverwandtschaften, Zwei Jahrhunderte musikalischer Wechselwirkungen zwischen Dänemark und Deutschland*, Copenhagen, Det kongelige Bibliotek 2004, p. 29.

Kerman, Joseph, "Reading Don Giovanni," in his *Write all These Down, Essays on Music*, Berkeley: University of California Press 1994, pp. 307–21.

Kreutzer, Hans-Joachim, "Der Mozart der Dichter: Über Wechselwirkungen von Literatur und Musik im 19. Jahrhundert," *Mozart Jahrbuch*, 1980–83, pp. 208–27.

Maragliulo, Marilena, *Eros in Musica: Kierkegaard e il Don Giovanni*, introduced by Giovanni Carlo Ballola, Milan: M & B Publishing 2005.

Osolsobe, Petr, "Kierkegaard's Aesthetics of Music: A Concept of the Musical Erotic," *Sbornik praci Filozofcke Fakulty Brnenske Univerzity*, nos. 27–8, 1992–93, pp. 97–106.

Petersen, Nils Holger, "Søren Kierkegaard's Aestheticist and Mozart's Don Giovanni," in *Interart Poetics*, ed. by Ulla-Britte Lagerroth, Hans Lund, and Erik Hedling, Amsterdam: Rodopi Bv Editions 1999, pp. 167–76.

—— "Seduction or Truth in Music? Mozart's *Don Giovanni* and Søren Kierkegaard's *Either/Or*," in *Kierkegaard Studies. Yearbook*, 2008, pp. 109–28.

Risum, Janne, "Towards Transparency. Søren Kierkegaard on Danish Actresses," trans. by Annette Mester, in *Kierkegaard and His Contemporaries, The Culture of Golden Age Denmark*, ed. by Jon Stewart, Berlin and New York: Walter de Gruyter 2003, pp. 330–42.

Rocca, Ettore, "Kierkegaard, Don Giovanni e la non verità," in *Ravenna Festival 2006: Mozart? Mozart!*, Ravenna: Fondazione Ravenna Manifestazioni 2006, pp. 57–61.

Rosenberg, Alfons, "Mozart in Kierkegaards Deutung," *Österreichische Muzikzeitschrift*, vol. 23, no. 8, 1968, pp. 409–12.

Schellong, Dieter, "Annäherungen an Mozart: Ein Beitrag zum Verhältnis von weltanschaulicher und praktischer Interpretation," *Anstosse*, vol. 27, no. 1, 1980, pp. 10–34.

Sousa, Elisabete M. de, "A Mão de Mozart," *DEDALUS—Revista portuguesa de literatura comparada*, vol. 9, 2004, pp. 147–71.

—— *Formas de Arte, A Prática Crítica de Berlioz, Kierkegaard, Liszt e Schumann*, Lisbon: Centro de Filosofia da Universidade de Lisboa 2008, especially pp. 179–223.

—— "Kierkegaard's Musical Recollections," in *Kierkegaard Studies. Yearbook*, 2008, pp. 85–108.

Stone, John, "The Making of *Don Giovanni* and its *Ethos*," *Mozart Jahrbuch*, 1984–85, pp. 130–4.

Tschnuggnall, Peter, *Søren Kierkegaards Mozart-Rezeption, Analyse einer philosophisch-literarischen Deutung von Musik im Kontext des Zusammenspiels der Künste*, Frankfurt am Main, et al.: Peter Lang 1992.

Tudvad, Peter, *Kierkegaards København*, Copenhagen: Politiken 2004, pp. 246–8; p. 262.

Utterback, Sylvia Walsh, "Don Juan and the Representation of Spiritual Sensuousness," *Journal of the American Academy of Religion*, vol. 47, no. 4, 1979, pp. 627–44.

Williams, Bernard, "Don Giovanni as an Idea," in *W.A. Mozart, Don Giovanni*, ed. by J. Rushton, Cambridge: Cambridge University Press 1994, pp. 81–91, see especially pp. 82–6.

Wiora, Walter, "Zu Kierkegaards Ideen über Mozarts *Don Giovanni*," in *Beiträge zur Musikgeschichte Nordeuropas: Kurt Gudewill zum 65. Geburtstag*, ed. by Uwe Haensel, Wolfenbütel: Möseler 1978, pp. 39–50.

Zelechow, Bernard, "Kierkegaard, the Aesthetic and Mozart's *Don Giovanni*," in *Kierkegaard on Art and Communication*, ed. by George Pattison, New York: St. Martin's Press 1992, pp. 64–77.

Eugène Scribe:

The Unfortunate Authorship of a Successful Author

Elisabete M. de Sousa

The posterity of Augustin Eugène Scribe, playwright and librettist (1791–1861), might well be a match to the fate of many of the characters in his 425 plays and almost 140 librettos or ballet scenarios[1]—they endure a few hardships in order to succeed rapidly in life, only to be forgotten as soon as they leave the stage. Though his name may hardly be recognized by modern theater spectators, Eugène Scribe was the most successful and prolific play writer of the nineteenth century, a feat rewarded by his election to the Académie Française in 1834 and by an impressive number of translations and performances of his plays on most European stages during his lifetime. This enabled him to be the first fully professional French dramatist, having built a fortune on his writings and earning revenues by attracting large audiences. Thus, Scribe is considered to have been the main contributor to the emergence of the theater industry,[2] making famous the Théâtre du Gymnase, founded in 1820, to the point that his comedies were labeled *comédies du Gymnase* by Jules Janin (1804–74) in his critical columns in the prominent Parisian *Journal des Débats*.[3] Not surprisingly, he was also a founding member of the *Société des Auteurs et Compositeurs Dramatiques* in 1827, which successfully negotiated with theater managers a quota of 15 per cent of the profit of each performance, establishing a fairer practice at least for the most successful authors.

Scribe also stands as a champion for co-writing, having written most of his plays together with other dramatists of his time,[4] sometimes using pseudonyms. This

---

[1]   For a complete list of his plays and co-authors, see Douglas Cardwell, "Eugène Scribe," in *French Dramatists 1789–1914*, ed. by Barbara T. Cooper, Detroit and London: Gale Research 1998 (*Dictionary of Literary Biography*, vol. 192), pp. 358–64. For a complete list of his librettos and ballet scenarios, see Christopher Smith, "Scribe, (Augustin) Eugène," in *The New Grove Dictionary of Opera*, vols. 1–4, London: Macmillan 1992, vol. 4, pp. 275–7.

[2]   For a detailed account of his determinant contribution to the development of theater industry, see Jean-Claude Yon, *Eugène Scribe: la fortune et la liberté*, Saint-Genouph: A.-G. Nizet 2000.

[3]   Neil Cole Arvin quotes Jules Janin's lengthy feuilleton from July 29, 1832 in *Eugène Scribe and the French Theater 1815–1860*, New York: Benjamin Bloom 1923, pp. 221–4.

[4]   Among these co-authors, the following maintained a lifelong collaboration: Jean Henri Dupin (1787–1887), Mélesville (Anne Honoré Joseph Duveyrier, known as Mélesville,

gift for co-authorship must have been seen as a natural advantage in his life-long collaboration with many different opera composers, from the very beginning of his theatrical career. Starting at the *opéra-comique*, he became the most demanded librettist of *grand opéra* composers, working with Vincenzo Bellini (1801–35), Gaetano Donizetti (1797–1848), Charles François Gounod (1818–93), Giuseppe Verdi (1813–1901), and especially Giacomo Meyerbeer (1791–1864), besides other less renowned composers, such as Jacques François Halévy (1799–1862) and D. Daniel François Auber (1782–1871), whose works constitute part of the history of the genre,[5] even if the modern public may consider them minor names. His dual career as playwright and librettist spanned the period between 1811 and 1861, the year of his death, and the degree of overlap between his theater plays and his musical works is yet to be analyzed.[6] It should be stressed, however, that Scribe's fame has survived until today mainly in opera thanks to the exact same skills which have made him fall into oblivion in theater history. According to Christopher Smith, Scribe applied the same principles of construction in his librettos and plays, developing plots in terms of rhythm, confrontation of situation, characters, and denouement, and all along he made clever use of the spectacular staging and settings available in the Paris Opera. Furthermore, Scribe paid more attention to the clarity of language, which could clearly be heard high above the orchestra, rather than to its poetic eloquence, a skill that made him a favorite among composers.

Eugène Scribe was left an orphan at an early age, but his mother, in the hope of his becoming a lawyer, secured for him a solid traditional education by means of a scholarship at the Collège Sainte-Barbe, a deeply influential background for his career as dramatist. While still at college, he quickly substituted the stage for the court and many of early school friends became co-authors in his twofold authorship. His very first *comédies-vaudevilles* present *in nuce* the characteristics of his "well-made plays" (*pièces bien-faites*) and thematize middle-class patterns of social behavior concerning marriage and money; the guiding norms are often directly related to parental control and child obedience especially in what concerns career choice and public virtues and private vices. The structural and formal characteristics of Scribe's well-made plays typically obey the following pattern: the plot culminates a long story, previous to the play, and observes a strict cause–effect logical development, based on a secret which is announced to the audience in soliloquies and asides, but only revealed to the main characters in a climactic scene. This secret is often based on the misunderstanding of a word, sentence or situation (the *quid pro quo* of the play) which is absolutely

1787–1865), Antoine François Varner (1789–1854), Joseph Xavier Saintine (1798–1865), Jean-François Bayard (1796–1853), Germain Delavigne (1790–1868), Ernest Legouvé (1807–1903) and for the librettos, Charles-Gaspard Delestre-Poirson (1790–1859), E.J. Mazères (1796–1863) and Benoît-Michel Decamberousse (1754–1841).

5   For a contextualization of Scribe's role as librettist, see "The Nineteenth Century: France," *The Oxford History of Opera*, ed. by Roger Parker, Oxford: Oxford University Press 1996, pp. 83–113.

6   His first play, *Les Dervis*, with Delavigne, is from 1811 and his first *opéra comique*, *La chambre à coucher*, music by Guenée (1757–1828) from 1813; his last play, *La Frileuse*, dates from 1861, as well as his last *opéra comique*, *La fiancée du roi de Garbe*, music by Auber, first performed in 1864.

topical, with no metaphysical or sociological concerns whatsoever, so as to allow for a perfectly logical denouement. The *pathos* unfolds itself by a dual increase in intensity, on the one hand, by means of the contrivance of entrances, exits, letters, revelations of identity, and, on the other hand, by a rise in emotional rhythm, due to the alternate good and bad turns of fortune experienced by the protagonist, whose lowest point of fortune (the *scène à faire*, the obligatory scene) should occur just before the highest. Most of his plays feature a couple, who are dissimilar on grounds of either social class, age, or education. They endure a sequence of incidents and are often exposed by compromising revelations which delay their happy reunion or a successful outcome in their careers, which takes place only at the end of the play. The audience is kept in a tense mood until the last scene, divided between the surprise and excitement caused by the attentiveness and sagacity required to foresee the concealed denouement, and the spiraling sequence of scenes which unravel the plot by frequently changing the whole situation quite unexpectedly. This sort of comic suspense is at the heart of the well-made play, and it proved effective to such an extent that the five-act comedies are built on a similar frame, though the latter give more emphasis to the intrigue than to the construction of characters. In fact, these *haute-comédies* often present a mere expansion of the sequence of the incidents, each act reproducing the same structural development of the one-act comedies, despite a more serious criticism of loose political or family morals.[7]

As early as 1911, Marcel Charlot divided Scribe's career into three periods.[8] The first, between 1816 and 1820, was dominated by light comedies, of which *L'Ours et le Pacha* (1820) may be the best-known example of *bouffonerie*, closer to the French vaudeville model. The second period, between 1820 and 1833, makes a point of the one-act comedies now known as well-made plays at the Théâtre du Gymnase, and includes *Les premières amours ou les Souvenirs d'enfance* (1825), the play extensively reviewed by Kierkegaard, under the pseudonym A, in the chapter "The First Love" of *Either/Or*, Part I.[9] The third period, from 1833 to 1861, develops the five-act comedy pattern which was successfully played on the stage of the Comédie-Française and thus, offered to Scribe the possibility of occupying a seat at the Académie Française from 1834 onwards. For Neil A. Arvin, Scribe's first *comédies-vaudeville* went beyond the entertaining contemporary model, since they dramatized current events, thus providing the dramatic structure for the presentation of what might be considered sketches of contemporary materialistic life. This pattern was also used in the history plays; in fact, Helene Koon and Richard Switzer point out that Scribe used historical plots as a metaphor for the present, rather than a study of the past, and the local color of his history plays would rather paint everyday life than taint history, since the intricate plots tend to focus on family matters, especially money and marriage, excelling when both these topics are joined together, just as

---

[7]   For a detailed analysis of the dramatic structure of the well-made play, see *French Dramatists 1789–1914*, ed. by Barbara T. Cooper, pp. 366–9.

[8]   Eugène Scribe, *Théâtre choisi d'Eugène Scribe, précédé d'une notice biographique et littéraire par Marcel Charlot*, Paris: Librairie Delagrave 1911, pp. 5–26.

[9]   [Eugène Scribe], *Den første Kjærlighed. Lystspil i een Act*, trans. by Johan Ludvig Heiberg, Copenhagen: Jens Hostrup Schultz 1832. See *SKS* 2, 225–71 / *EO1*, 231–79.

in any other well-made play[10] Therefore, whatever the social or historical context of a play, the public would watch the dramatic impact of common moral and/or financial dilemmas and laugh at them without endangering their bourgeois views. Scribe showed amusing pictures of middle-class manners and uses, well stitched together into a logically constructed story, even though the plot might sound too absurd or farcical and the dialogue too sentimental to convey the common-sense morals of the characters. For Alvin, the key to his success turned out to have been the result of the fortunate combination of his excellent knowledge of stage optics, his skilful, swift writing, and his intuitive awareness of the public taste.[11] In Koon and Switzer's words, Scribe's success traveled well, and his plays were effectively staged in theaters of many European countries. Besides the fact that these plays were widely translated and produced on stages across Europe during his lifetime, these critics believe that the social drama (the *pièce à thèse*) of Alexandre Dumas, fils (1824–95), as well as the plays of George Bernard Shaw (1856–1950) and Henrik Ibsen (1828–1906), show the influence of Scribe's technique, no matter how agonistic it might be,[12] and I believe Hollywood screwball comedies still feature many of the characteristics introduced by the Scribe comedy pattern.

Two studies are fundamental for an accurate understanding of the role of Scribe in Kierkegaard's work, and more generally for the reception of Scribe in Denmark, and will thus be repeatedly referred to in the current article: the first is Ronald Grimsley's comparative study "Kierkegaard and Scribe" (1966),[13] which presents an exhaustive account of the places in Kierkegaard's *corpus* where Scribe is mentioned or alluded to, including a detailed account of the references scattered in the journals, from the very first 1834 entries until 1855, where Scribe is mainly used, together with other authors, as a literary example to sustain different types of arguments. The second study is Peter Tudvad's "Dyrehavsbakken og det Kgl. Teater" (2004),[14] which includes a full description of the repertoire of the theatrical seasons between 1827 and 1855, with commentaries on the impact of Scribe's plays and *opéra-comiques* on Kierkegaard's work, side by side with other relevant playwrights whose influence is also acknowledged.

More recent data concerning Scribe's reception in Scandinavia have been compiled in *BREFS* which shows that, between 1830 and 1900, Scribe was the second most translated French author in Denmark with 89 translated plays, second only to Alexandre Dumas, père (1802–70), whose translations of plays and novels reached 106.[15] However, Scribe beat Dumas on stage, since he was the most staged

---

[10]   Helene Koon and Richard Switzer, "The History Plays," *Eugène Scribe*, Boston: Twayne Publishers 1980, pp. 86–110.

[11]   Arvin, *Eugène Scribe and the French Theater 1815–1860*, pp. 217–32.

[12]   Koon and Switzer, "Scribe's Influence," *Eugène Scribe*, pp. 111–22.

[13]   Ronald Grimsley, "Kierkegaard and Scribe," *Søren Kierkegaard and French Literature, Eight Comparative Studies*, Cardiff: University of Wales Press 1966, pp. 112–29.

[14]   Peter Tudvad, "Dyrehavsbakken og det Kgl. Teater," in his *Kierkegaards København*, Copenhagen: Politiken Forlag 2004, pp. 208–91.

[15]   *La BREFS: bibliographie RFS des traductions scandinaves de la littérature française de 1830 à 1900*, Odense: Institut for Litteratur, Kultur od Medier, Syddansk Universitet 2005 (*Cahiers du réalisme français en Scandinavie*, no. 6). The research involves five Scandinavian

playwright at the Royal Theater with 2,428 performances. According to *BREFS*, the most popular staged play between 1829 and 1855 was *Den første Kjærlighed* (*Les Premières Amours*, with 80 performances), followed by *Formynder og Myndling* (*Simple Histoire*, 61), *Familien Riquebourg*[16] (*La Famille Riquebourg*, 50), *Qvækeren og Dandserinden* (*Le Quaker et la Danseuse*, 47), *Statsmand og Borger* (*Bertrand et Raton*, 30), *Et Glas Vand* (*Le Verre d'eau*, 34), *Christen og Christine* (*Michel et Christine*, 32), and *For evig! eller medicin mod en Elskovsrus* (*Toujours ou l'Avenir d'un fils*, 30).[17] As a result of his success in Copenhagen, where he was acclaimed for the dramatic appeal of his well-developed plots and for his elegant yet witty dialogues,[18] Scribe managed to outdo the national hero Johan Ludvig Heiberg (1791–1860), who reached almost the same number of performances (2,279) but with only 32 titles. The popularity of Scribe and Heiberg may well be assessed by recalling the 385 performances of 15 Shakespeare plays, starting with *Hamlet* in 1813.[19] Heiberg was also the translator of 21 of Scribe's plays for the repertoire of the Royal Theater, out of a total of 38 performed on this stage, his first translation being *Favoriten* (*L'ours et le pacha*, which premiered on June 11, 1827) and his last *De Uafhængige* (*Les indépendants*, first performed on November 12, 1840).[20] In addition to the performances of Scribe's plays at the Royal Theater, it should be taken into consideration that during the summer seasons between 1836 and 1841, troupes of French actors performed several Scribe plays, including *Les premières amours*, which had already been first performed in Copenhagen on June 10, 1831. There were also private performances in salons, thus making it likely that Kierkegaard himself had assessed the effectiveness of Scribe's technique in the original text.[21]

As for his musical works, 28 of these operas were also performed in Copenhagen before 1855, among others, *Den hvide Dame* (*La Dame Blanche*, music by F.A. Boieldieu, in the repertoire since 1826), which was the most successful work in the genre across Europe, and quite a few with Auber, among them *Fra Diavolo*

---

universities under the supervision of Brinja Svane of the University of Oslo, and further research is yet to be published.

[16]   For Kierkegaard's commentary, see *SKS* 23, 263, NB18:20.

[17]   As sources, Grimsley mentions Thomas Overskou, *Den danske Skueplads i dens Historie fra de første Spor af danske Skuespil indtil vor Tid*, vols. 1–7, Copenhagen: Samfundet til den Danske Literaturs Fremme 1854–76, especially vol. 5 (1854); (Kierkegaard owned only vol. 1; vols. 6–7 entitled *Den kongelig danske Skuepladses Historie, fra dens Overdragelse til Staten i 1849 indtil 1874. Efter Forfatterens Død fuldført af Edgar Collin*, 1874–76) (*ASKB* 1395); and Peter Hansen, *Den danske Skueplads, illustreret Theaterhistorie*, vols. 1–3, Copenhagen: Ernst Bojesen 1891–96. Tudvad also mentions other sources: Arthur Aumont and Edgar Collin, *Det danske Nationalteater 1748–1889*, vols. 1–3, [Copenhagen]: J. Jørgensen 1896–99 and Jens Engberg, *Det Kongelige Teater i 250 år*, vols. 1–2, 2nd ed., Copenhagen: Frydenlund 1998.

[18]   Grimsley, "Kierkegaard and Scribe," p. 114.

[19]   See "4. Observations et perspectives, 4.1. Les favoris du people: Le palmarès des auteurs français 1830–1900," in *BREFS*.

[20]   Tudvad, *Kierkegaards København*, p. 236–7.

[21]   Grimsley, "Kierkegaard and Scribe," p. 113.

(which premiered on May 19, 1831), *Bruden* (*La Fiancée*, which premiered on April 22, 1831), *Den Stumme i Portici* (*La Muette de Portici*, which premiered on May 22, 1830), and *Murmesteren* (*Le Maçon*, which premiered on September 1,1827), as well as an *opéra-ballet*, *Brama og Bayaderen* (*Le Dieu et la Bayadère*, which premiered on May 28, 1833).[22] In Kierkegaard's library there were no French editions of Scribe's plays; however, there are five theater programs, which include the Danish translations of *Les premières amours*, *Bertrand et Raton*, *Oscar*, *Le Puff ou Mensonge et Vérité*, and *Les Contes de la Reine de Navarre*.[23]

The role of Scribe in Kierkegaard's writing enhances his aesthetic existence in multiple ways. It emerges as the result of Kierkegaard's frequent and regular visits to the Royal Theater to attend dramas, comedies, and operas. The frequent allusions to Scribe and the analogies with his plays and characters scattered in the journals allow the reader to understand Kierkegaard as a frequent member of the audience of his time, who shared opinions and exerted his views during his peripatetic practice along the *Strøget* or during a chat at the intermission of a play. Decisive for Scribe's popularity was the fact that this author became a favorite among famous actors and actresses of the time, who shared his success, since they would receive very good reviews of their performances,[24] and Kierkegaard himself praises the performances of some of them in his review of *Den første Kjærlighed* or *The First Love*. Moreover, Emmeline was one of the most successful roles of Johanne Luise Heiberg (1812–90),[25] and, as it is known, she plays the central role in Kierkegaard's "A Crisis and the Crisis in the Life of an Actress."

It should then be kept in mind that the plots of Scribe's plays and *opéra-comiques*, which focus on the dramatization of common situations, whether they are more materialistic or more sentimental, provided excellent terms of analogy which could sustain the discussion of contemporary issues in the Copenhagen milieu. Among other examples, Grimsley mentions that to discuss the topic "misunderstanding" as the essence of tragedy, Kierkegaard uses *Familien Riquebourg* (which premiered on December 30, 1831), together with Goethe's *Egmont*. A few allusions to arias of *opéra-comiques* in three entries from 1838 and 1843 reveal Kierkegaard's good knowledge of *Den hvide Dame*[26] and *Fra Diavolo*[27]—clear evidence of his regular attendance at opera performances at the Royal Theater and of the popularity of these

[22] A comparative analysis of Grimsley's and Tudvad's articles allowed for the data here presented.
[23] [Eugène Scribe], *Den første Kjærlighed. Lystspil i een Act*; [Eugène Scribe], *Statsmand og Borger. Skuespil i fem Acter*, trans. by Carl Borgaard, Copenhagen n.p. 1844; [Eugène Scribe and Mélesville, i.e., Anne Honoré Joseph Duveyrier], *Oscar. Skuespil i tre Acter*, trans. by A.V. Güntelberg, Copenhagen n.p. 1844; [Eugène Scribe], *Verden vil bedrages. Lystspil i fem Acter*, Copenhagen n.p. 1849; Eugène Scribe and E. Legouvé, *Dronning Marguerites Noveller. Lystspil i fem Acter*, trans. by F.L. Høedt, Copenhagen 1851.
[24] Grimsley cites Johan A.G. Stage, Jørgen P. Frydendahl, Nicolai P. Nielsen, Joachim L. Phister, Johanne L. Heiberg, and Anna Nielsen (Wexschall), see his "Kierkegaard and Scribe," p. 115.
[25] For a detailed account of the success of the first cast of *Den første Kjærlighed*, see Tudvad, *Kierkegaards København*, p. 240.
[26] *SKS* 17, 280–97, DD:208 / *KJN* 1, 272–89.
[27] *SKS* 18, 228, JJ:279 / *KJN* 2, 209.

works in Copenhagen circles. The same can be said about the allusions to arias from *Bruden* and *Murmesteren* in *The Battle between the Old and the New Soap-Cellars* from 1838.[28] More significantly, Tudvad comments that *Bruden* and *The First Love* engage in a double role as important subtexts for *Either/Or*. Both the performances at the Royal Theater attended by Kierkegaard and Regine and the actual texts of the plays must be taken into account if one wants to understand fully the allusions to their broken engagement, especially in "Diary of the Seducer."[29]

Tudvad also points out that Taciturnus provides a short summary of this play in *Stages in Life's Way*, drawing a parallel between the contradictions within the play and within the author himself. Taciturnus describes Scribe as a kind of talented poet who has misused his comedy skills while trying only to please his own age, thus failing to unite poetry and passion in his works.[30] Grimsley remembers that in *Stages in Life's Way*, Quidam uses the plot of *Oscar* (which premiered on August 7, 1844) to evaluate the quality and the idealistic fakeness of dying romantically and the inappropriateness of pursuing love and money.[31] Tudvad mentions allusions by Taciturnus to *Kostgængeren* (*La Pension Bourgeoise*, which premiered on October 4, 1832, and which saw 28 performances until February 27, 1841).[32] Another play, *Puf! eller Verden vil bedrages* (*Le Puff ou Mensonge et Vérité*, which premiered on March 27, 1849), which pictured once more the corruption of Parisian society, is used to scrutinize the light-heartedness of an age, which laughs at corruption instead of showing indignation.[33] Grimsley notes that as the period of publication in two series was drawing to a close and especially after the *Corsair* affair, Kierkegaard kept alluding or explicitly referring to Scribe in the journals, focusing more on the content rather than on the dramatic qualities of his works. That is the case of *Kammeraterne* (*La Camaraderie*, which premiered on November 14, 1839), which is the basis for a commentary on the biased, perverse nature of contemporary society, which praises Scribe's social moralizing and buffoonery instead of accepting Kierkegaard's own ethical criticism.[34] In a final commentary from 1855, Kierkegaard still compares the Grundtvigians to the society of "mutual admiration" presented in *Kammeraterne*.[35]

Undoubtedly, Scribe's play proved to be a resourceful tool for Kierkegaard to excel as literary critic and reviewer, since he proves to be well aware of the structure of the well-made play, and his scene-by-scene review of *The First Love* underlines the effect of each specific moment in the action. The above-mentioned commentaries which are scattered throughout Kierkegaard's writings, are very much in line with the essence of A's criticism in what concerns Emmeline and Charles, the two main characters of the play, which lends its name to the sixth chapter of *Either/Or*, Part I. By

---

28   See also Grimsley, "Kierkegaard and Scribe," p. 116.

29   Tudvad, *Kierkegaards København*, pp. 257–8; see also Grimsley, "Kierkegaard and Scribe," p. 121.

30   Tudvad, *Kierkegaards København*, p. 254; *SKS* 6, 379 / *SLW*, 409.

31   *SKS* 6, 443 / *SLW*, 225.

32   Tudvad, *Kierkegaards København*, p. 258.

33   *SKS* 21, 165, NB8:45. *SKS* 22, 20–1, NB11:25. *SKS* 22, 242, NB12:163.

34   *SKS* 21, 165, NB8:45. *SKS* 21, 166, NB8:47. Grimsley, "Kierkegaard and Scribe," p. 125.

35   *Pap.* XI–3 B 182. Grimsley, "Kierkegaard and Scribe," p. 128.

choosing to name the chapter after the play, Kierkegaard, as Eremita, the editor of A's papers, points toward different levels of reading: one focused on the actual review of Scribe's play, another on A's first love for writing, as critic or reviewer, another on A's experiences of a first erotic love, and at least another one at the intersection of these last two readings, which allows for positing the category of the accidental in literary and critical writing. Furthermore, this consummate literary review can also be read as an attempt to present the category of repetition to the reader; this is especially the case with the introductory part of the chapter, which anticipates the fundamental role of the theater in *Repetition* and argues for the autonomy of the author, both in terms of financial independence and freedom of thought, one of Kierkegaard's favorite topics in introductions and prefaces all through the authorship. This is a topic which may well have found the appropriate occasion to be here discussed thanks to Scribe's struggle for the financial and creative independence of the author. As a result, "The First Love" stands as a particular piece of writing in what concerns Kierkegaard's skills as critic and author, a dual category he would later try to hide when he looked back on his review of *Two Ages*.[36]

Before proceeding any further, a brief summary of the play proves to be essential for the sake of clarity. *Les premières amours* stands as an excellent example of the *pièce bien-faite* with a plot rich in all the ingredients that made the model successful. In the first scenes, we learn the background—Emmeline, the heroine, together with her cousin, Charles, were brought up by their virtuous Aunt Judith and had learned how to read with romantic novels; in fact, Emmeline had read up to four volumes a day. No wonder, then, that she and her cousin solemnly promised to love each other forever, firmly convinced that they would communicate just by looking at the moon, no matter where they might be, and recognize each other by the ring she gave him as a love token. During his eight years absence, she lived to believe in the validity of these vows and to make her father, Dervière, and their servants obey her whims. The action of the play begins with Dervière's decision to marry her to Rinville, a son of a dear friend of his, and Emmeline's determination not to obey her father. Therefore, before the happy union of Rinville and Emmeline, it has to be proved, to both audience and characters, that the reunion of Charles and Emmeline is out of the question and that this apparent unromantic fulfillment of their juvenile vows will be for the better of all, including the memory of the dead aunt. Scribe manages to do it by an amazing succession of scenes (scenes VI to XVII) in which Rinville, who has intercepted a letter and become aware of Emmeline's feelings, exchanges identity with Charles. Since Charles and Rinville are often both on stage, Emmeline will eventually be completely exposed; she first confesses that the false Charles is all virtue, only to profess the opposite opinion the moment she notices he is not wearing the ring. When the ring turns up on the false Charles's finger, Emmeline is ready to love him and to say loud and clear that the false Rinville is repulsive and unworthy of her affection. In the meanwhile, Emmeline has learned from Charles himself that he had got married and run into debt and was trying to make his uncle pay for it all. Although this would have been enough to make her come to her senses, Emmeline announces that she had been misled not by the exchange of identities and Charles's misconduct or her

---

[36]   *SV1* XIII, 498 / *PV*, 10.

predetermined disposition and feelings, but by a kind of literary anachronism, since she declares that she had misjudged the past by taking it as the future.

As mentioned previously, the chapter "The First Love" is more than an ordinary review of the play *The First Love*. In fact, "A," the author of the papers edited by Victor Eremita in *Either/Or*, Part I, offers an excellent example of Kierkegaardian practical criticism, and the chapter turns out to be an exercise in how to keep the tension alive and well between the *what* and the *how*, one of the hobby horses of Johannes Climacus in the *Concluding Unscientific Postscript*. The focus of A's criticism is on the content of the play, as well as on its dramatic development, and thus, on Scribe as author and as critic, who, however, stands out as a minor figure when compared to A's stance and skills as literary critic, since this Kierkegaardian *persona* turns out to be an accomplished theater reviewer. This is clear when one considers that his papers published by Eremita include reviews of comedies, ancient and modern tragedies, as well as operas. The tension between *what* A writes about and *how* he writes about it serves the purpose of placing the creativity of the critic at the same level, or even at a higher level than Scribe. In addition to this, the role of editor of "Diary of the Seducer" adds a touch of dramatic talent to A's skills as author since A claims in his introduction to the diary that, in order to clearly present the dangerous consequences of seducing and loving poetically, he has assembled Johannes' papers and Cordelia's letters in a hybrid novelistic form, a sort of epistolary novel dialogically structured but using both journal entries and letters, which often take the form of soliloquies.

The elaborate construction of "The First Love" makes way for the emergence of the critical reader according to the terms announced by Eremita in the preface, given that it actually presents itself as a piece of criticism structured as a set of Chinese boxes. The chapter begins by considerations on (1) A's own position as critic and the possible biographical motivation for this particular review, together with (2) the presentation of some exploratory topics concerning literary creation and literary criticism. These are narrated in the form of an intricate plot, full of characters who reduplicate roles from the play, whose actions are framed by a succession of unfortunate and fortunate events, thus blurring the borderlines between critic and author and between author and editor. Next comes (3) the review of the play, in form and content, which is ultimately presented as the result of A's experiences. The chapter ends by (4) a repetition of a few of the issues already dealt with in (1) and (2) while all along A goes on discussing Scribe's stance as an author. Hence, it should be kept in mind that all through this piece of literary criticism, two guiding lines are continually developed. In this way, "The First Love" contributes decisively to the emergence of Kierkegaard both as a critic of his age and as a theater reviewer, the actual review being structured as an evaluation of the ethical implications of an aesthetic experiment in criticism.

On the one hand, the review of the play is a link in the chain of critical writings on literary works and their aesthetic value, of which the highlights are *From the Papers of Ones Still Living* (1838), *Two Ages: The Age of Revolution and the Present Age. A Literary Review* (1846), and "The Crisis and a Crisis in the Life of an Actress" (1848). Among other topics in this chapter, A insists on the importance of a good performance, and he ends by praising the four actors who have made the play unforgettable,[37] even raising them to the creative status of the author. In addition, A claims that the performance makes the play and adds that a good performance is essential for a good theater review, thus claiming that any review that analyzes the play and subsequently the work of the actors fails to understand what the play is all about.

On the other hand, this chapter is posited as a key piece of *Either/Or*, a monumental work in two parts, given that it presents fundamental topics in both volumes concerning the idea of existential inwardness, with incidence on some dual concepts, such as erotic love and ethical love, living poetically and living responsibly, possibility and actuality, choosing, concealment and openness, imagination and actuality, thought and actuality, knowledge and action, as pointed out by Howard Hong.[38] As mentioned before, the whole chapter results in another peculiar experiment in repetition, concerning Victor Eremita's own feelings in the Preface of *Either/Or*. In addition, it can be read as an anticipation of Hilarius Bogbinder's excursions on recollection in "Lectori benevolo!" in *Stages on Life's Way*, and of Assessor William's discussion of marriage in *Either/Or*, Part II, with the whole being achieved as A manages to persuade the reader to come to terms with an understanding of *The First Love* by the excellence of his insight into Scribe's play.

A's review is very positive in the dramatic qualities he recognizes in the play, and implicitly in the well-made play, to the point that it produces similar statements to A's previous commentaries on Mozart's *Don Giovanni* in the chapter on the immediate musical erotic, since A defends the idea that in *The First Love* it is as useless to distinguish between form and content just as he had chosen to do with Mozart's *Don Giovanni* in the chapter "The Immediate Erotic Stages or the Musical-Erotic." This remark is quite interesting since it calls to mind Scribe's talent as librettist, the similarities residing in the usual attributes of Scribe's librettos, as pointed out by Christopher Smith. In fact, this musicologist emphasizes that in Scribe's librettos it is useless to distinguish the poetic character from the dialogue and the dramatic action from the plot, since they are fully intertwined. He further claims that the librettos are written in order that the audience might be naturally guided by the clarity of the lines and the transparency of the situation, thus rendering superfluous novelistic details or a more elaborate dialogue.[39] Going one step further, A suggests that any eventual flaws in Scribe's play actually help the audience to become aware of what is being performed on stage, and he proceeds to state that the play celebrates Scribe as a virtuoso and guarantees his immortality, another analogy with Mozart.

Notwithstanding his praise of the efficient dramatic structure of the play, which he fully analyzes in 14 pages, A is very critical of its actual content, and he uses the

---

[37]   Johanne Luise Heiberg, Peter Jørgen Frydendahl (1766–1836), John Adolph Gottlob Stage (1791–1845) and Johan Adolph Phister (1807–96), the actors on stage in 25 performances of the play between June 10, 1835 and March 5, 1836.

[38]   *EO1*, xii–xiii.

[39]   For a complete list of his plays and co-authors see Douglas Cardwell, "Eugène Scribe," in *French Dramatists 1789–1914*, ed. by Barbara T. Cooper, pp. 358–64. For a complete list of his librettos and ballet scenarios, see Christopher Smith, "Scribe, (Augustin) Eugène," in *The New Grove Dictionary of Opera*, vols. 1–4, London: Macmillan 1992, vol. 4, pp. 275–7.

characters and their power of illusion and mystification to structure two interwoven theoretical commentaries, one on the effects of literary works, taken here as the serious consequences of romantic novels for the character of the young, and another one on the nature and the production of the comic. The character faults of both Emmeline, who is immersed in illusion, and Charles, who has replaced illusion by mystification, are described as the inevitable outcome of their having taken the heroes and heroines of romantic novels as role models. This analysis is developed very much in line with Kierkegaard's criticism of romantic love, as it had been presented in *The Concept of Irony*,[40] where he dealt with Schlegel's *Lucinde*, while it foresees the future disclosure of the dangers of aesthetic love in the "Diary of the Seducer," the last chapter of *Either/Or*, Part I, and the presentation of the benefits of marriage in "The Esthetic Validity of Marriage," the first chapter of *Either/Or*, Part II. In A's opinion, Emmeline and Charles live within the limits of a circumscribed reality, determined by their untouchable beliefs in first love and family bonds. Each new scene in the play proves them to be wrong, allowing for actuality to disrupt their personal composure and social demeanor. In A's opinion, the comic is brought about by the unevenness of the situations, which the audience are the first to notice, and naturally from the clash between the concealment of identities and the de-concealment of beliefs versus the apparent openness of Rinville's and Emmeline's decisions to marry or not to marry. In this way, the whole is eventually presented as a caricature of the quintessence of all wisdom contained in "An Ecstatic Discourse,"[41] the last section of the "Diapsalmata," which follows Eremita's preface in *Either/Or*, Part I. In this sense, A's criticism stands out as a kind of theatrical cue for Assessor William's comment on Scribe at the beginning of the chapter, "The Esthetic Validity of Marriage" in *Either/Or*, Part II, where he criticizes Scribe's representation of first love in *Den forste Kjarlighed* and in *For Evig*! His harshest criticism is directed at Scribe's recurrent replacement of genuine love by a bourgeois mundane idea of romantic love without the adequate exposure of the lack of values of the romantic illusion their age lived in.[42]

In the chapter "The First Love," the analysis of the main characters is mainly centered on Emmeline and on her interaction with the other characters. In fact, the analysis unfolds as if A were keeping in mind Eremita's conviction that no correspondence between the outer and the inner can ever be found. Although Emmeline is considered to be the decisive character in terms of dramatic action, her comic effect relies on her being the antithesis of a tragic heroine, as defined in the previous chapter, "Silhouettes." Emmeline is described as being able only to chat instead of being a character capable of inducing *pathos*, as representing frivolity instead of passing on enthusiasm, and as deprived of an object or idea to which she may sacrifice herself. For A, she neither holds nor shows any kind of passion, having followed a phantasmatic belief since her childhood. In the beginning, Emmeline loves no one but Charles, because he was her first love; however, when she decides to love Rinville who is impersonating Charles, she has already replaced her first love by the idea of first love as the only true love.

---

[40]   *SKS* 1, 321–4 / *CIC*, 286–301.
[41]   *SKS* 2, 48–52 / *EO1*, 38–43.
[42]   *SKS* 3, 27–8 / *EO2*, 18–19. For more detailed commentaries, see Grimsley, "Kierkegaard and Scribe," pp. 120–1 and Tudvad, *Kierkegaards København*, p. 254.

Her final lines betray her as she confesses to have been wronged by the past, thus conveying the notion that true love can only take place in the future, an assertion which introduces categories of time in what concerns true love. This seems to imply that this concept can be lived both ethically and poetically.

Unquestionably, "*Je me suis trompée; j'ai pris le passé pour l'avenir*" ("I got it all wrong; I took the past for the future."), Emmeline's famous last line, refutes the validity of experiencing first love as true love and implicitly associates true love with the experience of future relationships, allowing for the possibility of a future life with Rinville as her husband, who obviously was not her first love. A's opinion corroborates this line of reading, since he claims that any eventual sense of morals is overcome by the infinite wit of Emmeline's final remark, a statement which challenges the possibility of simply believing that Emmeline will keep on looking in Rinville's character and figure for traits which might recall Charles. If that were the case, A would be convinced that the play was a mere mediocre example of bourgeois morality; instead, A defends an open end which allows Emmeline to prove that first love can be a numerical and a qualitative category at the same time.

Although A comments extensively on the characters of Dervière and Rinville, only his considerations on Charles will be mentioned in detail here, since they provide proof of Charles' relevance as evidence for the unethical and elusive nature of first love as true love. According to A, Charles depicts the criticism of the heroes of romantic novels more accurately than Emmeline, since he returns under an aura of mystery, which once unveiled, reveals a fallen character. For A, Charles manages to survive because he accepts showing himself as he actually is, thus preferring mystification to illusion to the point that he ends up as a reverse image of a romantic transfiguration by love. Not only has he developed into a worse being, but he has also come to believe that he is an extraordinary character, a state of affairs which, according to A, brings Charles back to his initial state of illusion. Another significant observation by A concerns the double elusiveness of Emmeline and Charles (as well as Dervière); although they are well-structured replicas of typical sentimental romantic characters, their social behavior is well anchored in actuality. Furthermore, Dervière's pragmatism, and especially Rinville's, contributes to transform their world into a mirror of actuality.

It is worth noting that when taken together with the central position of this chapter in *Either/Or*, Part I, Charles appears as the middle link in a chain of seducers in the volume. Compared to Don Giovanni and to Johannes the Seducer, Charles is depicted by A as the worst kind of aesthetic seducer, since he fails to represent erotic force and sensuality, as Don Giovanni does by music, and he is incapable of producing an indelible effect on Emmeline, as Johannes does on Cordelia by the use of the word. In addition, the deceptive identities of Rinville/Charles and Charles/Rinville, which eventually display the dissimulation and falsity of their feelings, may also be considered as reminders of the inevitability of Judge William's ethical stance concerning marriage with its strong emphasis on convention, which is fully developed in *Either/Or*, Part II. On the other hand, Emmeline lags behind Donna Elvira and Cordelia. Although her final lines manage to transform actuality into possibility by suggesting that a future love can effectively be taken as a first love, she plays a minor role as the seduced part. The effects of seduction on Donna Elvira and on Cordelia not only render them incapable of believing that the first love is true love, but deprive them of the chance of ever experiencing true love.

As previously stated, A claims that the only way to appreciate the irony in this play is to watch it, not to read it, an assertion which underlines the relevance of the performance for the making of the play. In order to evaluate A's stance as critic and author, I believe that special attention should be paid to his outstanding performance in the introductory section of the chapter "The First Love," where he carries out an impressive demonstration in favor of the fortunate authorship of an unsuccessful author. He begins by classifying authors into two types, depending on their interaction with the muse—those who may invoke the muse or those who are summoned by the muse. Only the latter are of interest to him since they may fall prey to the power of occasion, which stands for the accidental, itself a bounding requirement for the necessary. By contrast, trivial literature is the result of the trivialization of the occasion, a common procedure for authors who see an occasion in everything, usually with the single intent of making a profit from their writings. The more a writer acknowledges the occasion, the more suspicious the literary critic should be, for the occasion previous to the work of a great poet should only be known to the poet. According to A's point of view, the occasion lies at the heart of literary creation, and it also determines its aesthetic value, and consequently, the occasion is as relevant for the poet as it is for the critic. The occasion is defined in different terms from what is commonly understood as inspiration—it is more agile than exalting; further it is paradoxical, since it does not exist in itself but only in relation to an object. Within this perspective, a bad performance may turn out to be a better occasion to review a play than a good performance. However, for A, what counts is the good performance of *The First Love*; this puts the accent on the idea that the occasion is not a universal category, but a particular situation.

To account for the fragility of his condition as critic, in the context of the specific purpose of this piece of criticism, A identifies two sets of unfortunate factors, extrinsic and intrinsic that have made him a critic or reviewer. In fact, his fortune depends on the plans of an editor, which are actually described more as whims, and it is definitely connected to some crucial biographical incidents. At the end of this introductory section of "The First Love," before A finally manages to finish the review that he still believes will never be published; there is a digression on the role of the editor, who is taken as a devilish seducer, much like Mephistopheles who tempts Faust. A's review will only be published because the editor's first article for the first number of his newspaper was ruined by an unexpected accident, and eventually A's article turns out to be the editor's only solution to the problem of what to put on the front page. Thus, A sees his condition as author and reviewer repeatedly put at risk, just as his condition as seducer, lover, and fiancé emerges as a helplessly lost cause in the account of his love with a young lady who fails to keep her promise. This analogy combines the elusiveness of Emmeline and Charles' first love and Regine Olsen and Kierkegaard's broken engagement. In fact, though A himself believes there is no love like the first love, he writes extensively about the misfortunes and misunderstandings of his first love in a fictitious version of Kierkegaard's and Regine Olsen's encounters. This narrative moment should not be taken too literally as a biographical digression, and, in my opinion, it actually serves the purpose of demonstrating that A's creativity as critic is far richer than Scribe's as playwright, since he not only writes on Scribe's *The First Love*, but also lives and reflects on a real experience of a first love, and by so doing, he combines in himself more talents than Scribe could ever hope for. In fact, A narrates that his beloved is at the theater to attend a performance of *The First Love* and hopefully the play will make room for a conversation with her the following day; however, everything lies in the realm of the aesthetic since their coming to terms results not from their mutual understanding but from the fact that they both understood the poet. Besides, the effects of the play on the audience are taken more as a parody of the relation between Kierkegaard as author and the reader than as a parody of his broken engagement. Simultaneously, the category of repetition is summoned in different plans—life (their love) reduplicates fiction (the play), and the two lovers (A and his fiancée) swear to watch every coming performance of the play, as if in this way their mutual understanding might repeat itself with each new performance they attend.

As follows, A outdoes Scribe since he manages to produce an effect in his contemporary reader who contemplates the idea of repetition even before the publication of the next volume in the series. Moreover, he produces a completely distinct effect in the modern reader, who is placed under the spell of recollection, since the modern reader is obviously well aware of all the volumes published in the two series. In addition to this, the reader is persuaded to accept the value of repetition when A proceeds to explain that the incidental meeting with his fiancée did not provide the occasion to write the review. The category of occasion is thus further fictionalized, when A explains that the definite occasion for the present review was provided by the repeated encounter of the author with the play: at the theater, as performance, and as written text, since he came across the book, first at the inn and the following day at the home of a friend. These repetitions, together with another encounter with his fiancée, help him make up his mind about writing the review. To top it all, A eventually meets his former fiancée in the company of her new fiancé, whom she describes as her true first love, thus transforming her into the mouthpiece of Emmeline's final prophetic lines, which A had just read one time after the other.

In this manner, A manages to demonstrate that Scribe's success as an author may only be fully grasped by a reviewer who is capable of transforming his misfortunes as author and lover into a successful critical account of his condition as author. This is then followed by a detailed review of a play by Scribe, and as a result, A stands out as critic and as author. Moreover, A emerges as an author who continually writes on reflection, whereas Scribe fails to do so since he places the intrigue above the characters and excels in witticisms which never intend to confront the taste of the public or its behavioral patterns concerning marriage or parental obedience. Therefore, Scribe also fails to shape the public, whereas A leaves an indelible mark on his editor, on his former fiancée, on his reader, on the actors he praises, and on Kierkegaard's authorship, the whole providing proof that the actuality of his review establishes itself as more resilient and more effective than the fictitious possibility conveyed by Scribe's play.

Bibliography

I. Scribe's Works in The Auction Catalogue *of Kierkegaard's Library*

Den förste Kjærlighed. Lystspil i een Act, trans. by Johan Ludvig Heiberg, Copenhagen: Jens Hostrup Schultz 1832 (*ASKB* U 98).

Statsmand og Borger. Skuespil i fem Acter, trans. by Carl Borgaard, Copenhagen n.p. 1844 (*ASKB* U 99).

Verden vil bedrages. Lystspil i fem Acter, Copenhagen n.p. 1849 (*ASKB* U 101).

Oscar. Skuespil i tre Acter, trans. by A.V. Güntelberg, Copenhagen n.p. 1844 (*ASKB* U 100)

Scribe, Eugène and E. Legouvé, *Dronning Marguerites Noveller. Lystspil i fem Acter*, trans. by F.L. Høedt, Copenhagen n.p. 1851 (*ASKB* U 102)

II. Works in The Auction Catalogue *of Kierkegaard's Library that Discuss Scribe*

Heiberg, Johan Ludvig, *Om Philosophiens Betydning for den nuværende Tid. Et Indbydelses-Skrift til en Række af philosophiske Forelæsninger*, Copenhagen: C.A. Reitzel 1833, p. 41 (*ASKB* 568).

—— "Litterær Vintersæd," in *Intelligensblade*, ed. by Johan Ludvig Heiberg, Copenhagen: C.A. Reitzel 1843, vol. 2, no. 24, 1843, pp. 285–92, see p. 290 (*ASKB* U 56).

—— "Lyrisk Poesie," in *Intelligensblade*, ed. by Johan Ludvig Heiberg, Copenhagen: C.A. Reitzel 1843, vol. 3, nos. 25–6, 1843, pp. 25–72, see p. 44 (*ASKB* U 56).

Thomsen, Grimur, *Om den nyfranske Poesi, et Forsøg til Besvarelse af Universitetets æsthetiske Priisspørgsmaal for 1841: "Har Smag og Sands for Poesi gjort Frem- eller Tilbageskridt i Frankrig i de sidste Tider og hvilken er Aarsagen?,"* Copenhagen: Wahlske Boghandlings Forlag 1843, p. 73; pp. 96–8; p. 102; p. 104; p. 156 (*ASKB* 1390).

III. Secondary Literature on Kierkegaard's Relation to Scribe

Grimsley, Ronald, "Kierkegaard and Scribe," *Revue de Littérature Comparée*, vol. 38, 1964, pp. 512–30.

—— "Kierkegaard and Scribe," in his *Søren Kierkegaard and French Literature. Eight Comparative Studies*, Cardiff: University of Wales Press 1966, pp. 112–29.

Neiiendam, Klaus, "Kierkegaard og teatret," *Den danske Tilskuer*, Copenhagen: Selskabet for dansk Teaterhistorie 1990, pp. 83–100.

Tudvad, Peter, "Dyrehavsbakken og Det Kgl. Teater," *Kierkegaards København*, Copenhagen: Politikens Forlag 2004, pp. 208–91.

William Shakespeare:

Kierkegaard's Post-Romantic Reception of "the Poet's Poet"

Joel D.S. Rasmussen

When the dramatist Ben Jonson penned his dedication for the 1623 Folio edition of *Shakespeare's Comedies, Histories, & Tragedies*, he predicted a perennially enthusiastic reception for the plays of his friend and rival:

> Triumph, my *Britaine*, thou hast one to showe,
> To whom all scenes of *Europe* homage owe.
> He was not of an age, but for all time![1]

Jonson's expectation of an audience for William Shakespeare (1564–1616) beyond Britain's shores expresses a confidence that Shakespeare's works are charged with a power to augment our insights into broader human passions, projects, and relationships. But the translation of Shakespeare's works for "the scenes of Europe" (and later around the globe) has involved complex processes of recontextualization, such that subsequent readers and theater-goers have found in Shakespeare's plays meanings and resonances Jonson and his contemporaries might never have imagined. In the latter half of the eighteenth century, for example, German critics and audiences appropriated Shakespeare's Elizabethan dramas, first, in terms of the *Sturm und Drang* movement, and then, with the translations by August Wilhelm Schlegel (1767–1845) and Ludwig Tieck (1773–1853) that began appearing after 1795, according to a more fully articulated German Romanticism.[2] These Schlegel–Tieck translations gained for Shakespeare a literary status in nineteenth-century Germany that exceeded his reputation in England at the time.[3] A.W. Schlegel's

---

[1] Ben Jonson, "Ben Jonson on Shakespeare," in *Shakespeare: The Critical Heritage*, vols. 1–6, ed. by Brian Vickers, Abingdon: Routledge 1974–81, vol. 1, p. 24.

[2] Ernst Behler, *German Romantic Literary Theory*, Cambridge: Cambridge University Press 1993, p. 7; p. 92. See also the third chapter of Friederike von Schwerin-High's *Shakespeare, Reception and Translation: Germany and Japan*, New York: Continuum 2004.

[3] See Dennis Kennedy, "Shakespeare Worldwide," in *Cambridge Companion to Shakespeare*, ed. by Margreta de Grazia and Stanley Wells, Cambridge: Cambridge University Press 2001, p. 254. Incidentally, the trend of German "nostrification" (or spiritual appropriation) of Shakespeare continued into the twentieth century. In 1915 the dramatist Ludwig Fulda, observed "...Above all Shakespeare! He is more frequently performed in

brother, Friedrich Schlegel (1772–1829), gives us some sense for the Romantic enthusiasm for Shakespeare when, in his *Dialogue on Poetry*, he has one of the interlocutors ask us to "think on Shakespeare, in whom I would like to fix the actual centre, the core of the romantic imagination."[4] Thus, for the Romantics, Shakespeare and his works symbolized the emerging aesthetic of imaginative irony, a quasi-religious conception of human subjectivity in an indifferent world, wherein artistic creativity is believed to express the deepest truths of a dynamic reality. The Romantic reception was not without its detractors, however. For example, while Hegel agreed with the Romantics that "you will scarcely find any other modern dramatist who can be compared with Shakespeare,"[5] he was nonetheless a resolute critic of Romanticism generally, and of "Tieck and the brothers Schlegel with their premeditated irony" specifically.[6] For Hegel, Shakespeare's "universal interest"[7] consists not so much in his ability to express the truths of reality as such, as it lies in his genius for depicting the "depth of subjective inner life," together with a "breadth of individual characterization."[8] This inner life is an important dimension of reality, Hegel acknowledges. But, according to Hegel's form of absolute idealism, this subjective dimension needs to be mediated into a scientific system of knowledge that also accounts for the objective manifestations of Spirit in order truly to grasp the processes of reality. It was this, under Hegel's lights, that the Romantics failed to comprehend and that Shakespeare never intended to accomplish. Hamlet's well-known remark to his only dear friend is perhaps telling: "There are more things in heaven and earth, Horatio, than are dreamt of in your philosophy."[9]

Shakespeare's German reception proved decisive in the transmission of Shakespeare to other parts of Europe as well. This was arguably nowhere the case more than it was in Denmark, where Søren Kierkegaard received Shakespeare in a cultural bundle with Romantic irony and absolute idealism. Kierkegaard

---

Germany during a single year than during a whole decade in his native country. And, what is more important, he is incomparably better performed than over there, incomparably better understood than over there. Our Shakespeare! Thus we may call him, even if he happened to be born in England by mistake" (quoted in Wilhelm Hortmann, *Shakespeare on the German Stage: The Twentieth Century*, Cambridge: Cambridge University Press 1998, p. 4).

[4]		Friedrich Schlegel, *Dialogue on Poetry and Literary Aphorisms*, trans. by Ernst Behler and Roman Struc, University Park: Pennsylvania State University Press 1968, pp. 100–1.

[5]		[Georg Wilhelm Friedrich Hegel], *Hegel's Aesthetics: Lectures on Fine Art*, vols. 1–2, trans. by T.M. Knox, Oxford: Clarendon Press 1975, vol. 2, p. 1228. Kierkegaard owned Hegel's lectures on aesthetics, see *Georg Wilhelm Friedrich Hegel's Vorlesungen über die Aesthetik*, vols. 1–3, ed. by Heinrich Gustav Hotho, Berlin: Verlag von Duncker und Humblot 1835–38 (vols. 10.1–10.3 in *Georg Wilhelm Friedrich Hegel's Werke. Vollständige Ausgabe*, vols. 1–18, ed. by Philipp Marheineke et al., Berlin: Verlag von Duncker und Humblot 1832–45) (*ASKB* 1384–1386).

[6]		*Hegel's Aesthetics: Lectures on Fine Art*, vol. 2, p. 1175.

[7]		Ibid., p. 1176.

[8]		Ibid., p. 1177.

[9]		William Shakespeare, *Hamlet*, in *The Riverside Shakespeare*, ed. by G. Blakemore Evans et al., Boston: Houghton Mifflin Company 1974, Act I, scene 5; p. 1151.

customarily read Shakespeare's plays in his Schlegel–Tieck translation,[10] and the tributes his pseudonyms lavish upon Shakespeare—"great Shakespeare,"[11] "immortal Shakespeare,"[12] and "the poet's poet"[13]—echo the German esteem for him. A comment in Kierkegaard's dissertation about intellectuals who eulogize Shakespeare as "the grand master of irony" is a clear allusion to Romanticism.[14] And scattered remarks on the Shakespeare criticism of the post-Romantic Karl Ludwig Börne (1786–1837) and the Hegelian Heinrich Theodor Rötscher (1803–71) attest to Kierkegaard's familiarity with additional secondary literature on Shakespeare. Despite the fact that Kierkegaard received Shakespeare's works through German translation and critical mediation, however, Kierkegaard's critical appropriation of Shakespeare actually serves to establish a critical stance relative to the German traditions of Romanticism and absolute idealism. In one instance, Kierkegaard even hints that a distinctively Danish tradition of philosophy might begin with the "proposition" Hamlet poses to Horatio:

> Danish philosophy—should there ever be talk of such a thing—will differ from German philosophy in that in no wise will it begin with nothing or without any presupposition, or explain everything by mediating, since it begins, on the contrary, with the proposition that there are many things between heaven and earth which no philosophy has explained.[15]

Kierkegaard's allusion to Hamlet's adage is suggestive, for it seems to imply that he sees in Shakespeare's writings (or at least in *Hamlet, Prince of Denmark*) resources for gaining critical distance on "German philosophy." The task of this article, therefore, will be to elucidate Kierkegaard's appropriation of Shakespeare with respect to his efforts to disentangle his reading from quasi-religious Romantic interpretations of Shakespeare, on the one hand, and from the Hegelian insistence that subjective insights require mediation into a higher system of absolute knowledge, on the other hand. Then, with this interpretation in place, we should be in a better position to determine whether this conception of Shakespeare's authorship offers us any insights into Kierkegaard's own self-understanding as an author. First, however, so as not to become swamped in reception history from the outset, a brief consideration of Shakespeare's life and works apart from German and Danish categories will be helpful.

I. William Shakespeare's Life and Works in Brief

During Shakespeare's lifetime, he was "virtually unknown outside his island nation."[16] Indeed, even within England, where several of his works became famous

---

[10]   *Shakspeare's dramatische Werke*, trans. by August Wilhelm Schlegel and Ludwig Tieck, vols. 1–12, Berlin: G. Reimer 1839–40 (*ASKB* 1883–1888). For other translations of Shakespeare that Kierkegaard owned, see bibliography below.

[11]   *SKS* 4, 154 / *FT*, 61.

[12]   *SV1* XIII, 475 / *COR*, 77. *SKS* 6, 206 / *SLW*, 220.

[13]   *SKS* 11, 154 / *SUD*, 38.

[14]   *SKS* 1, 352 / *CI*, 324.

[15]   *SKS* 18, 217, JJ:239 / *KJN* 2, 199.

[16]   Hugh Grady, "Shakespeare Criticism, 1600–1900," in *The Cambridge Companion to Shakespeare*, p. 265.

within his lifetime, many details of his biography have remained obscure, and the historical reconstruction of his life has grown into a highly contested academic subfield unto itself.[17] He was born on April 26, 1564 in the market town of Stratford-upon-Avon, some 100 miles north-west of London. As the son of an upwardly mobile town alderman and bailiff, he likely attended a "grammar school" where he would have been educated primarily in Latin and some Greek. His plays and poems attest to an immersion in the works of Virgil, Ovid, Plutarch, Holinshed's *Chronicles*, and the Bible, all texts from which schoolboys read and memorized passages. After his schooling, Shakespeare married Anne Hathaway in 1582, and the couple had three children—a daughter named Susanna, and then twins named Judith and Hamnet. No documentation exists, however, to establish even such simple details as how Shakespeare supported his family, or where and how they lived. Neither is it known precisely when and why he left his family in Stratford, or how he quickly rose to such prominence as both an actor and a playwright in the London theatrical world by the early 1590s.

Shakespeare arrived in London during one of the most remarkable periods in English history. At the end of the sixteenth century, the capital city was becoming an unparalleled commercial success, and its population was growing exponentially.[18] At the same time, Queen Elizabeth's efforts to consolidate Protestant power following her accession to the throne in 1559 had given England the character of a police state, and religious-political intrigue reached deep into the theater world throughout her reign. Christopher Marlowe (1564–93), Shakespeare's first and main rival as playwright, was recruited to be a secret agent for the crown when he was still an undergraduate at Cambridge; the reasons for his assassination in 1593 remain murky to this day, but may well stem from suspicions of seditious allegory in his plays, and to allegations by an informant that he had expressed interest in spying for the Catholic dissenters. Thomas Kyd (1558–94), a fellow playwright who had once shared rooms with Marlowe, was in the same year interrogated and tortured, and he died from his injuries the following year.[19] Following Elizabeth's death and the succession of James I from Scotland to the crown of England in 1603, the poet and playwright Ben Jonson (1572–1637) was also incarcerated, with the Privy Council charging that Jonson had mocked the Scots in the play *Eastward Ho*. According to Harold Bloom, "The death of Christopher Marlowe was a lesson Shakespeare never forgot,

---

[17]   The periodic controversies over whether someone other than Shakespeare wrote the plays and poems bearing his name are not discussed in this article. Recent work in this area, however, seems to demonstrate that adequate historical evidence exists to link the events of Shakespeare's life unambiguously with his writings. See Stephen Greenblatt, *Will in the World: How Shakespeare Became Shakespeare*, New York: Norton 2004, and Michael Wood, *Shakespeare*, New York: Basic Books 2003. For a less conclusive exploration of "the authorship question," see John F. Mitchell, *Who Wrote Shakespeare?* London: Thames & Hudson 1996.

[18]   "From about 15,000 in 1550, [London's population] had leaped by Elizabeth's death in 1603 to an estimated 140,000 within the limits of the City itself, with another 40,000 inhabiting the suburbs" (Anne Barton, "The London Scene: City and Court," in *The Cambridge Companion to Shakespeare*, p. 117).

[19]   Wood, *Shakespeare*, pp. 154–5.

while the torture of Thomas Kyd and the incarceration of Ben Jonson doubtless also hovered always in Shakespeare's consciousness."[20] Surely, Shakespeare learned from the experiences of his colleagues the dangers of expressing his own opinions on matters of religion or politics in any but the most oblique fashion. "His instinct for keeping out of trouble was very agile,"[21] Northrop Frye has written, and in his plays especially, as Bloom says, Shakespeare "never permits us voyage to the undiscovered country of his self."[22]

Shakespeare's known works began pouring from his pen around 1589–90, with the composition and performance of *Henry VI, Part One*, and then of *Henry VI, Part Two*, and *Henry VI, Part Three* within the next two years. This initial productivity as a playwright was interrupted, however, when an outbreak of the plague necessitated a two-year closure of London's theaters beginning in 1592. During this closure, Shakespeare devoted his efforts to poetry, and enjoyed high acclaim upon the publication of his long narrative poems *Venus and Adonis* in 1593 and *The Rape of Lucrece* in 1594. Since it was poetry more than plays that would make or break an author's literary reputation in Elizabethan England (owing in part to the controversial status of the public theaters), the great success of these poems established Shakespeare's name among the educated classes. *Venus and Adonis* was especially popular among university students, and among the Cambridge in-crowd the dictum was, "We shall have nothing but pure Shakespeare."[23]

When the theaters reopened in 1594, Shakespeare resumed in London as an actor and playwright with the Lord Chamberlain's Men—later renamed the King's Men—the company with which he remained an actor, playwright, and shareholder for the rest of his career. *Richard II*, *Romeo and Juliet*, *A Midsummer Night's Dream*, *The Merchant of Venice*, *Henry IV, Part One*, *Henry IV, Part Two*, and *Henry V* were all written and performed within the following five years. By 1599, the company was profitable enough to build a theater for itself—the Globe—across the Thames River from London. And it was while the company was resident in the Globe that Shakespeare wrote what many consider his greatest plays: *Hamlet*, *Twelfth Night*, *Measure for Measure*, *Othello*, *King Lear*, *Macbeth*, and *The Tempest*. In all, Shakespeare composed at least 38 plays for the company, including some on which he collaborated with other playwrights. The plays are typically grouped into three categories—comedies, histories, and tragedies—following the divisions of the first folio edition of Shakespeare's plays (published by Jonson and other friends of Shakespeare in 1623, seven years after his death).

In addition to his prodigious work as an actor and playwright, Shakespeare remained a prolific writer of poetry during this same two-decade period. Apart from the two published narrative poems named above, however, most of Shakespeare's

---

[20]   Harold Bloom, *Shakespeare: The Invention of the Human*, New York: Riverhead Books 1998, p. 732.
[21]   Northrop Frye, *Northrop Frye on Shakespeare*, ed. by Robert Sandler, New Haven: Yale University Press 1986, p. 9.
[22]   Harold Bloom, *The Anxiety of Influence*, 2nd ed., New York and Oxford: Oxford University Press 1997, p. xlvi.
[23]   Wood, *Shakespeare*, p. 151.

poetry—comprising two more narrative poems entitled *The Phoenix and the Turtle* and *A Lover's Complaint*, and his sonnets—circulated for years in a "manuscript milieu" before ever going to press. Shakespeare finally selected and ordered 154 of his sonnets for publication in 1609. Yet, despite the fact that during his lifetime he "seems to have been almost as well known for his narrative and lyrical poems," he has received far more attention from subsequent generations for his plays.[24] This tendency has been even more pronounced in non-English-speaking lands, no doubt because the sonnet form presents more challenges to translators than the freer dialogue of the plays.

Around 1610 or shortly thereafter, Shakespeare returned to Stratford-upon-Avon to live with his wife and his two daughters and their husbands (Hamnet had died in 1596). Having earned income from his career as an actor, from the sale of his scripts, and from his shares in the company, he had over the years been able to purchase a large house and a considerable amount of property back in his home town. Only a few short years were left to him, however; he died on April 23, 1616, and was buried in Holy Trinity Church, Stratford.

II. Shakespeare in Kierkegaard's Authorship

Allusions to Shakespeare and quotations from several of his plays appear frequently in Kierkegaard's published writings. Kierkegaard seems to have had many passages from Shakespeare's plays at his fingertips, as it were, and the sheer number of plays to which he and his pseudonyms refer, and/or from which they quote, corroborates Kierkegaard's claim to have, as he says, "studied my Shakespeare."[25] When Kierkegaard studied Shakespeare, however, he did so not in terms of Elizabethan and Jacobean dramatic traditions, but in connection with the intellectual currents of late-eighteenth- and early-nineteenth-century German thought. Embedded within some of Kierkegaard's earliest references to Shakespeare are clear allusions to the German translators and interpreters of Shakespeare that mediated the plays to him. Mention was made in the introductory section of Kierkegaard's allusion in *The Concept of Irony* to those Romantic ironists who "eulogized" Shakespeare as "the grand master of irony."[26] Another Shakespearean-Germanic bundle appears early in Kierkegaard's authorship in the first volume of *Either/Or*, in a double reference to *Hamlet* and to Johann Wolfgang von Goethe (1749–1832). Here the aesthete makes passing reference to "what Goethe said somewhere about Hamlet, that his soul in relation to his body was an acorn planted in a flower pot, with the result, therefore, that it bursts the container."[27] This metaphor of organic development evokes a sense for the protracted

---

[24]   John Kerrigan, "Shakespeare's Poems," in *The Cambridge Companion to Shakespeare*, p. 65.
[25]   *SKS* 20, 24, NB:12–13 / *JP* 5, 5892, my translation. Kierkegaard's study appears to have been limited to Shakespeare's plays, however, as there is no evidence that he was familiar with Shakespeare's sonnets.
[26]   *SKS* 1, 352 / *CI*, 324.
[27]   *SKS* 2, 205 / *EO1*, 210. The reference is to a discussion in Johann Wolfgang von Goethe's *Wilhelm Meister's Apprenticeship* quoting Hamlet's lines, "The time is out of joint—O

and ultimately violent emergence of the self from its context, and it is precisely this ability to evoke such an overwhelming intensity of passion that first Goethe, then such Romantics as "Tieck and the brothers Schlegel,"[28] and following them Kierkegaard's aesthete, most admire in Shakespeare. In one of the "Diapsalmata" of *Either/Or*, for example, the aesthete complains that the age is wretched precisely because individuals lack passion, and on account of this, he says, "my soul always turns back to the Old Testament and to Shakespeare. There one still feels that those who speak are human beings; there they hate, there they love, there they murder the enemy, curse his descendants through all generations—there they sin."[29] In Kierkegaard's *Stages on Life's Way*, an admission of perfidy in love is embellished with a short quotation from Shakespeare's *Cymbeline*, and the anonymous writer reflects, "You, immortal Shakespeare; you are able to speak passionately."[30]

It should be observed, however, that references of this sort within Kierkegaard's writings do not have the character of "Shakespeare criticism" in any strict sense; they serve primarily to illustrate or emphasize some point within the context of a larger thematic development that is structurally independent from the specific Shakespearean reference. The great majority of the Shakespeare references in Kierkegaard's writings are of this sort, in fact, and do not so much *critique* features of the plays as they *appropriate* quotations and characters in order to illustrate, extend, and explore categories more apposite to Kierkegaard's writings than to Shakespeare's own.[31] What is true of Shakespeare's German-language interpreters also applies to Kierkegaard—they all interpret Shakespeare "through their own categories."[32] Yet, if the German-language lectures and treatises on Shakespeare that proliferated during the generations prior to Kierkegaard aimed primarily to understand some theme or

---

cursed spite, That ever I was born to set it right!" (*The Riverside Shakespeare*, Act I, scene v; p. 1151). And the interpretation is as follows: "In these words, I imagine, will be found the key to Hamlet's whole procedure. To me it is clear that Shakspeare [*sic*] meant, in the present case, to represent the effects of a great action laid upon a soul unfit for the performance of it. In this view the whole piece seems to me to be composed. There is an oak-tree planted in a costly jar, which should have borne only pleasant flowers in its bosom; the roots expand, the jar is shivered" (*Wilhelm Meister's Apprenticeship*, trans. by Thomas Carlyle, New York: P.F. Collier and Son 1917 (*Harvard Classics Shelf of Fiction*, vol. 15), pp. 248–9). Kierkegaard owned *Wilhelm Meisters Lehrjahre*, in *Goethe's Werke. Vollständige Ausgabe letzter Hand* [in 55 volumes], vols. 1–40, Stuttgart and Tübingen: J.G. Cotta 1827–30; *Goethe's nachgelassene Werke*, vols. 41–55, Stuttgart and Tübingen: J.G. Cotta 1832–33, vol. 19, p. 76 (*ASKB* 1641–1668).

[28]   *Hegel's Aesthetics: Lectures on Fine Art*, vol. 2, p. 1175.

[29]   *SKS* 2, 36 / *EO1*, 28.

[30]   *SKS* 6, 206 / *SLW*, 220. In this connection, see also Frater Taciturnus' remarks on Shakespeare's "definitive pathos" in depicting the "undialectical" passion of Romeo and Juliet (*SKS* 6, 378 / *SLW*, 407–8).

[31]   A catalogue of instances in Kierkegaard's writings where lines or scenes from Shakespeare's plays are cited primarily for purposes of illustration—sometimes almost imperceptibly vague—would run far too long to itemize here. For a list that is almost comprehensive, see *Cumulative Index to Kierkegaard's Writings*, ed. by Howard V. Hong, Edna H. Hong, Nathaniel J. Hong, Kathryn Hong, and Regine Prenzel-Guthrie, Princeton: Princeton University Press 2000, pp. 298–9.

[32]   Grady, "Shakespeare Criticism, 1600–1900," p. 265.

another in Shakespeare's plays, then the appropriation of Shakespeare by Kierkegaard and his pseudonyms tends more often to embellish and supplement the Kierkegaardian text itself.[33] There are certain notable exceptions to this generalization, however. For sometimes Kierkegaard's pseudonyms offer penetrating interpretations of key Shakespearean *dramatis personae*. And, while the extent of the commentary on these figures is better measured in paragraphs than in pages, such considerations serve *both* to supplement the specific discussion for which they are illustrations *and* to gloss features of these Shakespearean characters in new and insightful ways. What follows addresses the two most prominent of these short discussions—one on *Richard III* in *Fear and Trembling*, and another on *Hamlet* in *Stages on Life's Way*—taking these as representative of the ways Kierkegaard (through his pseudonyms) appropriates Shakespeare as a source for critical reflection.

In *Fear and Trembling*, within the context of a larger discussion contrasting "the ethical" with the silent religious faith of Abraham on the one side, and with the extreme aesthetic form of inwardness that is "demonic" on the other, Kierkegaard's pseudonym Johannes de silentio turns to Shakespeare's *Richard III* in order to help him flesh out his discussion of this latter "demonic" type of human "nature":

> In that kind of thing, Shakespeare is and remains a hero. That demoniac, the most demonic figure Shakespeare has depicted but also depicted in a matchless way—Gloucester (later Richard III)—what made him into a demoniac? Apparently his inability to bear the sympathy heaped upon him from childhood. His monologue in the first act of *Richard III* has more value than all the systems of morality, which have no intimation of the nightmares of existence or of their explanation.
>
>> ...I, that am rudely stamp'd, and want love's majesty
>> To strut before a wanton ambling nymph;
>> I, that am curtail'd of this fair proportion,
>> Cheated of feature by dissembling Nature,
>> Deform'd, unfinish'd, sent before my time
>> Into this breathing world, scarce half made up,
>> And that so lamely and unfashionable
>> That dogs bark at me as I halt by them—.
>
> Natures such as Gloucester's cannot be saved by mediating them into an idea of society. Ethics actually only makes sport of them....[34]

Despite the fact that it consists of fewer than twenty lines (eight of which quote from the play) the incorporation of this reference works on multiple levels. On one level, along with his earlier sketch of Agnes and the Merman, de silentio's reference to Gloucester helps provide a thick account of the demonic in relation to the ethical,

---

[33]   For an anthology of German-language scholarship on Shakespeare between 1741 and 1827, see *Shakespeare-Rezeption: Die Diskussion um Shakespeare in Deutschland*, vols. 1–2, ed. by Hansjürgen Blinn, Berlin: Erich Schmidt Verlag 1982.
[34]   *SKS* 4, 194 / *FT*, 105–6; Johannes de silentio cites from the Schlegel–Tieck translation, *Shakespeare's dramatische Werke*, vol. 3, pp. 235–6; *The Tragedy of Richard the Third*, in *The Riverside Shakespeare*, Act I, scene 1; pp. 712–13.

or "the universal." While de silentio's account is laden with theory (e.g., "The demonic has the same quality as the divine, namely, that the single individual is able to enter into an absolute relation to it"[35]; "A demoniac discloses himself without understanding himself,"[36] etc.), the category itself is borne by its exemplification. Gloucester finds himself "higher than the universal" by choosing his identity as a wicked individual ("Since I cannot prove a lover...I am determined to prove a villain"[37]) and thus, we might say, he exemplifies "the demonic" as its "ideal type," embodying specific human passions and a concrete narrative history. Gloucester simply exemplifies this condition more fully than any purely theoretical account could, indeed, in a "matchless way."[38]

At another level, this meditation is also a slice of Shakespeare criticism. Just as the Gloucester illustration furthers de silentio's discussion of the demonic, so too this discussion of the demonic reciprocally offers new insights into Shakespeare's play. By sketching an interpretation of Gloucester in terms of the way that he relates negatively both to "the ethical" and to "the religious," de silentio enriches our engagement with the play—potentially, at least—by expanding our interpretive horizon. Thus, readers of Shakespeare familiar with *Fear and Trembling* might interpret Richard not only as a "murtherer" and a "villain" (categories built into the play—Richard affirms and denies both[39]), but might also ask the question of whether de silentio's interpretation of Richard as a "demoniac" gives further insights into the play that would not otherwise be possible. Some will think so, and other will not; a critic such as Walter Kaufmann, for example, would find such an interpretation far too theologically freighted, whereas a Shakespeare critic like G.K. Chesterton might find the interpretation genial precisely because it contextualizes Gloucester theologically.

Despite the fact that de silentio contextualizes his interpretation of Gloucester in terms of his own reflections on religious faith, it should be noted that he does not think Shakespeare does so. On the contrary, de silentio says he does not find expressions of genuinely *religious* inwardness in any of Shakespeare's works. Almost as an aside to his deliberation on Abraham's "silent inwardness" during his journey to Mount Moriah to sacrifice Isaac, de silentio makes the following observation about Shakespeare's own silence on the theme of the "torment" of religious inwardness:

> Thanks to you, great Shakespeare, you who can say everything, everything, everything just as it is—and yet, why did you never articulate this torment? Did you perhaps reserve it for yourself, like the beloved's name that one cannot bear to have the world utter, for with his little secret that he cannot divulge the poet buys this power of the word to tell everybody else's dark secrets. A poet is not an apostle; he drives out devils only by the power of the devil.[40]

---

[35]   *SKS* 4, 186 / *FT*, 97.

[36]   *SKS* 4, 190–1 / *FT*, 101.

[37]   *Richard the Third*, in *The Riverside Shakespeare*, Act I; scene, p. 713.

[38]   *SKS* 4, 194 / *FT*, 105.

[39]   *Richard the Third*, in *The Riverside Shakespeare*, Act V, scene iii; p. 751.

[40]   *SKS* 4, 154–5 / *FT*, 61; see Mk 3:15–22.

Here we might ask whether it is noteworthy that de silentio does not say Shakespeare was unfamiliar with religious inwardness ("Did you perhaps reserve it for yourself?"), but only that none of his characters express the sort of passion indicative of what he calls a "collision" with an absolute requirement. The fact that Anti-Climacus modulates de silentio's remark six years later gives pause to wonder. "Read Shakespeare," he writes in *The Sickness Unto Death*, "and you will be appalled at the collisions. But even Shakespeare seems to have recoiled from essentially religious collisions."[41] Does de silentio (and does Anti-Climacus) imagine that Shakespeare was personally familiar with the kind of religious passion that he attributes to Abraham (or, *mutatis mutandis*, that Anti-Climacus attributes to a Christian), even though the characters in his plays never express it? The text surely seems to offer this interpretation as a possibility. At least one influential commentator, however, cautions that it would be a mistake to attribute such inwardness to Shakespeare. As Johannes Sløk puts it in *Kierkegaard og Shakespeare*, "Of course Kierkegaard does not believe that Shakespeare reserved the torment, Abraham's torment, for himself; this is just one poet's way of emphasizing the other poet's greatness."[42] So far as that goes Sløk may well be right, but when he goes on to distinguish between the two authors with respect to "inner" and "outer" worlds, he seems to risk overstating the differences. "Shakespeare does not in fact operate with an 'inner' world; all spiritual phenomena [*sjælelige fænomener*] are functions of the interpersonal drama," Sløk avers. "By contrast, Kierkegaard basically does not operate with an 'outer' world; anything external is trivial insofar as it can at most become an occasion for stirrings in the sole reality, the 'inner' universe of the individual."[43] On the one hand, Sløk is surely right to remind us that these authors had different interpretive "horizons," but on the other, the way he delineates between them looks somewhat too sharp. For instance, an allusion by Kierkegaard in *Four Upbuilding Discourses* to Cordelia, the third daughter of King Lear, clearly indicates an appreciation of her rich inner life: "If the good is silent this way, how easy for it to be misjudged! Unfortunately, it is frequently the case that the best people, who like that king's daughter certainly possess the heart's gold but have no small change to give away, sometimes suffer the most in the world simply because of others."[44] The question, therefore, is not whether Kierkegaard thinks Shakespeare "operates with an 'inner' world," but whether the inwardness that his most complete characters embody can be communicated in any unambiguous way. Perhaps the best way to pursue this question is through a consideration of the way Kierkegaard's pseudonym Frater Taciturnus assesses Shakespeare's *Hamlet*.

---

[41]   *SKS* 11, 238 / *SUD*, 127.

[42]   Johannes Sløk, *Kierkegaard og Shakespeare*, Copenhagen: Berlingske Forlag 1972, p. 182, my translation.

[43]   Ibid., pp. 180–1, my translation.

[44]   *SKS* 5, 356 / *EUD*, 371. Another reference to Shakespeare's Cordelia is found in the first volume of *Either/Or*, when Johannes discovers the name of the young woman he has been trailing: "Cordelia! That is really a splendid name—indeed, the same name as that of King Lear's third daughter, that remarkable girl whose heart did not dwell on her lips, whose lips were mute when her heart was full. So also with my Cordelia. She resembles her, of that I am certain" (*SKS* 2, 326 / *EO1*, 336).

In *Hamlet, Prince of Denmark* Shakespeare dramatized the conflict between reflective inwardness and external action in a way that appealed profoundly to late eighteenth- and early nineteenth-century audiences. In the words of Northrop Frye, "No other play has explored the paradoxes of action and thinking about action so deeply, but because it did explore them, literature ever since has been immeasurably deepened and made bolder. Perhaps, if we had not *Hamlet*, we might not have had the Romantic movement at all, or the works of Dostoyevsky and Nietzsche and Kierkegaard that follow it."[45] In large part, therefore, it is Hamlet's *inwardness*— what has been called his "most radical originality"—that inspired both the Romantic aesthetic sensibility and its critical successors.[46] Tasked by his spectral father to avenge his uncle's fratricidal slaying of the king and adulterous marriage to the queen, the play's action turns on Hamlet's inaction or, rather, on his interminable rumination over how to proceed in the face of his preposterous, madness-inducing, situation: what does it mean, subjectively, to be tasked with revenge *by a ghost?* Among some post-Enlightenment critics, this emerged as a question of whether the ghost in *Hamlet* should be considered a merely dramatic device, or whether it was not also a challenge to philosophical objectivity. Gotthold Ephraim Lessing (1729–1781), an important transitional between the Enlightenment and Romanticism, suggested in his *Hamburgische Dramaturgie* that the ghost and its directive have the power to make an audience/reader wonder along with Hamlet about the plausibility of such a thing, even in an age of Enlightenment.[47] Such association of Shakespeare and his art with a resurgent sense of enchantment in the post-Enlightenment era is one clear example of how *Hamlet* was appropriated to evoke the quasi-religious possibility of deeper realities than those of which Enlightenment figures allowed themselves to dream. And it was precisely for this reason that *Hamlet* came to be celebrated, to use Friedrich Schlegel's phrase, as "the actual centre, the core of the romantic imagination."[48] But the treatment of *Hamlet* in Kierkegaard's writings is more ambivalent and, therefore, somewhat more ambiguous than in the Romantic reception. On the one hand, Kierkegaard and Hamlet shared a certain "fellowship of

---

[45]   *Northrop Frye on Shakespeare*, ed. by Robert Sandler, pp. 99–100.

[46]   The characterization (cited earlier) of Hamlet in Goethe's *Wilhelm Meister* as an acorn from "an oak-tree planted in a costly jar," and reiterated by Kierkegaard's aesthete in *Either/Or*, still reverberates in contemporary literary criticism: "Hamlet, as a character, bewilders us because he is so endlessly suggestive. Are there any limits to him? His *inwardness* is his most radical originality; the ever-growing inner self, the dream of an infinite consciousness, has never been more fully portrayed" (Bloom, *Shakespeare: The Invention of the Human*, p. 416, emphasis in original). According to Hugh Grady, the interpretation of Hamlet in Goethe's *Wilhelm Meister's Apprenticeship* is "still the most influential interpretation of the play ever penned" (Grady, "Shakespeare Criticism, 1600–1900," p. 272).

[47]   Gotthold Ephraim Lessing, *Hamburgische Dramaturgie*, parts 11 and 12, in *Shakespeare-Rezeption: Die Diskussion um Shakespeare in Deutschland*, pp. 93–4 (Kierkegaard owned Lessing's collected works, see *Gotthold Ephraim Lessing's sämmtliche Schriften*, vols. 1–32, vols. 1–28, Berlin: Vossische Buchhandlung 1825–27; vols. 29–32 Berlin and Stettin: Nicolaische Buchhandlung 1828 (*ASKB* 1747–1762), *Hamburgische Dramaturgie* is in volume 24).

[48]   Schlegel, *Dialogue on Poetry and Literary Aphorisms*, pp. 100–1.

fate," as a number of readers have observed; each of them "had a tragic relationship to the woman he loved because his life in service of the idea claimed him completely."[49] But on the other hand, Kierkegaard himself is remarkably silent about any biographical parallel, and, when he does address *Hamlet* through a pseudonym, it is the only one of Shakespeare's plays that triggers any sort of critical response from Kierkegaard's pen. Taking these one at a time, let me first give a précis of an influential biographical reading of the Kierkegaard–Hamlet relation, and then explicate and assess the critique of *Hamlet* that Kierkegaard's pseudonym Frater Taciturnus offers in *Stages on Life's Way*.

The "fellowship of fate" reading first received critical expression in a 1955 essay by Denis de Rougemont entitled "Two Danish Princes: Kierkegaard and Hamlet." In order to identify a number of striking parallels between the lives of these two figures, de Rougemont begins with Shakespeare's play, and summarizes *Hamlet* as follows:

> A deeply melancholic young man is given a dreadful mission over which he hesitates a long time. This mission, which he may reveal only indirectly, isolates him from his fellows, forces him to break his troth with the very young Ophelia, and leads people to regard him as a dangerous madman. Finally, he sees himself impelled by the force of circumstances to perform the act before which he has been wavering. He kills the usurper and dies in the fight.
>
> Thus, we have the hero's melancholy, the secret he must keep and yet try to make others guess, the breaking of his troth, and finally the stupendous exposure of a usurpation that everyone tacitly agreed to gloss over.[50]

With this synopsis in place de Rougemont asks, "Could not this resumé of *Hamlet* stand as an exact resumé of the biography of Kierkegaard?"[51] Certainly, for starters, Kierkegaard's writings include expressions of a dark melancholy, and speak often of his life in terms of a mission that, among other things, entailed breaking his engagement with his fiancée, Regine Olsen. In addition, de Rougemont describes how both Hamlet and Kierkegaard employ "indirect communication" to carry out their respective secret missions:

> For Hamlet, it is very simple: he must say nothing, otherwise Claudius will have him murdered. For Kierkegaard, the matter is more complex. If he proceeded to attack immediately, nobody would listen to him. He must therefore start by inveigling the public; he must force it to become attentive, without betraying the real intention of his work. Kierkegaard lays his plan accordingly. He will first publish aesthetic works, works that are brilliant, paradoxical, and seemingly cynical, all of them signed with various pseudonyms. The Christian message, the only thing that matters to him, will always be present, though carefully dissimulated. In that way, he will attract the public and will lead it, without its knowledge, to the point most favorable for the decisive attack. Now, as the reader will recall, Hamlet lays a similar plan. He conceives the scheme of having a dumb play show performed before the court representing the murder of his father and the

---

[49]   Howard V. Hong and Edna H. Hong, translators' notes in *JP* 2, p. 576.
[50]   Denis de Rougemont, "Kierkegaard and Hamlet: Two Danish Princes," *The Anchor Review*, no. 1, 1955, p. 111.
[51]   Ibid.

usurpation. "The play's the thing wherein I'll catch the conscience of the king!" Thus, they both choose indirect means—Hamlet the players and Kierkegaard pseudonyms—in order to interest their publics and at the same time disturb them with a definite end in view, and to force the public or court to "give heedful note" despite itself.[52]

In each case, therefore, the manner in which the secret is communicated forces recipients to disclose something about themselves that they otherwise would not. Indeed, so remarkable is this particular parallel that another critic (without any apparent familiarity with de Rougemont's essay) has gone so far as to identify a relationship of influence here. "Indirect communication, the mode of Kierkegaard," Harold Bloom writes, "was learned by Kierkegaard from Hamlet."[53] Bloom's assertion folds nicely into de Rougemont's reading, but lacking textual evidence that this was the case it is hard to see how Bloom's claim can be anything but speculative or merely rhetorical. At any rate, we should not let it distract us from de Rougemont's final parallel, for his biographical reading entails one further and crucial element. Of the drama's denouement de Rougemont writes, "For Hamlet, a trivial incident sets off the catastrophe, a fencing match, in which Laertes' sword is poisoned, and the sporting duel turns into a duel to the death. Hamlet is wounded and can no longer hesitate. He kills the king."[54] In Kierkegaard's case, the equivalent to this climax is set off at the funeral of Bishop Jakob Peter Mynster, when Professor Hans Lassen Martensen eulogized the bishop as a "genuine witness to the truth." For most hearers this simple phrase might pass as little more than a cliché. But to Kierkegaard, as de Rougemont explains it, there was "poison" in the expression. Kierkegaard had worked assiduously in his writings to re-establish the conception of a "witness to the truth" in its apostolic sense, specifically, to mean a "martyr."[55] So when Martensen used the phrase to praise Mynster—a man rich in worldly goods, esteemed as a cultured gentleman, and decorated with titles—Kierkegaard regarded this as a complete usurpation of authentic Christianity by cultural Christendom. De Rougemont completes his biographical parallel this way:

> Kierkegaard felt he had been challenged. And here, too, what might have remained a simple fencing match, a polemic like any other, suddenly turned into a duel to the death. Kierkegaard immediately wrote an article of extreme violence. He waited months before publishing it, waited for Martensen to succeed Mynster and become Bishop in turn. Then he released it. And this article was his act, the direct attack, decisive and mortal, with the kind of exaggerated *élan* one might expect in a swordsman who stakes his life on a single thrust.[56]

The similarities as de Rougemont draws them are striking; he even confesses that while preparing his essay he began "to imagine that *Hamlet* had been written by

[52]   Ibid., pp. 114–15.
[53]   Bloom, *Shakespeare: The Invention of the Human*, p. 730.
[54]   de Rougemont, "Kierkegaard and Hamlet: Two Danish Princes," p. 117.
[55]   Here the translation into English entails a significant loss of meaning. The Danish term *Sandhedsvidne* is a translation of the Greek word *martyr*, meaning witness; in English, the term "martyr" seems largely to have lost the capacity to function synonymously with "witness."
[56]   de Rougemont, "Kierkegaard and Hamlet: Two Danish Princes," p. 118.

Kierkegaard and even that, vice versa, Kierkegaard's biography had been staged two-and-a-half centuries before it was lived."[57] But it is important to ascertain the respects in which these parallels break down, as well, precisely because *Hamlet* is not a script for Kierkegaard's life, and temptations to ascribe too fully to the analogy distract us from the more difficult task of coming to understand the more critical dimensions of Kierkegaard's reception of Shakespeare's most famous play.

As mentioned earlier, *Hamlet* is unique among Shakespeare's plays for being the only one that occasioned any extended critical attention within Kierkegaard's authorship. While Kierkegaard and almost all of his pseudonymous authors appropriate elements from various Shakespearean plays in order to illustrate or embellish some particular point or another, the pseudonymous author Frater Taciturnus alone devotes more than a page to anything approaching Shakespeare criticism in a strict sense, and he focuses on *Hamlet*. We come across it toward the end of *Stages on Life's Way*, in an appendix to Taciturnus' "Letter to the Reader" entitled "A Side-Glance at Shakespeare's *Hamlet*." On de Rougemont's resolutely biographical reading, this is "an appendix to the book in which Kierkegaard related the story of his engagement."[58] If that is the case, plain and simple, then perhaps de Rougemont appropriately summarizes the appendix as Kierkegaard's attempt to "correct" the biographical parallel:

> Kierkegaard reproaches Shakespeare with not having made of Hamlet a religious drama. For if Hamlet's scruples are not of a religious order, the hero ceases to be really tragic; he is merely irresolute or sick or, what is even worse, he is a dawdler, bordering on the comic. If, on the other hand, if his tergiversations were due to religious motives, they would become infinitely interesting, but then there would be no drama in the technical and aesthetic sense of the term. Indeed, "in the aesthetic order, the obstacle must be outside the hero, not within him." If the obstacle to his act is within him, then it involves a religious scruple. In that case, the hero is great only by virtue of his suffering and not of his triumph. There is no longer a thrilling poetic game. All that remains is the serious, the essential....In other words: if Hamlet were religious, we would have not Shakespeare's Hamlet, but purely and simply the biography of Kierkegaard.[59]

Thus, de Rougemont concludes, Taciturnus' appendix suggests that we should consider Hamlet an aesthetic hero at best (although even this seems to me a misreading of the appendix), whereas the life of Kierkegaard, whose "tragedy was not fictitious," was "the pure drama of a Christian vocation."[60]

It seems plausible that Kierkegaard would have appreciated some of the parallels between Hamlet's story and his own life that de Rougemont draws. It also seems likely that he would have appreciated the acknowledgment that the parallel is ultimately "wrecked by existence,"[61] since Hamlet's struggle is fictitious whereas his own was in actuality. However, regardless of whether or not we find a heroic account

---

Ibid., p. 120.
Ibid.
Ibid., pp. 120–1.
Ibid., p. 121.
Ibid.

of Kierkegaard's personal life persuasive, it should be noted that the resolutely biographical reading neglects important critical features of Taciturnus' appendix.[62] To begin, given the notorious complications of Kierkegaard's pseudonymous authorship, it seems somewhat rushed simply to identify Taciturnus' comments as "a note by Kierkegaard himself on Hamlet."[63] De Rougemont never mentions the pseudonymous nature of *Stages on Life's Way*, but the recognition that this "note" was penned under the name Frater Taciturnus, and published within a compilation of other pseudonymous papers by one Hilarius Bogbinder, should lead us back into the text itself, rather than straight to Kierkegaard's biography. And when we take a more direct look at this "Side-Glance," we see de Rougemont's mistake in saying that "Kierkegaard reproaches Shakespeare with not having made of Hamlet a religious drama,"[64] for the text in fact says that *Hamlet* ought *not* to be a religious drama. Taciturnus' short appendix, therefore, seems not so much to "correct" the parallel between Shakespeare's *Hamlet* and Kierkegaard's personal biography as to problematize a certain tradition in Shakespeare criticism.

Taciturnus structures his "Side-Glance" around a remark he finds in "a little review of *Hamlet*"[65] by the post-Romantic writer Karl Ludwig Börne (1786–1837). He writes, "Börne says of *Hamlet*, 'It is a Christian drama.' To my mind this is a most excellent comment. I substitute only the word a 'religious' drama, and then declare its fault to be not that it is that but that it did not become that or, rather, that it ought not to be drama at all."[66] Perhaps the first thing to note about this passage is how extraordinarily convoluted it is. Taciturnus begins with a quotation of Börne that is, in fact, a misquotation, as Gene Fendt has pointed out.[67] Börne actually says, "*Hamlet* is a Christian tragedy."[68] Taciturnus substitutes the more generic term "drama" for "tragedy." It is quite possible that Taciturnus makes this first substitution unwittingly, but he explicitly assumes responsibility for a second exchange: "I substitute only the

---

[62]   Both Gene Fendt and Richard Kearney offer helpful correctives to de Rougemont on this matter. On each of their readings, it is a mistake to say Taciturnus thinks Hamlet even *at best* an aesthetic hero. "For Kierkegaard [*sic*]," Kearney writes, "Hamlet is neither a religious hero nor an esthetic (tragic) hero but something in between. Neither fish nor fowl. A hybrid creature. In short an esthetic-religious mess. Perhaps not unlike Kierkegaard himself" ("Kierkegaard on Hamlet: Between Art and Religion," p. 230). Here, Kearney is more sensitive to the argument of the "Side-Glance" than de Rougemont is, and he also resists de Rougemont's tendency to portray Kierkegaard's life in heroic terms. His reading parallels Gene Fendt's in both of these respects. Gene Fendt's reading of the "Side-Glance," however, has the additional advantage that it more assiduously distinguishes between the words of Taciturnus and those of Kierkegaard than either de Rougemont or Kearney (see Fendt, "The Writ Against Religious Drama: Frater Taciturnus vs. Søren Kierkegaard").

[63]   de Rougemont, "Kierkegaard and Hamlet: Two Danish Princes," p. 120.

[64]   Ibid.

[65]   *SKS* 6, 417 / *SLW*, 452. See Ludwig Börne, "Hamlet, *von Shakspeare*," in Ludwig Börne, *Gesammelte Schriften*, vols. 1–8, 2nd ed., Hamburg: Hoffmann und Campe 1835–40, vol. 2, pp. 172–98 (*ASKB* 1627–1629).

[66]   *SKS* 6, 418 / *SLW*, 453.

[67]   Fendt, *Is Hamlet a Religious Drama?* p. 228.

[68]   Börne, "Hamlet, *von Shakspeare*," p. 197. See also *SKS* K6, 368   and *SLW*, 737, note 525.

word a 'religious' drama...."[69] All of this prompts a couple of questions. First, if Börne's characterization of *Hamlet* is "most excellent," as Taciturnus says, then why are these two substitutions necessary? And second, why does Taciturnus, even after these substitutions, declare the play's "fault" to be that it should not be drama at all? Let us address the second question first.

Given the way Taciturnus develops his criticism, the issue seems to revolve around a certain conception of what can and cannot be presented dramatically. He begins by saying, "If Shakespeare does not give Hamlet religious presuppositions that conspire against him in religious doubt (whereby the drama ceases), then Hamlet is essentially a vacillator, and the esthetic demands a comic interpretation."[70] In view of the fact that Taciturnus prefaces the sentence with "If," it is not completely clear whether or not he thinks Hamlet has either religious presuppositions or religious doubt. Indeed, one of the main interpretive difficulties that the "Side-Glance" presents is the fact that Taciturnus consistently casts his remarks in the subjunctive mood.[71] It is clearly the case, nonetheless, that Taciturnus thinks "the drama ceases" *if* Hamlet has religious presuppositions and doubts. Does this mean religiousness, as Taciturnus conceives it, cannot be presented dramatically? That would account for why he says *Hamlet* "ought not to be drama at all," but it would still leave unclear why he bothers to substitute "religious drama" for Börne's phrase "Christian tragedy" in the first place. Why not simply insist that Börne is wrong to call *Hamlet* a "Christian tragedy," and argue instead that the play should be interpreted in what Taciturnus calls "purely esthetic categories"?[72] Taciturnus' answer, although still not in the indicative mood, is that "If Hamlet is kept in purely esthetic categories, then what one wants to see is that he has the demonic power to carry out such a resolution."[73] Absent any inward religious misgivings or external obstacles, that is to say, Taciturnus thinks Hamlet should be able to carry out his plan without procrastination, much as Gloucester does in *Richard III*. But Hamlet does not do that. Instead, he vacillates and delays through four acts and most of a fifth. And, on "purely esthetic" grounds, such vacillation "demands a comic interpretation" because Hamlet looks to be *both* the would-be hero who "has conceived his grandiose plan" for vengeance, *and* the pathetic "loiterer" or "self-torturer" who either "does not know how to act" or "torments himself for and with wanting to be something great."[74] It is for this very reason, in fact, that the Hegelian theater critic Heinrich Theodor Rötscher (1803–71) called Hamlet "morbidly reflective," another characterization that Taciturnus regards as

---

[69]   *SKS* 6, 418 / *SLW*, 453.
[70]   *SKS* 6, 418 / *SLW*, 453.
[71]   Fendt rightly observes, "Taciturnus' entire argument is subjunctive, containing not a single objective premise about Shakespeare or *Hamlet*" (*Is Hamlet a Religious Drama?* p. 228). It is interesting to note that in a deleted passage of a sketch for the "Side-Glance," this is cast in the indicative mood: "The mistake in Shakespeare is precisely that Hamlet does not have religious doubts" (*Pap.* V B 148:16 / *JP* 2, 1561). In the process of revision, however, Kierkegaard seems to have recognized that this presumes knowledge about Hamlet's inwardness that, strictly speaking, no one but Hamlet could have.
[72]   *SKS* 6, 419 / *SLW*, 453.
[73]   Ibid.
[74]   *SKS* 6, 418 / *SLW*, 453.

"excellent."[75] And so it is clear that, according to Taciturnus, Hamlet cannot be regarded as an "esthetic hero." But is it equally clear that Hamlet cannot be regarded as a "religious hero"? Taciturnus makes one final stab at this question:

> If Hamlet is to be interpreted religiously, one must either allow him to have conceived the plan, and then the religious doubts divest him of it, or do what to my mind better illuminates the religious (for in the first case there could possibly be some doubt as to whether he actually was capable of carrying out his plan)—give him the demonic power resolutely and masterfully to carry out his plan and then let him collapse into the religious until he finds peace there. A drama, of course, can never come from this; a poet cannot use this subject, which should begin with the last and let the first shine through it.[76]

This is perhaps the most befuddling passage of the entire "Side-Glance." Taciturnus first scripts two possible scenarios that would make Hamlet conform to his notion of religiousness. The first is to have Hamlet conceive of the plan for vengeance and then, before he carries it out, to have him repent of the plan. (Taciturnus is not explicit about what exactly should prompt Hamlet's religious doubt and repentance, but the editors are likely correct to indicate the biblical injunctions against revenge.[77]) The limitation of this first alternative, however, is that one would never be sure whether it was in fact religious scruples or lack of courage that deterred Hamlet from his plan. Consequently, a second scenario that "better illuminates the religious" would be to have Hamlet carry out his revenge upon Claudius, and then to repent of his hubris in having usurped God's role as avenger. Yet, despite having just suggested these two possibilities, Taciturnus insists a drama "can never come from this." Why not? Here again, we find ourselves on shifting sands. "A poet cannot use this subject," he writes, "which should begin with the last, and let the first shine out through it."[78] What Taciturnus seems to mean is that in order for "this subject" to be considered authentically religious, a poet should reverse the order of what he has just suggested. Thus, instead of first carrying out the plan of vengeance and then repenting, Hamlet should "begin with the last," that is, he should first "collapse into himself and into the religious until he finds peace there," and then let his plan of action (presumably a new

---

[75]   *SKS* 6, 418–19 / *SLW*, 453. See Heinrich Theodor Rötscher, *Die Kunst der dramatischen Darstellung. In ihrem organischen Zusammenhange*, vols. 1–3, Berlin: Wilhelm Thome 1841–46; for vol. 1 (1841) see *ASKB* 1391; vol. 2, *Der Kunst der dramatischen Darstellung Zweiter Theil, welcher das Gesetz der Versinnlichung dramatischer Charaktere an einer Reihe dichterischer Gestalten wissenschaftlich entwickelt* [also entitled as *Cyclus dramatischer Charactere. Nebst einer einleitenden Abhandlung über das Wesen dramatischer Charactergestaltung*], 1844; vol. 3, *Der Kunst der dramatischen Darstellung Dritter Theil, welcher eine neue Reihe dramatischer Charaktere entwickelt* [also entitled as *Cyclus dramatischer Charactere. Zweiter Theil. Nebst zwei Abhandlungen über das Recht der Poesie in der Behandlung des geschichtlichen Stoffes und über den Begriff des Dämonischen*], 1846, vol. 2, p. 99 (*ASKB* 1802–1803).
[76]   *SKS* 6, 419 / *SLW*, 454.
[77]   *SKS* K6, 368 and *SLW*, 737, note 527. See Rom 12:19 "Beloved, never avenge yourselves, but leave room for the wrath of God; for it is written, 'Vengeance is mine, I will repay, says the Lord.'" See also Deut 32:35; Heb 10:30.
[78]   *SKS* 6, 419 / *SLW*, 454.

plan, other than revenge) "shine out" through the religious peace he has found. Is this an answer to our question of why Taciturnus thinks *Hamlet* "ought not to be drama at all"? Taciturnus never answers this question explicitly, but he seems to mean that the religiousness that exists (if and when it exists) "in the interior being" cannot "shine out" in way that a poet could employ it dramatically in an external action with the beginning, middle, and end that drama requires. As both Fendt and Richard Kearney point out, Taciturnus assumes these dramatic criteria directly from Aristotle's *Poetics*.[79] Whether his conclusion that a poet "cannot" use this subject is equivalent to his earlier assertion that *Hamlet* "ought not" to be drama, however, is far from clear.

Another important matter that is far from clear is to what extent Taciturnus' abstract discussion of *Hamlet* remains faithful to the actual text of Shakespeare's *Hamlet*. Obviously, the two scenarios Taciturnus suggests would revise Shakespeare's play dramatically. But one important and ostensibly descriptive comment seems to depart significantly from the play as well. According to Taciturnus, "Hamlet says he has conceived his grandiose plan of being the avenger to whom vengeance belongs."[80] But Shakespeare's Hamlet never says this. In fact, it is crucial to Shakespeare's play that Hamlet does *not* conceive the plan of revenge himself, but that the ghost of his father tasks him with revenge.[81] Moreover, while it is true that Hamlet promises the ghost he will discharge his task swiftly, by the end of the next scene in which Hamlet appears he is experiencing doubts about what he has seen, and misgivings about what he has promised:

> The spirit that I have seen
> May be a dev'l, and the dev'l hath power
> T' assume a pleasing shape, yea, and perhaps,
> Out of my weakness and my melancholy,
> As he is very potent with such spirits,
> Abuses me to damn me.[82]

Hamlet's qualm here may not qualify as "religious doubt" in the strict sense to which Taciturnus might wish to reserve that category. But his anxiety about his possible damnation seems to suggest that Shakespeare has, in fact, given Hamlet what

---

[79]   Fendt, *Is Hamlet a Religious Drama?* pp. 36–7; Kearney, "Kierkegaard on Hamlet: Between Art and Religion," p. 231.

[80]   *SKS* 6, 418 / *SLW*, 453.

[81]   "*Ghost*: List, list, O list! If thou didst ever thy dear father love— *Hamlet*: O God! *Ghost*: Revenge his foul and most unnatural murther." (*Hamlet*, in *The Riverside Shakespeare*, Act I, scene v; p. 1149.)

[82]   Ibid., Act II, scene ii; p. 1159. C.S. Lewis comments helpfully on a certain tradition of reception of this passage: "Critics have disputed whether Hamlet is sincere when he doubts whether the apparition is his father's ghost or not. I take him to be perfectly sincere. He believes while the thing is present: he doubts when it is away" (C.S. Lewis, "Hamlet: The Prince or the Poem?" in *Interpretations of Shakespeare: British Academy Shakespeare Lectures*, ed. by Kenneth Muir, Oxford: Clarendon Press 1985, p. 134.

Taciturnus calls "religious presuppositions," at least in a vague sense, and that these conspire against him to make him doubt the legitimacy of his errand.[83]

Strangely, Taciturnus nowhere mentions the ghost and his directive, but his role in the play surely makes a difference for interpreting both Hamlet's agonizing uncertainty, and for understanding why Börne would have interpreted *Hamlet* in religious categories. Lessing, we have seen, suggested that the ghost in *Hamlet* was not merely a dramatic device, but a character that could evoke a belief in ghosts and the supernatural more generally, even among modern audiences. And, as a ghost story of sorts, *Hamlet* was particularly attractive to the Romantics who "deployed it," in Paul Coates' words, "to demonstrate the presence of other worlds than those of which the Enlightenment dreamt, yet without committing the believer (or merely credulous) to any constraining religious system."[84] In some measure, therefore, the Romantic idea that art discloses the deepest truths of the nature of reality conforms to a religious (or at least quasi-religious) sensibility and elucidates why certain Romantics appropriated *Hamlet* as "the actual centre, the core of the romantic imagination."[85] For the Romantics and such post-Romantics as Börne, *Hamlet* warrants a religious interpretation, in part because the ghost evokes the possibility— objectively uncertain to be sure—that "There are more things in heaven and earth... than are dreamt of in your philosophy."[86]

Kierkegaard's Taciturnus is sympathetic to the Romantic rejection of reductionism. But he is hostile toward the Romantic tendency to conflate the aesthetic with the religious in what he takes to be "semiesthetic categories,"[87] or "esthetics with imitation religious gilding."[88] Is this why Taciturnus ignores the role of the ghost entirely, and mistakenly attributes "the grandiose plan of being the avenger" to Hamlet himself? There is perhaps no way to be sure about these specific questions. But if we return to the first of the two questions posed earlier, it appears we now have reason to suspect a heavy dose of irony in Taciturnus' remark that Börne's comment is a "most excellent" one. Indeed, the "Side-Glance at Shakespeare's *Hamlet*" begins to read not so much as Shakespeare criticism as an oblique critique of Börne himself. As Fendt wittily observes, Taciturnus "considers that the play's the thing that catches out Börne's misunderstanding of the religious, and it is this field, in particular, that area where the religious life and literary art intersect, that is the brother's interest and forte."[89]

We might surmise, therefore, that what Taciturnus truly finds "excellent" about Börne's comment is that it offers him a rhetorical conceit. His substitutions of

---

[83] Fendt is surely right that the play itself is "highly spiced with Christian echoes and references" (*Is Hamlet a Religious Drama?* p. 161). This, of course, does not mean that Hamlet appropriates them as *his* presuppositions.
[84] Paul Coates, *Cinema, Religion, and the Romantic Legacy: Through a Glass Darkly*, Aldershot: Ashgate 2003, p. 144.
[85] Schlegel, *Dialogue on Poetry*, pp. 100–1.
[86] *Hamlet*, in *The Riverside Shakespeare*, Act II, scene i; p. 1159.
[87] *SKS* 6, 429 / *SLW*, 465.
[88] *SKS* 6, 432 / *SLW*, 468.
[89] Fendt, "The Writ Against Religious Drama: Frater Taciturnus vs. Søren Kierkegaard," p. 51.

"religious" for Börne's term "Christian," and of "drama" for Börne's term "tragedy," are not innocuous modifications, but are in fact the first two steps in a Trojan horse critique of the quasi-religious cult of literature that emerges with German Romanticism. He wants his criticism to cover more broadly than the specifically Christian in the sphere of religiousness, and more broadly than the specifically tragic in the sphere of the aesthetic. And he further wants to stipulate that if one delineates between "the religious" and "the aesthetic" in the strict senses that he reserves for them, then a dramatist could never depict the inwardness of the former through the dramatic action required by the latter. According to this view, as Kearney quips, "Trying to make a good drama out of the religious struggles of subjective inwardness is like trying to make a silk purse from a pig's ear. It simply cannot be done."[90]

Does this mean that we should, after all, concede Sløk his opinion that in the light of Kierkegaard's authorship "Shakespeare does not in fact operate with an 'inner' world"?[91] Again, this would go too far, for it is precisely to evoke an inner world that Shakespeare gives Hamlet his famous soliloquies and has him, as Hamlet says, "unpack my heart with words."[92] Moreover, Taciturnus makes an aside (prior to the "Side-Glance") that shows he, too, recognizes Hamlet's inwardness.[93] The question, therefore, is not whether Hamlet has an "inner world," but whether the inwardness he embodies can be expressed in language in any unambiguous way. Bloom is correct that, "Shakespeare, through Hamlet, has made us skeptics in our relationships with anyone, because we have learned to doubt articulateness in the realm of affection."[94] Consequently, *Hamlet* may well be gilded with religious imagery and expressions, its ghost may be richly evocative of unseen realities, and Hamlet's soliloquies may well indicate deep inward passion of some kind or another, but these outward manifestations can never establish the truth or untruth of whether Hamlet himself has religious presuppositions and religious doubt. According to Taciturnus, it is a mistake in the Romantic reception to think otherwise, and therefore a mistake to consider *Hamlet* a religious drama. The underlying assumption for this judgment seems to be that any combination of the poetic and the religious is a fundamental misalliance: "the poetic is glorious, the religious still more glorious, but what lies between is silly talk, no matter how much talent is wasted on it."[95] He thus concludes that any attempt to combine religiousness and drama fails both on aesthetic grounds and on religious grounds.

III. "A Poet is not an Apostle"

It remains to ask whether we should ascribe Taciturnus' anti-Romantic appropriation of Shakespeare directly to Kierkegaard himself. On the one hand, Sløk speaks for

---

90   Kearney, "Kierkegaard on Hamlet: Between Art and Religion," p. 229.
91   Sløk, *Shakespeare og Kierkegaard*, pp. 180–1, my translation.
92   *Hamlet*, in *The Riverside Shakespeare*, Act II, scene ii; p. 1159.
93   "The esthetic hero must have his opposition outside himself, not in himself. That this is not the case in Hamlet is perhaps precisely the anomaly...." *SKS* 6, 377 / *SLW*, 407.
94   Bloom, *Shakespeare: The Invention of the Human*, p. 715.
95   *SKS* 6, 383 / *SLW*, 413.

many commentators when he writes, "Although this critique is written by Frater Taciturnus, there is hardly any mistake in assuming Kierkegaard shares the brother's opinion."[96] On the other hand, the relationship between the poetic and the religious gets cast in a variety of ways by the various voices in Kierkegaard's authorship, and it is tricky to identify Kierkegaard's position directly with any one of them. For example, compare Taciturnus' "Side-Glance" with an essay Kierkegaard published two years later under the initials H.H. entitled "The Difference between a Genius and an Apostle." H.H. appropriates Shakespeare (along with Plato) in order to contrast the intellectual genius of "a poet or a thinker" with the specifically Christian religiousness of the Apostle Paul:

> [A]n erroneous scholarship has confused Christianity, and from the scholarship the confusion has in turn sneaked into the religious address, so that one not infrequently hears pastors who in all scholarly naiveté *bona fide* [in good faith] prostitute Christianity. They speak in lofty tones about the apostle Paul's brilliance, profundity, about his beautiful metaphors etc.—sheer esthetics. If Paul is to be regarded as a genius, then it looks bad for him....As a genius, Paul cannot stand comparison with either Plato or Shakespeare; as a stylist, he is a totally unknown name.... Paul is an apostle. And as an apostle he again has no affinity, none whatever, with either Plato or Shakespeare or stylists...they all...are without comparison to Paul.[97]

Obviously, there are important differences between the way H.H. distinguishes "sheer esthetics" from apostolicity, on the one hand, and the way Taciturnus distinguishes between the aesthetic and the generically religious on the other. While Taciturnus' critique turns on the apparent misalliance between Aristotelian categories and religious inwardness, H.H. invokes the qualitative difference between immanent human creativity and transcendent divine authority. Nonetheless, Kierkegaard uses these two pseudonyms in order to explore closely related issues from different points of view, and what is common to both of them is (1) an insistence that the combination of poetry and religiousness (as each sees it) is a fundamental misalliance, and (2) the appropriation of Shakespeare to make this point. And still another one of Kierkegaard's pseudonyms uses Shakespeare to make this point in an even more oblique fashion. The epigram for Johannes Climacus' *Philosophical Fragments*— "Better well hanged than ill wed" (*"Bedre godt hængt end slet gift"*)—is a shortened gloss on a Danish translation of the Schlegel–Tieck translation of the fool's comment to Maria in Shakespeare's *Twelfth Night, or What You Will*: "Many a good hanging prevents a bad marriage."[98] Ostensibly, Climacus invokes the line to imply that it is better for a thinker of his kind to be hanged than to be "married" into a system of speculative philosophy with its conception of consummate religion. And this is indeed how he interprets it two years later in the preface to *Concluding Unscientific Postscript to Philosophical Fragments*. There he comments on the lackluster critical reception of *Philosophical Fragments* saying, "better well hanged than by a hapless

96   Sløk, *Shakespeare og Kierkegaard*, p. 183, my translation.
97   *SKS* 11, 97–8 / *WA*, 93ff.
98   *SKS* 4, 214 / *PF*, 3. See also the notes concerning this transmission history: *SKS* K4, 197–8 / *PF*, notes, p. 274.

marriage to be brought into systematic in-law relationship with the whole world."[99] Within the pages of *Philosophical Fragments*, therefore, the epigram capitalizes on Shakespeare's propensity to speak the truth through the mouth of the fool in order to indicate what Climacus considers the fundamental misalliance of systematic philosophy and Christian faith.

It may have been tempting at times for Kierkegaard to affirm fully as his own the positions of some of his pseudonyms regarding their views about the misalliance of human imagination and Christianity. Indeed, it is not always clear precisely where Kierkegaard stands vis-à-vis the views of one pseudonym or another and, just as Sløk attributes the view of Taciturnus directly to Kierkegaard, it is not uncommon to come across other commentators who have identified Kierkegaard's personal view directly with those of other pseudonyms. Kierkegaard, however, was notoriously cagey on this issue, and this may well have been because he recognized the respects in which his own authorship could be implicated in the pseudonymous critiques of "esthetics with imitation religious gilding."[100] But if Kierkegaard were to insist that poetry could *never* come into productive relationship with religiousness, then this would create an irreconcilable contradiction within his own authorship.[101] The point is that a strict dichotomy between the aesthetic and the religious cannot account for the "special case" of "the religious poet" which Kierkegaard adumbrates in *Works of Love*.[102] Neither can it help us make sense of Kierkegaard's description of himself as a "Christian poet and thinker"[103] who crafts his writings for purposes of inward awakening, edification, and encouragement in Christian living. Thus, while it is important to be able to distinguish between the various voices within Kierkegaard's authorship (including whatever we take to be his own), it is also clear that these voices often work together, problematizing an issue from different perspectives. Shakespeare's appearance within Kierkegaard's authorship offers a case in point. The more substantive references to Shakespeare tend to come bundled along with the German reception and celebration of Shakespeare: Frater Taciturnus uses *Hamlet* as a proxy to critique Romanticism; Johannes Climacus invokes a line from *Twelfth Night* as a cipher to satirize speculative philosophy; and Johannes de silentio, who eulogizes "Great Shakespeare" as one who "can say everything, everything, everything just as it is," nonetheless prefigures the anti-Romantic view

---

[99]   *SKS* 7, 9 / *CUP1*, 5.

[100]   *SKS* 6, 432 / *SLW*, 468.

[101]   On this point, I'm in agreement with Gene Fendt, who avers, "If Kierkegaard believes any connection between religion and poetry is a misalliance, he is in trouble." Fendt, "The Writ Against Religious Drama: Frater Taciturnus vs. Søren Kierkegaard," p. 49, note 2, emphasis in original.

[102]   *SKS* 9, 53 / *WL*, 46. "But is the poet, then, no Christian? We have indeed not said this, neither do we say it but say only that *qua* poet he is no Christian. Yet a distinction must be made, for there certainly are religious poets. But these do not sing about erotic love [*Elskov*] and friendship; their songs are to the glory of God, about faith, hope, and love [*Kjerlighed*]." For a typology of the different senses of the term "poet" in Kierkegaard's writings, see Chapter 5 of Joel D.S. Rasmussen, *Between Irony and Witness: Kierkegaard's Poetics of Faith, Hope and Love*, New York: T&T Clark International 2005.

[103]   *SKS* 21, 368, NB10:200 / *JP* 6, 6391.

of H.H. in his avowal that "a poet is not an apostle."[104] Therefore, while each voice says something somewhat different about Shakespeare as far as the specifics are concerned, the synoptic consideration of these voices reveals a consistent strategy of appropriation designed to combat what was, as Kierkegaard saw it, a creeping cult of "genius" stemming from the different strands of German idealism. What is distinctive about Kierkegaard's use of Shakespeare as a source is not that he offers any novel interpretation of the playwright's works, but rather that he invokes Shakespeare in order to oppose the idealist synthesis of nature and spirit common to Romanticism and Hegelianism. In general outline, the formula for how Kierkegaard deploys Shakespeare is to echo the idealist reverence for Shakespeare as an unsurpassed poet or "genius," but to cast this in such a way as to deny the Romantic identification of creative genius with divine revelation. Thus, while he assiduously resists any identification of Shakespeare as an "apostle," Kierkegaard is happy to agree in the estimation of him as "that most profound poet."[105] Or, as Taciturnus writes in his "Side-Glance at Shakespeare's *Hamlet*":

> On a specific point, one may have a doubt, another opinion, and yet agree on the one opinion that has been the opinion of one and two and three centuries—that Shakespeare stands unrivaled, despite the progress the world will make, that one can always learn from him, and the more one reads him, the more one learns.[106]

---

[104]   *SKS* 4, 155 / *FT*, 61.
[105]   *SKS* 8, 198 / *UD*, 93.
[106]   *SKS* 6, 419 / *SLW*, 454.

Bibliography

I. Shakespeare's Works in The Auction Catalogue *of Kierkegaard's Library*

Dramatische Werke, vols. 1–8, trans. by Ernst Ortlepp, Stuttgart: L.F. Rieger 1838–39 (*ASKB* 1874–1881).

Vierzig Kunstblätter zu Shakespeares dramatischen Werken (in Stahl grawirt) [steel engravings supplementary by Ernst Ortlepp to *ASKB* 1874–1881], *Gratis-Beigabe zur Stuttgarter Ausgabe von Ernst Ortlepp*, Stuttgart: L.F. Rieger 1840 (*ASKB* 1882).

Shakspeare's dramatische Werke, vols. 1–12, trans. by August Wilhelm von Schlegel and Ludwig Tieck, Berlin: G. Reimer 1839–40 (*ASKB* 1883–1888).

William Shakspeare's dramatiske Værker, vols. 1–9, trans. by Peter Foersom and Peter Frederik Wulff, Copenhagen 1825 (*ASKB* 1889–1896).

Macbeth, Tragedie i fem Akter, trans. and interpreted by N. Hauge, Christiania: Johan Dahl 1855 (*ASKB* 1897).

William Shakspeare's dramatiske Værker, vols. 1–11, trans. by Peter Foersom and P.F. Wulff, (vols. 6–11 ed. by Offe Høyer), Copenhagen: J.H. Schubothes Boghandling 1845–50 (*ASKB* U 103).

II. Works in The Auction Catalogue *of Kierkegaard's Library*
that Discuss Shakespeare

Adler, Adolph Peter, *Theologiske Studier*, Copenhagen: I Commission hos Universitets-Boghandler C.A. Reitzel 1846, p. 20, note; p. 81 (*ASKB* U 12).

Baader, Franz von, *Vorlesungen, gehalten an der Königlich-Bayerischen Ludwig-Maximilians-Hochschule über religiöse Philosophie im Gegensatze der irreligiösen, älterer und neuer Zeit*, vol. 1, Munich: Giel 1827, p. 61, note (*ASKB* 395).

—— *Revision der Philosopheme der Hegel'schen Schule bezüglich auf das Christenthum. Nebst zehn Thesen aus einer religiösen Philosophie*, Stuttgart: S.G. Liesching 1839, p. 59 (*ASKB* 416).

[Becker, Karl Friedrich], *Karl Friedrich Beckers Verdenshistorie, omarbeidet af Johan Gottfried Woltmann*, vols. 1–12, trans. by J. Riise, Copenhagen: Fr. Brummer 1822–29, vol. 10, p. 512; p. 518; p. 565 (*ASKB* 1972–1983).

Börne, Ludwig, "Hamlet, *von Shakspeare*," in Ludwig Börne, *Gesammelte Schriften*, vols. 1–8, 2nd ed., Hamburg: Hoffmann und Campe 1835–40, vol. 2, pp. 172–98 (*ASKB* 1627–1629).

Flögel, Karl Friedrich, *Geschichte der komischen Litteratur*, vols. 1–4, Liegnitz and Leipzig: David Siegert 1784–87, vol. 1, p. 184; vol. 4, pp. 213–14 (*ASKB* 1396–1399).

Frauenstädt, Julius, *Die Naturwissenschaft in ihrem Einfluß auf Poesie, Religion, Moral und Philosophie*, Leipzig: F.A. Brockhaus 1855, pp. 38–40 (*ASKB* 516).

[Goethe, Johann Wolfgang von], "Shakspeare und kein Ende," and "Erste Ausgabe des Hamlet," in *Goethe's Werke. Vollständige Ausgabe letzter Hand* [in 55 volumes], vols. 1–40, Stuttgart and Tübingen: J.G. Cotta 1827–30; *Goethe's nachgelassene Werke*, vols. 41–55, Stuttgart and Tübingen: J.G. Cotta 1832–33, vol. 45 (*Nachlaß*, vol. 5), pp. 38–57 and pp. 58–63 respectively (*ASKB* 1641–1668).

—— *Wilhelm Meisters Lehrjahre*, in *Goethe's Werke. Vollständige Ausgabe letzter Hand* [in 55 volumes], vols. 1–40, Stuttgart and Tübingen: J.G. Cotta 1827–30; *Goethe's nachgelassene Werke*, vols. 41–55, Stuttgart and Tübingen: J.G. Cotta 1832–33, vol. 19 (*ASKB* 1641–1668).

[Hamann, Johann Georg], *Hamann's Schriften*, vols. 1–8, ed. by Friedrich Roth, Berlin: G. Reimer 1821–43, vol. 2, p. 38; p. 53; p. 83; p. 96; p. 197; p. 219; p. 269; p. 287; p. 366; p. 433; p. 500; p. 515; vol. 3, p. 27; p. 64; p. 193; vol. 5, p. 248 (*ASKB* 536–544).

Hebbel, Friedrich, *Mein Wort über das Drama! Eine Erwiderung an Professor Heiberg in Copenhagen*, Hamburg: Hoffmann und Campe 1843, pp. 4–10 passim; pp. 33–8 passim (*ASKB* 454).

Hegel, Georg Wilhelm Friedrich "Ueber *Solger's nachgelassene Schriften und Briefwechsel*. Herausgegeben von Ludwig Tieck und Friedrich v. Raumer. Erster Band 780 S. mit Vorrede XVI S. Zweiter Band 784 S. Leipzig, 1826" [1828], in *Georg Wilhelm Friedrich Hegel's vermischte Schriften*, vols. 1–2, ed. by Friedrich Förster and Ludwig Boumann, Berlin: Duncker und Humblot 1834–35 (vols. 16–17 in *Georg Wilhelm Friedrich Hegel's Werke. Vollständige Ausgabe*, ed. by Philipp Marheineke et al., Berlin: Duncker und Humblot 1832–45), vol. 1, pp. 436–506 (*ASKB* 555–556).

—— *Georg Wilhelm Friedrich Hegel's Vorlesungen über die Aesthetik*, vols. 1–3, ed. by von Heinrich Gustav Hotho, Berlin: Verlag von Duncker und Humblot 1835–38 (vols. 10.1–10.3 in *Georg Wilhelm Friedrich Hegel's Werke. Vollständige Ausgabe*, vols. 1–18, ed. by Philipp Marheineke et al., Berlin: Duncker und Humblot 1832–45), vol. 1, p. 244; pp. 296–7; p. 302; pp. 312–13; p. 344; p. 352; p. 356; p. 371; p. 524; pp. 539–40; vol. 2, p. 187; pp. 196–207 passim; p. 215; p. 218; vol. 3, p. 84 p. 353; p. 489; p. 491; p. 498; p. 504; p. 506; p. 520; pp. 566–72 passim; p. 579 (*ASKB* 1384–1386).

Heiberg, Johan Ludvig, *Om Philosophiens Betydning for den nuværende Tid. Et Indbydelses-Skrift til en Række af philosophiske Forelæsninger*, Copenhagen: C.A. Reitzel 1833, pp. 42–3 (*ASKB* 568).

—— "Om den romantiske Tragedie af Hertz: *Svend Dyrings Huus*. I Forbindelse med en æsthetisk Betragtning af de danske Kæmpeviser," in *Perseus*, vols. 1–2, ed. by Johan Ludvig Heiberg, Copenhagen: C.A. Reitzel 1837–38, vol. 1, pp. 165–264, see p. 259 (*ASKB* 569).

[Herder, Johann Gottfried von], *Johann Gottfried von Herder's sämmtliche Werke. Zur schönen Literatur und Kunst*, vols. 1–20, Stuttgart and Tübingen: J.G.

Cotta'sche Buchhandlung 1827–30, vol. 17, pp. 228–44 (*ASKB* 1685–1694; see also *ASKB* A I 125–133).

Lessing, Gotthold Ephraim, *Hamburgische Dramaturgie*, in *Gotthold Ephraim Lessing's sämmtliche Schriften*, vols. 1–32, vols. 1–28, Berlin: Vossische Buchhandlung 1825–27; vols. 29–32 Berlin and Stettin: Nicolaische Buchhandlung 1828, vol. 24, parts 11 and 12 (*ASKB* 1747–1762).

[Lichtenberg, Georg Christoph], *Georg Christoph Lichtenberg's auserlesene Schriften*, Baireuth: bei Iohann Andreas Lübecks Erben 1800, p. 85; pp. 87–8; pp. 96–100; p. 106; p. 127; p. 132; p. 135; p. 145; p. 153; pp. 209–13 (*ASKB* 1775).

Martensen, Hans Lassen, *Den christelige Dogmatik*, Copenhagen: C.A. Reitzel 1849, p. 298; pp. 571–2 (*ASKB* 653).

[Møller, Poul Martin], *Efterladte Skrifter af Poul M. Møller*, vols. 1–3, ed. by Christian Winther, F.C. Olsen and Christen Thaarup, Copenhagen: C.A. Reitzel 1839–43, vol. 3, p. 175; p. 319 (*ASKB* 1574–1576).

Nielsen, Rasmus, *Forelæsningsparagrapher til Kirkehistoriens Philosophie. Et Schema for Tilhørere*, Copenhagen: P.G. Philipsen 1843, p. 71 (*ASKB* 698).

Ørsted, Hans Christian, *Aanden i Naturen*, vols. 1–2, Copenhagen: Andr. Fred. Høst 1850, vol. 1, p. 96 (*ASKB* 945).

Overskou, Thomas, *Den danske Skueplads, i dens Historie, fra de første Spor af danske Skuespil indtil vor Tid*, vols. 1–7, Copenhagen: Samfundet til den danske Literaturs Fremme 1854–76, vol. 1, 1854, p. 140 [Kierkegaard owned only vol. 1; vols. 6–7 were entitled *Den kongelig danske Skuepladses Historie, fra dens Overdragelse til Staten i 1849 indtil 1874. Efter Forfatterens Død fuldført af Edgar Collin*, 1874–76] (*ASKB* 1395).

[Richter, Johann Paul Friedrich], Jean Paul, *Vorschule der Aesthetik nebst einigen Vorlesungen in Leipzig über die Parteien der Zeit*, vols. 1–3, 2nd revised ed., Stuttgart and Tübingen: J.G. Cotta 1813, vol. 1, p. 7; p. 74; p. 84; p. 140; p. 170; p. 240; p. 251; p. 304; vol. 2, p. 393; p. 407; p. 422; pp. 468–9; p. 474; p. 483; p. 503; p. 508; vol. 3, p. 791; p. 932; p. 945 (*ASKB* 1381–1383).

Rötscher, Heinrich Theodor, *Die Kunst der dramatischen Darstellung. In ihrem organischen Zusammenhange*, vols. 1–3, Berlin: Wilhelm Thome 1841–46, vol. 1, 1841 (*ASKB* 1391; for vols. 2–3, also entitled *Cyclus dramatischer Charaktere. Nebst einer einleitenden Abhandlung über das Wesen dramatischer Charaktergestaltung*, see *ASKB* 1802–1803).

Die Kunst der dramatischen Darstellung. In ihrem organischen Zusammenhange, vols. 1–3, Berlin: Wilhelm Thome 1841–46; vol. 2, *Der Kunst der dramatischen Darstellung Zweiter Theil, welcher das Gesetz der Versinnlichung dramatischer Charaktere an einer Reihe dichterischer Gestalten wissenschaftlich entwickelt* [also entitled as *Cyclus dramatischer Charactere. Nebst einer einleitenden Abhandlung über das Wesen dramatischer Charactergestaltung*], 1844, pp. 71–178; pp. 247–69; pp. 298–339 (vols. 2–3, *ASKB* 1802–1803; for vol. 1 see *ASKB* 1391).

—— "Jago in *Othello*," "Coriolan in Shakespeare's *Coriolan*," and "Constanze in Shakespeare's *König Johann*," in his *Die Kunst der dramatischen Darstellung. In ihrem organischen Zusammenhange*, vols. 1–3, Berlin: Wilhelm Thome 1841–46, vol. 3, *Der Kunst der dramatischen Darstellung Dritter Theil, welcher eine neue Reihe dramatischer Charaktere entwickelt* [also entitled as *Cyclus dramatischer Charactere. Zweiter Theil. Nebst zwei Abhandlungen über das Recht der Poesie in der Behandlung des geschichtlichen Stoffes und über den Begriff des Dämonischen*], 1846, pp. 142–56; pp. 220–61; and pp. 295–323 respectively (vols. 2–3, *ASKB* 1802–1803; for vol. 1 see *ASKB* 1391).

Schlegel, August Wilhelm, *Ueber dramatische Kunst und Litteratur. Vorlesungen*, vols. 1–2 [vol. 2 in 2 Parts], Heidelberg: Mohr und Zimmer 1809–11 (*ASKB* 1392–1394).

[Schlegel, Friedrich], *Friedrich Schlegel's sämmtliche Werke*, vols. 1–10, Vienna: Jakob Mayer und Compagnie 1822–25, vol. 2.1, p. 113; vol. 2.2, pp. 19–242 (*ASKB* 1816–1825).

Schopenhauer, Arthur, *Die Welt als Wille und Vorstellung*, vols. 1–2, Leipzig: F.A. Brockhaus 1844; vol. 1, p. 20; p. 234; p. 288; p. 445; vol. 2, p. 66; p. 100; p. 118; p. 125; p. 236; p. 300; p. 432; p. 436; p. 584 (*ASKB* 773–773a).

—— *Parerga und Paralipomena: kleine philosophische Schriften*, vols. 1–2, Berlin: Druck und Verlag von A.W. Hayn 1851, vol. 1, p. 198; p. 311; p. 331; p. 360; p. 375; p. 445; p. 465; vol. 2, p. 197; p. 206; p. 262; p. 364; p. 383; p. 385 (*ASKB* 774–775).

Solger, Karl Wilhelm Ferdinand, *Solger's nachgelassene Schriften und Briefwechsel*, ed. by Ludwig Tieck und Friedrich von Raumer, vols. 1–2, Leipzig: F.A. Brockhaus 1826, pp. 493–628 (*ASKB* 1832–1833).

—— *K.W.F. Solger's Vorlesungen über Aesthetik*, ed. by K.W.L. Heyse, Leipzig: F.A. Brockhaus 1829, p. 106; p. 155; p. 165; pp. 170–2; pp. 176–7; p. 222; p. 227; p. 230; p. 233; p. 243; p. 248; p. 254; p. 320 (*ASKB* 1387).

Steffens, Henrich, *Anthropologie*, vols.1–2, Breslau: Josef Max 1822, vol. 2, p. 190 (*ASKB* 795–796).

—— *Was ich erlebte. Aus der Erinnerung niedergeschrieben*, vols. 1–10, Breslau: Josef Max und Comp. 1840–44, vol. 3, pp. 268–9; pp. 271–2; vol. 4, p. 310; vol. 5, p. 199; vol. 6, p. 114; vol. 7, p. 304 (*ASKB* 1834–1843).

[Sulzer, Johann George], *Johann George Sulzers vermischte philosophische Schriften. Aus den Jahrbüchern der Akademie der Wissenschaften zu Berlin gesammelt*, vols. 1–2, Leipzig: Weidmann 1773–81, vol. 2, pp. 115–17 (in "Vorbericht") (*ASKB* 807–808).

—— *Allgemeine Theorie der Schönen Künste, in einzeln, nach alphabetischer Ordnung der Kunstwörter auf einander folgenden, Artikeln abgehandelt*, vols. 1–4 and a register volume, 2nd revised ed., Leipzig: Weidmann 1792–99, vol. 1, p. 145; p. 151; p. 458; p. 568; p. 684; p. 707; vol. 3, p. 269; vol. 4, p. 434; p. 596 (*ASKB* 1365–1369).

Thiersch, Friedrich, *Allgemeine Aesthetik in akademischen Lehrvorträgen*, Berlin: G. Reimer 1846, p. 185; p. 507 (*ASKB* 1378).

Thomsen, Grimur, *Om den nyfranske Poesi, et Forsøg til Besvarelse af Universitetets æsthetiske Priisspørgsmaal for 1841: "Har Smag og Sands for Poesi gjort Frem- eller Tilbageskridt i Frankrig i de sidste Tider og hvilken er Aarsagen?,"* Copenhagen: Wahlske Boghandlings Forlag 1843, p. lxiii; p. 5; p. 56; p. 57, note; pp. 65–7; p. 107; pp. 109–10; p. 112; p. 145 (*ASKB* 1390).

Zeuthen, Ludvig, *Om den christelige Tro i dens Betydning for Verdenshistorien. Et Forsøg*, Copenhagen: Gyldendal 1838, p. 39; p. 41 (*ASKB* 259).

III. Secondary Literature on Kierkegaard's Relation to Shakespeare

Agajanian, Shaakeh, "The Problem of Hamlet. A Christian Existential Analysis," *Religion in Life*, vol. 46, 1977, pp. 213–24.
Bellessort, André, "Le crepuscule d'Elseneur," *Revue de Deux Mondes*, 84, 1914, pp. 49–83.
Bennett, William E., "Shakespeare's Iago. The Kierkegaardian Aesthete," *The Upstart Crow*, vol. 5, 1984, pp. 156–9.
Bielmeier, Michael G., *Shakespeare, Kierkegaard, and Existential Tragedy*, Lewiston: Edwin Mellen Press 2000.
—— "Ethics and Anxiety in Shakespeare's *Troilus and Cressida*," *Christianity & Literature*, vol. 50, 2001, pp. 225–45.
Boehlich, Walter, "Søren, Prinz von Dänemark," *Der Monat*, 6, 1954, pp. 628–34.
Børge, Vagn, "Kierkegaard und Hamlet," *Wissenschaft und Weltbild*, vol. 23, 1970, pp. 50–8.
Cheung, King-kok, "Shakespeare and Kierkegaard: 'Dread' in 'Macbeth,' " *Shakespeare Quarterly*, vol. 35, 1984, pp. 430–9.
Christensen, Villads, *Søren Kierkegaard i Lyset af Shakespeares Hamlet*, Copenhagen: Rosenkilde & Bagger 1960.
Erichsen, Valborg, "Hamlet og Søren Kierkegaard," *Edda*, vol. 15, no. 1, 1921, pp. 75–80.
Faber, Bettina, *La contraddizione sofferente. La teoria del tragico in Søren Kierkegaard*, Padova: Il Poligrafo 1998, p. 73; p. 94; p. 96.
Fendt, Gene, *Is Hamlet a Religious Drama? An Essay on a Question in Kierkegaard*, Milwaukee, Wisconsin: Marquette University Press 1998.
Hannay, Alastair, "Hamlet without the Prince of Denmark Revisited: Pörn on Kierkegaard and the Self," *Inquiry: An Interdisciplinary Journal of Philosophy and the Social Sciences*, no. 28, 1985, pp. 261–71.
Heller, Ágnes, "Two Episodes from the Shakespeare–Kierkegaard Relationship," *Kierkegaard Studies Yearbook*, 2000, pp. 361–72.
Henriksen, Jan-Olav, *The Reconstruction of Religion. Lessing, Kierkegaard and Nietzsche*, Grand Rapids, Michigan: Eerdmans 2001.
Hohlenberg, J., "Søren Kierkegaard og Hamlet," in his *Den trange port. Naar saltet mister sin kraft. Essays*, vols. 1–2, Oslo: Aschehoug 1948, vol. 2, pp. 273–83.
Kearney, Richard, "Kierkegaard on Hamlet. Between Art and Religion," in *The New Kierkegaard*, ed. by Elsebet Jegstrup, Bloomington, Indianapolis: Indiana University Press 2004, pp. 224–43.
Kjær, Grethe, *Søren Kierkegaards seks optegnelser om den Store Jordrystelse*, Copenhagen: C.A. Reitzel 1983, see pp. 69–72.
Madariaga, Salvador de, "Noch einmal: Kierkegaard und Hamlet. War Hamlet melancholisch?" *Der Monat*, vol. 6, no. 66, 1954, pp. 625–8.

McCarthy, Robert Eugene, *The Wonder-Wounded Hearer: The Problem of Communication in Kierkegaard's Authorship and Its Application to an Understanding of Hamlet*, Ph.D. Thesis, Syracuse University, Syracuse, New York 1977.

Micheletti, M., "Wittgenstein, Kierkegaard e il 'problema di Lessing,' " in *Kierkegaard e la letteratura*, ed. by Massimo Iiritano and Inge Lise Rasmussen, Rome: Città nuova 2002, pp. 143–54.

O'Meara, J., " 'And I Will Kill Thee / And Love Thee After.' Othello's 'Sacrifice' as Dialectic of Faith," *English Language Notes*, no. 8, 1990, pp. 35–42.

Oppel, Horst, "Shakespeare und Kierkegaard. Ein Beitrag zur Geschichte der Hamlet-Deutung," *Shakespeare-Jahrbuch*, vol. 76 (Neue Folge, vol. 17), 1940, pp. 112–36.

Rougemont, Denis de, "Kierkegaard und Hamlet," *Der Monat*, vol. 5, no. 56, 1953, pp. 115–24.

—— "Hamlet and Kierkegaard: Two Danish Princes," *The Anchor Review*, vol. 1, 1955, pp. 109–27.

—— "Two Danish Princes: Kierkegaard and Hamlet," in his *Love Declared. Essays in the Myth of Love*, New York: Pantheon 1963, pp. 77–98.

Ruoff, James E., "Kierkegaard and Shakespeare," *Comparative Literature*, vol. 20, 1968, pp. 343–54.

Sløk, Johannes, *Shakespeare og Kierkegaard*, Copenhagen: Berlingske 1972 (*Berlingske Leksikon Bibliotek*).

Sobosan, Jeffrey G., "One Hand Clapping...: A Study of the Paradoxical in *Lear* and Kierkegaard," *Laval Théologique et Philosophique*, vol. 30, 1974, pp. 47–53.

Percy Bysshe Shelley:

Anxious Journeys, the Demonic, and "Breaking the Silence"

Bartholomew Ryan

> This kind of despair is rarely seen in the world; such characters really appear only in the poets, the real ones, who always lend "demonic" ideality—using the word in its purely Greek sense—to their creations.[1]

Percy Bysshe Shelley's complete works, like Lord Byron's, were to be found in Kierkegaard's library in German.[2] Although Shelley is rarely mentioned in Kierkegaard's entire corpus, two of his works, *Prometheus Unbound* and *The Cenci*, help to illuminate Kierkegaard's thought on anxiety, the demonic and "breaking the silence." There are also connections to be drawn between Shelley's role as a poet and wanderer *par excellence* and Kierkegaard's interest (which Shelley shared) in the myth of the "Wandering Jew."

I. A Brief Introduction to Shelley

In 1792, Percy Bysshe Shelley was born into an aristocratic family at Field Place near Horsham in Sussex. His father, Timothy Shelley, was a Sussex squire and Member of Parliament. Shelley was educated at Syon House Academy, Eton and lasted one year at Oxford University before being expelled for publishing the pamphlet *The Necessity of Atheism* (1811), which he co-wrote with Thomas Jefferson Hogg (1792–1862). Shelley was an absolute non-conformist: after eloping with the 16-year-old Harriet Westbrook, he traveled to Ireland, preaching political reform, and estranged himself from his family. Shelley's first major poem, *Queen Mab*, was published in 1813.[3] The marriage to Harriet rapidly deteriorated when Shelley met Mary Wollstonecraft (1759–97), daughter of the author of the classic feminist treatise, *A Vindication of the Rights of Women* (1792). Unable to annul the marriage to Harriet,

---

[1]   *SKS* 11, 186 / *SUD*, 72.

[2]   *Percy Bysshe Shelley's Poetische Werke in einem Bande*, trans. by Julius Seybt, Leipzig: Verlag von Wilhelm Engelmann 1844 (*ASKB* 1898).

[3]   There is an interesting connection between Shelley and Kierkegaard in that, in *Queen Mab*, Shelley acknowledges the poem "Der Ewige Jude" (The Wandering Jew) by C.F.D. Schubarth who serves as a figure of despair and defiance for Kierkegaard.

Shelley eloped to Switzerland in 1814 with Mary, soon to be Mary Shelley, author of *Frankenstein* (1818). Shelley spent the summer of 1816 by Lake Geneva with Byron composing *Mont Blanc* and *Hymn to Intellectual Beauty*. The Shelleys joined Byron again in Italy in 1818 and spent extended time in Rome and Pisa. Shelley's life was not without tragedy: Harriet (apparently pregnant by another man) drowned herself. Shelley lost custody of the two children he had with Harriet to her family, and the Shelley's infant daughter Clara and son William died in Italy in 1818. But it was also in Italy where Shelley composed his greatest poetical works, publishing *Ozymandius* (1818), *Ode to the West Wind* (1819), and *Prometheus Unbound, The Cenci*, and *Ode to a Skylark* (all 1820). In 1822, at the age of 29, Shelley drowned at sea off the coast of Italy, leaving his final work, *The Triumph of Life*, almost complete.[4]

II. Kierkegaard's Mentions of Shelley

The only explicit place in the whole of Kierkegaard's published corpus where Shelley is mentioned is in *The Concept of Anxiety* (1844), in the section "Anxiety about the Good (The Demonic)," where he is placed alongside Byron and Shakespeare. Kierkegaard, under the guise of the pseudonym Vigilius Haufniensis, writes, "Even though the word was terrible, even though it were a Shakespeare, a Byron, or a Shelley who breaks the silence, the word always retains its redeeming power, because all despair and all the horror of evil expressed in a word are not as terrible as silence."[5] It is significant that Kierkegaard places the two poets alongside Shakespeare, who, for him, may well be the greatest poet of them all.[6] It can be ascertained then that Kierkegaard held these two poets in high esteem. All other references to Shelley are to be found in Kierkegaard's vast and labyrinth-like journals and notebooks.

Kierkegaard refers directly to Shelley twice in the journals in his preparations for *The Concept of Anxiety*. The two works mentioned are *Prometheus Unbound* and *The Cenci*. Like Byron, Shelley is viewed also as the great rebellious poet of defiance who deeply understands the demonic, anxiety, and despair. The first entry reads:

> In the introduction to his poem "Prometheus" Shelley remarks that the idea of Prometheus seems to him far more beautiful than the idea of the Devil because Prometheus is pure and lofty, not corrupted and corrupting like Satan. This is true, but there is an entirely different problem: vis-à-vis God to think an idea as justified as the idea of Prometheus.

---

[4]   For the most complete biography of Shelley, see Richard Holmes, *Shelley: The Pursuit*, London: HarperCollins Perennial 2005.

[5]   *SKS* 4, 432 / *CA*, 131.

[6]   See *SKS* 6, 419 / *SLW*, 454: "...Shakespeare stands unrivalled, despite the progress the world will make, that one can always learn from him, and the more one reads him, the more one learns." See also *SKS* 4, 154 / *FT*, 61: "Thanks to you, great Shakespeare, you who can say everything, everything just as it is...."

Satan is indeed great, but his corruptedness is precisely what makes it possible to think of him together with God. [7]

The second reference to Shelley comes under the forbidding excluded sections of *The Concept of Anxiety* to be found in the journals and notebooks under the title: "Vocalizations for *On the Concept of Anxiety*,"[8] with an epigraph underneath which reads "*loquere ut videam te*" (speak, that I may see you). The first of the "vocalizations" is "Examples of the Consequences of the Relations of Generations," which includes an entry "*Cenci* by P.B. Shelley."[9]

III. A General Interpretation of Kierkegaard's Use of Shelley

What room did Kierkegaard have for Shelley in his workshop? There are a few important concepts in Kierkegaard's writings that can be illuminated by tracing his reading of Shelley. These include the categories of anxiety, "inclosing reserve" (*det Indesluttede*), "breaking the silence," rebelling against God, sinning in sorrow, and the poet's ideal as "wanderer."

First, let us take a look at Kierkegaard's connection to Shelley's *Prometheus Unbound*. As a poet of defiance, Prometheus is a natural choice of topic for Shelley. Here we have the idea of rebelling against God. But Satan is more appealing to Kierkegaard than to Shelley, because Satan can be cast on the same scale as God, while Prometheus is lower than both. What draws the Romantic poet to Prometheus over and above both God and Satan is in Prometheus' very inferiority—*this* is what draws humankind to him, both in the break of Man with God, and the emergence of the anti-hero as hero. The symbol of Prometheus reveals the defiance of Shelley that would also fit the criteria of the analysis in *The Sickness unto Death*, in what Kierkegaard views as the highest form of despair. Prometheus is great, because, while he does rebel against the gods, he remains true and noble. Shelley and Kierkegaard part ways due to Shelley's attempt to strive on behalf of humanity, as he would see it, and to use the story of Prometheus to help human beings break free from an oppressive God; by contrast, Kierkegaard, by the time of writing *The Sickness unto Death*, attempts to show the despair of prioritizing humanity over and above God, and to demonstrate that every individual instead "exists *before God*."[10]

The second piece of literature in reference to Shelley in Kierkegaard's writings is *The Cenci*. The use of Shelley here makes its way quite profoundly from Kierkegaard's journals to *The Concept of Anxiety*. This text was written and published in the year that Kierkegaard was reading *Prometheus Unbound* and *The Cenci*. The latter,

---

[7]   *SKS* 18, 228, JJ:280 / *KJN* 2, 209. Kierkegaard read the German version, *Der entfesselte Prometheus*, from his copy of *Percy Bysshe Shelley's poetische Werke in einem Bande*, pp. 55–92.

[8]   See Joakim Garff, *Søren Aabye Kierkegaard. A Biography*, trans. by Bruce H. Kirmmse, Princeton, New Jersey: Princeton University Press 2005, pp. 348–9, for a discussion of these "vocalizations."

[9]   *Pap.* V A 104 / *JP* 5, 5716.

[10]   *SKS* 11, 197 / *SUD*, 85.

Shelley's only tragedy, has been referred to as the "theater of anxiety."[11] It is the story of Beatrice Cenci who has her father killed because he raped her and because of his overall diabolical treatment of his family. She is subsequently sentenced to death. In Kierkegaard's sinister and macabre "Vocalizations for *The Concept of Anxiety*" from his journals, Beatrice Cenci is one of the examples chosen (alongside characters from Shakespeare), and it is easy see why when one is familiar with both the biography and writings of Kierkegaard. With *The Cenci*, Shelley was giving more of his own personality and temperament, developing further the masculine role assigned to his heroines such as in his other characters, Cythna and Asia. Indeed, in his biography of Shelley, Richard Holmes makes this explicit: "The identity between male and female, or at least the transposable or interchangeable elements between the two sexes had long been an under-theme of Shelley's writing."[12] *The Cenci* is shrouded in melancholy. Its themes of the oppressive father, anxiety, and despair, and the great sin that is unspeakable—all are very much situated in Kierkegaardian territory. But apart from its biographical resonances, the play can also be viewed as an important inspiration and influence on *The Concept of Anxiety* on a number of points.

First of all, as one of the "real poets," Shelley is someone who is able to "break the silence" and to show how Beatrice tries to break free from her horrific predicament. What does this mean—to break the silence? Kierkegaard, as Haufniensis, knows himself that this is a question that is extraordinarily difficult to answer.[13] Instead, he gives himself and the reader categories, creations, and poets to help bring us closer to understanding what breaking the silence might mean. An essential category is "inclosing reserve," which is most prominent in the section on the demonic in *The Concept of Anxiety* and appears again in *The Sickness unto Death*. The person of inclosing reserve or encapsulation is one who cannot speak, who is entangled in muteness, or who is, as described in *The Sickness unto Death*, "an inwardness with a jammed lock."[14] The "real poet" is able to break this silence, is able to create characters of the most profound case of "inclosing reserve" and articulate them on the page. Such examples in Shakespeare are, of course, King Lear, Richard III, and Hamlet, who all occupy a significant place throughout Kierkegaard's thought. In *The Concept of Anxiety*, Hamlet is referred to as "the inclosed Hamlet,"[15] who attempts to break the silence of his own encapsulation, his own demonic anxiety for both the past and the future. These major Shakespearian characters all meet violent and bloody ends. In Shelley's *The Cenci*, the violence and the horror exceed all three of the above Shakespearian characters.

Second, the main character from Shelley's tragedy is a woman, and this might have special interest and inspiration for Kierkegaard in his study of anxiety. As Haufniensis, he writes: "*Woman is more anxious than man.* This is not because of her

[11]   See Remy Roussetzki, "Theater of Anxiety in Shelley's *The Cenci* and Musset's *Lorenzaccio*—Percy Shelley, Alfred de Musset," *Criticism: A Quarterly for Literature and the Arts*, vol. 42, no. 1, 2000, pp. 31–58.
[12]   Holmes, *Shelley: The Pursuit*, p. 517.
[13]   *SKS* 4, 429 / *CA*, 128.
[14]   *SKS* 11, 186 / *SUD*, 72.
[15]   *SKS* 4, 429 / *CA*, 128.

lesser physical strength etc., for that kind of anxiety is not the issue here, but because she is more sensuous than man and yet, like him, essentially qualified as spirit."[16] Beatrice is sexually violated by her own father, and it is this act that she tries to keep secret. How can Beatrice break the silence? She does it through violence. For Kierkegaard, this "breaking the silence" becomes a terrible and violent rupture. We might understand the "vocalizations" better by seeing the anxiety that is in certain characters who are created by the "real poets" and to whom horrific, unspeakable injustices have been done.

The third point then becomes a combination of the use of vocalizations and their connection with anxiety and the "inclosing reserve," which also continues the theme of "breaking the silence." The "vocalizations" caption, *loquere ut videam te*—asking the one to speak so that that one can be seen—echoes the "inclosing reserve" of Beatrice. Beatrice Cenci is unable to speak of the crime afflicted upon her. She sighs, "If I try to speak I shall go mad."[17] Later, she says,

> I have endured a wrong,
> Which, though it be expressionless, is such
> As asks atonement; both for its past,
> And lest I be reserved, day after day,
> To load with crimes an overburdened soul,
> And be...what ye can dream not.[18]

Her articulation finally comes in murdering her own father, as the tragedy itself moves from melancholy to anxiety to despair to resolution. There is something "demonic," spiritually understood in *The Concept of Anxiety*, in Beatrice: not only in her way of keeping her father's violation of her secret, but also in her anxiety about what would be right to do. We may go as far as to say that "the demonic" in Beatrice is her anxiety about the good—the theme that makes up most of chapter four of *The Concept of Anxiety*. When Beatrice does finally decide that she must disclose her secret and act, the result is death for both herself and her father. If we bear this play in mind, and imagine it on Kierkegaard's desk, we can read with interest the following lines from *The Concept of Anxiety*:

> The demonic is inclosing reserve, the demonic is anxiety about the good. Let the inclosing reserve be x and its content x, denoting the most terrible, the most insignificant, the horrible, whose presence in life few probably even dream about, but also the trifles to which no one pays attention. What then is the significance of the good as x? It signifies disclosure.[19]

Another area that can be of interest to readers of Kierkegaard and his connection to *The Cenci* is in the use of time and its crucial relation to anxiety. Beatrice is anxious about the past and cannot forget the terrible deed that was done to her within

---

[16]   *SKS* 4, 370 / *CA*, 66.
[17]   *The Cenci*, in *The Complete Poems of Percy Bysshe Shelley*, annotated by Mary Shelley, New York: Modern Library 1994, p. 324, Act III, scene i, lines 85–6.
[18]   Ibid., Act III, scene i, lines 213–18.
[19]   *SKS* 4, 427–8 / *CA*, 127.

her own family. She cannot get rid of the past. The past remains in the face of her father, and her secret is her past, which is still present. With this thought of Beatrice in mind, we read in *The Concept of Anxiety*: "If I am anxious because of a past offense, it is because I have not placed it in an essential relation to myself as past and have in some deceitful way or another prevented it from being past."[20] Reading *The Concept of Anxiety* further, we can see Beatrice as being anxious about the future too. She trembles for what is to come, and she begins to foresee the tragedy that lies ahead. Her only salvation to escape from her "inclosing reserve" and her past is to sin, to strike a blow at her despair. Kierkegaard's Haufniensis writes:

> Anxiety is ahead; it discovers the consequence before it comes, as one feels in one's bones that a storm is approaching. The consequence comes closer; the individual trembles like a horse that gasps as it comes to a halt at the place where once it had been frightened. Sin conquers. Anxiety throws itself despairingly into the arms of repentance. Repentance ventures all. It conceives of sin as suffering penalty and of perdition as the consequence of sin. It is lost. Its judgement is pronounced, its condemnation is certain, and the augmented judgement is that the individual shall be dragged through life to the place of execution. In other words, repentance has gone crazy.[21]

Beatrice's revenge and breaking out of her inclosing reserve becomes her repentance and salvation; but she too sins, and her redemption also brings to her a sentence of death.

There are other passages from *The Cenci* that might have appealed to Kierkegaard, given what we know about his work and biography. One example is of the unspeakable despair that is passed on from one generation to another, such as in the treatment of the continuation of sin in *The Concept of Anxiety*, and Kierkegaard's own torment with the brooding presence of his father, "Who, if a father's curses, as men say, / Climb with swift / wings after the children's souls, / And drag them from the very throne of Heaven, / Now triumphs in my triumph!"[22]

Kierkegaard's "great earthquake" entry in 1838 shows his own affinity and empathy with Shelley's tragedy:

> It was then the great earthquake occurred, the terrible upheaval which suddenly pressed on me a new infallible law for the interpretation of all phenomena. It was then I suspected my father's great age was not a divine blessing but rather a curse; that our family's excellent mental abilities existed only for tearing us apart from one another....[23]

A second example is a magisterial description by Shelley of the destructive force of despair eating up the human being not unlike the "inclosing reserve" in *The Concept of Anxiety* and *The Sickness unto Death*. Despair hides itself from itself and cannot speak so that it will be seen; it "closes itself off more and more from communication," and is in the realm of the demonic and anxiety about the good:[24]

---

[20]   *SKS* 4, 394–5 / *CA*, 93.
[21]   *SKS* 4, 417–18 / *CA*, 115–16.
[22]   *The Cenci*, Act I, scene iii, lines 84–7.
[23]   *Pap.* II A 805 / *JP* 5, 5430.
[24]   *SKS* 4, 427 / *CA*, 126. *SKS* 4, 430 / *CA*, 129. *SKS* 11, 177 / *SUD*, 63.

> The air
> Is changed to vapours such as the dead breathe
> In charnel pits! Pah! I am choked! There creeps
> A clinging, black, contaminating mist
> About me...'tis substantial, heavy, thick,
> I cannot pluck it from me, for it glues
> My fingers and my limbs to one another,
> And eats into my sinews, and dissolves
> My flesh to a pollution, poisoning
> The subtle, pure, and inmost spirit of life![25]

Finally, there is a passage from *The Cenci* that reveals an uncanny likeness to *The Sickness unto Death* in its portrait of the dangers of erring in sorrow. In *The Sickness unto Death*, Anti-Climacus writes, "In his sorrow, he may sink into the darkest depression—and a fool of a spiritual counsellor may be on the verge of admiring his deep soul and the powerful influence good has on him."[26] Kierkegaard's interest in this theme was not a minor one; he planned to write seven discourses on the "most beautiful and noble, humanly speaking, forms of despair" under the title "Let not the heart in sorrow sin."[27] Once again, the influence of *The Cenci* can be felt: "And let mild, pitying thoughts lighten for thee / Thy sorrow's load. Err not in harsh despair, / But tears and patience."[28]

A final point to make concerns the motif of the poet and the wanderer. The Romantic poets consider themselves wanderers of the world and of the spirit (as John Keats once wrote: "Great spirits now on earth sojourning"[29]), sacrificing happiness and security, and choosing instead the path of discovery in the endless search for truth. This romantic idea has not only inspired generations of young people around the world; it has also influenced, and indeed been assimilated into, the writings of several major thinkers of the late nineteenth and twentieth centuries, including Friedrich Nietzsche, Martin Heidegger, and Walter Benjamin.

This "wanderer" motif was not neglected by Kierkegaard; nor could he withstand its allure and aesthetic quality. From his earliest journal entries to his last publications, the image of the poet as wanderer, reflected both in Kierkegaard himself and in his great predecessors, never vanishes from his writings. Both Shelley and Kierkegaard showed an interest in the myth of the "Wandering Jew,"[30] and both moved on from this interest. Interestingly, all that remains of this interest in both men's writings are fragments on the topic. Both Shelley and Kierkegaard studied, reflected upon deeply, and ultimately abandoned the motif of the Wandering Jew. However, this

---

[25]   *The Cenci*, Act III, Scene i, lines 14–23.

[26]   *SKS* 11, 224 / *SUD*, 112.

[27]   *SKS* 21, 166, NB8:46 / *JP* 6, 6277.

[28]   *The Cenci*, Act IV, scene iv, lines 144–5.

[29]   John Keats, "Addressed to the Same," in *Poems of John Keats*, selected and ed. by Henry Newbolt, New York: T. Nelson 1900, p. 292.

[30]   Kierkegaard notes in his journal: "How beautifully the preparatory relationship of the Jews to Christianity is intimated in the legend of the Wandering Jew (see *Ein Volksbuchlein*, p. 27), which relates how in the latter part of his life he continually guides those who come from afar to visit the holy land." See *Pap.* I A 299 / *JP* 2, 2210.

abandonment can also be interpreted as a *metamorphosis* into the homeless, restless pursuit of the poet (Shelley) or the homeless, restless Christian (Kierkegaard). We find fragments in Shelley with titles such as "The Wandering Jew's Soliloquy," "Song from a Wandering Jew," and "Fragment from the Wandering Jew." We similarly find sketches on the subject in *Either/Or*, along with echoes of Kierkegaard's abandoned project on the figures of the Master Thief, Don Giovanni, Faust, and Ahasverus the Wandering Jew. Kierkegaard described the latter three figures as the "three great ideas."[31] In his first book on Kierkegaard, Josiah Thompson described the figure of Ahasverus (the Wandering Jew) as something essential for his thesis and as a central figure in Kierkegaard's workshop:

> The figure of Ahasverus probably stands closer to the center of Kierkegaard's mental landscape than all the others. This pitiful figure doomed by Christ to spend eternity wandering an alien world is the perfect exemplar of that frozen, timeless world Kierkegaard knew so well. In 1835 he described Ahasverus in words from Hoffmann's *Meister Floh* as, "the Eternal Jew who wandered through the gay tumult of the world without joy, without hope, without pain, in dull indifference, which is the *caput mortuum* of despair, as though through a dreary and disconsolate desert" (*Pap.* I C 60). How closely this description of Ahasverus's sufferings parallels Kierkegaard's own.[32]

Like Ahasverus, Kierkegaard complains of his suffering, vagabonding fate (at least of the mind) in 1839:

> you will never imagine what must be suffered by one who, having wasted the strength and courage of youth in disobedience toward him, now begins to retreat through devastated lands and ravaged provinces, exhausted and powerless, surrounded on all sides by abominable desolation, by razed towns and the smoking ruins of disappointed hopes, by what was once prosperous but is now trodden down, and what was once pleasant but is now shattered, a retreat as slow as a bad year, as long as an eternity monotonously interrupted by the constantly repeated sigh: these days have no pleasure for me.[33]

Shelley and Kierkegaard shared an interest in the Wandering Jew's transformation into a figure who, though equally lonely, nevertheless became somewhat triumphant. A year before his death, Shelley wrote a short poem, "Fragment: A Wanderer" which runs as follows: "He wanders, like a day-appearing dream, / Through the dim wilderness of the mind; / Through desert woods and tracts, which seem / Like ocean, homeless, boundless, unconfined."[34]

And in Kierkegaard's last pseudonymous work, Anti-Climacus brings to life beautifully a parallel image of the homeless, Christian wanderer: "He walks like a dreamer, and yet one can see by the fire and flame in his eyes that he is wide awake;

---

[31]   *Pap.* I A 150 / *JP* 2, 795.

[32]   Josiah Thompson, *The Lonely Labyrinth: Kierkegaard's Pseudonymous Works*, Carbondale: Southern Illinois University Press 1967, pp. 64–5.

[33]   *SKS* 18, 27, EE:64 / *KJN* 2, 23.

[34]   Shelley, "Fragment: A Wanderer," in *The Complete Poems of Percy Bysshe Shelley*, p. 697.

he walks like a stranger, and yet he seems to be at home."[35] Although their respective journeys take them to different worlds, there remains a commonality in their shared motif of the "wanderer" as homeless, awake, restless and on the move. In coming to understand the Wandering Jew, Shelley and Kierkegaard came to understand themselves and their roles as the lonely, travelling poet and homeless, Christian wanderer respectively.

In conclusion, we can view Kierkegaard's reading of Shelley, most notably *Prometheus Unbound* and *The Cenci*, as inspiration for his reflections on "breaking the silence," his project for the "vocalizations," his use of "inclosing reserve," his understanding of the form of despair known as rebellious defiance, and his analysis of anxiety and sin. We might also see Shelley and Kierkegaard as sharing an interest in the homeless wanderer from their early readings about the Wandering Jew to their later mature works. Kierkegaard viewed Shelley, alongside Byron and Shakespeare, as one of the "real poets" who understood, embraced and experienced the sufferings of existence and transformed this into his art, and for this reason we should not ignore the English poet when reading Kierkegaard.

---

[35]   *SKS* 12, 188 / *PC*, 189.

Bibliography

I. Shelley's Works in The Auction Catalogue *of Kierkegaard's Library*

Percy Bysshe Shelley's Poetische Werke in einem Bande, trans. by Julius Seybt, Leipzig: Verlag von Wilhelm Engelmann 1844 (*ASKB* 1898).

II. Works in The Auction Catalogue *of Kierkegaard's Library that Discuss Shelley*

Adler, Adolph Peter, *Populaire Foredrag over Hegels objective Logik*, Copenhagen: C.A. Reitzel 1842, p. 61, note (*ASKB* 383).
[Becker, Karl Friedrich], *Karl Friedrich Beckers Verdenshistorie, omarbeidet af Johan Gottfried Woltmann*, vols. 1–12, trans. by J. Riise, Copenhagen: Fr. Brummer 1822–29, vol. 10, p. 238 (*ASKB* 1972–1983).
Heiberg, Johan Ludvig, "Lyrisk Poesie," in *Intelligensblade*, ed. by Johan Ludvig Heiberg, vol. 3, nos. 25–6, 1843, pp. 25–72, see p. 38 (*ASKB* U 56).

III. Secondary Literature on Kierkegaard's Relation to Shelley

Pattison, George, "The Joy of Birdsong or Lyrical Dialectics," in *Without Authority*, ed. by Robert L. Perkins, Macon, Georgia: Mercer University Press 2007 (*International Kierkegaard Commentary*, vol. 18), pp. 111–25.
Roussetzki, Remy, "Theater of Anxiety in Shelley's *The Cenci* and Musset's *Lorenzaccio*—Percy Shelley, Alfred de Musset," *Criticism: A Quarterly for Literature and the Arts*, vol. 42, no. 1, 2000, pp. 31–58.
Thorlby, Anthony, "Imagination and Irony in English Romantic Poetry," in *Romantic Irony*, ed. by Frederick Garber, Budapest: Akadémiai Kiadó 1988, pp. 131–55, see pp. 143–9.

Richard Brinsley Sheridan:

A Story of One Review—Kierkegaard on *The School for Scandal*

Nataliya Vorobyova

Kierkegaard's use of the Irish playwright Richard Brinsley Sheridan represents an unexplored field in Kierkegaard studies. In order to examine this relation and fill out the necessary background, I will need to address a number of questions. The first one is what was the reason for the success of Sheridan's *The School for Scandal* in Britain? This classic work was performed for the first time on May 8, 1777 in Drury Lane and clearly constitutes the main, if not sole, point of contact with Kierkegaard's thought. Next, we will have a look at the staging of *The School for Scandal* in Denmark in 1846. Kierkegaard owned the Danish translation of the play,[1] and it is clear that he attended the performance. The question here is what captivated the philosopher's attention in the text in the work's character development and plot. Moreover, why did he deliberately make a mistake in the review of *The School for Scandal*, which appeared in the "Writing Sampler," where he names William Shakespeare as the author of the play?

I. Sheridan's Life

Richard Brinsley Sheridan was born in September 1751 in Dublin; however, the exact date of his birth is unknown. His biographers are only sure that he was baptized on November 4 of that year. He was a son of Thomas Sheridan, an actor, playwright, theater director, and obsessive scholar of eloquence, rhetoric, and the English language. His mother, Frances, was a prominent and popular writer of sentimental novels and plays. Some of her plays remained unfinished, and it is often suggested that Sheridan's debut play, *The Rivals*, was partially based on one of his mother's unfinished manuscripts. The Sheridans had five children, the eldest, Thomas, died shortly after birth; the second, Charles, was the father's only hope and love; the youngest daughter, Ann Elizabeth, quickly acquired the same status. There was also Alicia, known in the family as Lissy, who was Richard's younger and equally neglected sister.

---

[1]   Richard Brinsley Sheridan, *Bagtalelsens Skole. Comedie i fem Acter*, trans. by N.V. Dorph, Copenhagen n.p. 1841 (*ASKB* U 104).

When Richard turned 11, his parents decided that it was time for him to begin to look out for himself. They placed him in Harrow boarding school, while they left for France in 1764 with three other children. At that point Sheridan's parents were escaping the creditors, but it is probable his father hoped that moving to a more favorable climate would improve his wife's failing health. At the school Richard did not receive any information from the family for almost two years. The news about the death of his mother reached him through the headmaster of Harrow, since no one else took the trouble to inform him about the event. The young Sheridan had to cope with his grief by himself and could not count on much sympathy from the side of his peers for whom he had always remained the son of a bad and impoverished actor. Altogether, this certainly does not sound like a promising beginning for a young man with ambition, and as O'Toole summarizes in his monumental biography of the playwright:

> If he wanted love, he would have to dazzle for it. If he wanted money, he would have to discover some alchemy that could turn his own base prospects as the unfavored second son of a poor player, into gold. If he wanted power, he would have to be watchful and clever, to play subtle games, to turn every opportunity to advantage.[2]

In 1769 Sheridan's father returned with his children to London, and in the autumn 1770 the family moved to Bath. After the reunion Richard was largely left alone except for when he was attending the classes in language and rhetoric given by his father along with supplementary classes in mathematics and Latin provided by other tutors. In Bath Thomas Sheridan set out on a quest to realize one of his oldest ambitions connected with the reformation of the English education system and the improvement of speech: he opened an Academy where young gentlemen could receive instruction in reading, reciting, and grammar. However, the project never succeeded, and the notion of an Irishman trying to teach the English how to speak properly was ridiculed. As O'Toole eloquently concludes: "the idea that an Irishman could provide a passage into English society may have made sense in Scotland, or even in Dublin, but in Bath it was merely risible."[3] The collapse of the Academy meant for Richard the regaining of his freedom and the chance to devote himself to the activities which would influence or help his future prospects. His ambition was to get into politics, an idea very difficult to achieve without money, social connections, or a position in the society. He was aware that for a young man with a low social status and no fortune, there were only five ways to attain a political career:

> He could make money in trade, usually by securing government contracts. He could become a war profiteer. He could join the East India Company and come home with his pockets full of loot. He could marry a wealthy landed heiress. He could work his way up through the legal profession and eventually leap the narrow chasm that separated a leading barrister from a member of parliament.[4]

---

[2]   Fintan O'Toole, *A Traitor's Kiss: The Life of Richard Brinsley Sheridan*, London: Granta Books 1997, p. 28.
[3]   Ibid., p. 45.
[4]   Ibid., pp. 81–2.

Neither of the first two options was possible for Sheridan. He had no connections to start with and managed to run up debts quite early. He rejected the third possibility by declining an offer to take a position in the East India Company in favor of staying in England. His decision was determined by the fact that at that time he was in love with Eliza Linley, his future wife. Eliza came from the family of a musician, Thomas Linley, whose income depended upon his daughter's talents. Besides being extraordinarily beautiful, she was a fabulous and popular singer. Such a choice of a spouse could bring Sheridan neither a desirable position nor capital. By getting married, Richard rejected the last possible way of advancing into politics, namely, by deciding not to enter law school. At that point it was more crucial to find a way of supporting his family. The most obvious road to success was through the theater.

It is impossible to omit the premarital affair between Richard and Eliza, which was truly in the sentimental spirit of the time. Thomas Linley more than once tried to use his daughter to secure the family's financial future. In 1770, he made the first attempt by announcing the engagement of his daughter and a 60-year-old Wiltshire squire, Walter Long. As the outcome Thomas was supposed to receive £1,000 as a compensation for the loss of his daughter as a source of income: it was unspeakable that the wife of a gentleman would perform in public. The engagement with an aristocrat meant for Eliza a complete withdrawal from public performances, which quickly made the whole arrangement public.

The most violent reaction came from Samuel Foote, an actor and manager of the Haymarket Theatre in London, who used the story in *The Maid of Bath*. The play became a great success, and Walter Long, not relishing the idea of being the talk of the town, broke the engagement, settling it with £3,000 and a present of jewelry worth £1,000. Shortly thereafter Eliza acquired a new admirer, Captain Thomas Mathews, who did not seem to have any reason for reproach since he himself had been married for seven years. Eliza became desperate, trying to avoid Mathews' seduction, deciding that the best solution to resolve the situation would be to escape. Sheridan's sisters, with whom Eliza was very intimate, gladly supplied the idea of a flight to St. Quentin in France, where the girls had acquaintances dating back to the time when the family had lived there. An escape required an escort, and Richard agreed to accompany Eliza.

The escape succeeded; however, it did not clear up the situation. Eliza's poor health was undermined by a rough voyage to the Continent. She got very sick in Lille, where an English doctor took her to his house until she recovered. Back in Bath, Thomas Linley was agitated, making various attempts to get his daughter to return, since her escape put him in financial difficulty. At the same time the town was full of gossip and rumors, which of course meant that it would be impossible for Richard and Eliza to return to England without being married. Whether encouraged by social convention or not, the young couple got married in a Catholic church in France. Weeks passed, but Mathews did not show any sign of remorse for his behavior. On the contrary, he wrote an offensive letter about Sheridan to the *Bath Chronicle*,[5] after the publication of which there was nothing left for Sheridan to do but to challenge him to a duel. After Mathews broke multiple promises to issue an apology, the duel

5   Ibid., p. 56.

eventually took place in London. With respect to the insult, Sheridan had a perfectly
good reason for killing Mathews, and he almost did so during the duel. As a result
Mathews was forced to write and sign a letter which was supposed to end the affair.
Yet, upon his return to Bath, Mathews was eager to present his own account of
the event, so that his stubbornness resulted in a second duel, in which both he and
Sheridan were seriously injured. It is difficult to understand why Sheridan insisted
on the second duel. The first one was a consequence of his courtship of Eliza, while
the second one was most likely, as O'Toole underlines, a way of defending the status
of a gentleman. "To deserve the treatment of a gentleman, it was necessary to be
recognized as a gentleman. And without that recognition, Sheridan had no chance at
all of fulfilling any of his ambitions to be a public man."[6] Therefore, it was significant
that the duel was transformed in time into a memorable public event, and the whole
story acquired the status of a real-life melodrama, which in the end permitted the
main characters to exchange roles. Eliza withdrew from public life, as the wife of a
gentleman, while Richard moved into the public sphere.

At that time he was already determined to earn his living as a writer; now he
had enough material to write *The Rivals*, which was performed for the first time
at Covent Garden on January 17, 1775. O'Toole wittily summarizes Sheridan's
theatrical debut: "The reality of his life as a penniless, unqualified, Irish actor's son,
famous only for his involvement in some romantic but vaguely disreputable scrapes,
is expanded into a gigantic joke and then explodes in a burst of laughter."[7] The play
was not a success the first night, but, after it was revised, it ran for 15 nights and
probably brought Sheridan much needed income. Sheridan's second successful play
was *St. Patrick's Day*, after which came a real triumph, an opera *The Duenna*, which
was truly a family production. Eliza helped with writing songs, while her father and
brother composed the music.

The three plays determined Sheridan as a man of great prospects, which might
have been one of the reasons why David Garrick, an actor and manager of Drury
Lane, considered him as a possible candidate to purchase his share in the theater
upon his retirement. Sheridan did not have enough capital for such an investment,
but after a series of complicated financial arrangements, in mid January 1776, he
became a part owner of one of the greatest European theaters. This is where his 35
years of dubious theater management got started. Sheridan began his new role as
a manger by reviving a number of William Congreve's (1670–1729) plays, which,
with respect to their mood, are said to anticipate *The School for Scandal*, a play

> which would nevertheless make more explicitly and more profoundly the point Sheridan
> had implied in his staging of the Congreve plays: that the cult of sensibility was abused
> when it became a front for prudery and hypocrisy. It would do so by turning on its head
> the received idea that society was virtuous and the stage corrupt. Sheridan would show
> that the world of "fact"—the world as it appeared in the newspapers—was full of lies,
> while the inventions of the theatre could reveal a kind of truth.[8]

---

[6]   Ibid., p. 64.
[7]   Ibid., p. 86.
[8]   Ibid., p. 125.

With the increase of the social significance of the Georgian theater, Sheridan had a chance to open doors into society and earn his much desired fortune. He became and remained a playwright purely due to practical reasons. Since his talent was mainly exercised because of financial considerations, it was money that forced Sheridan to get back to writing. In the season of 1777, in Drury Lane there was a demand for a new comedy.

II. The School for Scandal *in 1777*

The School for Scandal ran for altogether 114 performances over four seasons, in the period between 1777 and before Sheridan entered Parliament in 1780. But before having a look at what exactly assured its success, it is worth summarizing briefly this still popular comedy of manners.

The School for Scandal has three vivid plot lines, which make the performance very catchy. An elderly gentleman and an old bachelor, Sir Peter Teazle, had been married six months previously. He has chosen for his spouse the young daughter of a country squire, who is drastically transformed under the influence of fashionable London society. In her everyday life, Lady Teazle is preoccupied mainly with scolding her husband and spending time with her acquaintances, who are busy creating and spreading malicious gossip. The play opens in the boudoir of one of the most dangerous fabricators of rumors, Lady Sneerwell. There she and a forger Snake are plotting a breakup between Charles Surface and Sir Peter's ward Maria. With the help of letters, Snake is to spread a rumor that is intended to destroy the romance between the young lovers. Maria's hand would then go to Charle's elder hypocritical brother with excellent reputation, Joseph, whose interest in the girl lies purely in her fortune. Yet, he is also backed by Sir Peter, who is fooled by Joseph's perfect exterior. If she succeeds, Lady Sneerwell would be able to keep "extravagant" Charles for herself. Meanwhile Sir Oliver Surface, the rich uncle of Charles and Joseph, arrives unexpectedly from Australia, because he has heard rather conflicting reports about the nephews who are his prospective heirs.

Before making a final decision regarding the recipient of his fortune, he wants to test both of them. He approaches them in disguise, first arranging to see a deeply in debt Charles pretending to be a moneylender. Although at the start of the negotiations Sir Oliver is disappointed that Charles, without any regret, sells his whole collection of family portraits, his heart melts when the young man insists on keeping the portrait of Sir Oliver for himself, explaining that he has obligations and appreciates the support received from his uncle. This convinces Sir Oliver that even though Charles is less fortunate and not careful with money, he has retained a sense of honor that is so crucial for a gentleman. When Sir Oliver approaches Joseph, presenting himself as a poor relation from Ireland in need of financial support, the young man reveals his true selfish, greedy, and sly nature.

Yet, another rumor has been spread by the company of scandalmongers. It concerns Lady Teazle and states that she is involved in an affair with Charles, while in reality she flirts with Joseph. However, she does this not because of any romantic involvement, but for the sake of fashion. When the rumor reaches the ears of Sir

Peter, he goes to Joseph's apartment to consult with him. When he unexpectedly arrives, Lady Teazle, who has been enjoying Joseph's company, hides in haste behind the screen. Shortly after his arrival, Charles comes for a visit, which forces Sir Peter to hide in a closet. Yet the damage to Joseph's affair is already done, as Sir Peter openly speaks about his approval of Joseph as Maria's suitor. Accidentally, Charles reveals Lady Teazle behind the screen, and later Sir Peter is forced to come out of the closet, with a completely revised estimate of the young man. This is the culminating point of the play, which is conventionally known as the Screen Scene: when the screen falls all secrets begin to be exposed. At this point Lady Teazle asks her husband for forgiveness for being so blinded by the demands of fashion. And meanwhile, Sir Oliver succeeds in getting a confession out of Snake about the plot; this eliminates all the objections from Sir Peter's side about this match and brings about a reconciliation between Charles and Maria.

There is a balance between the three main plots, all of which in their own way provide enjoyment to the audience. The story of two brothers can be referred to as a "comedy of merit rewarded."[9] But unfortunately it is the least aesthetically valuable element of the play, for "it contains the potentially improbable, the excessively sentimental and the facilely moral."[10] The story of the Teazles is told via the "punitive comedy of exposure" and a "comedy of self-adjustment."[11] Moreover, there is a thoroughly structured satirical attack on fashionable society and those who, due to boredom, get involved in scandalmongering.[12] And it is not only the disclosure of the mild villainy of Joseph that captures the audience's attention, but also the hope for the reconciliation of Sir Peter and Lady Teazle and the resolution of the situation of Charles (with the help of Sir Oliver), who not once loses face and yet remains faithful to his ethical convictions. Auburn explains the complex and perfectly developed plot by the fact that the play was a unification of the two different sketches, written earlier, entitled the "The Slanderers" and "The Teazles,"[13] which together produced a perfect comedy of manners. Having a difficult task in front of him, on the one hand, to exploit scandals and, on the other, to provide witty entertainment, Sheridan completed it with brilliance.

The School for Scandal is not original in its topic or its choice of material, but the way Sheridan treated it was outstanding: "Slander and scandal-mongering, both of the eternal sort characteristic of all mankind and of the special sort brought to

---

[9]   Mark S. Auburn, *Sheridan's Comedies: Their Context and Achievements*, Lincoln and London: University of Nebraska Press 1977, p. 126.

[10]   Ibid.

[11]   Ibid., p.146.

[12]   "In the elaborate false details with which Sir Benjamin and Crabtree describe the after effects of the Screen Scene (see Richard Brinsley Sheridan, *The School for Scandal: A Comedy in Five Acts*, Boston: Walter H. Baker 1915, V. ii.I I–95, pp. 78–9), Sheridan dramatizes the vulnerability of facts, the valued underpinnings of accurate communication. In the malice and exaggeration of the similes by which the scandal cabal lacerates its victims (II. ii. 29–69, in ibid., p. 28), he displays the corruption and misapplication of figurative language." Cf. Jack D. Durant, "Sheridan and Language," in *Sheridan Studies*, ed. by James Morwood and David Crane, Cambridge and New York: Cambridge University Press, p. 108.

[13]   Auburn, *Sheridan's Comedies: Their Context and Achievements*, p. 112.

devilish perfection in the paragraphs and '*tete-à-tetes*' of 1770s journalism, had already served a number of Georgian dramatists."[14] Even though the subject had the potential to become morally serious, in the moments when such a threat exists, Sheridan masterly uses "wit" and satire to ridicule social conventions, and this mostly happens when we encounter the company of scandalmongers. Around a century later George Bernard Shaw would write a review for the *Saturday Review* (that appeared on June 27, 1896) of the Lyceum production, in which he claims that he could not avoid moralizing, when speaking about Sheridan's play:

> Everything has its own rate of change. Fashions change more quickly than manners, manners more quickly than morals, morals more quickly than passions, and in general, the conscious, reasonable, intellectual life more quickly than the instinctive, wilful, affectionate one. The dramatist who deals with the irony and humour of the relatively durable sides of life, or with their pity and terror, is the one whose comedies and tragedies will last longest—sometimes so long as to lead a book-struck generation to dub him "Immortal," and proclaim him as "not for an age, but for all time."[15]

Even though Shaw's understanding of the play "re-writes" it completely, not only via moralizing but also showing the way in which it "dated," he is still forced to admit its perfection. Moreover, his perception of the Georgian comedy of manners confirms the alteration of taste and interpretation.

In order to be able to illuminate Sheridan's theatrical achievement, it is crucial to have a look at theatrical tradition in London at that time and consider what shaped and influenced the performances. The first factor, which is impossible to ignore, is that the theater in those days performed roughly the same role in shaping the public's tastes and opinions as the mass media today. Secondly, in order to interpret the play it is crucial to have a look at the raw material which the playwright had at his disposition.

Auburn calls the Georgian period "the age of repertory" and "the age of acting."[16] The first criterion was determined by the popular taste of the audience, which was capricious with respect to new plays. As in all times, the theater could exist only as long as it earned money, and it could earn it only if people wanted to pay for the experience. The revival of old, well-known plays guaranteed support from the audience, who were always eager to see a varying interpretation or a new casting of a favorite performance.

With the appearance of David Garrick on the stage of the Theatre Royal on Drury Lane, not only had the style of acting changed,[17] but also the way the audience

---

[14]   Ibid., p. 135.

[15]   *Sheridan: Comedies: The Rivals, A Trip to Scarborough, The School for Scandal, The Critic, A Casebook*, ed. by Peter Davison, Basingstoke: Macmillan 1986, p. 147.

[16]   Mark S. Auburn, "Theatre in the Age of Garrick and Sheridan," in *Sheridan Studies*, ed. by James Morwood and David Crane, p. 17.

[17]   As Auburn points out: "Garrick's amazing achievements would influence dramatic performance for the next three decades. His emphasis upon ensemble acting countered a tradition of formal and individualistic presentation which had marked London acting for several decades: actors portrayed the universal rather than particular truths of their characters;

perceived their favorites. The biggest change employed by Garrick might seem very straightforward nowadays. Every play has to come alive, and in order for this to happen actors have to collaborate, work in unison, and support each other in such a manner as to create a dramatic presentation that will imitate reality. Moreover, in most cases the success of a new play depended upon its cast. Simultaneously, a number of actors had established themselves in certain roles, in the eyes of the audience, reviewers and playwrights. As a playwright Sheridan was no exception; he remembered to keep in mind the versatile skills and associations of the cast, crafting the parts to match the abilities of the performers.

The Georgian period was quite particular for theater development, for it was then that a tremendous shift of focus could be observed: it was not the text that ruled the stage, but the actor together with a class of theater-goers: "Londoners loved their theatre with a passion, discussed it endlessly, and were as personally attached to the actors and managers as today's fans are to football players or cricketers or television stars."[18] Such a change led to numerous adaptations and re-writings of, for instance, Elizabethan plays. Yet it also diminished the quality of the newly written, contemporary texts. Even as talented and skillful a playwright as Sheridan had to rework *The Rivals*—a play that was withdrawn after its first night.[19] A successful production relied on the actor's skills, enhanced by changes of the stage, light and the way of the performing, as well as on the favorable disposition of the audience. This might be the reason why very few plays of the period are of literary value, but nevertheless they provide an insight into the theatrical art and what we can today call a "social sentiment." In the last forty years of the eighteenth century there were a number of talented actors who, besides setting social fashions, raised their theatrical occupation to the level of an honorable profession.

Its success was assured by the play's cast, which can be considered as the strongest at that time. Sir Peter Teazle was played by Thomas King (1730–1805), who from the 1760s had become Drury Lane's chief comedian after Garrick. He was at his best performing the character of an aristocratic eccentric. One of the actors and critics, Francis Gentleman, praised King's affable disposition and cherished the special warm sensibility in his acting. And it might have been those two qualities that influenced King's conception of Sir Peter Teazle, a role he acted 254 times. Auburn confirms this opinion: "I once gave credence to the report that King's Sir Peter was an 'old fretful dotard,' but I now doubt that report. King's roles as warm if eccentric old men confirm him in a line of amiable humorists for which he was much beloved."[20]

The role of Lady Teazle was performed by Frances Abington (1737–1815), who not only won regular applause from the audience, but was first and foremost an influential figure when it came to what to wear or how to wear one's hair. Not a few fashionable ladies of the capital followed and consulted her in matters of fashion.

they represented the passion which they found in their roles; they acted exemplars rather than people." Ibid., p. 19.
[18]   Ibid., p. 15.
[19]   Stanley Ayling, *A Portrait of Sheridan*, London: Constable 1985, p. 45.
[20]   Auburn, "Theatre in the Age of Garrick and Sheridan," p. 25.

She typically played young heroines—parts which matched the humor, elegance, and grace of her nature.

John Palmer (1744–98) created the character of Joseph Surface. But he had a tendency to remain in real life as hypocritical and *intrigant* as his characters, which gave him a name of a "Plausible Jack."[21] For instance, at some point in his career Palmer took a great risk and made an attempt to build his own theater, creating a source of competition for both the Theatre Royal and Covent Garden. However, his enterprise failed in the same manner as did the great plans of Joseph Surface. All in all, Palmer's true nature could be briefly but wittily summarized as follows:

> There is an anecdote which ought to be true but sounds too neat. Palmer seeks his old acting job back at Drury Lane and apologizes to Sheridan for his attempt to break the patent monopolies: Jack says, "If you could but see my heart, Mr. Sheridan—" "Why Jack!" replies Sheridan, "you forget: I wrote it."[22]

Since almost fifty years had passed between the first production of *The School for Scandal* with the original cast and the time when Lamb writes, "On the Artificial Comedy of the Last Century" (in the *London Magazine*, in April 1822)[23] and declares that the hero of *The School for Scandal*, when "Palmer had the part, was Joseph Surface," the following comment is fitting when it comes to understanding the perceptual differences of the play:

> Joseph Surface, to go down now, must be a downright revolting villain—no compromise—his first appearance must shock and give horror—his specious plausibilities, which the pleasurable faculties of our fathers welcomed with such hearty greetings, knowing that no harm (dramatic harm even) could come, or was meant to come, of them, must inspire a cold and killing aversion.[24]

Finally, we should mention the role of Charles Surface, played by William Smith, and the part of Maria, which was intended to be performed by Mary Robinson, but she was pregnant and therefore unable to perform. As a result, the role went to the daughter of Drury Lane prompter William Hopkins, that is, Priscilla Hopkins, who was not a prominent actress. Many critics believe that such a change in cast influenced the fact that Maria's part in itself is rather disappointing:

> If Sheridan really doubted Miss Hopkins's capacities in a love scene, why did he not call upon a more experienced and presumably more trustworthy actress such as Sophia Baddeley to take that part? I think the truth is that he never intended a love scene between Charles and Maria, not because performers capable of handling such a scene were unavailable, but because he realized that such a scene was aesthetically improper in the particular kind of comedy he had designed.[25]

---

21 Ibid., p. 28.
22 Ibid., pp. 29–30.
23 Ibid., p. 30.
24 Ibid., p. 139.
25 Ibid., p. 133.

Sheridan chose with great care the cast of all the slanderers, which suggests that they were to bear the most weight of the text. James Dodd (1740–96) brilliantly recreated Sir Benjamin Backbite. He was "the prince of pink heels, and the soul of empty eminence,"[26] tottering about on slim legs. If one judges by his earnings of £8 a week, it is possible to conclude that he was a substantial asset to the company as a comedian. As Auburn concludes, "although he would occasionally descend to low comedy or attempt, usually for his benefits, to rise into tragedy, it was as coxcombs, fops, country boobies, and silly beaux in comedy of manners and sentimental comedy that Dodd excelled."[27] Jane Pope's Mrs. Candour was one of her most famous roles. William Parson as Crabtree "played the wasp to Dodd's butterfly."[28]

Lady Sneerwell was recreated by Katherine Sherry, a rather young and not very experienced actress. For this role Sheridan could have chosen Mrs. Elizabeth Hopkins, wife of the Drury Lane prompter. She was the one who recreated Mrs Malaprop and in general was an "experienced portrayer of malicious ladies."[29] "But clearly Sheridan wanted the younger actress who was more capable than Mrs. Hopkins of portraying a woman of an age delicately balanced between the freshness of youth and the sad cynicism of middle age."[30]

All in all, as Bernard Shaw would, many years later, beautifully write, this play was written "for the actor as Handel wrote for the singer, setting him a combination of strokes which, however difficult some of them may be to execute finely, are familiar to all practiced actors as the strokes which experience has shown to be proper to the nature and capacity of the stage-player as a dramatic instrument."[31] This is exactly why critics believe that it provides magnificent opportunities for individual and ensemble playing. *The School for Scandal* is a perfect example of a highly theatrical play which flourishes when it is acted, not read. To this we should add that one of the ways in which Georgian theater functioned was that actors insisted on their own interpretation of the character in such a manner that they could show their own merits from the best possible way and gain as much applause as possible, which of course, was directly correlated with what they earned.

Yet, of course, each epoch or generation of spectators and critics saw in the play the reflection of the human nature of their own contemporaries. This opinion could be confirmed while reading various reviews collected in the casebook by Peter Davidson. The mastery of *The School for Scandal* lies, on the one hand, in its ability to adapt to new circumstances and interpretations and, on the other, in the universality of the satire of human vices: hypocrisy, villainy, and adultery. But, of course, such a reading might imply something that was not meant to be seen in the original performance. Some critics argue that the play was meant to have a

---

[26]   Christian Deelman, "The Original Cast of The School for Scandal," *Review of English Studies*, no. 13, August 1962, p. 263.

[27]   Auburn, "Theatre in the Age of Garrick and Sheridan," p. 27.

[28]   Deelman, "The Original Cast of The School for Scandal," p. 264.

[29]   Auburn, "Theatre in the Age of Garrick and Sheridan," p. 145.

[30]   Ibid.

[31]   George Bernard Shaw, "The Second Dating of Sheridan," in his *Dramatic Opinions and Essays*, vols. 1 2, New York: Brentano 1913, vol. 2, p. 34.

sentimental tone, while others insist that Sheridan wanted to write a high comedy of manners, which he failed to do because he accepted the morality of his time. If one wants to agree with the latter opinion, as the Auburn suggests, then one has to read *The School for Scandal* in a very specific manner, seeing "the foolishness of Sir Peter, a stereotypical old bachelor marrying a young and lusty wife, the physical implications of Lady Teazle's relationship with Joseph, the hearty but undisguised (i.e., 'natural') rakishness of Charles contrasted with the Tartuff-like (i.e., 'affected') hypocrisy of Joseph."[32] Yet, this interpretation leaves no room for satire, the exposing of the villainy and hypocrisy which is so obviously present in the play.

III. Kierkegaard on The School for Scandal

On December 15, 1846 in Copenhagen's most popular newspaper, the *Berlingske Tidende*, there appeared the following review of the performance of Sheridan's revived *The School for Scandal*:

> *The Theater*. Again one of the old English comedies has been put on stage to please the Danish audience, and the full house entirely confirms that the taste of the audience in every respect has not changed. Last night after a long break Sheridan's splendid comedy *The School for Scandal* was performed, and in every respect the given example proves that the performance without doubt will for some time remain in the repertoire of our theater. Mr. *Nielsen*'s Sir Peter Teazle is much superior to Frydendal's and can stand next to Schwartz's, and with that everything is said. We have never seen a better Lady Teazle; Mrs. *Heiberg* exceeded herself, so that we do not know which scene we should accentuate, for she was remarkable in all of them. Mr. *Holst* performed the role of Charles with good nature, jollity and humor, all the qualities that the role demands, however, without the smallest hint of exaggeration. Mad. *Nielsen* and Miss *Ryge* were splendid and Madam *Larcher* gave us a superb performance of a natural and amiable young girl. Mr. *Wiehe* performed his role excellently, which was also the case with Mr. *Rosenkilde, Schneider* and *Kragh*; to put it in a nutshell, everyone ensured that the performance was as complete and perfect as possible.[33]

The review strikes the reader as rather dim, lacking originality and beautifully avoiding the presentation of any opinion. It would not have been of any value to the contemporary reader if Kierkegaard had not decided to write a short satire on this piece. Kierkegaard's mocking review appears twice in his writings. Once it pops up in the "Writing Sampler" and another time in an abstract from his papers that is associated with an essay, "The Crisis and a Crisis in the Life of an Actress."

Since these are the only references to *The School for Scandal* in the whole of Kierkegaard's works, we are bound to conclude that Sheridan's plays or polemical, satirical, political writings had no direct influence on him. There is likewise no evidence that he was familiar with any other plays by Sheridan beyond *The School for Scandal*. Therefore, the only definite link between the two authors remains the theatrical performance itself. A keen theater-goer, the Danish philosopher attended

---

[32]   Auburn, *Sheridan's Comedies: Their Context and Achievements*, pp. 107–8.
[33]   See *Berlingske Tidende*, no. 292, December 15, 1846.

most of the events at Copenhagen's Royal Theater, showing great interest in both drama and opera. Obviously, he deeply admired several contemporary actors, including Johanne Luise Heiberg (1812–90) and Joachim Ludvig Phister (1807–96), to whom he devoted two short essays respectively: "The Crisis and a Crisis in the Life of an Actress" and "Phister as Captain Scipio." These works were intended to appear in a small collection of essays, which at first glance seems to be devoted to the theater stars of the day, but in fact the collection "would have centered on esthetic considerations and been an example of the compatibility of esthetic and religious interests in the stages of an individual's life."[34] It was supposed to be a so-called "mystification," which was intended to appear under a pseudonym with a name that in translation meant "the lucky one from St. Victor." We read in Kierkegaard's journal in 1847:

> I would like to create a little literary mystification by, for example, publishing something I would call "The Writings of a Young Man"; in the preface I would appear as a young author publishing his first book.
> I would call myself Felix de St. Vincent. The contents would include:
> 1. The Crisis in the Life of an Actress
> 2. A Eulogy on Autumn
> 3. Rosenkilde as Hummer
> 4. Writing Sampler[35]

Though Kierkegaard never finished this book, the first essay was published separately in *Fædrelandet*.[36] The "Writing Sampler" was drafted twice, as a sequel to Kierkegaard's satirical *Prefaces*. Written between 1844 and 1847, neither of the drafts was ever published during Kierkegaard's lifetime. "Considering a variety of pseudonyms before settling on 'A.B.C.D.E.F. Godthaab,' Kierkegaard first turned to this work shortly after the publication of *Prefaces*. Apparently seriously considering publication, he prepared a substantially altered fair copy sometime in the period 1845–47."[37] The "Writing Sampler" appears to be a collection of polemical works in which the Danish philosopher put even stronger emphasis on the satirical and ironical elements than he had done before in *Prefaces*. Today we find it rather difficult to understand the humor of *Prefaces* and the "Writing Sampler," because the books are filled with small details and cultural references to the life of Copenhagen of that period. As a part of these books a short review of *The School for Scandal* could be both representative and challenging:

> **The Theater**. Last evening Shakespeare's [*sic*] glorious masterpiece, *The School for Scandal*, was performed for the first time. For every connoisseur and patron of true classical poetry, it ought to be true classical pleasure to take part in so rare an artistic pleasure. It is another question whether it would not have been altogether proper for someone with a loving and artistic hand to have undertaken one or two little changes, so that at least one or two expressions shocking to a cultured public would have been

[34]   Todd W. Nichol, "Historical Introduction," in *WS*, p. xiv.
[35]   *SKS* 20, 225, NB2:217 / *JP* 5, 6060.
[36]   See "Historical Introduction," in *CD*, p. xv.
[37]   See "Historical Introduction," in *WS*, p. xiv.

omitted. But we do not wish to detract from this pleasure, but rather, in the name of the most esteemed public, to thank the directors of the theater for this rare pleasure while at the same time to take the liberty of suggesting that it produce a piece by Iffland as soon as possible.

As for the production, it was so excellent in every respect that it would be difficult to find its equal outside Copenhagen, at least not according to what the reviewer knows of scenic presentation in other cities. The reviewer recalls seeing the same piece produced in Corsør, but this performance was in no way a match for that of the Royal Theater.

Limited space unfortunately does not permit us to enter into profound or exhaustive evaluation of details; we will therefore be brief. Herr. Dir. Nielsen's performance as Sir Oliver Surface was masterful and far surpassed that of his predecessor in Corsør, Herr Rasmussen. Madame Nielsen's performance was also very good and Herr Phister as Snake was likewise excellent. But Fru Heiberg's mastery surpassed them all and every description. We would have to describe all that she did with the role if we were to give the reader a sense of the way in which she delivered her lines or of the lines she spoke. But since this would be too prolix, and moreover we do not have the script at hand, we will limit ourselves to transcribing from the *Berlingske Tidende*, which so admirably says, "We would have to transcribe the entire role if we were to give the reader a sense of the masterly performance by Herr Wiehe."[38]

The School for Scandal had been in the repertoire of the Danish Royal Theater since 1784. As Robert Neiiendam points out in the introduction to the Danish edition of the play, it is most likely that it came to Denmark via France or Germany, since during that period the country had only very loose ties with England.[39] However, there was a break in the staging of the performances between 1835 and 1846. Interestingly enough, during this break there appeared a new translation of the play by N.V. Dorph (1783–1858).[40] It was precisely this translation that Kierkegaard bought on January 11, 1847,[41] and it was the version used for the new performance that he saw around the same time. Peter Tudvad noted that it is likely the philosopher had attended "one of the four performances given in December or one of the two staged at the beginning of January."[42] Yet it seems most likely that he saw the first performance of the play given on December 14, which would explain the attention he paid to the review in *Berlingske Tidende* on December 15.

Kierkegaard's review starts with an outrageous mistake, where he names the author of *The School for Scandal* as Shakespeare. The purpose of such confusion could have been to stress the ignorance and to ridicule the poor knowledge and skills of the newspaper reviewers, for it is hard to believe that it was an innocent slip of a pen. If it was not on purpose, such a change could emphasize the hidden similarity in the perception of human nature by the English playwrights. Even though

[38]   *Pap.* VII–2 B 274, 6, pp. 322–3 / *WS*, 78–9.
[39]   Robert Neiiendam, "Omkring Bagtalelsens Skole," in Richard B. Sheridan, *Bagtalelsens Skole: Komedie i 11 Billeder*, trans. by N.V. Dorph, revised by Holger Rørdam and Edvin Tiemroth, Copenhagen: Carit Andersen 1945, p. 5.
[40]   Sheridan, *Bagtalelsens Skole. Comedie i fem Acter.*
[41]   Peter Tudvad, *Kierkegaards København*, Copenhagen: Politikens Forlag 2004, p. 274.
[42]   Ibid.

Shakespeare's comedies are not satirical, there is always present there an ironic turn of fortune similar to the Screen Scene when Lady Teazle is discovered. We can also see it the way Henry James did, when commenting in 1874 on how when one talks about "intellectual brilliancy on the English stage,"[43] one is most likely to end up mentioning the names of only two playwrights for the obvious reason: their plays are being continuously revived:

> There is Shakespeare, of course, but Shakespeare stands apart, and it never occurs to the critic to call him brilliant. We commend him in less familiar phrase. There are the old English comedies just mentioned....But for real intellectual effort, the literary atmosphere and the tone of society, there has long been nothing like *The School for Scandal.*[44]

Another confusing reference lies in the definition of the play as a perfect example of "classical poetry." The language of *The School for Scandal* is witty, full of similes and could be called "poetic," for in general Sheridan's language is highly eloquent, with numerous wordplays and exploitations of the ambiguities of the English language. However, the play is written in prose. The satirical mode of the review is also confirmed in a note made on the margins next to the name of the "Fru Heiberg," which says: "It could produce a droll effect if one called her Madam Heiberg instead of Fru."[45] This could be a pun which was hidden in the comparison with another famous actress of the time, Anna Nielsen, who although being married, insisted on being referred to as "madam" because as an actress she did not consider herself a person of rank. Johanne Luise Heiberg, on the contrary, due to her marriage with a professor changed her title to "Fru." Tudvad confirms that such a dismissal of the professor's wife might have indeed produced "a droll effect."[46]

Interestingly, Kierkegaard chose to mention in the review only some of the actors and characters. According to the *Berlingske Tidende*, Sir Peter Teazle[47] was played by Nicolai Peter Nielsen (1795–1860), a well-known Danish actor. Nielsen debuted in 1820, performing the main part in *Axel and Valborg*. In his youth he played a variety of roles from pirates to nobleman. Besides, at the start of his theatrical career he was frequently employed as a singer. His high base was especially good for parts that were not so demanding (he sang Leporello's part in *Don Giovanni*). Nielsen neglected any additional education required for an actor and relied primarily on his talent. At the time when Heiberg was a director, Nielsen was appointed as a drama director at the Royal Theater. But he was dismissed from his post in 1849, and it has been widely thought that he served as prototype for the character of an actor in Heiberg's "Soul after Death" published with *New Poems*.[48] According to

---

[43]   Henry James, *Essays on Art and Drama*, Scholar Press, 1996, p. 50; see also *Sheridan Comedies*, p. 144.
[44]   Ibid.
[45]   *Pap.* VII–2 B 274,6, p. 323 / *WS*, 79.
[46]   Tudvad, *Kierkegaards København*, p. 276.
[47]   The first Danish Sir Peter had been created by a famous actor Frederik Schwarz (1753–1838). He was familiar with English culture, and it was not by accident that he had chosen this part as his last role when the play was staged for the first time in 1810.
[48]   Johan Ludvig Heiberg, *Nye Digte*, Copenhagen: C.A. Reitzel 1841 (*ASKB* 1562).

Kierkegaard's review, Herr Nielsen performs Sir Oliver Surface. Such a discrepancy might serve as a hint towards the lack of professionalism of the Danish reviewers, but it could also suggest which characters the philosopher admired the most. For Kierkegaard, the role of Sir Oliver, a practical, sturdy man of common sense, free from any sort of sentiment could be more appealing than the kind-hearted and even naive, Sir Peter.

Nielsen's wife, the aforementioned Anna Helene Dorothea Nielsen (1803–56), was a member of the Royal Theater Company from 1821 until her death. A great favorite of the critics, she was able to combine her personal genius with the most diverse performance skills and was especially noted for her portrayal of women at various stages in their lives, such as Lady Macbeth, Donna Elvira in Mozart's *Don Juan*, Maria Stuart in the Schiller's play of the same title. She is remembered for creating a character of a mistress, so typical for Oehlenschläger's (1779–1850) plays. She came from a noble family, which gradually lost its fortune, a circumstance that without doubt made a tremendous impact on the development of her character. Later she was twice married, the first time with the violin player Friederich Torkildsen Wexschall (1798–1845), and the second with Nicolai Peter Nielsen. Anna's appearance was not intriguing. She was tall, with proud bearing, but her body retained undeveloped features of youth. Yet she glowed with inborn nobility, calmness, and femininity, the qualities which allowed her to reach out to the audience's hearts. She was a typical Nordic type, blonde with expressive blue eyes, the complete opposite of the dark-haired, Jewish Fru Heiberg. She had a captivating mezzo-soprano voice, perfectly suited for operas. She was the only actress who could compete with the talent of Johanne Luise Heiberg at that time. In addition to rivalry on stage, there was a rivalry between the Heibergs and the Nielsens, since the latter attempted to resist and change the conservative politics of Johan Ludvig Heiberg. Devoting herself entirely to performing, Anna was never concerned about the judgment of the audience. Due to the existence of Lehmann's painting, it is easy to visualize her being on stage. She stands with a slightly lowered head and glance that stressed the density of a highly dramatic scene. The picture recreates what Kierkegaard understood by "the essential femininity," as he wrote in 1845 in *Stages on Life's Way*. Here Kierkegaard claimed that Anna Nielsen's art of performing was hidden neither in her beauty nor in her voice or even in her erotic glow, but in her whole presence on stage.[49]

---

[49]   Klaus Neiiendam, *Romantikkens Teater i Danmark: Belyst gennem Edvard Lehmanns scenetegninger, Skuespil og ballet*, Copenhagen: Selskabet for Dansk Teaterhistorie 1994, p. 31. See also *SKS* 6 / *SLW*, 131: "The character she presents, but not immediately, the voice she uses so skillfully in the play, the inwardness that animates the interaction, the introverted absorption that makes the spectator feel so secure, the calmness with which she grips us, the authentic soulfulness that disdains all sham mannerism, the even, full sonority of mood that does not come in gusts, does not strain by coyly absenting itself, does not drift into wild ranting, does not pretentiously procrastinate, does not violently erupt, does not pant for the inexpressible, but is true to herself, is responsible to herself, always promptly at every moment and continually reliable—in short, her whole performance brings to a focus what could be called the essentially feminine."

Johanne Luise Heiberg was one of the actors whom Kierkegaard valued and praised most, which he proved by writing an essay devoted to her profession. "The Crisis and a Crisis in the Life of an Actress" is full of extraordinary intuitions and insights about the actors, their development during their careers and the way they are perceived. He talks about a metamorphosis which can happen only to the most talented actors, proving that their eminence originates from within and has very little to do with pure craft. As an example Kierkegaard describes the part of Juliet in *Romeo and Juliet*. He stresses, "in order to represent Juliet an actress must essentially have a distance in age from Juliet."[50] This role is particularly demanding because it requires from the actress the understanding of the complexity of feelings. To play this character is to overcome time. A young Juliet does not know what weight Shakespeare's Juliet must bear. Only a mature actress, through her inwardness, is able to produce an ideal, eternally unforgettable performance, since she is able dialectically to relate herself to Juliet. There are roles to which one has to mature.

One can say that the role of Lady Teazle required a maturity similar to the role of Juliet, since she is a mixture of purity and wit. Most of Lady Teazle's problems appear because of her excessive attachment to fashion and lack of insight into the inner nature of gossiping London society. Coming from the countryside, she is naive and naturally inexperienced. But we cannot call her cold-hearted or calculating. Fashion made a shrewish wife out of her and encouraged her to follow social clichés, but she did not realize the full meaning of her behavior and its moral inappropriateness before the Screen Scene. Even though she is associated with the company of those whose main pastime is plotting against each other, she is not fully aware of their devious nature. Lady Teazle is not experienced in the matters of love, but she would never allow herself to be seduced. There is no real sexuality in her relationship with Joseph, since they are "lovers not more than Fashion requires."[51] He is to her "a mere Platonic Cicisbeo—what every London wife is entitled to."[52] Johanne Luise Heiberg had a long relationship with the role of Lady Teazle. She was only 22 when she performed this part for the first time. The next time she impersonated the English Lady, she was 34 years of age. This is how Neiiendam describes her return:

> When Fru Heiberg had her comeback after the theater disputes in 1859, she preferred to appear in the role of Lady Teazle. It was a great night, and the city has been taken to such a degree that a new magazine *Illustreret Tidende* even used a picture of the performance—at that time something completely unknown in Danish journalism. Heiberg was not present at the performance, but at 8 p.m. a secretary sent the following message to him: "Your wife was, upon her entry, received with such tremendous amount of flowers and laurel wreaths that it surpassed all previous occasions. Your assistant has collected four big tightly filled baskets from all over the stage...."[53]

The character of Lady Teazle must have been captivating, for it is mentioned in the actress' memoirs. She writes, with years it seems to obtain "a new mental clothing

---

50   *SV1* X, 340 / *C*, 321.
51   Sheridan, *The School for Scandal*, p. 33.
52   Ibid.
53   Robert Neiiendam, "Omkring Bagtalelsens Skole," p. 7.

which was formed out of the reflections of my own soul."[54] The role had a number of personal undertones for Johanne Luise, who, upon her return, was able to add more flavor to the part by bringing personal experience from her life with her much older husband, Heiberg. The role is considered to be one of her greatest creations, and that is why it was a rather ungrateful task for Josephine Hortensia Eckardt (1839–1906) to recreate it in 1865 when she took over this part.

If Johanne Luise Heiberg was as captivating in *The School for Scandal* as portrayed by Lehmann,[55] it does not come as a surprise that Kierkegaard's attention was caught by her performance. Even in the satirical review he praises her skills, remembering with admiration her impersonation, where he also mentions his other favorite Herr Phister, who debuted in 1825. By his twenties he already had 119 of the most varied roles in his repertoire. In Sheridan's play, Phister appeared in a secondary, yet prominent role of Snake. As Joseph characterizes him: "that fellow hasn't virtue enough to be faithful even to his own villainy."[56] This role permitted Phister to engage his sparkling humor and sharp intelligence. Kierkegaard believed that Phister's greatest strength as an actor and comedian was "reflection,"[57] which he used not simply to study his role but to put extra weight into the recreation of the character in such a manner that it became "a thoroughly reflected totality."[58] He possessed an ability to dissect the role into single lines, giving new meaning to each and every one of them. Such effort and manner of performing require a special type of admiration, notes Kierkegaard, and it is not enough to say bravo, which is an immediate admiration. Reflective performance demands reflective admiration, because "the reflective performance is a pure consciousness; to admire in this case, therefore, is akin to undergoing an examination: whether one has understood or not, whether one knows anything or not."[59] This type of consciousness the philosopher called, among other things, "irony," an ability to open a paradox in every character and build comic relief on such discrepancies.

The last to be mentioned in the review is Herr Wiehe. This is a reference to one of the three Wiehe brothers, Michael, who was particularly interested in the role of Joseph Surface, for it was not a typical role of the romantic lover, and therefore it was rather refreshing for him to impersonate a hypocritical young fellow, a role for

---

54   Quoted from ibid.

55   Klaus Neiiendam, *Romantikkens Teater i Danmark: Belyst gennem Edvard Lehmanns scenetegninger, Skuespil og ballet,* p. 26: "Fru Heiberg dominates the picture with her feet in a beautiful second position. Her straw hat sits at a rakish angle on the back of her head, while her face is outlined by two long black braids. She is carrying a basket with flowers under her right arm and is reaching for a violet with her left hand. At the same time her upper body and head are declined slightly backwards to catch the glance of the on-duty officer of the Guards. Lehmann has captured the plastic and refined erotic element in Fru Heiberg's acting. On the stage it was subtlely emphasized by the romantic contrasts such as her dark hair with braids against her striking blue eyes."

56   Sheridan, *The School for Scandal,* p. 12.

57   *Pap.* IX B 68, p. 383 / *C,* Supplement, p. 329.

58   *Pap.* IX B 68, p. 385 / *C,* Supplement, p. 330.

59   *Pap.* IX B 68, p. 388 / *C,* Supplement, p. 333.

which he never lacked veneration. On May 30, 1864 Michael Wiehe gave his last performance, and it happened to be in *The School for Scandal.*

It is refreshing to read Kierkegaard's opinions on theatrical performances and the perfomances of the actors he appreciated most, since his reviews and essays express an untypical approach to theatrical art. He incorporates philosophical terminology into the presentation of the most valuable qualities and skills of various performers, building on paper almost intimate relationships with the prominent actors of his time. Even though the review of *The School for Scandal* does not have the mentioned depth of reflection, there is no doubt that the philosopher greatly admired the performance. Among its cast one can find the names of the most prominent and talented actors of the Golden Age.

Bibliography

I. Sheridan's Works in The Auction Catalogue *of Kierkegaard's Library*

Bagtalelsens Skole. Comedie i fem Acter, trans. by N.V. Dorph, Copenhagen n.p. 1841 (*ASKB* U 104).

II. Works in The Auction Catalogue *of Kierkegaard's Library that Discuss Sheridan*

[Becker, Karl Friedrich], *Karl Friedrich Beckers Verdenshistorie, omarbeidet af Johan Gottfried Woltmann*, vols. 1–12, trans. by J. Riise, Copenhagen: Fr. Brummer 1822–29, vol. 10, p. 289; vol. 11, p. 373 (*ASKB* 1972–1983).

III. Secondary Literature on Kierkegaard's Relation to Sheridan

Risum, Janne, "Towards Transparency: Søren Kierkegaard on Danish Actresses," in *Kierkegaard and his Contemporaries: The Culture of Golden Age Denmark*, ed. by Jon Stewart. Berlin and New York: Walter de Gruyter 2003 (*Kierkegaard Studies. Monograph Series*, vol. 10), pp. 330–42; see p. 336.
Tudvad, Peter, *Kierkegaards København*, Copenhagen: Politikens Forlag 2004, pp. 276–7.

Johan Herman Wessel:

Kierkegaard's Use of Wessel, or The Crazier the Better

Tonny Aagaard Olesen

> Everything that you desired from the favor of fate
> was to joke through the course of life.[1]

Kierkegaard has been called "the funniest man in Denmark"![2] If this is true, it must mean, according to Kierkegaard's own pseudonymous theory of the comic, which is developed in the *Concluding Unscientific Postscript* (1846), that he was also the most serious man. For, as he has Johannes Climacus emphasize, the greater the comical force, the deeper the seriousness, and vice versa: the truer the pathos, the more *vis comica*. One gladly grants him this elastic unity of reflection (comic) and ethical-religious pathos (seriousness).

There are certainly only a few authors who, like Kierkegaard, can reveal the fundamentally comic relation in this world's misfortunes, and only a few who, like him, can get the reader to tremble at the most intense address. There are only a few who are so infinitely witty, so thoroughly ironic, so comically offended—that is, sarcastic, satirical, polemical—but there are also only a few, who, like him, can grip the reader's heart with an almost naïve, credulous cheerfulness. On the other hand, there are also only a few, who can, like him, frighten a reader out of his or her wits with his unceasing demand for self-denial, with his almost Pietistic ethic of duty and melancholic disposition; but admittedly there are likewise not many who, after having demolished even the smallest bit of pride in the human constitution, can again build up the creation with a mild, affectionate, often entirely touching pathos.

Kierkegaard's character, or perhaps better, his author persona is entirely special with his inner distinction and subsequent dialectical intensification of the two basic moments: the comic and the pathetic. Kierkegaard's sense for the comic is acute due to the pathos it presupposes, and its pathos or elevated seriousness is precisely so

---

[1]   "*Alt hvad Du af Skjæbnens Gunst begjerte, / Var at spøge Livets Bane hen.*" From an anonymous elegy on occasion of Wessel's death with the title, "Ved en Vens Grav," printed in Rasmus Nyerup and Knud Lyne Rahbek, *Bidrag til en Udsigt over dansk Digtekunst under Christian VII*, Part 1, *Indbefattende Tidsrummet 1766–75*, Copenhagen: Jens Hostrup Schultz 1828, pp. 150–4; pp. 295–310, see p. 153 (*ASKB* 1389).

[2]   See Helge Hultberg, "Kierkegaard som humorist," *Kierkegaardiana*, vol. 14, 1988, pp. 49–56, see p. 49.

mature by always being purified in the comic reflection. This is the way things stand regarded ideally. The readers themselves must decide to what degree Kierkegaard lived up to this norm in praxis.

The history of literature, however, does not provide many examples of the Socratic demand that the same poet ought to write both tragedy and comedy. The two fundamental dialectical moments are seldom unified in a single person such that the same author wins fame both in the one and in the other literary genre. By contrast, there are great comic poets, just as there are poets whose elevated pathos has passed the test of history. Danish literature provides outstanding examples of this.

The father of modern Danish literature, Ludvig Holberg (1684-1754), thus made himself immortal through a number of comic works. It was—one can say—a classicistic comedy, which took pathetic (or ethical) legitimacy from the common sense of the Enlightenment. Among Holberg's contemporaries there was another poet, namely, the pastor and later bishop Hans Adolf Brorson (1694–1764), whose Pietistic psalms have shown a genuine durability. The age's Pietistic movement also captured King Christian VI, who soon after mounting the throne in 1730 outlawed the theater and thus the performance of Holberg's comedies. However, laughter could not be driven out with royal power. One should instead imagine the situation thus: Holberg's victorious comedy turned against Brorson's pathos, and Brorson's elevated seriousness turned against Holberg's laughter. It is this confrontation and unstoppable dialectic which comes together and fights its battle in the works of Kierkegaard. Therefore, it is not surprising that precisely Holberg is one of the most quoted Danish authors in Kierkegaard, while it is from Brorson's psalms, which Kierkegaard claims to know by heart, that he takes the text for his gravestone. If Kierkegaard thus has Holberg's sense for the comic, then this comic is first secured, that is, legitimized in Brorson's inward, Christian seriousness.

There are several analogies in the history of Danish literature. Strongly stamped by the Pietistic tradition and the new German *Sturm und Drang* poets, especially Klopstock, a worthy interpreter of the literary, heroic pathos appeared in the 1770s, namely, the son of a pastor, Johannes Ewald (1743–81). In spite of his short life, he stands as one of this period's great figures, a kind of Romantic genius, which Denmark had never had before. At the same time Holberg received a worthy successor, with respect to comedy, in the person who is called "Denmark's most indolent poet,"[3] namely, Johan Herman Wessel (1742–85). We shall return to him presently. This standing and in many ways productive opposition between Ewald and Wessel has for all times challenged every Dane's, including Kierkegaard's, sense for inner accommodation.

Before Wessel died, he himself managed to name the young Jens Baggesen (1764–1826) as the new king of comic poetry, since the latter had achieved great success with his *Comic Stories* (1785).[4] In the following decades Baggesen was undisputedly the country's greatest author, whose trademark was the playful wit of sentimentality. He was one of reflection's wittiest authors. Opposite him, Adam Oehlenschläger (1779–1850) appeared at the beginning of the 1800s, one of the

---

[3]   See Leif Ludwig Albertsen, "Kærlighed uden lægge," *Danske Studier*, 1969, p. 99.
[4]   Jens Baggesen, *Comiske Fortællinger*, Copenhagen: August Friderich Stein 1785.

greatest poets Denmark ever produced. With him literary Romanticism had arrived, and soon after he reigned as the sovereign king of poetry, who, just as Holberg had founded Danish comedy, now wanted to found Danish tragedy. There arose a great conflict between Baggensen and Oehlenschläger, a conflict, which, so to speak, divided the waters. It was called a conflict between the men of reflection and the followers of Oehlenschläger's immediate genius.

The tensions that lay in the Wessel–Ewald and Baggesen–Oehlenschläger oppositions were significant enough for literary controversies, but they were also productive for someone who wanted to unite the opposites. In these relations, however, it was exclusively a question of literary authors, which, with respect to Kierkegaard, not so much impeded the comic side (Wessel–Baggesen), which lay in the aesthetic ahead of time, as it undeniably took away from the pathetic side (Ewald–Oehlenschläger) the legitimacy to secure the ethical-religious pathos.

Kierkegaard as the dynamic unity of the acute, healthy common sense and the Pietistic-religious seriousness also finds a fitting analogy in his own time. In any case the early Kierkegaard, perhaps even up to 1848, could certainly be presented as a tense unity of Johan Ludvig Heiberg (1791–1860), with his certain aesthetic and comic reflection, and Bishop Jakob Peter Mynster (1775–1854), with his sensitive, orthodox seriousness. In any case, Kierkegaard was stamped in this way in the 1830s, but, as we know, after 1848 Heiberg and Mynster (and Hans Lassen Martensen) melted together with a Goethe-humanistic coterie in Kierkegaard's eyes. Nonetheless Mynster's sermons must be that which can best represent the ethical, pathos-filled moment since Brorson's psalms were, of course, themselves poetic products.

If after this general overview we turn to the comic tradition, then we find here a line: Holberg–Wessel–Baggesen–Heiberg. This was the literary canon that triumphed during the Heiberg period, especially in the 1830s when Kierkegaard received his literary schooling. Kierkegaard's affinity for this tradition is thus beyond doubt. They are the witty masters of reflection and possibly equals to Kierkegaard with respect to comic force. But where Professor Holberg had a great, unique personality, and where Professor Heiberg had an almost so famed, independent character, Baggesen was a more demonic individual, who, however, revealed himself in a powerful authorship of fiction and philosophy. There were three great authors, whose inner and outer lives virtually belonged to the reading public. This was not the case with Wessel. He was not a professor, not a philosopher, indeed, hardly an author, but more of a mystical figure. The great contrast between Wessel as the defender of refined taste, as his age saw him, and posterity's popular anecdotes,[5] in which he is presented as the always drunken entertainer with the crass joke, would not have been possible if one were concerned with Holberg, Baggesen or Heiberg.

---

[5]   See, for example, *Morsomme Historier af og om J.H. Wessel*, Copenhagen: Jul. Strandbergs Forlag [1879]. This kind of collection of anecdotes appeared in numerous editions throughout the 1800s.

I. Wessel's Life and Works

Johan Herman Wessel bore a hero's name. He was the grandson of the brother of the legendary naval hero Peter Wessel, also called Tordenskjold, whose noteworthy deeds put Johan's fate in relief. Indeed, in spite of his hero's name, Johan was anything but a man of action. While the popular anecdotes tell of Tordenskjold's heroic courage and cunning, about his military achievements and erotic conquests, the later anecdotes portray the poet as a loafer in the service of humor. Of the sea hero it is told—in an anecdote that Kierkegaard loved—that before taking a fortress he made the enemy believe that he had an extraordinarily large number of soldiers in his force. The enemy then sent a captain to see if it was true. Tordenskjold got the captain drunk and paraded in front of him marching soldiers, who were standing all down the street. Every time the captain had seen a full street, the troops marched over to another street, where they were shown to him again. The enemy, which was thus convinced of his superiority, immediately surrendered. While the naval hero Wessel was able to get so much out of so little, the fate of the poet Wessel seems to be just the opposite: he got far less out of much or nothing out of something. This also marks his rare sense for the comic.[6]

Johan Herman Wessel was a Norwegian, born in 1742 in Vestby parish south of Kristiania (Oslo). As early as his school years, he had as a boy shown an extraordinary talent for language, with which he would nourish himself for the rest of his life under precarious circumstances, but which also became the foundation for his poetic works. In 1761 he traveled, like to many of those his age, to Copenhagen to study at the university. He passed the first year examinations with an excellent result, but he never really got started with an actual course of studies for a profession. As far as we know, he instead used his time to study English and French, immersing himself in the literature of the age, while he also cultivated the free life of a student. In a way he remained a *studiosus* throughout his life, not in the sense of endlessly immersing himself in the field of science but as someone with a kind student disposition, whose cheerfulness or humor, freedom from duty and responsibility, virtually became his trademark.

In 1772 the hardly 30-year old Wessel became famous with a single blow. He published his debut work, the comic tragedy *Love without Stockings*,[7] which recalled the comic spirit of the unreachable Holberg. The piece, which was a great success, has ever since been regarded as a masterpiece of Danish literature. What is odd is that, according to contemporary witnesses, Wessel did not write the work with an eye

---

[6]   A further comparision of Tordenskjold and Johan Herman Wessel is found in the conclusion to "Om Wessels Levnet og Skrifter" (1832), in *Johan Herman Wessels samlede Digte*, 3rd ed., Copenhagen: Otto B. Wroblewskys Forlag 1861, pp. 71–2.

[7]   Johan Herman Wessel, *Kierlighed uden Strømper: Et Sørge-Spil i 5 Optog*, Copenhagen: Det Kongelige Universitets-Bogtrykkerie 1772; for translations, see *Der Bräutigam ohne Strümpfe. Ein Trauerspiel in fünf Acten von Johann Hermann Wessel. Aus dem Dänischen übersetzt von Anton Martini*, Copenhagen: Friedrich Brummer 1827; J.H. Wessel, *Gedichte*, Itzehoe: Schönfeldt 1827; *L'amant sans bas. Tragedie. D'apres "Kjerlighed uden Strömper"* de Wessel, par h. de. B. [sc Buchwald], Kiel: C.F. Mohr 1838; *Lieb' ohne Strümpfe. Tragi-Comödie, frei nach Joh. Heinr. Wessel von Ad. Oehlenschläger*, Leipzig: Ernst Fleischer 1844.

towards publication, and only after his friends' animated persuasion along with his own need for money did he let it be printed.[8] It first appeared anonymously (1772), and then again anonymously (1774), and then finally the third time with Wessel's name on the title page (1776). It is strange that Wessel did not use the opportunity to assert himself as an author. It seems as if the event was merely something that happened to him. As far as we know, he earned no money from his masterpiece and never converted his fame into a secure existence. By the same token he was rewarded with the great expectations of those who surrounded him, a reward which he presumably would have liked to do without.

In 1772 The Norwegian Society was established—a literary club, which Wessel became the focus of for posterity. To use Oehlenschläger's oft quoted words: he was "the flower and the crown of its cheerfulness and mood."[9] This collection of cultivated Norwegians conceived of itself as the bulwark of classic and French aesthetics against the German influence of Klopstock and Ewald. They met over a glass of wine or punch and competed for the best improvised occasional poem on a given rhyme or theme. The verses were recorded in the society's verse proceedings, in which several of the poems which came to constitute Wessel's humble authorship were originally conceived.[10] From 1774 the society began to hold prize competitions, and the results were published, together with other material, in three *Poetic Collections* (1775, 1783, and 1793), of which the first contains two "serious" poems by Wessel, the didactic poem "Moderation" [*"Nøisomhed"*] and the poem "The Sleep" [*"Søvnen"*].[11] Finally, in the society whose members cultivated the ambition of creating a drama in the serious style, that is, where the Norwegian father Holberg had founded the national comedy, one now wanted to create a corresponding tragedy. Several of the society's members were influential in this ambition, but the works they delivered soon became a matter of only historical interest. We know only a little about Wessel's views on these pieces. Without Wessel, they would certainly be forgotten. Kierkegaard presumably did not know them.

Wessel's production is not impressive with regard to its volume. In 1776 he published the comedy *Happiness is better than Reason*,[12] but it disappointed expectations. The same is true of the next and last of his dramatic works, the play *Anno 7603*,[13] which appeared a few months before his death in 1785. One of the causes of the lack of comic force in this work is probably that Wessel used prose and not verse. Wessel's comedy is straightforwardly founded on versification, on the

---

[8]   See the explanatory notes by Christen Pram on Wessel's "Elegie ved Wessels Grav" (1786), in which there are a number of biographical pieces of information which since then have been handed down orally from one person to another. The elegy with the notes is printed in *Johan Herman Wessels Udvalgte Digte*, Copenhagen: Seidelin 1801, see pp. XVIII–XIX.

[9]   See Adam Oehlenschläger, "Om Evalds Liv og Værker," *Athene*, vol. 1, 1813, p. 308. See also Flemming Conrad, *Om Smagen og det nationale,* Copenhagen: Museum Tusculanum, 1996, p. 408, note 37.

[10]   On the basis of the surviving copies, there was also published *Det Norske Selskabs Vers-Protokol*, Oslo: Norske Selskab 1935.

[11]   Later collected and printed in Oslo: Norske Selskab 1922.

[12]   Johan Herman Wessel, *Lykken bedre end Forstanden*, Copenhagen: P. Horrebow 1776.

[13]   Johan Herman Wessel, *Anno 7603*, Copenhagen: P. Horrebow 1785.

portentous verse feet and striking rhymes. In fact, the disappointment about Wessel's last two dramatic works was so great that people did not want to count them as belonging to his authorship. In the numerous editions of Wessel's collected writings, which continue right up until our times, they are—with only a few exceptions—not even included! Kierkegaard presumably did not know them either.

We do not know why Wessel never again reached the heights of his debut work. The reason is probably to be found in his personal circumstances, which we, however, know very little about. We believe, however, that Wessel in 1776 became ill with a painful disease in his teeth and jaw. Contemporary witnesses tell that he was bedridden for a year and a half on this occasion and that after this event he never regained his good humor. We cannot know whether this is true. However, there is much that indicates that it was not so much a sudden reversal in Wessel's disposition but rather a gradually increasing despair about his own situation. He did not live up to people's expectations, and his work conditions were not the best. It was later to the great indignation of Wessel's friends that such a genius was obliged to earn a living by means of the most tiring private tutoring in language at an elementary level. They believed that the state should—as it had on so many occasions both before and since—support the genius with a fixed stipend. When this is said in this way, one ought, however, not claim—as many have done—that Wessel's supply of comedy was exhausted. In the following years he wrote (if he did not have them lying in his drawer from an earlier period) several of his almost classic short stories, which—admittedly—have been judged very differently, most often negatively, by the professors of later times. However, they were popular, widely disseminated, and learned by heart like nothing else from the period.

From 1774 until his death Wessel translated seven agile French *Singspiele*. In 1779 he was appointed as translator for the Royal Theater and thus had a prospect of a stable income if he could deliver three translations per year. But Wessel was not like Johan Ludvig Heiberg, who a half century later received a similar appointment, which he used to create one success after the next. Wessel was not successful in this. His productivity was too small; indeed, he only managed to translate three pieces in this position. We do not know the reasons for this. At 38 years of age, he got married in 1780, but this marriage was not happy. He had a son, however, whom he loved dearly. Perhaps it was this relation that came to expression after Wessel's death, when his friends organized a large collection, not for his wife, who was never mentioned, but for his son!

In 1784 Wessel finally published an entertaining weekly journal with the title *Votre Serviteur. Otiosis*, that is, "Your Servant for Leisure Hours." It consisted of Wessel's own comic stories, with six short pages per issue, and it immediately created a stir. The first five issues had to be quickly reprinted, but in the interim it looked as if Wessel had become exhausted. We do not know if this was due to the fact that he ran dry of poems, which he had left over from an earlier time, or if he no longer could or wanted to keep up the pace of publication. The weekly stopped a year later, with Wessel having published 54 issues. He died in 1785 at the age of 43. Even if he lived a half a year longer than Kierkegaard, he only managed to produce a fraction of works in comparison to him. Wessel never found an idea for which he could live or die.

Wessel's authorship, or rather the texts that survive from him, can easily fit into a single volume. In Kierkegaard's time it consisted of the comic tragedy, *Love without Stockings*, the roughly 40 comic stories in verse, and finally a series of lesser miscellaneous poems, epigrams, impromptu compositions, fragments, epitaphs, all for the most part improvised *pièces d'occasion*. It was Wessel's three friends, Peter Johan Monrad (1758–1834), Jens Baggesen, and Christen Pram (1756–1821), who collected Wessel's many, often unpublished short verses, and it was they who judged how much should be included in the first edition of Wessel's *Collected Writings* from 1787.[14] In the preface the editors explain that they have not included a biography of the author since the three friends felt that they would be criticized for being prejudiced in Wessel's favor. They therefore left it to unbiased posterity to write such a biography, and added mysteriously that this posterity "as far as we are able, will not be lacking in data, although it perhaps will not be in print, and although it will not be given here."[15]

Ten years later an anonymous article by Hans Christian Ørsted (1777–1851) appeared with the title "Attempt at a Portrayal of the Poetic Character of Johan Herman Wessel," in which it is argued that no Danish author has contributed more to the ennoblement of taste and morality than Wessel.[16] One also finds a trace of this positive Wessel portrait, which is not built up from empirical data but rather pieced together through a reading of the works, in the next Wessel editor, Knud Lyhne Rahbek (1760–1830). Even if his introduction was substantially enlarged every time he edited the *Collected Writings*,[17] to the end he shies away from providing an actual biography, while his general observations on the poems virtually swell to a monograph. In the preface to Wessel's *Selected Poems* from 1801,[18] he had declared that he had nothing to say about Wessel's "person, circumstances and works," which was not already said better in Pram's elegy at the grave of the poet.[19] In 1828 Rahbek's colleague Rasmus Nyerup (1759–1829), who had only met Wessel a few times, had been given the task of writing Wessel's biography. However, he refers to the fact that the first editors' "necessary data" had never appeared, and that the best person to deliver a surrogate for this data was Rahbek.[20] Thus, he never got started, while the historical Wessel became more and more mysterious. The first person to address this problem was Adolph Engelbert Boye (1784–1851), whose edition from 1832 set

---

[14]   *Johan Herman Wessels samtlige Skrivter*, vols. 1–2, ed. by P.J. Monrad, Jens Baggesen, and C. Pram Copenhagen: Abraham Soldins Forlag 1787.

[15]   See ibid., vol. 1, [p. 8].

[16]   Hans Christian Ørsted, "Forsøg til en Skildring af Johan Herman Wessels digteriske Karakter." The article was printed under the signature "..st..," in the journal *Mennesket. En Journal af blandet Indhold*, ed. by P.P. Hempel & Komp., [Odense] 1797, pp. 73–101; see especially pp. 99ff.

[17]   *Johan Herman Wessels samtlige Skrivter*, vols. 1–3, ed. by Knud Lyhne Rahbek, 2nd ed., Copenhagen: Abraham Soldins Forlag 1799–1800 (3rd ed., Abraham Soldins Forlag 1817).

[18]   Johan Herman Wessel, *Udvalgte Digte*, foreword by K.L. Rahbek, Copenhagen: K.H. Seidelin 1801.

[19]   Ibid., p. IV.

[20]   Nyerup and Rahbek, *Bidrag til en Udsigt over den danske Digterkunst*, p. 151.

new standards.[21] Boye delivered an extensive account of Wessel's life, established the texts with new philological mysteriousness and wrote elucidating commentaries to the texts. This is the edition which Kierkegaard research generally uses.

By 1855, when Kierkegaard died, Wessel's collected writings had appeared in a dozen editions, each of which was often reprinted in new revised printings. In 1848–50 there appeared an edition by Peder Ludvig Møller (1814–65) with sketches by Peter Christian Klæstrup (1820–82). As Møller was one of Kierkegaard's opponents during the conflict with *The Corsair*, Kierkegaard presumably did not want to touch this edition with a ten-foot pole.[22] In 1862, some years after Kierkegaard's death, his competent secretary, the linguist Israel Levin (1810–83), published a new edition, which in ever new, revised versions, has become the standard edition that is used to this very day. It is strange that there was no edition of Wessel's writings in the private library that Kierkegaard left behind. It seems entirely absurd to imagine that Kierkegaard never owned such an edition.

II. Love without Stockings

Wessel's main work is, as noted, *Love without Stockings*.[23] In 1842, P.L. Møller wrote an article about Wessel, in which one reads:

> Without doubt many people have had the same experience as I, namely, that at an early age we read *Love without Stockings* and later, due to such an acquired familiarity with the poem, the frequent discussion of and quotation from it in oral conversations, did not find occasion to renew our familiarity with the work itself. But I also believe that most people will experience the same thing as I did, when they, as I have done in these days, take down and reread the work after a significant passage of time. I was genuinely struck by the wonderful power with which it captivated me, indeed, sweep me off my feet while reading; so fresh and charming so everlastingly comical is the hilarity which once let this poem fall like a ripe fruit from the tree.[24]

Even if Kierkegaard did not like P.L. Møller, one can imagine that he nevertheless had a similar relation to Wessel's comic tragedy. He read it in his youth, perhaps

---

[21]   Johan Herman Wessel, *Samlede Digte*, ed. by A.E. Boye, Copenhagen: C.A. Reitzel 1832 (2nd ed., Copenhagen: C.A. Reitzel 1845; 3rd ed., Copenhagen: C.A. Reitzel 1861).
[22]   See, for example, how Kierkegaard immediately sent P.L. Møller's *Kritiske Skizzer fra Aarene 1840-47*, Copenhagen: P.G. Philipsen 1847 back to the bookstore. Cf. *SKS* 20, 266, NB3:41 / *JP* 6, 6080.
[23]   See Alexandra Bänsch: "Wessels *Kærlighed uden Strømper:* ein progressiver Rückfall," *Skandinavistik. Zeitschrift für Sprache, Literatur und Kultur der nordischen Länder*, 1992, no. 2, pp. 107–21; James Massengale: "Johan Herman Wessel," in *Danish Writers from the Reformation to Decadence, 1550–1900*, ed. by Marianne Stecher-Hansen, Farmington Hills, Michigan: Thomson Gale 2004 (*Dictionary of Literary Biography*, vol. 300), pp. 477–84; P.M. Mitchell, *A History of Danish Literature*, 2nd ed., New York: The American-Scandinavian Foundation 1971, p. 97; *A History of Danish Literature*, ed. by Sven H. Rossel, Lincoln and London: University of Nebraska Press 1992, pp. 151–2.
[24]   See P.L. Møller, "Johan Herman Wessel," *Figaro. Journal for Literatur, Kunst og Musik*, 1842, vol. 1, pp. 91–6; pp. 111–20; pp. 205–13; pp. 217–24; see p. 92.

even learned it by heart in order later to reproduce it for renewed pleasure. In his youth he could also have seen it performed at the Royal Theater, where it played 57 times until 1830, and after this six times until January 19, 1833, and once at a summer performance on June 3, 1847. In the following we will present the positive testimony about Kierkegaard's relation to Wessel's masterpiece.

Love without Stockings calls itself a tragedy, which it also is with respect to its form. According to its content, it is, however, a parody or a travesty on a tragedy or, more generally, on heroically stilted pathos. The piece was organized following the stiff rules of French tragedy about the unity of time, place, and action, about the choice of hero and villain, about the main characters and the supporting characters (the confidants). It follows the pompous versification (the elegant, rhyming Alexandrians), the proverb-like diction, the courteous form of address, and the antithetical reasoning in the portrayal of the struggle in the soul of the hero. Precisely in the contrast between this beautiful form and the everyday content, the base motifs, the laughable driving force of the plot, etc., arose the almost unmanageable comical power of the piece.[25] It is a refined comedy of bad timing. And since the piece itself is conscious of these contrasts, and the characters gradually step more and more out of their roles in order to comment upon the form, the whole thing ends in a kind of higher madness.

In itself the piece remains a comic work, which does not presuppose any specific knowledge of other concrete works.[26] However, indirectly it can be considered a parody. It is not only French tragedy (the tradition running through Corneille, Racine, and Voltaire) and its Danish-Norwegian epigones, which are indirectly parodied, and not only the bombastic German *Schwärmerei* (the heroic, *schwärmerish* Klopstock tradition), which is indirectly ridiculed, but the Italian opera (the Pieto Metastasio tradition) likewise does not escape unscathed. New music was composed for *Love without Stockings*, when the piece was to be performed at the Royal Theater. The composer Paolo Scalabrini (1713–1803), who, although having worked in Denmark for 25 years and having composed music for a half dozen operas, had to suffer the irony of fate of being remembered only for *Love without Stockings*. It is, however, a question of whether the half dozen arias and duets, which play a significant role in the performance of the piece, in spite of the comic deployments and the humorous content, have gained anything with the help of the packaging of them as serious opera. Professor Rahbek, who saw the first performances, was among those who did not think so.[27] Perhaps one could go further and ask whether the piece needed to be performed at all. Just as the piece can be read without knowledge of the literature

[25]   See, for example, C.A. Thortsen, *Historisk Udsigt over den danske Litteratur indtil Aar 1814*, Copenhagen: C.A. Reitzel 1846 [1839, *ASKB* 970], pp. 109–11.
[26]   An excellent account of the piece's intertextual aspect is found in Fr. Orluf's treatise "Wessel og Poul Møller," *Danske Studier*, 1940, pp. 59–95.
[27]   See K.L. Rahbek, "Fortale til nærværende Udgave," in *Johan Herman Wessels samtlige Skrivter*, 3rd ed., 1817, vol. 1, pp. VII–VIII. In opposition to Rahbek's downplaying of the music stands A.E. Boye. See Boye's introduction, "Om Wessels Levnet og Skrifter," in Wessel, *Samlede Digte*, 3rd ed., 1861, pp. 10ff.

which is being parodied, so also can it to a large extent be *read*—without music or theater.

Let us now briefly give an account of the plot of the piece, in the course of which we will frequently insert references to the work that appear in Kierkegaard's writings.

The curtain rises! The heroine of the piece, Grete, wakes up on her chair from a horrible daydream: "You will never marry, if it does not happen today!" (Act I, Scene 1). She reveals her mental anguish in a despairing monologue, where she tells that her fiancé, the tailor Johan von Ehrenpreis, has not returned from a journey, where he was supposed to mend a pair of trousers for a major. What unforgivable infidelity! Then her confidante, Mette, appears. She tries in vain to tackle her heroine, but then she hits upon the idea that Grete should instead marry her rejected suitor, Mads. The man-hunting Grete now regards heroically such a marriage as a blow from fate. Mads appears and is told of his good fortune. He hastens "galloping" home for his wedding clothes, after which Grete expresses her resignation in an aria.

The second act begins at the home of Mads, who breaks out in song and "shouts with joy." He tells his friend, Jesper, what has happened. Grete struggles heroically with frightened premonitions, which Mette attempts to drive away. There is a knock at the door, and in comes Johan. The reunion of the lovers is exuberant. They exchange compliments with each other in good style until Grete tells him that they must get married on that very day. Then Johan turns pale, became he does not own the obligatory knee stockings. Grete faints, is revived, and orders that they be married on that day, even if Johan has to wear boots! The hero breaks out in a monologue that reveals how he is caught in a tragic conflict: either to obey honor or to follow the god of love. If he shows up in boots, then he will be condemned to laughter. According to the age's codex of heroes, one demonstrated one's manhood by means of one's strutting legs. Since Johan's legs are as thin as straw, people would have to believe that he was not only concerned with the lack of stockings but also with obtaining some suitable filler. We know the frightening scenario—thin legs planted in the middle of long boots—from *The Corsair*'s caricature of Kierkegaard. The artist, Peter Klæstrup, was, as noted above, the Wessel illustrator of the day.

The third act is introduced with a despairing monologue by Mads, who has been transported from heaven to hell. Jesper is accused of mocking the hurt Mads, who draws a knife in order to kill him. Jesper, however, has good news. They will confront Grete with the shameful fact that she will marry a man without stockings. Immediately Mads' spirits are raised, and he sings an aria about the fire of love in his heart and about how everyone who sees the smoke—"the smoke is my aria"—must be assured about how hot it is inside him. It is this song, or this safety valve against overheating that Constantin has in mind in "*in vino veritas*," where the mechanism is transferred to a woman, which should, indeed, be regarded as a joke.[28] Now Mads meets with Mette: he asks for an audience with the heroine, since she cannot marry someone without stockings. Mette, by contrast, asks Mads to borrow a pair of stockings, a proposal which he straightforwardly rejects. The heroine becomes perplexed.

---

[28]   See *SKS* 6, 54, lines 28–33 / *SLW*, p. 52.

The madness picks up steam in the final two acts. Gradually the characters relate not only to *what* is happening and being said but also to *how* it happens or should happen. It seems especially to be these final acts with a more pronounced "dramatic irony"[29] which Kierkegaard enjoyed. In any case we have several references to them from Kierkegaard's hand.

One of these is a reference to the beginning of the fourth act, where Mette suggests to Johan that he steal a pair of stockings from Mads. She expects the hero's reaction, which falls short in relation to the heroic standard. Johan assumes a genuinely tragic posture and expresses his inward division between virtue (which "is my life") and love ("my favorite"). He expresses himself with the heroic lines: "I am otherwise accustomed to depart where there is a fight, but I carry those fighting with me in my heart" (Act IV, Scene 1). He can neither flee nor reconcile the split, but must choose. When Johannes Climacus in the *Postscript* invokes Wessel's words by wanting to keep out of the speculative "jostling crowds,"[30] that is, fight, then he could well have quoted the rest of Johan's line. Certainly, it is a question of choosing, even if we hear it from the mouth of Johan von Ehrenpreis! Oddly, this Wessel reference in Kierkegaard has since been used to characterize Wessel as an isolated genius.[31]

After his excellent hero monologue, Johan gets permission to leave, since Mette is to sing an aria about the frightening premonitions that are haunting her. Johan, however, immediately returns with a pair of stockings, which he has stolen from

---

[29]   It is this relation that Christian Molbech refers to in the following characterization of the piece: "The goal of the poet—to amuse by means of an absolute comic contrast between the parodied pompous form and the laughable in the everyday nature of the material, between the characters' triviality and cothurni, which they put on along with the tragic mask, which is so ill-suited to their faces that they themselves feel and express it—is completely achieved; but the piece is also with more refined art raised above the usual parodies due to the fact that in a way a *double* comedy is being played out: the characters are not only really ironic; they are not merely travestied heroes who are presented with dramatic objectivity for the audience; but they have themselves, so to speak, a kind of consciousness about the irony that the poet has placed in the piece. They feel the laughable in their tragic role; for a moment they step out of it with subjective reflections and remarks, and do so by means of these, and sometimes by means of an uttered hint that they, so to speak, cannot completely manage in their mask character, even more, that they do not exist *seriously* but only as *ironic characters*," Christian Molbech, *Dansk poetisk Anthologie, eller Udvalg af danske og norske lyriske Digteres Arbeider, efter Tidsfølgen, og ledsaget med biographisk-kritiske Efterretninger*, vols. 1–3, Copenhagen: C.A. Reitzel 1830–40, vol. 1, pp. 264–92; p. 273. H.C. Ørsted had already in 1797 emphasized this innovation by Wessel, "to let the characters comment upon their ways of acting in order to determine if they fit with the tragic hero or not"; cf. Ørsted, "Forsøg til en Skildring af Johan Herman Wessels digteriske Karakter," p. 82.

[30]   See *SKS* 7, 34, line 27 / *CUP1*, 27.

[31]   See N.M. Petersen, *Bidrag til den danske Literaturs Historie*, vols. 1–5, ed. by C.E. Secher 2nd ed., Copenhagen: Wøldikes Forlag 1867–72, vol. 5, p. 317: "Søren Kierkegaard says (in the *Concluding Postscript*): 'Wessel has said that he stays out of jostling crowds'; this would also befall him after death; he stands alone, outside all jostling in accordance with immortality. This is what Kierkegaard calls 'the melancholy of the distinction of genius,' and 'it cannot be made into a paradigm'; there is no pattern of conjugation, it is the sole exception that is itself the highest rule. We know of no greater praise," p. 317.

Mad's chest. He attempts to explain away the improbable leap in time—since he had already stolen the stockings—by remarking that heroes are not slaves of time like "cobblers and tailors." He falters but is immediately supported by Mette: "Finish what you have to say; be not ashamed of it" (Act IV, Scene 3). A tailor, who is a hero, is namely no longer a tailor, she reasons, since one only needs to use one's highest title. When Martensen, during the attack on the church, came to respond in *Berlingske Tidende,* he claimed, among other things, that Kierkegaard sought Christ "in private rooms."[32] In a draft to a polemical rejoinder Kierkegaard pauses at this statement: What does it mean? "It practically says: 'You S. Kierkegaard, you poor, wretched, mediocre man, you have only a private Christianity, you have a private religion; you have'—I beg Your Reverence, 'Finish what you have to say; be not ashamed of it'....so, out with it; is it not true that I have no official Christianity no royally privileged Christianity, that I am a nonunion Christian?"[33] Here one sees Wessel's refinement can be used elegantly in a new context.

While we wait for our hero to put on his stockings, we follow a conversation between Grete and Mette. The heroine makes a sublime speech in excellent Alexandrine feet about how she cannot escape grief; it always follows her, even into the dining room, where she is accustomed to seek consolation for all complaints, so she both received the smoked pork and grief stuck in her throat. Then follows the great culminating scene (Act IV, Scene 5), where the hero, Johan, appears dressed in stockings. Grete, who feels "doubt, hope and fear and joy," turns to Mette: "Where did he get the stockings?" Then to Johan: "I have a doubt!" At which Mette says to Johan: "Answer her like a hero in the grand style!" Now Grete again asks Johan where he got the stockings from. When Martensen in the summer of 1854 published his sermon on the deceased Bishop Mynster, the editor Mendel Levin Nathanson (1780–1868) reviewed the sermon in his paper, *Berlingske Tidende*, with great praise.[34] This got Kierkegaard to go to the inkwell to write up a polemic, which was never printed. He notes how Martensen since he has become bishop has apparently advanced in Nathanson's eyes, a fact which is directly reflected in the treatise: "Read this review. There you see what merchant N. is able to do—the finest and most delicate butter—it is the genuine grand style, the kind Mette speaks of when she says to Johan v. Ehrenpreis: Speak in grand style."[35] One must confess that the editor's stylistic pathos does have a comic touch.

Johan answers the question in heroic style by avoiding it. First he goes on the attack: if anyone other than precisely the heroine had raised the question, the person would have to die. Then he goes on the defensive: how can a heroine think so badly of a hero? Finally, he tries a new tack, where he shows his hurt feelings at the unheard of insult to his honor of being accused of theft: "At Easter I let my head be shaved, /

---

[32]   H.L. Martensen, "I Anledning af Dr. S. Kierkegaards Artikel i *Fædrelandet* Nr. 295," *Berlingske Tidende*, no. 302, 28 December, 1854.
[33]   *Pap.* XI–3 B 89, p. 139 / *M*, Supplement, p. 502.
[34]   Anonymous [Mendel Levin Nathanson], "*Bispevielse i Frue Kirke* paa anden Pindsedag, den 5te Juni 1854. Reitzels Bo og Arvinger," *Berlingske Tidende*, no. 141, June 21, 1854.
[35]   *SKS* 25, 351-2, NB29:93 / *JP* 6, 6874.

The stubble left over in fear is raised, / And my wig an inch from its place does lift, / Who worries not at being called a thief" (Act IV, Scene 5). How can a man with the hero's name Johan von Ehrenpreis commit theft? It is a self-contradiction, according to Johan's argument. This is followed by an appeal to sympathy, since he, while he was an apprentice, was called an ass by his master, but never had anyone dared to call him a thief. Then he stops: "Are you crying, Grete?" She answers, "No!" But Grete nonetheless cries out of joy for this heroic speech, after which they get ready for the wedding. When the young Kierkegaard in Heiberg's journal was locked in a polemic with *Kjøbenhavnsposten*, a wit wrote the *Humoristiske Intelligensblade,* in which all the parties in the conflict were made to look ridiculous. In his response to this satirical attack, which was never printed, Kierkegaard makes use of the above quoted four lines from Johan's defense against the insult to honor, in that he replaces "thief" with "sophist."³⁶ Kierkegaard here used Wessel to get laughter on his side, just as incidentally the *Humoristiske Intelligensblade* had also made use of Wessel.

The final act of the piece begins with Mads and Jesper. They have heard the report that Johan has arrived with a pair of stockings. Mads gets ready to kill himself with a knife. But, Jesper asks, where did Johan get the stockings? And then they begin, as a last chance, to look into the contents of Mads' chest, which happens accompanied by a beautiful duet. In a journal entry from 1854 Kierkegaard remarks, "if one were to search thoroughly the consciences of the countless mass, one would probably begin to feel like a person rooting around in an ancient chest full of all kinds of trifles, as in that trunk in the play, *Love without Stockings*."³⁷ Now Mads and Jesper go through a longer list, and ultimately discover that there is a pair of white stockings missing, "into which Grete has previously sewn my name with silk." Mads wants to rise up against his hated rival.

For the hero and the heroine everything is merry until Grete suddenly has a cruel premonition. Mette appears immediately to warn the heroine that she, with two premonitions in one day, "oversteps the strict law of heroines" (Act V, Scene 4). Nonetheless they agree that the new premonition and the earlier dream are due to the fact that Grete ate herring, peas, and pork. In Quidam's diary " 'Guilty?'/ 'Not Guilty?' " we are reminded of these dreams, which have the same cause as Grete's.³⁸ And we approach now the grand finale.

Mads appears: "Madam, there stands a thief," to which Grete responds: "There stands a hero, traitor." Mads: "I say now as before, Madam, there stands a tailor" (Act V, Scene 5). We also find this exchange in the young Kierkegaard in his polemic against *Kjøbenhavnsposten:* "The energetic reforming spirit going through *Kjøbenhavnsposten* has now been spoken about for a long time, but I must admit I have never yet been able to find it, and should *Kjøbenhavnsposten* continue with 'Mette' to maintain 'there stands a hero, traitor,' then I say as before, 'Madam, there stands a tailor.' "³⁹ One notes how Kierkegaard here assumes the position of the

---

³⁶   *SKS* 17, 38, AA:21 / *KJN* 1, 32.
³⁷   *SKS* 26, 181, NB32:92 / *JP* 3, 3362.
³⁸   *Stages on Life's Way*, in *SKS* 6, 299 / *SLW*, 321.
³⁹   See "Kjøbenhavnspostens Morgenbetragtninger i Nr. 43," *Kjøbenhavns flyvende Post, Interimsblad*, no. 76, February 18, 1836 / *EPW*, 10.

villain, Mads, which was also the correct one in this context. But it shows how Wessel's piece could be used almost anywhere. That Kierkegaard has come to exchange Mette for Grete one can interpret as one wants.

Mads begins to mock Grete, who wants to marry a thief. However, he is prevented from saying his piece by the hard-pressed hero. If Grete would just listen to him, Mads swears, he promises never to say another word: "May the golden peas in my hungry mouth turn to stone" (Act V, Scene 5). With this oath, Grete becomes so afraid that he has Mette go to fetch pork and peas, so she, so to speak, can get back on her feet again. In the final scene (Act V, Scene 7) we meet this mad tableau: Mads reminds Grete, who is energetically eating peas, of the white stocking which she once gave him with insewn initials. These are the stockings that Johan is wearing. Grete faints and asks someone to take the bowl with the peas. This grips the hungry Mads, who now eats away, while Grete again is revived. Crying, Johan confesses his misdeed, after which he stabs himself with a knife. The heroine is offended by Mads, after which she stabs herself. "Get these peas away from me," Mads exclaims, after which the bowl is with Mette, who also gives Jesper permission to eat. Then Mads stabs himself to death, and Mette gives the bowl to Jesper since she "dies with no proverb." Ultimately, Jesper remains alone. He pushes the bowl away and states the moral of the piece, "May your love never lack stockings!"—and stabs himself.

Wessel wrote an epilogue to the second edition of the piece, which appeared in the subsequent editions. Here Mercury comes down from Olympus, sees the terrible scene, takes the bowl with the peas, while he begins to awaken all the dead. In a final song (called "Vaudeville") all the actors sing in their turn a verse in the chorus: "the crazier, the better!"[40] Even if this expression was known in Wessel's time, it was difficult to use it in later periods without thinking of *Love without Stockings*. Kierkegaard uses this expression several times.[41] There can be no doubt that for Kierkegaard—as for most of those in his age—*Love without Stockings* designated a sublime form of madness.

---

[40]   Johan von Ehrenpreis sings, for example, "A wise man like Socrates one ought to be, / And mad, like him, in time and place, / the crazier, the better." ["*Man viis, som Socrates, bør være, / Og gal, som han, til Tid og Sted, / jo galere, jo bedre.*"]

[41]   Around 1838 Kierkegaard makes use of the expression in connection with the dramatic fragment *The Conflict between the Old and the New Soap-Cellar*, which was first supposed to have the title "The All-Encompassing Debate of Everything against Everything," a well-known expression from F.C. Sibbern's philosophy, while the subtitle was supposed to be: "The Crazier the Better" (*SKS* 17, 280, DD:208 / *KJN* 1, 272). In the following year the formulation is used in an entry "concerning the category of higher madness" (*SKS* 18, 70, EE:195 / *KJN* 2, 64), and in the second preface in *Prefaces* (1844) it is used of the reading public in Copenhagen (*SKS* 4, 481 / *P*, 17). Finally, we find the expresson in a journal entry from 1849, which concerns the endeavor to want to let the world be destroyed with a joke (*SKS* 21, 294–5, NB10:70 / *JP* 2, 1761).

III. Comic Stories, Poetry, and Verse

There is no doubt that *Love without Stockings* is Wessel's untouchable masterpiece. He also wrote 40 stories in verse form, many of which became very popular, although they were not always to the taste of the critics. For the sake of background information, one can mention how the former professor of aesthetics, Rahbek, diplomatically attempted to characterize these stories. He writes:

> If one assumes the tasteful definition that Marmontel in his *Elements de la Litterature* gives for the three words "comic," "funny" and "foolish" (*comique, plaisant,* and *bouffon*) namely, that *the comic* is that laughable which comes from weakness, error, foolishness or character defect; *the funny*, a striking special and new contrast, which is discovered between two objects, or an object and the heteroclite idea that it awakens; an unexpected manner, which in an inexplicable situation awakens in us laughter's sweet cramp; and *the foolish*, the exaggeration of the two others; one must without doubt call these stories *funny* rather than *comic*; likewise, it cannot be denied that Wessel who knew his readers, many times for the sake of greater emphasis or greater ease, availed himself of *the foolish*, without, however, ever *slightly* overstepping the limits of the *decent*, let alone falling into the *vile*, which otherwise is so often the case even with great comic writers, among whom I need merely mention Pope, Swift, Holberg, Plautus, and Aristophanes. Now and then in these stories by Wessel the reader runs across a very fine taste for things, which he perhaps does not know well, or that he wishes he had said or written; but more easily he comes across something he should regret or be ashamed or have read or laughed at.[42]

One notes how Rahbek is extremely cautious when he at the end speaks of "a reader of very fine taste," who even only "now and then" finds something offensive! Professor Molbech, one of the age's theorists of comedy, could not avoid commenting on this characterization of the stories in his portrayal of Wessel. He writes,

> One can agree that he [sc. Rahbek] is right in this, even if one does not agree with him in the explanation that he, following Marmontel, gives of these terms, which one now frequently uses in another sense than in the definition from this French aesthetician. But if we could assume his three kinds of poetic presentation of the laughable (*le comique, la plaisant* and *le bouffon*) to be more for three classes or degrees of the laughable or of humorous poetry than for three different elements, then without doubt Wessel's stories would far more belong to the second and third than to the first.[43]

Molbech is thus in agreement with Rahbek that in these stories one does not find *the comic*, which one knows from classical comedy, which chastises vices or moral misrelations. For "a reader of very fine taste" this is of course not something positive. Wessel was not a moralist, even the moral points of his stories are more of a joke than something edifying.

Which stories does Kierkegaard refer to? There was the story "The Blacksmith and the Baker" (1777/84), which Kierkegaard's friend, the actor C.N. Rosenkilde (1786–1861) loved so much that he often read it aloud from the stage of the Royal

---

42   Rahbek, "Fortale til nærværende Udgave," pp. XXVI–XXVII.
43   See Molbech, *Dansk poetisk Anthologie*, vol. 1, pp. 288–9.

Theater. It is the story of the hot-tempered blacksmith, who beats his enemy to death but escapes punishment. The town's judges and citizens were in agreement that a life must be paid for with a life. However, since the town only had one blacksmith, but two bakers, they condemned instead the elder baker to his "well-deserved punishment" and "like-minded people to abhorrence and fear." The moral of the story is: Always be prepared for death, for it comes when you least expect it! Kierkegaard had planned for this humoristic anecdote[44] to appear in the *Postscript*,[45] but it was not included in the final version. The story "The Gentleman from Jutland" (1785), is about a man from Jutland who bought a pair of shoes but who was too miserly or self-respecting to wear them. It begins with the familiar words: "that we, unfortunately, / are all Jutlanders in the eyes of our Lord." Judge Wilhelm makes use of this line in a humorous manner in his second letter in *Either/Or*.[46]

Finally, one should mention the parody of Goethe, "Stella" (1785), which begins with the proverb: "What do the Germans not do for money!" It is thought somewhat provocative to see Goethe made comical, who in the next century would come to dominate intellectual life so profoundly. In his critical discussion of Goethe, Kierkegaard could have taken several humorous arrows, "many funny and apposite satirical views,"[47] from Wessel's poem if he did not think—as Georg Brandes did later—that the poem was "less witty than coarse."[48] In any case Kierkegaard sticks only to the first line of verse. These anti-Socratic words Kierkegaard turns in the *Postscript* against un-Socratic speculation,[49] while in *The Moment* he directs these words against the Danish career pastors.

A final group of poems by Wessel can be grouped under the lose designation "miscellaneous poems." These were typically short verse works, which were intended for a closed circle of friends, and which therefore were not written with an eye towards publication. Nonetheless it is in these poems that one likes "to find Wessel again, so unpretentious and cheerful as he was."[50] One can count among these poems two fragments which Kierkegaard recalls in his books. Towards the end of his dissertation *The Concept of Irony*, Kierkegaard says that one should take care with letting negation fall in the incorrect place, "like the caesura in that famous verse."[51] When in a scholarly treatise one can make these kinds of references, then one should believe that the reader of course knew the poem, which is referred to, not least of all when what is at issue is a poem by Wessel, which, since it is lacking a

---

[44]   In Søren Holm's *Humor. En Æsthetisk Studie* (Copenhagen: Graabrødre Torv's Antikvariat 1964, pp. 20–1), the moral is used in this story to illustrate how humor is distinguished from irony.

[45]   See *Pap.* VI B 40, 10.

[46]   See *SKS* 3, 218 / *EO2*, 228. Behind this proverb lies the expression: "We are all sinners in the eyes of Our Lord," which has its root in Rom 3:23: "all have sinned and fall short of the glory of God."

[47]   See Møller, "Johan Herman Wessel," column 210.

[48]   Georg Brandes, "Goethe og Danmark" (1881), in *Samlede Skrifter*, vols. 1–18, Copenhagen: Gyldendal 1899–1910, vol. 1, p. 270.

[49]   *SKS* 7, 134 / *CUP1*, 144.

[50]   Rahbek, "Fortale til nærværende Udgave," pp. XXIXff.

[51]   *SKS* 1, 342 / *CI*, 310.

title, is often referred to by its first line, "I sing of a man; as such it is the old tone" or merely "Abelone." The poem is for the most part a play on words, for example, when it makes the joke which Kierkegaard refers to: "I sing of a woman—the hemistich falls." [*"Jeg synger om en Kone —Hemistichen faldt."*] When the caesura, the pause, in the Alexandrian meter, which Wessel uses, is supposed to fall after the third verse foot (iamb), then the line, that is, the part of the verse which the caesura separates ("the hemistich") reads: "I sing of a cow!" [*"Jeg synger om en ko–"*].

In the first part of *Either/Or* there is a short treatise on Scribe's popular comedy *The First Love.* The aesthete begins by philosophizing about the significance of the occasion, and in connection with the discussion of the poet's invocation of the muse it is noted: "what Wessel once said still holds concerning the god of taste 'whom all invoke,' that he 'so rarely comes.' "[52] This refers to Wessel's fragment "The Jewish Girl" or "About a Jewish Girl," in which the witty lines are found: "You god of all bards, and the Judge of Wit, / who are invoked so often and who so rarely come." If the god, however, had no time, Wessel suggests that he instead send a muse, but just not one of these "street tarts," who is immediately willing, "when some Jack whistles." Kierkegaard wrote down these lines in the *Journal FF* (1838), possibly for use in the imagined polemic surrounding his book on Andersen.[53] Curiously enough, at the time when Kierkegaard was working on *Either/Or*, P.L. Møller had discussed "The Jewish Girl" as a fragment which was not worthy of Wessel's name![54]

However, it was not only in his journals or in his works that Kierkegaard made use of Wessel. In a letter to his sick relative, the widow Julia Augusta Thomsen (1810–84), from January 1849, he interrupts his jesting and garrulousness with the words: "if I were to say that now I had no more to add, then, in the words of the poet, it would be 'all sorts of—lying in my throat.' "[55] This refers to a versified piece of domestic advice by Wessel, which in 1776 appeared in *Aftenposten*, and which, as such, must have been intended for the general interest. "Drink mead with ground carnations, then your whooping cough will disappear, if not, then you can call me a liar."[56]

IV. Kierkegaard's Use of Wessel: Some Preliminary Points

We can ascertain that Wessel was present for Kierkegaard as early as his polemical debut with the journals in the mid-1830s. Furthermore, there are constant references to Wessel's poetry all the way up to the attack on the church in the mid-1850s. From Kierkegaard's quotations it is not possible to identify the edition that he was using, but a reasonable guess would be A.E. Boye's edition from 1832, which awakened great attention with its theretofore unmatched critical standard. Even if Kierkegaard's

---

[52]   *SKS* 2, 227 / *EO1*, 233.

[53]   *SKS* 18, 116, FF:214 / *KJN* 2, 107.

[54]   Møller, "Johan Herman Wessel," columns 209–10.

[55]   *B&A*, vol. 1, p. 222 / *LD*, Letter 197, p. 282.

[56]   The verse runs thus in Levin's edition: *"Tør jeg besvære Aftenposten / Med ringe Raad imod Kiighosten: / Stød Nelliker en Morgen smaae, / Kom dem i Miød, og drik dem saa. / Hvis du er ikke inden Aften / Som den, der aldrig haver havt'en; / Saa kan du sige allenfals: / Hr. Medicus! Løgn i jer Hals!"*

quotations are for the most part correct, there are now and again enough deviations to lead one to believe that he quoted from memory rather than made a direct copy from a written text. The work by Wessel which Kierkegaard most often has recourse to and which he constantly refers to through a period of almost twenty years is *Love without Stockings*. Of the dozen references that he has to this piece, most of them were not published. This is true primarily of the references from the attack on the church where the piece belongs to the potential artillery. With what concerns the rest of the comic stories and short verse works, Kierkegaard's selection seems more random: for example, several of the most famous stories are never even touched.

If one wants to evaluate Kierkegaard's way of using Wessel, then it is not enough merely to register all of the references to his writings. The question that immediately pops up is how Kierkegaard's use of Wessel is distinguished from the common use made by others at the time. We have already seen P.L. Møller imply that Wessel was an author whose works people knew by heart, especially his *Love without Stockings*. There are other testimonies to the same effect. In the foreword to his edition from 1819 Professor Rahbek writes that he still recalls

> the time when it was common to know *Love without Stockings*...virtually by heart; when everywhere, in the most serious and the most unserious places in and out of season, at the gaming table, at the bench [sc. in a court of law], in learned conflicts as in jesting conversations one heard allusions to it and quotations from it.[57]

A.E. Boye recalled these works in the preface to his edition from 1832 and added: "Even now it has not...disappeared from the lips of the living, but is often used for a joke in everyday life, although no longer in such unsuitable places as at the bench."[58] Just as Kierkegaard's contemporaries took pleasure in quoting Wessel, so also did Kierkegaard himself. However, in Kierkegaard this was not a case of an exaggerated use of Wessel, and one does not find Wessel used in unsuitable places. Kierkegaard quotes *Love without Stockings* over a period of 20 years without repeating himself a single time! On the contrary, he demonstrates a good ability to find an always surprising passage. Several of the references to the comic stories are, by contrast, almost proverbial, for example, "We are all Jutlanders in the eyes of our Lord" and "What wouldn't the Germans do for money." But this says nothing in itself about any special appropriation of the poem. This is different with the various short verse works, which are used very precisely in their respective contexts. All this seems to imply that Kierkegaard clearly knew his Wessel.

V. Wessel's Epitaph and Kierkegaard's Aesthete

There are also references in Kierkegaard to a last poem by Wessel, which, however, is so central that it demands a somewhat extensive treatment. It concerns what one can call the very essence of Wessel's literary activity, that is, the picture that

---

[57]   Rahbek, "Fortale til nærværende Udgave," pp. V–VI.
[58]   A.E. Boye, "Om Wessels Levnet og Skrifter," in Wessel, *Samlede Digte*, 3rd ed., pp. 6–7.

the poems reflect of their author's unique character. It was the greatest annoyance for the energetic philologist Levin that the first editors of Wessel's writings ran from the promise to provide a characterization of the poet's life, which they, if anyone, had the immediate qualifications for providing. Thus later ages were deprived of the foundation upon which later Wessel research could build. Several characteristics of Wessel's personality are, however, handed down in testimonies from his contemporaries. Of the positive characteristics, one finds an almost naïve good nature, which never wanted to attack or hurt concrete people. The negative characteristics were, however, those which became almost legendary: the fruitless idleness, the social but also private drinking, the unstoppable wit, and the increasing melancholy, which was not in the least grounded in a dissatisfaction with his own situation.[59] From the earliest time until our own day it has been a common practice to interpret Wessel's character and disposition from his poetic products. One of the central verses in this context has been "Epitaph for the Poet, Written by Himself." This jesting text has always been taken seriously in the biographical sense.

Let us put Kierkegaard's use of this poem into perspective by connecting it with some introductory remarks about the different versions that this epitaph has appeared in. We do this not because the text-critical versions are decisive for Kierkegaard, but because the reception that is tied to it casts a light on Kierkegaard, on Wessel, and on Kierkegaard's reception of Wessel. In the first edition of Wessel's writings from 1787 there is a version of the epitaph that has since become the most common.[60] It runs as follows:

> He ate and drank, was never glad,
> Wore down his boots from time to other,
> He never bothered do good or bad,
> To live he even didn't bother.[61]

> *Han aad og drak, var aldrig glad,*
> *Hans Støvlehæle gik han skieve,*
> *Han ingen Ting bestille gad,*
> *Tilsidst han gad ei heller leve.*

---

[59]   These are the characteristics that one finds in C.A. Thortsen's sketchy overview of Wessel, where he portrays him as admired for his "Quiet and unpretentious being, good-nature spirit and naïve wit," but portrays him as dying of "despondency, sickness and alcoholism." Then follows a characterization that certainly tacitly, as a guilty conscience, has always been present in everything that has been written about Wessel, namely, that he was "a magnificent talent, who was destroyed due to a lack of the proper encouragement and care," *Historisk Udsigt over den danske Litteratur indtil Aar 1814*, pp. 109–10.

[60]   The edition provides no information about the textual basis from which the epitaph comes. When Sigurd Thomsen (in *Kun en Digter. En Bog om Johan Herman Wessel*, Copenhagen: Jespersen og Pios Forlag 1942, p. 134) mentions that Wessel composed an epitaph in the verse proceedings of The Norwegian Society, it cannot be confirmed from the copies of the proceedings that survive.

[61]   Quoted from *Norwegian Poetry in English*, ed. by Liv Nordem Lyons, Minneapolis: Sons of Norway Heritage Programs n.d. (*Information Bank*, no. 14), p. 5.

One can well understand why this famous verse has tempted every Wessel biographer, but what kind of picture is it that is sketched of the poet here? Molbech in 1830 found in this poem a characteristic "tendency toward melancholy and indifference for life."[62] He regrets that the poet has done nothing to make his fate more bearable, and that he has "a disproportionately larger drive and desire to spend money, than to earn it by constant industry."[63] The old testimonies claim that Wessel's capricious cheerfulness is replaced by an ineffective melancholy and is precisely the mood "which he himself with few, sharp and lively characteristics, has portrayed in his aforementioned epitaph."[64] The tremendously hard-working Molbech had difficulties understanding how a poet could waste his genius with "strong drink" and cheerful idleness, but explains it by the fact that this "tone and way of life...was preferred by many of the age's poets and good minds."[65] Some years later P.L. Møller protested against this attempt by Molbech to paint "unusual natures" according to the "prosaic rules of life" which are valid for common citizens.[66]

One of the age's most interesting treatments of Wessel is found in the neglected essay "On Wessel's Wit" written by Ludvig Zeuthen (1805–74), which was originally given as a lecture in the Student Association in the spring of 1831.[67] It is possible that the young Kierkegaard could have been present.[68] Zeuthen's presentation of Wessel's character is an engaged interpretation of the epitaph. First he recalls the table, around which people were gathered, not to eat or drink but to enjoy conversation. This situation is witnessed in Plato and Xenophon in their symposiums, and later in Luther in his *Tischreden*. This joy for conversation is not found in our more recent poets. "Wessel was not happy, but ate and drank and told witticisms."[69] He was a melancholy character, who could not be livened up with witticisms.[70] His inner nature did not consist of cheerfulness, which he evoked in others. He did not have "a truly *positive* higher or deeper sense for the eternal truth and beauty."[71] All of Wessel's witticisms are "absolute products of the moment."[72] They are "attractive" but also "light as soap bubbles."[73] Kant (and Jean Paul) have defined the laughable as a tense expectation that is suddenly dissolved into nothing.[74] Everything that Wessel has written "seems determined solely to evoke laughter about nothing, in which an

---

[62]   Molbech, *Dansk poetisk Anthologie*, vol. 1, p. 277.
[63]   Ibid.
[64]   Ibid., p. 285.
[65]   Ibid., p. 278.
[66]   Ibid., pp. 223–4.
[67]   F.L.B. Zeuthen, "Om den Wesselske Vittighed," in his *For Æsthetik og Philosophie*, Copenhagen: C.A: Reitzel 1831, pp. 22–39.
[68]   See Peter Tudvad, *Kierkegaards København*, 2nd ed., Copenhagen: Politikens forlag 2005 [2004], p. 199, column 2.
[69]   Zeuthen, "Om den Wesselske Vittighed," p. 28.
[70]   Zeuthen has, without comment, co-opted this characterization from Pram's "Elegie ved Wessels Grav" (1786), ibid., p. XXIII.
[71]   Ibid., p. 29.
[72]   Ibid., p. 30.
[73]   Ibid.
[74]   Ibid., pp. 30–1.

awakened expectation is dissolved."[75] One finds this in the comic stories: "the few lines over which there stands the moral, are usually the most trivial of all, indeed sometimes, so to speak, *nothing at all*."[76] One finds this in *Love without Stockings*: "In the presentation of feelings, characters and action one has nothing fixed to hold on to. Everything is, so to speak, fluid. Therefore, laughter follows upon laughter, as one wave replaces the next."[77] With Zeuthen's description of Wessel's despairing witticism, which awakened laughter outwardly, but inwardly only tears, we come very close to the figure which Kierkegaard some years later called "the aesthete."

In Professor Rahbek's edition of Wessel's writings one finds another version of the epitaph. Rahbek could not get the first line, that is, that he "ate and drank," to fit with his picture of his friend, "who could not with truth refer to himself as a glutton." Rahbek continues: "From an authentic hand I have the first line thus: *He was seldom happy without drink* [*Han uden Drik var sjælden glad*] and thus it fits better with the fiery self-hatred, which is generally dominant."[78]

Rahbek's "improvement" of the text, the credibility of which has never been determined, was adopted by several later editors, first by Rahbek's successor Rasmus Nyerup, who in 1828 gave the new reading an increased authority.[79] Then it was co-opted by A.E. Boye, who in the introduction to his edition called Rahbek's verse line "more characteristic," since Wessel ended his life in a silent melancholy, discontent and withdrawn: "only wine could now make him cheerful."[80] Later in his edition P.L. Møller declared Rahbek's textual modification as a "more genuine reading,"[81] without, however, dwelling on it. In L.J. Flamand's *Gallery* from 1850, Wessel is well on his way to becoming a drinker. It is told that in his later days Wessel was "very quiet and melancholy, and only the wine evening could bring him into an excited mood," which indeed is what is written in the epitaph, "which quite characteristically expresses the despondency, the boredom and indifference which had taken possession of him."[82] Finally, the literary historian N.M. Petersen thought that Wessel was too much of a genius to "eat": He drank! Ultimately, Levin attempted to refute Rahbek's version. In his edition Levin correctly points out that the expression, "to eat and drink" ["*æde og drikke*"] (in Norwegian) should be interpreted neutrally, merely designating that Wessel was a loafer.[83] Levin put a stop

---

[75]   Ibid., p. 32.

[76]   Ibid., p. 34.

[77]   Ibid., p. 39.

[78]   Rahbek, "Fortale til nærværende Udgave," p. XXXV. Rahbek, however, does not make his textual correction in the edition from 1799–1800, but discussed it in his foreword.

[79]   See Nyerup, *Bidrag til en Udsigt over dansk Digtekunst*, p. 167, p. 295; cf. p. 169.

[80]   A.E. Boye, "Om Wessels Levnet og Skrifter," in Wessel, *Samlede Digte*, 3rd ed., p. 60.

[81]   P.L. Møller in his edition *J.H. Wessels Værker*, Copenhagen: Brødrene Berling 1848, p. 259.

[82]   L.J. Flamand, *Galleri af berømte og mærkelige danske Mænd og Qvinder*, Copenhagen: Trykt i det Berlingske Bogtrykkeri 1850, pp. 173–4.

[83]   See Israel Levin's notes to *J.H. Wessels samlede Digte*, Copenhagen: C.A. Reitzel 1862, p. 330. Levin could also have referred to the Bible, where "*æde*" merely means "to eat"!

to this version of the text,[84] without critically taking a position on his own version, that is, the first version.

When in 1925–30 the diaries which B.W. Luxdorph (1716–88), one of Wessel's friends, had written were published, under the date February 24, 1784 a third version of Wessel's epitaph is found, where the first line reads: "He liked to drink, was seldom happy" [*"Han giærne drak, var siælden glad"*].[85] The Norwegian literary historian Francis Bull has argued for this version, since it is the earliest known written draft.[86] While "ate and drank" [*"aad og drak"*] in a neutral sense express that life passes, while one does nothing, and where "without drink" [*"uden Drik"*] designates straightforward alcoholism, "liked to drink" [*"gierne Drak"*] seems to contain a deeper contrast. This tension is also apparent in the Wessel portrait that Bull conjures up. Wessel was, he writes,

> pale and sickly, a city person and a bohemian without any sense for nature, a quiet intellectual, who found his consolation in a bottle, and his happiness in the world of thought, with books and conversations, an outsider, who did not have the drive of ambition to participate in the race, but regarded life and human beings with an ironic and self-ironic smile, a linguistic artist without equal, and a humorist who had the rare gift of being funny and witty without being mean, who fought neither for nor against anything, except when art and good taste were in danger.[87]

As the Norwegian professor of literature Alvhild Dvergsdal has correctly remarked, this Wessel portrait is very "romantically" inclined. It is "the picture of the urbane, enlightened and intellectual artist type, Schiller's sentimental poet, Kierkegaard's aesthete, who is sketched."[88] We will return to this "romantic" conception of Wessel, but first we must have a look at Kierkegaard's part in the matter.

In *The Concept of Irony* (1841) Kierkegaard discusses the difference between "dying from" in the moral (Christian) and intellectual (Greek) sense. He shows how the ironic life view is really revealed in the conception of death, and how the Socratic or ironic longing for death is grounded in depression and apathy. He writes:

> In my view, that well-known epitaph by Wessel, "At last he did not care to live," contains irony's perception of death. But he who dies because he cannot be bothered to live certainly would not wish for a new life either, since that would indeed be a contradiction. Obviously the languor that desires death in this sense is a snobbish sickness found only in the highest social circles and in its perfectly unalloyed state is just as great as the

---

[84]   In his chapter on Wessel's alcoholism in his book *Vesen gjennom vidd og vers. Om Johan Herman Wessel* (Vestby: Vestby historielag 1992, p. 51), Bjørn Linnestad presents Rahbek's version.

[85]   See [B.W. Luxdorph], *Luxdorphs Dagbøger indeholdende Bidrag til det 18. Aarhundredes Stats-, Kultur- og Personalhistorie*, ed. by E. Nystrøm, vols. 1–2, Copenhagen: G.E.C. Gad 1915–30, vol. 2, p. 304.

[86]   Francis Bull and Fredrik Paasche, *Norsk Litteraturhistorie*, vols. 1–6, Kristiania: H. Aschehoug & Co. 1923–55, vol. 2, 1928, p. 463.

[87]   Ibid., p. 457.

[88]   Alvhild Dvergsdal, "Johan Herman Wessel: Klassisist? Romantisk? En drøfting med utgangspunkt i hans versfortellinger," *Nordlit*, no. 11, 2002, [p. 6].

enthusiasm that sees in death the transfiguration of life. Ordinary human life moves drowsily and vaguely between these two poles. Irony is healthiness insofar as it rescues the soul from the snares of relativity; it is a sickness insofar as it cannot bear the absolute except in the form of nothing, but this sickness is an endemic disease that only a few individuals catch and from which fewer recover.[89]

As is apparent, this is not a matter of a peripheral use of a Wessel quotation. On the contrary, this last line of the epitaph, to which Kierkegaard probably was the first to give a heavy emphasis, is tied to the entirely central issue with the ironist, namely, this longing for the Absolute, but "in the form of nothing." It is as if Wessel's epitaph were chiseled into the gravestone of irony and moved over to the cemetery of Romanticism, where negativity haunts. It is the same absolute indolence, the same "noble sickness," which in the second part of the dissertation is sketched in the portrait of the Romantic ironist. This is expressed in Friedrich Schlegel's *Lucinde,* where "to live poetically" is exemplified in the idealized portrayal of Lisette's life. But the most dominant characteristic, writes Kierkegaard, "is the superior indolence that cares for nothing at all, that does not care to work...does not care to engage its mind."[90] Of course, Lisette or Schlegel is no Socrates, and it is a long way from the first negativity to the absolute negativity. The Romantic ironist, which Kierkegaard ultimately conjures up, is thus intensified in negativity such that the relative indolence ("He did not care to do anything") reaches the absolute ("ultimately he did not care to live either"). Indolence, this demon of the will, is also accompanied by other phenomena: idleness, melancholy, boredom, wit, etc., all designations that we know from Wessel. This is not to say that Kierkegaard tried to change Wessel into a Romantic ironist, but due to the fact that he has changed Wessel's epitaph, every new application of this to Wessel will get it to change character. Two examples will be given to show that this really did happen in the wake of Kierkegaard's dissertation.

The first is P.L. Møller's Wessel portrait from 1842. He goes back to Zeuthen's presentation, is tacitly inspired by Kierkegaard, and then arrives at the following description:

> I have previously referred to the fact that in a single direction such a gifted poet cannot have been lacking what we in his works certainly most often miss, a sense for what is deeper and more serious in existence, but that just as his nature constantly let him see what was funny, thus perhaps his uninterrupted dissatisfaction with life led him more often than would otherwise have happened to make this limitless irony the foundation for his poems, this irony, which does not belong to the form but to the content; for this is in general a lively expectation which is dissolved into nothing in order to thus awaken laughter. That this irony was always without bitterness must certainly be ascribed to his nature more than to his will. He seems to feel it as the principle of his entire existence to promise much and keep little, and he tried to explain his natural dissatisfaction with this, as it seems, with games to realize the same principle in his poems. Thus he often seemed in the poetry to forget that this in the long run demands much more than a merely momentary "pleasure" from its practioners, just as he in life sought to hide himself and his higher vocation in momentary amusements, instead of creating for his mind true

---

[89]   *SKS* 1, 136 / *CI*, 77–8.
[90]   *The Concept of Irony*, in *SKS* 1, 328 / *CI*, 295.

nourishment and fullness. But this, his ironizing game with himself, which, if one stops with his works, is so often amusing, while its repetition in his personal fate awakens melancholy, sometimes went further; and he is thus perhaps the only one of all the poets who has felt, or affected, disdain for the beauty of nature.[91]

Under Møller's hand, Wessel had become an ironist. He was not in possession of the fullness of existence, of humor, which "in an apparently trivial and empty existence shows us a glimpse of the eternal."[92] He can only amuse us, not satisfy us with "an, in truth, refreshing material of life."[93] Wessel was "an original nature, but no character."[94] It is Kierkegaard's Romantic ironist who here steps forth for us, that is, the figure, whom Kierkegaard a year later called "the aesthete."

A second example of a presentation of Wessel as an ironist can be found in the Norwegian professor and poet J.S. Welhaven (1807–73), who in a treatise from 1849 emphasized "Wessel's irony." He notes that the more recent times have "everywhere acknowledged the full significance and penetrating power of irony in *Love without Stockings*," but adds that Wessel occupied such a "free and superior standpoint" that it has offended the age's aesthetic authorities.[95] Wessel drove, he writes,

> negation to the extreme; he gave nugaries an appearance of importance and let small things appear with great gesticulations. All the unreasonable value that people in that age's poetic productions ascribed to the material and that people gave as the direction and goal of poetry, found its counterweight in this feather-light matter, whose entire content ultimately is a completely unveiled triviality or a mere oddity or nothing at all.[96]

One immediately fastens on to the claim that Wessel drove "negation to the extreme." There was certainly no one else who, like Kierkegaard, had shown how irony drove negation to the extreme and has given a presentation of what that meant. When Wessel's tragedy, his comic stories and manifold short poems end in "nothing at all," then one recalls involuntarily—without comparison, incidentally—the Socratic discussions in Plato's early dialogues, in which Kierkegaard had found precisely this ironic characteristic feature. Thus something points to the fact that Kierkegaard was, if not the originator, then an indispensable moment in the development of the Romantic Wessel portrait. Kierkegaard, however, was not done with Wessel's epitaph, since it made its way into *Either/Or* (1843), where the ironist/Romanticist of the dissertation was transformed into the aesthete.

One does not have to read far into *Either/Or* before one runs across a Wessel dictum. Already in one of the first diapsalmata, in which one takes in the aesthete's lyricism, his despairing basic mood, one meets the sublime indolence:

---

[91]   Møller, "Johan Herman Wessel," column 220.

[92]   Ibid., column 222.

[93]   Ibid.

[94]   Ibid.

[95]   J.S. Welhaven, "Om Betydningen af det norske Selskabs Opposition mod den Ewaldske Poesi," *Norsk Tidskrift for Videnskab og Litteratur*, 1849, pp. 225–90; p. 278. Also published as a separate monograph.

[96]   Ibid.

I don't feel like doing anything. I don't feel like riding—the motion is too powerful. I don't feel like walking—it is too tiring; I don't feel like lying down, for either I would have to stay down, and I don't feel like doing that, or I would have to get up, and I don't feel like doing that, either. *Summa Summarum*: I don't feel like doing anything.[97]

The dissertation's sketch of the ironist is developed into a full portrait of the aesthete. By means of the variegated material, which the first part of *Either/Or* consists of, the aesthete reveals his fine intellectual cultivation, his aesthetic ideality, and his critical gifts. But under the surface of all this there works a omnivorous negativity. Every "will-to-something" is dissolved into a far deeper "will-to nothing." Every positivity that this intellect grasps, slips out again like sand running through one's fingers. Actuality is dissolved under ideality, but this ideal does not lead to a new actuality. The disinterested reflection gnaws like a worm in the decision, in the choice, and prevents any real action. The aesthete is a superior spirit but at bottom a despairing existence.

If one jumps over into the second part of the work, where one often has the feeling that the Christian humanist Judge Wilhelm's criticism of his young friend does not really hit the mark of the figure, whom we met in the first part, then one nonetheless finds a chastisement of A's indolence. Wilhelm protests against the aesthete's vampirelike manner of sucking all nourishment out of the true immediacy, but he who in the final account suffers the greatest loss is the aesthete himself: "you lose your time, your serenity, your patience for living, because you yourself know very well how impatient you are, you who once wrote to me that patience to bear life's burdens must indeed be an extraordinary virtue, that you did not even have the patience to want to live."[98] When Wilhelm can directly refer to a letter in which the aesthete has declared that he did not *care* to live, then one immediately hears the entire constellation of these from Wessel's epitaph, as it is interpreted by Kierkegaard. Judge Wilhelm's moral criticism of the aesthete thus corresponds to Molbech's, but especially to Zeuthen's corresponding criticism of Wessel. Zeuthen's moral criticism of Wessel's wittiness—that is, that it was without the true (Christian) joy—could straightforwardly be put into the mouth of Wilhelm.

Professor Thomas Bredsdorff has recently called Wessel "our first literary nihilist."[99] If one makes the epitaph the basis of the discussion, as has been done in the foregoing, one can hardly limit this nihilism to the literary field. It is certainly more a kind of existential nihilism, which one finds in Kierkegaard's aesthete. That Bredsdorff in fact means something similar is apparent from the following characterization:

> In spite of all wit and sharpness there is, in Wessel's world, a sense of it being late in the world, that everything has been tried and nothing really leads to anything. Wessel

---

[97]   *Either/Or*, in *SKS* 2, 28 / *EO1*, 20.

[98]   See "The Aesthetic Validity of Marriage," *SKS* 3, 20 / *EO2*, 11.

[99]   See Thomas Bredsdorff, *Den brogede oplysning*, Copenhagen: Gyldendal 2004, p. 170. As Bredsdorff himself notes, there is a similar argument in Liv Bliksrud, *Den smilende makten. Norske Selskab i København og Johan Herman Wessel*, Oslo: Aschehoug 1999, pp. 216–19.

is not enlightenment; he is rather the Danish Enlightenment's *fin de siècle:* Feelings are laughable, but reason does not lead to anything better. Let us therefore cultivate art for its own sake.[100]

VI. Conclusion

Every development ends in its own parody,[101] or the comic view is always the concluding one.[102] Kierkegaard did not need Hegel or Heiberg to tell him about this experience. It is an old truth that the ancient Greeks and later the Romans knew well and thus is found in the course of history, where Wessel is an excellent example. Kierkegaard's use of Wessel cannot be reduced to the textual ornament of the witticisms. Wessel is one of the allies of reflection or the intellectual comic. If he was not as great, for Kierkegaard, as a Holberg, a Baggesen or a Heiberg, then he nevertheless seems with his epitaph to strike more deeply.

Translated by Jon Stewart

---

[100]   Ibid., p. 171.
[101]   Kierkegaard claims this in *The Concept of Irony*, in *SKS* 1, 179 / *CI*, 128.
[102]   Kierkegaard claims this in the *Concluding Unscientific Postscript*, in *SKS* 7, 42 / *CUP1*, 35.

Bibliography

I. Wessel's Works in The Auction Catalogue *of Kierkegaard's Library*

None.

II. Works in The Auction Catalogue *of Kierkegaard's Library that Discuss Wessel*

Nyerup, Rasmus and Knud Lyhne Rahbek, *Bidrag til en Udsigt over dansk Digtekunst under Christian VII*, Part 1, *Indbefattende Tidsrummet 1766–75*, Copenhagen: Jens Hostrup Schultz 1828, pp. 150–4; pp. 295–310 (*ASKB* 1389).
Steffens, Henrich, *Was ich erlebte. Aus der Erinnerung niedergeschrieben*, vols. 1–10, Breslau: Josef Max 1840–44, vol. 2, pp. 116–21 (*ASKB* 1834–1843).
Thortsen, Carl Adolph, *Historisk Udsigt over den danske Litteratur indtil Aar 1814*, Copenhagen: C.A. Reitzel 1839, pp. 109–12 (*ASKB* 970).

III. Secondary Literature on Kierkegaard's Relation to Wessel

None.

Edward Young:

Kierkegaard's Encounter with a Proto-Romantic Religious Poet

Joseph Ballan

Between the Augustan period typified by Alexander Pope and the Romantic one exemplified by William Wordsworth, in what Shaun Irlam deems the "black hole of English poetry between neoclassicism and romanticism," "poetry of sensibility" of the eighteenth century or of "enthusiasm" flourished.[1] The age of "sensibility," along with its poetic expression, earned its name by its reaction against the aesthetic and epistemological prejudices produced by the Enlightenment, the age of "reason." Many of this epoch's brightest lights, for instance James Thomson, Christopher Smart, and Edward Young (1683–1765), have not enjoyed the posthumous fame, nor their works the canonical status, of a Pope or a Wordsworth, but, taken together, their works nevertheless constitute a transitional period without which Romanticism would scarcely be thinkable. In Germany as well as in England, the Romantic poets looked to Young in particular as a source of inspiration as well as a literary point of departure for their own work. Not more than a few decades after Young's death, Samuel Johnson articulated the challenge facing anyone endeavoring to summarize the poet's work: "Of Young's Poems it is difficult to give any general character; for he has no uniformity of manner: one of his pieces has not great resemblance to another. He began to write early, and continued long; and at different times had different modes of poetical excellence in view."[2] Indeed, Young employed several different poetic modes at various points during his long career, beginning as a dramatist (e.g., *The Brothers*), then authoring a number of satirical works (for example, *Love of Fame*) before composing the long moral-didactic poem for which he is most well known, *Night Thoughts*. His last major work is a lively piece of literary criticism addressed to the famous eighteenth-century prose writer, Samuel Richardson (1689–1761), *Conjectures on Original Composition*.

In 1724, after having written several plays and begun a more conventional career in law, Young was ordained in the Church of England. The rectorship he assumed at

---

[1]   Shaun Irlam, *Elations: The Poetics of Enthusiasm in Eighteenth-Century Britain*, Stanford, California: Stanford University Press 1999, p. 1. Enthusiasm in this context must be understood in its etymological sense of being possessed by or filled with God or a god.

[2]   Samuel Johns, *Lives of the Poets*, London: George Bell & Sons 1900 [1779–81], pp. 341–2.

Welwyn, Hertforshire, in 1730, would provide the setting for and the material means supporting the composition of the literary work of his maturity, including *Night Thoughts*.³ As a prime instance of the poetics of "unworlding" characteristic of the poetry of sensibility, *Night Thoughts* presents itself as the insomniac reflections of a poet reflecting on "life, death, and immortality,"⁴ to cite the subtitle, and disputing the rationalist, Enlightenment criticism of Christianity. Young does this in a rhetorical style designed to intensify the effect, to awaken the imagination and, in short, to encourage epiphanic experience in the reader. An immensely popular work in its day, *Night Thoughts* has since undergone a quite variegated reception, with figures as diverse as John Wesley and William Blake producing their own editions of it, Wesley with explanatory notes for a popular readership and Blake with 43 of his singular engravings, the most he devoted to any individual author's work other than his own.⁵

With its ruminations upon death and its graveyard setting, a generation of Romantic poets in both England and Germany looked to *Night Thoughts* for inspiration, often bracketing or regarding as of secondary importance the Christian, pedagogical content of the work. This reading of Young was in evidence in Germany by the period of *Sturm und Drang* and of Goethe, who found in *Night Thoughts* "nothing more than a gloomy weariness with life" and a characteristically English morbidity and misanthropic outlook.⁶ Young's English reception was not wholly laudatory, either. Without overlooking or minimizing the Christian content of *Night Thoughts*, George Eliot attacks the more pernicious effects, replicated in both poetry and popular religion in the time that had elapsed between Young's lifetime and hers, of Young's particular "style" of Christianity. In summarizing her argument, which presents Young in contradistinction to another eighteenth-century religious poet, William Cowper, Eliot avers that "in Young we have the type of that deficient human sympathy, that impiety towards the present and the visible, which flies for its motives, its sanctities, and its religion, to the remote, the vague, and the unknown."⁷

Søren Kierkegaard's earliest citation of Young is also the latter's most prominent appearance in his *oeuvre*. On the frontispiece of the first volume of *Either/Or*, Victor Eremita, the pseudonymous editor of that work, includes two lines from the fourth of

³   Edward Young, *Night Thoughts*, ed. by Stephen Cornford, New York: Cambridge University Press 1989. Chapter and verse will be cited from this edition.
⁴   The text originally appeared as *The Complaint, or Night Thoughts on Life, Death and Immortality*, London: R. Dodsley and T. Cooper 1742–45.
⁵   Jon Mee, "Blake and the Poetics of Enthusiasm," in *Cambridge Companion to English Literature, 1740–1830*, ed. by Thomas Keymer and Jon Mee, New York: Cambridge University Press 2004, pp. 199–201. In all, Blake actually produced 256 engravings to accompany Young's *Night Thoughts*.
⁶   Johann Wolfgang Goethe, *Aus Meinem Leben: Dichtung und Wahrheit*, ed. by Klaus-Detlef Müller, Frankfurt am Main: Deutscher Klassiker Verlag 1986 (vol. 14 in Goethe, *Sämtliche Werke, Briefe, Tagebücher und Gespräche: vierzig Bände (Frankfurter Ausgabe)*, ed. by Dieter Borchmeyer et al., Frankfurt am Main: Deutscher Klassiker Verlag 1985–99), pp. 631–2.
⁷   George Eliot, "Worldliness and Other-Worldliness: The Poet Young," in *Essays and Leaves from a Notebook*, ed. by Charles Lee Lewes, New York: Harper and Brothers 1883 [1857], p. 64.

nine "nights" comprising Young's *Night Thoughts*: "Is reason then alone baptized,/ Are the passions pagans?"[8] Since he did not read English, Kierkegaard encountered Young in a translation produced by Young's earliest German translator, Johann Arnold Ebert (1723–95), who is also considered to be one of the more faithful translators of Young in any European language.[9] Ebert's edition of *Night Thoughts* sets this long poem in prose, presumably in order to convey as precisely as possible the semantic content of the lines without attempting to reproduce the blank verse of the original. A bilingual edition, Ebert's volumes leave the English text in verse form, allowing Kierkegaard to construct a versified epigraph for his first pseudonymous work. Inexplicably, he reverses the lines he quotes. Neither Ebert nor the Danish translators of Young whom Kierkegaard may have read provide a precedent for this reversal.[10] Young's text reads, "Are *Passions*, then, the Pagans of the Soul? *Reason* alone baptiz'd."[11] These lines nicely capture both the program of the eighteenth-century poetics of enthusiasm in general and a central argument of this didactic poem in particular, which includes a dialogue between the poet and Lorenzo, a fictional character representing a deistic, rationalist position regarding religious matters. In debate with Lorenzo, Young offers an argument for the imagination and the passions as alternatives to the epistemological paradigm furnished by the natural sciences.[12] He echoes the lines quoted by Kierkegaard in the seventh night:

> Ye gentle Theologues, of calmer Kind![13]
> Whose Constitution dictates to your Pen,
> Who, Cold yourselves, think Ardor comes from Hell!
> Think not our Passions from *Corruption* sprung,
> Tho' to Corruption, now, they lend their Wings;
> That is their *Mistress*, not their *Mother*. All
> (And justly) *Reason* deem Divine: I see,
> I feel in the *passions*, too...[14]

The poet goes on to argue that the passions "lend their wings" to corruption because of the fall of Adam and Eve, and, while conceding that reason does have a role to

---

[8] *SKS* 2, 9 / *EO1*, 1.

[9] [Edward Young], *Einige Werke von Dr. Eduard Young*, vols. 1–3, trans. and revised by Johann Arnold Ebert, Braunschweig and Hildesheim: bey sel. Ludw. Schröders Erben 1767–72 (*ASKB* 1911). For an assessment of Ebert as translator of Young's *Night Thoughts*, see John Louis Kind, *Edward Young in Germany*, New York: Columbia University Press 1906, pp. 62–9.

[10] [Edward Young], *Forsøg til en Oversættelse af Dr. Edward Youngs Klager eller Nattetanker om Liv, Død og Udødelighed: Forfattet i 9 Sange*, trans. by Emanuel Balling, Helsingøer: Trykt udi det Kongel. allene privil. Bogtrykkerie 1767; [Edward Young], *Edward Youngs Klage eller Natte-tanker om Liv, Død og Udødelighed*, trans. by Barthold Johan Lodde, Copenhagen: Gyldendal 1783.

[11] Young, *Night Thoughts*, ed. by Stephen Cornford, p. 107 (Chapter IV, verses 629–30).

[12] For the poetry of sensibility as an epistemological program see Irlam, *Elations*, pp. 4–6.

[13] The gentleness and calm of which Young speaks here refers to the rationalist's lack of enthusiasm and passion for things religious.

[14] *Night Thoughts*, Chapter VII, verses 521–8.

play in reining in and moderating the passions in so far as they lead one into corrupt ways of life,[15] he maintains that "boundless *Passion* speaks" of eternal life in the presence of God where "*Reason*" remains "silent."[16] In rehabilitating the role of the passions in religious life, Young's project resonates with that of his fellow Anglican and contemporary, the devotional writer William Law (1686–1761), whose *Treatise on Christian Perfection* Kierkegaard also owned in German translation.[17]

What, however, does Young's polemic with deism and the European Enlightenment have to do with the contents of the first volume of *Either/Or*? Because it serves as an epigraph and not as a citation supporting an argument or a passage that the author opens for discussion, the context, or lack thereof, does not allow for a conclusive answer to this question. From Judge William's mention of Young in the context of a discussion of Goethe's autobiography, whose judgment of Young we mentioned above, we can surmise that Kierkegaard did not ignore the explicitly Christian content of Young's work, as did other eighteenth- and nineteenth-century writers. In Judge William's contribution to *Stages on Life's Way*, the essay "Reflections on Marriage to Objections by a Married Man," he writes that Goethe "expressly laments that the age and he as a part of it have become depressed by reading English authors—Young, for example. Well, why not? If one is so constituted, one can become depressed by listening to a sermon, if it really has substance, as Young has, but Young is far from depressing."[18] Stephen Cornford describes, in the introduction to his edition of *Night Thoughts*, how, "ironically, a poem of specifically Christian intent became a seminal work in a secular cult of sepulchral melancholy."[19] The reference to Young vis-à-vis Goethe demonstrates that Kierkegaard did not read Young in this exclusively secular, melancholy way, but he would likely have been familiar with such readings as he found them as represented by Goethe, if not in the primary sources. Knowing that, at least among readers of German, Young was associated with a certain "secular cult of sepulchral melancholy" possibly led him to believe that a citation from Young could aptly set the tone for the collection of A's aesthetic essays, which include three addresses to be delivered before the Συμπαρανεκρωμενοι the fellowship of the dead. One of these essays, "The Unhappiest One" chooses as its subject for meditation "not...that sacred sepulchre in the happy East [i.e., Christ's] but...that mournful grave in the unhappy West," a grave located in England which bears the inscription from which the Συμπαρανεκρωμενοι address derives its title.[20] The parallels between a secularized Young and the aesthete of *Either/Or* are especially notable in the "Silhouettes" essay, in which sorrow is lauded and celebrated with

[15]   Ibid., Chapter VII, verse 539.
[16]   Ibid., Chapter VII, verse 549.
[17]   William Law, *Eine practische Abhandlung von der Christlichen Vollkommenheit: aus dem Engländischen der fünften Edition übersetzt*, Halle: Gebauer 1770 (*ASKB* 611).
[18]   *SKS* 6, 141 / *SLW*, 151.
[19]   *Night Thoughts*, ed. by Stephen Cornford, op. cit., p. 17.
[20]   *SKS* 2, 215 / *EO1*, 220.

ritualistic fervor,[21] and in which night itself is apostrophized and praised[22] in a way that echoes the opening address to "*Night*, sable Goddess" in *Night Thoughts*.[23]

In addition to the two appearances discussed above, Kierkegaard mentions Young four times, all of which have some relation to the text of *Concept of Anxiety*. In fact, three of these instances offer variations on the theme of language's function and purpose. Unfortunately, these three discussions of Young are misreadings (or very strong readings, at best) that serve as little more than a foil against which Kierkegaard and his pseudonyms have opportunity to articulate their own views. The prototype for these discussions may be found in a journal entry from 1844, which associates Young with a view that Kierkegaard also ascribes to Charles Maurice de Talleyrand (1754–1838), namely, that "men do not seem to have acquired speech in order to conceal their thoughts (Talleyrand, and Young before him in *Night Thoughts*) but in order to conceal the fact that they have no thoughts."[24] *Night Thoughts*, however, rarely discusses language as such; the second "night" contains the longest exposition of this topic, placed in the context of an exposition of the theme of friendship. Here the poet admonishes his interlocutor, Lorenzo, for what Vigilius Haufniensis might call his "self-enclosure [*det Indesluttende*]."[25] Without friendship and the opportunities it affords for the expression of one's thoughts, "*Good Sense* will Stagnate: Thoughts shut up want Air."[26] Young defines language, and specifically spoken language (*parole* rather than *langue*; the latter seems to be Kierkegaard's concern in his journal entry) not as that which conceals thought, but as the instrument allowing for its expression and communication, or what Young memorably calls its "ventilation":

> Speech, Thought's Canal! Speech, Thought's Criterion too.
> Thought, in the Mine, may come forth Gold or Dross;
> When coin'd in Word, we know its *real* worth...
> *Speech* ventilates our Intellectual fire;
> *Speech* burnishes our Mental Magazine...[27]

It is possible, then, that Kierkegaard does not give the correct citation when he ascribes such a position to Young's *Night Thoughts*. In the text of *Concept of Anxiety*, he repeats nearly verbatim the description of language he finds in Talleyrand and Young, but he

---

21	*SKS* 2, 194 / *EO1*, 174. *SKS* 2, 209 / *EO1*, 214.
22	*SKS* 2, 166–7 / *EO1*, 168.
23	*Night Thoughts*, Chapter I, verse 18.
24	*SKS* 18, 208, JJ:212 / *KJN* 2, 191. Given what we described above as the poetry of sensibility's defense, in reaction against the poets and theologians of the Age of Reason, of the imagination and the affects' role in procuring religious knowledge, it should be noted that the journal entry we cite here is followed by one in which Kierkegaard argues along very similar lines that "understanding disdains everything that imagination and feeling hit upon.... It is therefore just as arbitrary to do homage exclusively to the understanding as to do homage exclusively to feeling and imagination." (*SKS* 18, 208, JJ:213 / *KJN* 2, 192.)
25	See, for example, *SKS* 4, 425–37 / *CA*, 123–35.
26	*Night Thoughts*, Chapter II, verse 466.
27	*Night Thoughts*, Chapter II, verses 469–71; verses 477–8.

omits the reference to *Night Thoughts* specifically.[28] The reference to the source for this sentiment, supposedly expressed by Young, is also missing from the British poet's last appearance in Kierkegaard's works, specifically in " 'Guilty?'/'Not Guilty?' " the third section of *Stages on Life's Way*. Here Quidam, whose diary constitutes the section in question, voices his dissent[29] from the theory that he attributes to Young, Talleyrand, and "a more recent author" (i.e., Vigilius Haufniensis) and which holds that language conceals thought rather than disclosing it. Instead, in discussing the possibility of repentance for one's behavior in an erotic relationship, Quidam notes that the age to which he belongs has overlooked or forgotten that repentance consists in action and not, for instance, in expressions of mere regret or apology. Language, then, does not conceal thought, but rather serves to "strengthen and assist people in abstaining from *action*."[30] The passage sounds a critical note regarding Young's alleged theory of language, but it does not offer in its place a more positive view of language's social function than the corresponding earlier passages do.

If Kierkegaard did not read this theory in *Night Thoughts*, as his later omissions of this title suggest, in which of Young's works might he have found it? Ebert's German edition contains, in addition to *Night Thoughts*, two of Young's more well-known satires, including *Love of Fame, The Universal Passion*. In this text we read:

> With generous scorn how oft hast thou survey'd
> Of court and town the noontide masquerade;
> Where swarms of knaves the vizor quite disgrace,
> And hide secure behind a naked face;
> Where Nature's end of language is declined,
> And men talk only to *conceal* the mind....[31]

As in the discussion of communication between friends, however, this poem evokes a function of language specific to the particular social-historical context it satirizes without venturing to say anything at all about language's essence. If anything, these verses posit the contemporary corruption of the true "end [*Zweck* in Ebert's translation] of language" as the obscuring of thought by disingenuous speech.[32] That

---

[28]   Vigilius Haufniensis refers to what Kierkegaard takes to be the Talleyrand-Young theory of language in the context of a discussion of genius, specifically the distinction between the "pagan" and the Christian genius. In a work that influenced the Romantic poets and thinkers of the nineteenth century, Young's *Conjectures on Original Composition* also meditate on the subject of genius. Ebert did not, however, translate this prose work of Young's and, furthermore, the thematic of genius developed in that text bears little resemblance to Haufniensis' account in *Concept of Anxiety*.

[29]   The draft for this statement of dissent may be found in an 1844 journal entry: *Pap*. V B 115, 2 / *JP* 3, 2322.

[30]   *SKS* 6, 315 / *SLW*, 339, my emphasis.

[31]   *Love of fame, the universal passion. In seven characteristical satires*, London: Jeremiah and R. Tonson and S. Draper, 1752, p. 38 (book II, verses 203–8).

[32]   It should be noted that, in his notes to the text, Ebert directs the reader to Jer 9:3–5 as expressing a criticism of the use of language in a given historical situation similar to that condemned, in a more playful voice, by Young: "They bend their tongues like bows; they have

Kierkegaard may have realized that he had not only misquoted Young earlier by citing *Night Thoughts* in connection with this particular theory of language, but had misread Young altogether by merely attaching his name to this theory, may be evidenced by a late (1854) reflection on the relation between theory and practice. Here, he posits that "what Talleyrand said about speech, that it is given to men to conceal their thoughts, can be said far more truthfully of the relation between theory and practice in the domain of ethics."[33] What was formerly considered to be the Talleyrand–Young theory of language is eventually attributed to the French diplomat alone.

Before offering some concluding remarks, we note one final appearance that Young makes in Kierkegaard's writings. From the final draft of the section of *The Concept of Anxiety* that includes Haufniensis' definitions of certitude, inwardness, earnestness, and the relation between these three terms, Kierkegaard deletes a long quotation from another of Young's satires, *The Centaur not Fabulous*. Haufniensis takes Qoholeth's declaration in Ecclesiastes that "All is vanity" as an example of a statement that, when uttered with inwardness, denotes earnestness, but which can also be spoken in a melancholy or frivolous mode, in which earnestness as an essential element is absent from the assertion.[34] Kierkegaard found a discussion of Ecclesiastes in this late satire by Young, directed against the deistic opponents of Christianity as well as against the "men of pleasure" of his day; "in such [men as these], as in the fabled Centaur, the brute runs away with the man."[35] The final letter, entitled "The dignity of man resumed," cites Qoholeth and the "*last* sentiment, the sum of his Divine philosophy," which, as Kierkegaard correctly notes, refers to Ecclesiastes 12:13: "Fear God, and keep his commandments; for that is the whole duty of everyone." Having referred to the author of Ecclesiastes, whom he takes to be Solomon, Young contends that "many a philosopher may justly be reputed a fool; that as there is but one God, one trial, one great tribunal, one salvation, so there is but one wisdom; that all which devoid of *that*, assumes the name, is but folly of different colors and degrees."[36] In all likelihood, this text was omitted from the final version of *The Concept of Anxiety* because of its length (the entire paragraph is quoted), its lack of immediate relevance to the larger discussion (i.e., the definition of the terms inwardness, earnestness, and certitude), a certain dogmatic tone uncharacteristic of Haufniensis, and because Kierkegaard apparently had little to offer by way of commentary on this mostly rhetorical passage of Young.

It would be difficult to count Young as a major source of inspiration for or influence on Kierkegaard, given that the latter's citations of him consist of an epigraph, a simple quotation with practically no commentary, a somewhat questionable interpretation of

---

grown strong in the land for falsehood, and not for truth....They all deceive their neighbors, and no one speaks the truth; they have taught their tongues to speak lies."
[33]   *SKS* 26, 283, NB33:42 / *JP* 4, 3870.
[34]   *SKS* 4, 446 / *CA*, 146–7.
[35]   The preface to the work continues: "And farther, I call them 'Centaurs NOT FABULOUS,' because by their scarce half-human conduct and character, that enigmatical and purely ideal figure of the ancients is not unriddled only, but realized" p. ii. *The Centaur not Fabulous. In six letters to a friend, on the life in vogue*, London: A. Millar and R. and J. Dodsley 1755, pp. i–ii.
[36]   Ibid., p. 246.

an isolated verse, and a very broad, general characterization of his religious poetry. One could speculate that Kierkegaard would have found rather salutary what Harriet Guest describes as the effect of "desocialization" and "isolation" that Young's poems were intended to have on his audience, downplaying their identity as members of ecclesiastical communities in order to provoke the self-examination and reflection of individual Christian readers *as individuals*.[37] One could also cite the graveyard scene that furnishes the *topos* for *Night Thoughts* as a literary precedent for Kierkegaard's own discourse "At a Graveside" (1845).[38] Without attempting such extrapolations, interesting though they may be, a more modest conclusion can be drawn from the use that Kierkegaard *does* make of Young's work. Judge William's reference to Young may give the best indication of the hermeneutic principle governing Kierkegaard's reading of the British pastor-poet. As noted above, the Judge disputes Goethe's claim that Young's poetry suffers from an inherent, innately English melancholy or morbidity. Were one predisposed toward depression, Young's works would elicit this particular mood, but this would say more about the reader in question than about Young himself, whose work Judge William finds "far from depressing."[39] Similarly, that Kierkegaard associates Young with a very negative (even depressing) view of language and communication probably says more about Kierkegaard's intentions as a reader and thinker than it does about Young as a poet. By suggesting that "empty talk" [*Passiaren*] expresses Young's theory of language as well as his poetry supposedly does,[40] Kierkegaard does acknowledge the social dimension of Young's satirical verses on language, but by not engaging these lines closely, it must be concluded that he does not approach them on their own terms, but only in so far as they have use-value for his own work.

---

[37]   Harriet Guest, A *Form of Sounds Words: The Religious Poetry of Christopher Smart*, New York: Oxford University Press 1989, p. 65 and p. 67.
[38]   *SKS* 5, 442–69 / *TD*, 69–102.
[39]   *SKS* 6, 141 / *SLW*, 151.
[40]   *SKS* 4, 409 / *CA*, 108.

Bibliography

I. Young's Works in The Auction Catalogue *of Kierkegaard's Library*

Einige Werke von Dr. Eduard Young, vols. 1–3, trans. and revised by J.A. Ebert, Braunschweig and Hildesheim: Schröder 1767–72 (*ASKB* 1911).

II. Works in The Auction Catalogue *of Kierkegaard's Library that discuss Young*

Flögel, Karl Friedrich, *Geschichte der komischen Litteratur*, vols. 1–4, Liegnitz and Leipzig: David Siegert 1784–87, vol. 2, pp. 404–5 (*ASKB* 1396–1399).

[Goethe, Johann Wolfgang], *Goethe's Werke. Vollständige Ausgabe letzter Hand*, vols. 1–40, Stuttgart and Tübingen: J.G. Cotta 1827–30; *Goethe's nachgelassene Werke*, vols. 41–55, Stuttgart und Tübingen: J.G. Cotta 1832–33, vol. 25, p. 213 (*ASKB* 1641–1668).

[Hamann, Johann Georg], *Hamann's Schriften*, vols. 1–8, ed. by Friedrich Roth, Berlin: G. Reimer 1821–43, vol. 1, p. 53; p. 131; vol. 2, p. 135; p. 173; p. 188; p. 198; p. 266; p. 329; p. 515; vol. 3, pp. 109–10; p. 393; vol. 4, p. 114; vol. 6, p. 365; vol. 7, p. 216 (*ASKB* 536–544).

Heiberg, Johan Ludvig, "Det astronomiske Aar," in his *Urania. Aarbog for 1844*, ed. by Johan Ludvig Heiberg, Copenhagen: H.I. Bing & Söns Forlag 1843, p. 106 (*ASKB* U 57).

[Richter, Johann Paul Friedrich], Jean Paul, *Vorschule der Aesthetik nebst einigen Vorlesungen in Leipzig über die Parteien der Zeit*, vols. 1–3, 2nd revised ed., Stuttgart and Tübingen: J.G. Cotta 1813, vol. 1, p. 214; vol. 2, p. 355; p. 363; p. 597; p. 629 (*ASKB* 1381–1383).

Steffens, Henrich, *Was ich erlebte. Aus der Erinnerung niedergeschrieben*, vols. 1–10, Breslau: Josef Max 1840–44, vol. 2, p. 137; vol. 3, p. 267 (*ASKB* 1834–1843).

Sulzer, Johann Georg, *Allgemeine Theorie der Schönen Künste, in einzeln, nach alphabetischer Ordnung der Kunstwörter auf einander folgenden, Artikeln abgehandelt*, vols. 1–4 and a register volume, 2nd revised ed., Leipzig: Weidmann 1792–99, vol. 1, p. 75; vol. 2, p. 367; vol. 3, p. 200; p. 302; p. 561; p. 628; vol. 4, p. 189 (*ASKB* 1365–1369).

III. Secondary Literature on Kierkegaard's Relation to Young

None.

Index of Persons

Abington, Frances (1737–1815), English
actress, 232.
Abraham, 194.
Abrahams, Nicolai Christian Levin (1798–
1870), Danish actor and theater
director, 143, 144.
Adorno, Theodor W. (1903–69), German
philosopher, 157.
Agnete, 6, 192.
Andersen, Hans Christian (1805–75),
Danish poet, novelist and writer of
fairy tales, 149, 261.
Aristophanes, 259.
Aristotle, 202, 205.
Auber, Daniel François (1782–1871),
French composer, 156, 170, 174.

Bach, Johann Sebastian (1685–1750),
German composer and organist, 137.
Baggesen, Jens (1764–1826), Danish poet,
73, 85, 246, 247, 251, 270.
Beaumarchais, Pierre (1732–99), French
dramatist, 143.
Beethoven, Ludwig van (1770–1827),
Austrian composer, 137.
Bellini, Vincenzo (1801–35), Italian
composer, 142, 170.
Benjamin, Walter (1892–1940), German
philosopher, 221.
Berlioz, Hector (1806–69), French
composer, 147, 150, 155–9 passim,
161.
Bertung, Birgit, 88.
Biehl, Charlotte Dorothea (1731–88),
Danish author and translator, 14.
Billeskov Jansen, Frederik Julius (1907–
2002), Danish literary scholar, 77,
86, 88, 89.
Blake, William (1757–1827), English poet,
274.
Blanc, Louis (1811–82), French politician,
96.

Blicher, Steen Steensen (1782–1848),
Danish author, 51.
Bloom, Harold, 188, 197, 204.
Boieldieu, F.A., 173.
Bonaparte, Joseph-Napoleon (1768–1844),
Napoleon's elder brother, 113.
Börne, Karl Ludwig (1786–1837), German
writer, 187, 200, 203, 204.
Bournonville, August (1805–79), Danish
ballet choreographer, 143.
Boye, Adolph Engelbert (1784–1851),
Danish author, 251, 252, 261, 262,
265.
Brandes, Georg (1842–1927), Danish author
and literary critic, 260.
Bredsdorff, Thomas, 269.
Brorson, Hans Adolph (1694–1764), Danish
Pietistic poet, 246, 247.
Bruun, Niels Thorup (1778–1823), Danish
author and translator, 143.
Bull, Francis (1887–1974), Norwegian
literary historian, 266.
Buloz, François (1803–77), French editor,
35.
Byron, George Gordon Noel (1788–1824),
English poet, 1–11, 120, 131, 215.

Carstens, Adolph Gotthard (1712–95),
Danish author, 66.
Cervantes, Miguel de (1547–1616), 13–29,
70.
Cetti, Giovanni Battista (1794–1858),
Italian-Danish opera singer, 145.
Charles IX, King of France (1550–74), 111.
Charles X, King of France (1757–1836),
111.
Charlot, Marcel, 171.
Chateaubriand, Vicomte François-René de
(1768–1848), French writer and
statesman, 31–62.
Chodowiecki, Daniel Nicolaus (1726–
1801), Danish painter, 71.

Christ, 23, 75, 100, 222, 256.
Christian VI, King of Denmark (1699–1746), 68, 81, 82, 246.
Close, Anthony, 26.
Colette, Jacques, 155.
Congreve, William (1670–1729), English playwright, 228.
Corneille, Pierre (1606–64), French poet and dramatist, 125, 126, 253.
Cowper, William (1731–1800), English poet, 274.

Dahlhaus, Carl, 137.
Da Ponte, Lorenzo, i.e., Emanuele Conegliano (1749–1838), Italian librettist and poet, 138, 139, 143, 144, 155, 163.
Defoe, Daniel (1660–1731), English author, 63, 70.
Descartes, René (1596–1650), French philosopher, 125.
Diderot, Denis (1713–84), French philosopher and Encyclopedist, 70.
Dodd, James (1740–96), English actor, 234.
Donizetti, Gaetano (1797–1848), Italian composer, 142, 170.
Dorph, Niels Vinding (1783–1858), Danish educationist and translator, 85, 237.
Dostoevsky, Fyodor Mikhailovich (1821–81), Russian author, 195.
Dumas, Alexandre, père (1802–70), French author, 112, 114, 172.
Dumas, Alexandre, fils (1824–95), French author, 172.
Dvergsdal, Alvhild, 266.

Ebert, Johann Arnold (1723–95), German translator, 275, 278.
Eliot, George, i.e., Mary Ann Evans (1819–80), English author, 274.
Elisabeth, Queen of England (1533–1603), 188.
Ewald, Enevold (1696–1754), Danish theologian, Johannes Ewald's father, 63.
Ewald, Johannes (1743–81), Danish poet, 63–76, 246, 247, 249.

Faust, 3, 4, 117, 149, 181, 222.
Fendt, Gene, 199, 202, 203.

Fétis, François (1784–1871), Belgian musicologist, 147.
Fenger, Henning (1921–85), Danish literary scholar, 122.
Fielding, Henry (1707–54), English author, 70.
Flamand, Ludvig Joseph (1800–79), Danish author, 265.
Frederik IV, King of Denmark (1671–1730), 81, 82.
Frederik V, King of Denmark (1723–66), 64, 65, 68, 82.
Frye, Northrop (1912–91), Canadian literary critic, 189, 195.

Garrick, David (1717–79), English actor, 231, 232.
Gautier, Théophile (1811–72), French poet, author and literary critic, 32.
Gluck, Christoph Willibald (1714–87), Czech composer, 148.
Goethe, Johann Wolfgang von (1749–1832), German poet, author, scientist and diplomat, 3, 9, 16, 87, 111, 117, 174, 190, 191, 247, 260, 274, 276, 280.
Gounod, Charles François (1818–93), French composer and organist, 170.
Grimsley, Ronald, 36, 109, 120, 172, 174, 175.
Grundtvig, Nikolai Frederik Severin (1783–1872), Danish poet and theologian, 175.
Gutenberg, Johannes (ca. 1400–69), German goldsmith and printer, 101.
Gyllembourg-Ehrensvärd, Thomasine Christine (1773–1856), Danish author, 100, 122.

Hage, Johannes (1800–37), editor of the Danish newspaper *Fædrelandet*, 84.
Halévy, Jacques François (1799–1862), French composer, 142, 170.
Hamann, Johann Georg (1730–88), German philosopher, 87.
Hamlet, 4.
Handel, Georg Friedrich (1685–1759), German-English composer, 148.
Haydn, Joseph (1732–1809), Austrian composer, 137.

Hegel, Georg Wilhelm Friedrich (1770–1831), German philosopher, 48, 126, 155–7, 163, 186, 207, 270.

Heiberg, Johan Ludvig (1791–1860), Danish poet, playwright and philosopher, 78, 121–3, 131, 140, 141, 173, 237–41 passim, 247, 250, 257, 270.

Heiberg, Johanne Luise (1812–90), Danish actress, 174, 235–41 passim.

Heidegger, Martin (1889–1976), German philosopher, 221.

Heine, Heinrich (1797–1856), German poet and author, 15–19 passim.

Hérold, Ferdinand (1791–1833), French composer, 148.

Hobbes, Thomas (1588–1679), English philosopher, 125.

Hoffmann, Ernst Theodor Amadeus (1776–1822), German Romantic author, jurist, composer, 138, 139, 145, 163, 222.

Hogg, Thomas Jefferson (1792–1862), British biographer, 215.

Hojer, Andreas (1690–1739), Danish historian and lawyer, 87.

Holberg, Christian Nielsen (1620–86), Ludvig Holberg's father, 79.

Holberg, Ludvig (1684–1754), Danish dramatist and historian, 69, 70, 77–92, 246–9, 259, 270.

Holm, Bent, 83.

Homer, 16.

Hong, Howard V., American translator, 178.

Horace, 68.

Hotho, Heinrich Gustav (1802–73), German art historian, 159.

Hugo, Victor (1802–85), French author, 111.

Hulegaard, Arendse, 63, 64, 70, 71.

Ibsen, Henrik (1828–1906), Norwegian playwright, 172.

Iffland, August Wilhelm (1759–1814), German actor and dramatist, 237.

James, Henry (1843–1916), American-British author, 238.

Janin, Jules (1804–74), French critic and novelist, 170.

Jean Paul, i.e., Johann Paul Friedrich Richter (1763–1825), German author, 16, 264.

Jesus, see "Christ."

Johnson, Samuel (1709–84), English author, 273.

Jonson, Ben (1572–1637), English playwright, 185, 188, 189.

Kant, Immanuel (1724–1804), German philosopher, 87, 264.

Kaufmann, Walter (1921–80), American philosopher, 193.

Kearney, Richard, 202, 204.

Keats, John (1795–1821), English poet, 221.

Kierkegaard, Michael Pedersen (1756–1838), Søren Kierkegaard's father, 220.

Kierkegaard, Søren Aabye (1813–1855), "Our Journalistic Literature" (1835), 17.

The Battle between the Old and the New Soap-Cellars (ca. 1837), 141, 175.

From the Papers of One Still Living (1838), 51, 71, 75, 177.

The Concept of Irony (1841), 179, 187, 190, 260, 266, 267.

Johannes Climacus, or De omnibus dubitandum est (ca. 1842–43), 37.

Repetition (1843), 41, 72, 176.

Either/Or (1843), 2–9 passim, 18, 19, 31–3, 38, 41–8 passim, 51–8 passim, 71, 121, 128, 131, 132, 146–54 passim, 159–61, 171, 175–82 passim, 190, 191, 222, 260, 261, 268, 269, 274, 276.

Fear and Trembling (1843), 6, 192, 193.

Two Upbuilding Discourses (1843), 47.

Three Upbuilding Discourses (1843), 72.

Four Upbuilding Discourses (1844), 194.

Philosophical Fragments (1844), 132, 205, 206.

The Concept of Anxiety (1844), 2, 6, 72, 85, 216–20 passim, 277, 279,

Prefaces (1844), 236.

"A Cursory Observation Concerning a Detail in *Don Giovanni*" (1845), 150.

"The Activity of a Traveling Esthetician and How He still Happened to Pay for the Dinner" (1845), 20.

Three Discourses on Imagined Occasions (1845), 73, 280.

Stages on Life's Way (1845), 5, 19, 60, 84, 85, 89, 132, 148, 175, 178, 191, 192, 196–207 passim, 239, 254, 257, 276, 278.

Concluding Unscientific Postscript (1846), 17, 21, 22, 26, 84–6, 177, 205, 245, 255, 260.

A Literary Review of Two Ages (1846), 100, 101, 176, 177.

"The Difference between a Genius and an Apostle" (1847), 205.

Works of Love (1847), 103, 127, 206.

"The Crisis and a Crisis in the Life of an Actress" (1848), 177, 235, 236, 240.

The Point of View for My Work as an Author (ca. 1848), 102.

The Lily in the Field and the Bird of the Air (1849), 6.

The Sickness unto Death (1849), 5, 6, 194, 217, 218, 220, 221.

Practice in Christianity (1850), 223.

The Moment (1855), 260.

Journals, Notebooks, *Nachlaß*, 3, 17, 22, 31, 38, 39, 73–5, 85–8, 106, 117, 131, 149, 175, 216–18, 222, 256, 277.

King, Thomas (1730–1805), English actor, 232.

Kingo, Thomas (1634–1703), Danish poet, 79.

Klæstrup, Peter Christian (1820–82), Danish artist, 252, 254.

Klopstock, Friedrich Gottlieb (1724–1803), German poet, 65, 68, 246, 249, 253.

Kolderup-Rosenvinge, Janus Lauritz Andreas (1792–1850), Danish legal historian, 32, 104, 107.

Kruse, Laurids (1778–1839), Danish author, 144, 145.

Kyd, Thomas (1558–94), English playwright, 188, 189.

Lamartine, Alphonse Marie Louis de Prat de (1790–1869), French poet and statesman, 93–107.

Lamb, Lady Caroline Ponsonby (1785–1828), 1.

Law, William (1686–1761), English writer and mystic, 276.

Lehmann, Edvard (1815–92), Danish painter, 239, 241.

Lem, Karen (1647–95), Ludvig Holberg's mother, 79.

Lenau, Nicolaus, see "Strehlenau, Niembsch von."

Lennox, Charlotte (1730–1804), British author, 19.

Lessing, Gotthold Ephraim (1729–81), German writer and philosopher, 195, 203.

Levin, Israel (1810–83), Danish philologist, 252, 263, 265.

Licht, Johan Friedrich (1699–1764), Danish school principal, 63.

Liebenberg, F.L. (1767–1828), editor of Johannes Ewald's collected works, 71.

Liszt, Franz (1811–86), Hungarian composer and pianist, 140, 162.

Loménie, Louis de (1815–78), French author, 35.

Louis XIV, King of France (1638–1715), 125, 126.

Luther, Martin (1483–1546), German religious reformer, 264.

Luxdorph, Bolle Willum (1716–88), Danish historian and poet, 66, 266.

Marlowe, Christopher (1564–93), English playwright, 188.

Marmontel, Jean-François (1723–99), French historian and writer, 259.

Martensen, Hans Lassen (1808–84), Danish theologian, 4, 197, 247, 255.

McCarthy, Vincent A., 56.

Mencke, Johann Burkhard (1674–1732), Danish professor of history, 80.

Mephistopheles, 4, 9.

Mérimée, Jean-François-Léonor, (1757–1836), French painter, Prosper Mérimée's father, 109.

Mérimée, Prosper (1803–70), French writer, 109–24.

Merman, the, 6, 192.

Meyerbeer, Giacomo (1791–1864), German composer, 142, 156, 170.

Mickiewicz, Adam (1798–1855), Polish poet, 111.

Mohammed, 99.

Molbech, Christian (1783–1857), Danish philologist and literary scholar, 65, 66, 73–5, 259, 264, 269.

Molière, i.e., Jean Baptiste Poquelin (1622–73), French dramatist, 125–35, 139, 144, 150, 160, 163.

Møller, Peder Ludvig (1814–65), Danish critic, 20, 21, 26, 252, 261–8 passim.

Montaigne, Michel de (1533–92), French essayist and philosopher, 109.

Montesquieu, Charles-Louis de Secondat baron de la Brède et de (1689–1755), French political philosopher, 70.

Monrad, Peter Johan (1758–1834), Danish civil servant, 251.

Mörike, Eduard (1804–75), German poet, 139.

Mozart, Constanze (1762–1842), Wolfgang Amadeus Mozart's wife, 146.

Mozart, Maria Anna (1751–1829), Wolfgang Amadeus Mozart's sister, 146.

Mozart, Wolfgang Amadeus (1756–91), Austrian composer, 2–7 passim, 120, 131, 132, 137–67, 178, 239.

Munthe, Ludvig (1597–1649), bishop in Bergen, 79.

Musset, Alfred de (1810–57), French author and poet, 138.

Mynster, Jakob Peter (1775–1854), Danish theologian and bishop, 197, 247, 256.

Napoleon, I also Napoleon Bonaparte (1769–1821), French emperor, 4, 43, 110.

Napoleon III also Charles Louis Napoleon Bonaparte (1808–73), President of the French Republic, 94, 117.

Nathanson, Mendel Levin (1780–1868), Danish editor, 256.

Neefe, Christian Gottlob (1748–98), German opera composer, 139.

Neiiendam, Robert (1880–1966), Danish theater historian, 237, 240.

Newton, Isaac (1642–1727), English mathematician and physicist, 98.

Nielsen, Anna (1803–56), Danish actress, 145, 235–9 passim.

Nielsen, Nicolai Peter (1795–1860), Danish actor, 237–9.

Niemetschek, Franz Xaver (1766–1849), Czech philosopher and music critic, 146.

Nietzsche, Friedrich (1844–1900), German philologist and philosopher, 4, 195, 221.

Nissen, Georg Nikolaus von (1761–1826), Danish diplomat, 146.

Nyerup, Rasmus (1759–1829), Danish literary historian, 251, 265.

Oehlenschläger, Adam (1779–1850), Danish poet, 65, 66, 140, 141, 239, 246, 247, 249.

Olsen, Regine (1822–1904), 39, 175, 181, 196.

Ørsted, Hans Christian (1777–1851), Danish scientist, 102, 251.

Oulibicheff, Alexandre (1794–1878), 146, 147.

Ovid, 39, 188.

Palmer, John (1744–98), English actor, 233.

Pascal, Blaise (1623–62), French mathematician, physicist and philosopher, 109, 125.

Paul, 85, 205.

Petersen, Niels Matthias (1791–1862), Danish literary historian, 265.

Phister, Joachim Ludvig (1807–96), Danish actor, 145, 236, 237, 241.

Pindar, 68.

Plato, 157, 158, 205, 253, 264, 268.

Plautus, 259.

Plutarch, 188.

Pope, Alexander (1688–1744), English poet, 259, 273.

Pope Pius VII (1740–1823), 43.

Pram, Christen (1756–1821), Danish author, 251.

Proust, Marcel (1871–1922), French author, 55.

Pushkin, Alexander (1799–1837), Russian author, 2, 111, 117.

Racine, Jean (1639–99), French dramatist, 40, 110, 121, 125, 253.

Radbodus of the Goths (d. 719), 89.

Rahbek, Knud Lyne (1760–1830), Danish writer and literary scholar, 65, 129, 131, 251, 253, 259, 262, 265.

Reicha, Anton (1770–1836), Czech-French composer, 157.

Reitzer, Christian (1665–1736), Danish professor of law, 80.

Richardson, Samuel (1689–1761), English author, 273.

Richelieu, Armand-Jean du Plessis de, also known as Cardinal Richelieu, (1585–1642), French clergyman and statesman, 125.

Rochlitz, Johann Friedrich (1769–1842), German author and editor, 139, 144, 146.

Rohde, H.P. (1915–2005), Danish art historian, 31, 51.

Ronchaud, Louis de, 99.

Rosenkilde, Christian Niemann (1786–1861), Danish actor, 259.

Rossel, Sven H., 80, 83.

Rossini, Gioacchino (1792–1868), Italian composer, 142, 148.

Rötscher, Heinrich Theodor (1803–71), German theater critic, 187, 200.

Rougemont, Denis de, 196, 197, 199.

Rousseau, Jean-Jacques (1712–78), French philosopher, 53, 109.

Rung, Henrik (1807–71), Danish composer, 143.

Sainte-Beuve, Charles Augustin (1804–69), French literary critic, 35, 44.

Scalabrini, Paolo (1713–1803), Italian composer, 253.

Schelling, Friedrich Wilhelm Joseph von (1775–1854), German philosopher, 15, 16.

Schikaneder, Emanuel born Johann Joseph Schikaneder (1751–1812), German impresario, 138.

Schiller, Friedrich von (1759–1805), German poet, 239, 266.

Schlegel, August Wilhelm von (1767–1845), German critic, 15, 185, 187, 191, 205.

Schlegel, Friedrich von (1772–1829), German Romantic writer, 15, 16, 145, 179, 186, 191, 195, 267.

Schlichtegroll, Friedrich (1765–1822), German philologist, 146.

Schmieder, Heinrich Gottlieb (1763–1811), German author and theater director, 139.

Schopenhauer, Arthur (1788–1860), German philosopher, 1, 157, 158, 163.

Schröder, Friedrich Ludwig (1744–1816), German actor and theatrical manager, 139.

Schubarth, Karl Ernst (1796–1860), German philosopher, 3, 4.

Schumann, Robert (1810–56), German composer, 138, 155, 158–62 passim.

Scott, Walter (1771–1832), Scottish author, 110, 111.

Scribe, Augustin Eugène (1791–1861), French dramatic author, 109, 122, 140, 141, 149, 156, 169–83, 261.

Shakespeare, William (1564–1616), English dramatist, 6, 9, 14, 110, 111, 121, 141, 173, 185–207, 216–18, 225, 228, 229, 236–41 passim, 246, 247, 266–8, 273–80.

Sharp, Sutton (1797–1843), English lawyer, 113, 116.

Shaw, George Bernard (1856–1950), Irish playwright, 172, 231, 234.

Shelley, Mary (1797–1851), English author, 216.

Shelley, Percy Bysshe (1792–1822), English poet, 6, 113, 215–24.

Sheridan, Richard Brinsley (1751–1816), Irish playwright, 225–43.

Sheridan, Thomas (1719–88), Irish actor and theatrical manager, 225, 226.

Sibbern, Frederik Christian (1785–1872), Danish philosopher, 126.

Sløk, Johannes (1916–2001), Danish theologian, 194, 204, 206.

Smart, Christopher (1722–71), English poet, 273.

Socrates, 44, 78, 246, 266–8.

Stanhope, Lady Hester Lucy (1776–1839), English traveler, 93.

Stendhal, i.e., Marie-Henri Beyle (1783–1842), French author, 110, 113, 116, 121.

Sterne, Laurence (1713–68), Irish-English author, 70.

Strehlenau, Niembsch von, i.e., Nicolaus Lenau (1802–50), Austro-Hungarian poet, 4.

Struensee, Johann Friedrich (1737–72), King Christian VII's personal physician, 69.

Swift, Jonathan (1667–1745), Irish-English author, 70.

Talleyrand, Charles Maurice de (1754–1838), French diplomat, 278, 279.
Thomson, James (1700–48), Scottish poet and playwright, 273.
Thompson, Josiah, 222.
Tieck, Ludwig (1773–1853), German poet, 15, 185, 186, 191, 205.
Tudvad, Peter, 172, 175, 237, 238.

Vega, Lope de (1562–1635), Spanish playwright and poet, 14.
Verdi, Giuseppe (1813–1901), Italian opera composer, 142, 170.
Viallaneix, Nelly, 106.
Vigny, Alfred de (1797–1863), French poet, 112.
Vinding, Poul (1658–1712), Danish professor of Greek, 80.
Virgil, 188.
Voltaire, i.e., François-Marie Arouet (1694–1778), French Enlightenment writer, 70, 253.

Wagner, Richard (1813–83), German composer, 147, 153, 161, 162.
Welhaven, J.S. (1807–73), Norwegian professor and poet, 268.
Wesley, John (1703–91), English clergyman, 274.

Wessel, Johan Herman (1742–85), Danish playwright and poet, 245–71.
Wessel, Peter, also called Tordenskjold (1690–1720), Danish naval hero, 248.
Wexschall, Friedrich Torkildsen (1798–1845), Danish violin player, 239.
Wiehe, Michael (1820–64), Danish actor, 235, 237, 241.
Winckelmann, Johann Joachim (1717–68), German archaeologist and art historian, 138.
Wollstonecraft, Mary (1759–97), English author and feminist, 113, 215.
Wordsworth, William (1770–1850), English poet, 273.
Wulff, Marie Matthiasdatter (1715–91), Johannes Ewald's mother, 63.

Xenophon, 264.

Young, Edward (1683–1765), English author, 273–81.

Zeuthen, Frederik Ludvig Bang (1805–74), Danish philosopher and theologian, 264–9 passim.
Zrza, Eleonora Christina (1797–1862), Danish opera singer, 145.

Index of Subjects

aesthetics, 44, 47.
Ahasverus, see "Wandering Jew."
Anfægtelse, see "spiritual trial."
anxiety, 72, 215–20 passim, 223.
appropriation, 129.
Archimedean point, 103.
atheism, 47.
Athenæum, 129.
attack on the church, 89, 256, 262.
authenticity, 126, 129.

Baroque, 148, 157.
Bible,
    Ecclesiastes, 279.
    Job, 35, 36.
Borchs Collegium, 80.
boredom, 267.

Catholicism, 43, 95.
Christendom, 17, 23, 197.
Christianity, 17, 21–3, 26, 45, 47, 99, 100,
    103, 107, 197, 205, 206, 256, 274,
    279.
Classicism, 137, 145, 157, 246.
comedy, 16–26 passim, 77, 81, 83–7 passim,
    97, 125–33, 171, 179, 198, 200, 241,
    245–70 passim.
communication, indirect, 78, 88, 90, 196,
    197.
The Corsair, 20, 86, 88, 175, 252, 254.
Court Theater in Copenhagen, 143.
crowd, 88, 100, 107.

death, 266.
Deer Park, 41.
deism, 276.
demonic, 8, 9, 192, 193, 215–19 passim.
despair, 4, 5, 9, 126, 149, 216–22 passim.
doubt, 117, 202, 204.
drama, 77, 82, 83, 86, 110, 121, 125–33,
    169–82 passim, 185–207 passim,
    225–42 passim, 245–70 passim.

Enlightenment, 70, 126, 195, 203, 246,
    270–6 passim.
equality, 102, 103.
evil, 4.

faith, 17, 45, 192, 193, 206.
The Fatherland, 20.
freedom, 126, 129,
French Revolution of 1848, 94, 96, 104,
    116.

great earthquake, 220.

history, 112, 115, 116.
Huguenots, 111, 112.
humor, 268.

idealism, 187, 207.
imitation, 22.
immortality, 47.
individual (see also "single individual, the"),
    107, 131.
inner/outer, 155, 179.
inwardness, 23, 48, 178, 192–5, 204, 205,
    279.
irony, 3, 78, 186, 187, 190, 241, 255, 267,
    268.
    Socratic, 88.

July Revolution in France (1830), 114.

Königstädter Theater, 41.

language, 278–80.
leveling, 100.
love, 6, 7, 23, 56, 103, 126, 127, 149–53
    passim, 176–80 passim, 182.

marriage, 6, 54, 153, 178, 180.
martyr, 107.
mediation, 48.

melancholy, 32, 36–9, 50, 53, 59, 66, 152, 196, 218, 219, 245, 263–5, 267, 276, 279, 280.
Middle Ages, 17, 19, 132.
monasticism, 95.
music, 8, 137–63 passim, 180, 253.

negativity, 267, 269.

Ottoman Empire, 2, 13.

pantheism, 103, 107.
Pietism, 63, 68, 125, 246.
poetry, 5, 36, 63–75 passim, 99, 189, 205, 206, 273–80 passim.
politics, 93–107.
Providence, 98, 99.
pseudonym, 109, 121, 122.
public, 101.

reason, 96, 98, 99, 126, 273.
recollection, 178.
Reformation, 106.
repetition, 72, 106, 176, 182.
romantic/romanticism, 1, 5, 6, 9, 15–25 passim, 32, 35, 36, 52, 53, 56, 84, 94, 98, 102, 107, 110, 112, 137–41 passim, 145, 147, 157, 175–80 passim, 185–213 passim, 247, 267, 273.

Royal Theater in Copenhagen, 65, 68, 77, 84, 121, 122, 129–31, 141–5 passim, 150, 163, 173–5, 236–9 passim, 250, 253, 259.

seducer, 7, 9.
seduction, 5, 56.
sin, 191, 218, 220, 221, 223.
single individual, the, 101–5 passim, 193.
Sorø Academy, 82.
speculation, 22, 205.
spiritual trial, 23.
stages, 59.
Strandveien, 41.
subjectivity, 186.
suffering, 5, 22, 38, 40.

theater, see "drama."
Turks, see "Ottoman Empire."

University of Copenhagen, 84.

Valkendorfs Collegium, 64, 71.

Wandering Jew, 215, 221–3.
woman, 218.
women's equality, 83.